EARLY YEARS CARE AND EDUCATION

S/NVQ LEVEL 3

Penny Tassoni
Kath Bulman
with
Kate Beith
Louise Burnham
Harriet Eldridge

Heinemann
Child Care

Student Handbook

Heinemann Educational Publishers
Halley Court, Jordan Hill, Oxford, OX2 8EJ
Part of Harcourt Education

Heinemann is the registered trademark of
Harcourt Education Limited

First published 1999

07 06 05 04
20 19 18 17 16 15 14

A catalogue record for this book is available from the British Library on
request.

ISBN 0 435 401602

Designed by Wendi Watson
Cover designed by Sarah Garbett

Typeset by TechType, Abingdon, Oxon

Printed and bound in the UK by CPI Bath

Contents

Acknowledgements

Kate Beith would like to thank Cathy Wakely, Chris Lawrence, Carryl Sabine, Karen Hillier, Myra Fowler, Lisa Bedlow, Alan and Sandra Gough, Pat Ardrey and all the staff, students and children at The Chiltern College for their endless support. Thanks too to her mum, husband and children.

Kath Bulman would like to thank her children, Joanne and Andrew, for providing endless inspiration and ideas for examples and case studies.

Louise Burnham would like to thank Penny Tassoni for getting her started and for all her help. Also Gill Mallard and staff at Pickhurst Infant School for their support and advice, and Jayne Carvell for her assistance. Many thanks too to Francis, Thomas and Lucy for all their encouragement.

Penny Tassoni wishes to thank her family and friends for their continued support, Beaky's Nursery in Hastings for their advice, and all those at Bexhill College – the staff for their help over the past year, and the many students for their inspiration. Thanks also to Jan Nikolic at Heinemann for her support and patience during this project.

The authors and publishers would like to thank the following for permission to reproduce photographs:

Haddon Davies (pages 20 and 48)
Glaxo Wellcome (page 31)
Collections/Sandra Lousada (page 193)
Gary Boden for all other photos

Introduction

Welcome to this handbook for the National Vocational Qualification (NVQ) or Scottish Vocational Qualification (SVQ) Level 3 in Early Years Care and Education. The fact that you are reading this means that you are setting out or have already begun to train for work with young children.

Some background information

As you may know, any NVQ has formal, nationally set standards. To achieve your NVQ you will register with a particular awarding body. Your awarding body will award you a certificate when you have successfully completed your NVQ.

About this book

This handbook will provide you with the knowledge you need for *each* mandatory unit. To achieve this aim, the text has been linked closely with the performance criteria within all the elements. In addition, you will find various activities in the text which test your understanding of this knowledge. We strongly advise that you do carry out these activities as they will also support your practical, work-based portfolio.

It is important to remember that the standards are the same across the country and *do not vary*, whichever awarding body you happen to be with, although the appearance of the documentation or style of approach may be different.

The standards themselves are divided into **units**. The unit is given a letter, for example C (Care), P (Parental Involvement), M (Management), E (Environment), and a number. Each unit is then divided into **elements** which break down the work into manageable chunks. Within each element are 'performance criteria'. These tell you what you have to do to achieve the standard for that element in a safe, professional manner. In addition to performance criteria, each element also has a '**range**'. The range explains in what circumstances you are expected to carry out the performance criteria.

You will notice that the units are either 'mandatory' or 'optional'. To achieve your NVQ you have to complete all **eleven** of the mandatory units and three out of fourteen optional units. All the mandatory units are covered in this handbook.

Each unit for the NVQ in Early Years Care and Education (Level 3) is given a separate chapter, which is then divided into elements. You will find that for each element we have identified what you need to learn and then you are given information and activities related to these items of learning. At the end of each unit, there is also a Unit test that you can use to check your understanding overall. This means that each unit can stand alone and therefore you can work through the units in any order.

Throughout this chapter, there are a number of features to help you with your studies:

Active knowledge

Activities that ask you to check things or try things out in your own work setting. They will help to make the links between your knowledge and what happens in practice.

Keys to good practice

Checklists of the key points to remember and carry out at work.

Consolidation

Questions to check your understanding and give practice in the kinds of questions your assessor may ask you.

Getting started

There are some fundamental items of knowledge and understanding which are relevant to all the units. These are:

Values

- Appreciation of rights of the child and the parents/carers of that child
- Understanding of the need for confidentiality when working with children and their parents/carers
- Understanding of the need for high standards of personal behaviour, commitment and reliability when working with children
- Understanding of your role and responsibilities towards children, their parents/carers, your colleagues and other professionals in the early years sector
- Understanding and appreciation of the wide range of parenting styles, customs and cultures that co-exist in society.

These values will be addressed as you work through your units.

The rights of individual children must always be respected and you must aim to treat all children with equal concern for their overall needs. It is also important to appreciate that work in the early years sector must involve positive relationships with parents and other primary carers wherever possible, and this is stressed throughout the book. Finally, remember that respect for your colleagues and other professionals is also essential.

Working with children brings with it particular responsibilities, as children look to adults as their role models for behaviour and attitudes towards others. You will find that your own behaviour and/or attitudes may come under scrutiny or question. This does not infringe your rights as a unique individual, but is a recognition of the particular sensitivity of working with children and the power of adults in their lives. It means it is necessary to ensure high standards of professional behaviour within early years work settings.

Unit C2
Provide for children's physical needs

Successful completion of this unit will demonstrate that you can satisfactorily care for the basic physical needs of children in your care. Young children, in common with all humans, have basic physical needs, but unlike adults they are unable to deal with their own needs for nutrition, personal hygiene, sleep, rest and prevention of illness, and they rely on their adult carers for support and provision until they are older. From birth, children are constantly developing in all areas, including personal skills. A baby very quickly learns to communicate when he or she is hungry, for example. You need to understand the underpinning knowledge relating to these areas to be able to provide the correct support at appropriate ages.

It is essential to relate the physical care given to children to their individual needs. The age and stage of development a child has reached, and the wishes and beliefs of the child and his or her family, must be considered in providing for any aspect of a child's physical needs.

The elements for this unit are:

C2.1   Plan, prepare and provide food and drink for children

C2.2   Contribute to children's personal hygiene

C2.3   Respond to illness in children

C2.4   Plan and provide quiet periods for children

Element C2.1   Plan, prepare and provide food and drink for children

Food and drink are essential elements of life. Children vary widely in their approach to eating and drinking, which is often determined by family and cultural issues. As an early years worker you can make a difference to a child's enjoyment of food, and also support parents in ensuring that a child develops the right foundations for life.

WHAT YOU NEED TO LEARN

- Ensuring food and drinks are nutritious and meet the needs of cultural and religious practices.
- Presenting food and drinks that are attractive and appetising to all children.
- Preparing food and using equipment within the health, safety and hygiene requirements of the setting.
- Using food and meal times as a learning tool.

To support children with their intake of suitable food and drink, you need to be aware of the stage of development of the children you are working with. Throughout this element you will need to refer to the following chart.

Age	Stage of development	Effect on eating and drinking
0–3 months	Immature digestive and renal system – cannot tolerate anything other than milk, which must be human or modified formula. Kidneys unable to cope with high salt and mineral levels. Strong instinct to suck. Starts to recognise breast or bottle and makes eager movements on approach.	Diet consists entirely of breast or bottle milk. Routine based on demand feeding.
3–6 months	Sucks or licks lips in response to preparations for feeds. Starts to sit with support. Takes everything to the mouth. Puts hand to bottle and pats it when feeding.	May need to start eating supplements to milk diet. Will need to be held on carer's lap and fed with smooth, puréed foods. Shows an interest in different tastes; starts to show an interest in food.
6–12 months	Sits alone without support from nine months. Develops inferior pincer grasp, increasing in skill. Puts hands round cup or bottle. Tries to grasp spoon when being fed, eventually able to hold and put to mouth. Understands simple instructions.	Can sit in high chair to eat. Starts to use fingers to feed himself or herself with small pieces of food – bread, fruit, cheese, etc. Shows great interest in food and drink. Can chew food with lumps, but needs care to prevent choking.
1–2 years	By 18 months can use spoon efficiently and chews well. Can use cup alone with care. By two years, spoon-feeds well, lifts cup and drinks well. Asks for food and drink.	Should be largely self-sufficient in self-feeding with spoon and cup. Able to eat meals with family, or other children. All normal foods as eaten by care group and family.
2–4 years	At two years starts to use fork; proficient within a year. Little understanding of dangers at two to three years, very curious.	Skill with relevant eating implements developing. Care required to avoid child attempting to eat unsuitable items or drink dangerous liquids.
5 years +	Uses knife and fork. General behaviour should be well controlled. Will sit for reasonable period of time. Has a sense of time in relation to the day's programme.	Should be socialised fully into eating a full diet. Able to make choices of foods, and request favourites. Should be reliable, diet wise, in most social situations, for example parties, family meals. Knows when mealtimes are due.

Ensuring food and drinks are nutritious and meet the needs of cultural and religious practices

Food is a fuel, and without it living organisms, including humans, will die. Food gives children the fuel to grow and develop, and the energy they need for the hard work involved in playing and learning. When they are young, children need help to ensure they have the right amount and balance of food. They are incapable of providing the food for themselves, and to begin with are unable to eat without help. All babies start life on a pure milk diet, either through breast-feeding or bottle-feeding. By the time they are 12 months old, most children are eating a normal diet. The change from a liquid diet to a mixture of liquids and solids is called **weaning**.

Providing a balanced diet

In order to grow and develop, children need to eat a balanced diet containing a range of different nutrients, as outlined in the chart below.

Nutrient	Function	Examples
Carbohydrates	Provide energy for growth and activity, heartbeat and circulation, warmth and movement, the making and functioning of all body cells Aids digestion of other food	Starches – potatoes, pasta, rice, pulses, etc. Sugars – fruit, milk, sweets, etc.
Fats: saturated from animal sources; unsaturated from vegetable sources	Provide energy, body heat, insulation (some fats contain vitamins A, D and E)	Saturated – butter, cheese, meat Unsaturated – olive, vegetable and fish oils; polyunsaturated in sunflower seeds, corn, wheatgerm
Proteins	Aid growth and repair of the body Replace and build all body cells, enzymes and tissues	Meat, fish, soya, pulses, cheese, eggs, nuts, pulses, cereals, milk, yoghurts, edible seeds
Vitamins: fat soluble (A, D, E and K) water soluble (C and all Bs)	A – aids vision and healthy skin B – aids blood formation, nerve and muscle function; takes part in the release of energy from food C – binds cells together; absorbs iron from intestines; helps with resistance to viral infections D – aids absorption of calcium, growth of bones and teeth E – protects cells from damage; prevents early breakdown of essential fatty acids K – aids blood clotting	A – liver, oily fish, butter, margarine B – whole cereals, yeast, yoghurt, milk, meat, fish, bread, potatoes C (easily destroyed by air) – potatoes, tomatoes, citrus fruits, green vegetables, salads D (added to margarine) – oily fish, fish liver oils, liver E – wheatgerm, wholewheat flour and bread, sesame and sunflower seeds and oils K – present in most vegetables
Minerals: calcium, iron, sodium, potassium, magnesium, sulphur, fluoride, trace elements	Build bones and teeth; also aid balance of fluids, energy production, control of nerves and muscles	In nearly all foods in differing amounts Calcium – milk, cheese, tinned fish, bread and flour Iron – liver, kidney, red meat, nuts, whole cereals, white flour Sodium – salt, meat, fish, bread Fluoride – water
Fibre	Adds bulk to food, keeps bowels functioning by aiding muscle tone in the gut; thought to help in prevention of heart disease and cancer	Oats, wholewheat bread, beans, leafy vegetables, prunes, apples
Water	Maintains fluid balance, main transport system of the body; helps in waste elimination	All foods and drinks

A lot of advice is available on the subject of healthy diets, some of which may seem to be confusing. Much that is reported in the media tends to relate to the adult diet, and some of the advice to adults could be harmful if applied to children. The COMA report (1991), issued by the Committee on Medical Aspects of Food Policy, advised the following:

- Children need nutrient-dense foods, in small, frequent amounts.
- Fibre intake should be as part of normal family foods, and not supplied in addition to these.
- Low-fat products should not be given to the under fives. Children under two years should have full-fat milk, and skimmed milk should not be given to a child under five. The diet should include the full range of fats, not polyunsaturated fatty acids only.
- Care should be taken not to give too much salt after weaning.
- Children need some sugar and sugar products, especially during periods of high activity, but they should not be allowed to interfere with a child's intake of other foods.

What does a balanced diet mean? The answer to this will vary between cultures, countries, regions and areas. But think about the most regular feature of every meal that you eat – there will be a 'staple' food in most of them. Most diets include a staple food that is high in carbohydrate, providing most of the body's energy needs, with some protein and vitamins. A country's staple food is usually based on a crop that is easily grown there, for example potatoes in Britain, rice in India and China, yams in the Caribbean, and will be from one of the following groups:

- cereal grains – wheat, oats, barley, rice, corn
- root crops – potatoes, yams
- pulses and seeds – lentil, millet
- some tree crops – sago, plantain or okra.

However, improved transport systems and storage facilities have resulted in the range of available staple items being much wider than even a few years ago. A trip to the supermarket offers you the chance to try most of the staple items listed above. Among the group of children you work with, there may be a range of staple foods that the children are used to.

Certain proportions of foods are required for a healthy diet. All need to be eaten in balanced quantities. The chart below gives quantities for a child from the age of 12 months who is eating a normal, full diet.

Food groups	Nutrients	Portions per day
1 Staple food, for example bread, potatoes, cereals, pasta, lentils, rice	Fibre, vitamins, minerals, carbohydrates	3–5 (one at each meal)
2 Fruit and vegetables	Fibre, vitamins, minerals, carbohydrates	3–4
3 Milk and milk products	Proteins, fats, vitamins, minerals	2–3 1 pint milk 1 small yoghurt 28 g cheese
4 High-protein foods – meat, eggs, fish, pulses	Proteins, vitamins, minerals, fats	2–3
5 Fats and oils	Essential fatty acids	Small amounts, infrequently

A balanced diet will be based on the information in the chart, and include a staple food with the addition of other foods to provide nutritional balance, flavour, texture and interest.

Key issues

The amount of food and particular nutrients needed varies with the age, size and sex of a child. Nutritionists calculate recommended daily intakes – the following figures were published in the 1991 COMA report:

	Boys less than 1 year	Boys 1–10 years	Girls less than 1 year	Girls 1–10 years
Energy (kcals)	545–920	1230–1970	515–865	1165–1740
Protein (g)	12.5–14.9	14.5–28.3	12.5–14.9	14.9–28.3
Calcium (mg)	525	350–550	525	350–550
Iron (mg)	1.7–7.8	6.9–8.7	1.7–7.8	6.9–8.7
Vit A (μg)	350	400–500	350	400–500
Vit B1 (mg)	0.2–0.3	0.5–0.7	0.2–0.3	0.5–0.7
Vit C (mg)	25	30	25	30
Vit D (μg)	8.5	7.0	8.5	7.0
Fibre (g)	There is no recommended figure for children under 5 years of age. Older children should increase their fibre intake as a percentage of their overall food consumption			

Key issues

What about junk food?

'Junk food' is often dismissed as not providing a healthy diet, yet just think about what is in a burger or a pizza or fish and chips. So-called 'junk food' can provide a useful contribution to a child's diet, but just as a constant diet of shepherd's pie or meat curry and rice every day would not meet all dietary needs, eating nothing but burgers is not healthy. Think about how fast food can be included in a healthy diet, by balancing it with fresh fruit and vegetables.

Case study

1   Jehan's parents were very worried, as all their son seemed to be eating was Rice Krispies and cream crackers and cheese. At the end of a week of making a note of everything he had eaten, they discovered Jehan's diet had contained:

Rice Krispies (carbohydrate, minerals, vitamins)
Milk (protein, fat, carbohydrate, vitamins A and B)
Sugar (carbohydrate)
Cream crackers (carbohydrate, fat)
Margarine (fat, vitamins A and D)
Cheese (as milk)

Bananas (carbohydrates, Vitamin C, fibre)
Dahl and rice (protein, carbohydrate, vitamin B, iron, calcium, fibre)
Fresh orange juice (vitamin C, fibre, fruit, sugars).

In fact, Jehan had been taking all the nutrients he needed, perhaps not in the form his parents would have preferred or in family meals. He was active, full of energy and well, and his weight was within the normal range for his age and height.

2   Marietta's parents were worried about her weight. She weighed twice the expected amount for her height and age. Her parents thought that she had some 'gland' problem. All Marietta ate, they claimed, were normal family meals. A weekly diary of food revealed that in addition to normal family meals, Marietta ate almost continually – bags of crisp, chocolate, extra sandwiches, sugary drinks – and that her normal family meals were often fried, with chips and heavy puddings. In fact, Marietta was consuming almost three times her required daily calories.

How could each of the situations be dealt with?

Active knowledge

Have a look at the menus for meals at your place of work. How are they planned and by whom? What is the range of diets eaten by the children in your workplace? What happens if a child needs a different diet? Analyse the nutritional content of the menu for one week.

Cultural and religious considerations

When planning a balanced diet, one of the most important considerations is to ensure that the food offered to a child is appropriate to his or her cultural background. Faced with an unfamiliar food, a child may be reluctant to eat. A survey of different types of cooking will reveal surprising similarity between cultures, however, even if the food is presented in a slightly different way. For example, meat and potato pie, or Cornish pasty, is the same as a samosa, spring roll or ravioli – a staple item of potato or pasta with meat and/or vegetable added.

An awareness of different cultural eating habits is important to make sure that you respect cultural or religious practices. The best way to make sure that you are providing the most appropriate diet for any child in your care is to ask the parents. If there is a language barrier, find someone to translate. The dietary guidelines for some religious and cultural groups are shown in the chart below, but it is worth doing more research when you need to, by consulting with local leaders of cultural groups.

Cultural group	Dietary code	Related religious practices
Buddhism	Usually vegetarian, but eat dairy produce and eggs	
Hinduism	Mostly vegetarian – some fish No beef or eggs No alcohol	Caste system affects who may cook and handle crockery, etc. Festival of Hoil in spring, Divali in autumn

Cultural group	Dietary code	Related religious practices
Islam (Muslim)	No pork, meat produced in halal tradition No shellfish No alcohol	Festival of Eid, ends Ramadan (period of fasting during the day for one month) in the spring
Judaism	No pork, kidney, shellfish or gamebirds Meat must be produced in the kosher manner Meat and dairy produce must not be eaten in the same meal or cooked in the same pans	Saturday is the week's main holy day Passover and Yom Kippur (a day of fasting) are important festivals
Sikhism	No beef or pork Mostly vegetarians No alcohol	New Year in April, Festival of light in autumn

Consolidation

Considering that it is unlikely that children have all their meals at nursery or school, plan a full week's menu for a child aged three years who attends daily, building in the typical menu at nursery or school as well as at home. How would this need changing for an 18-month-old, or a six-year-old child?

Involving parents

While it is essential to comply with cultural requirements in relation to diet, it is also important to share this knowledge with other children. As long as there is no flouting of cultural rules, it is a good idea to encourage children to try foods from cultures other than their own. There is plenty of scope for children to learn about countries and widen their awareness of other cultures through food, and to broaden their taste in food in the process. Involving parents in bringing in or preparing food in school or nursery is an excellent opportunity for parental involvement. Whole activity plans can be developed around a country or culture, for example.

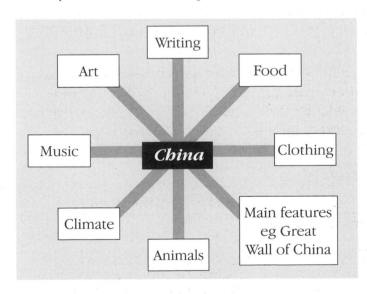

Learning about the food of another culture can act as the basis for a range of activities about other countries and cultures

Presenting food and drinks that are attractive and appetising to all children

Variety of food preferences

Apart from cultural variations, it is unusual to find two people who have exactly the same tastes in food. We all have preferences for different foods, often at different times. For example, the choice of what you like to eat may vary according to:

- the weather – hot or cold
- time of day
- amount of money available for food
- what was eaten at the previous meal
- time available for preparation and eating
- activities to be done after the meal
- what is available
- state of health
- emotional upsets.

Food preference changes with time. For example, a child who steadfastly refuses to eat cheese one week may surprise you by eating huge chunks the following week. If a food is definitely refused, remove it without a fuss and offer an alternative that is readily available in the kitchen. Think about how your own likes and dislikes have changed over the years.

Keys to good practice
Meal times

- Eating habits are developed in early childhood – children should be encouraged to try different types of food before the age of two years.
- New foods that are rejected the first time should be offered again later.
- Avoid making a fuss about food. Meal times should not involve a battle of wills between adults and children.
- Make sure that a child is comfortable, sitting at a table and chair of suitable height, or safely strapped into a high chair.

Remember

- Meal times should be an enjoyable part of the day.
- A hungry child will eat.

Encouraging positive eating habits

Food is a very emotional topic for most parents – with a tiny baby, feeding is an obvious demonstration of a mother's love for her child, especially breast-feeding. A child who rejects food can make his or her parents feel that they are being rejected. As an early years worker, you may work with children for whom meal times have become a battleground of emotions. Often parents do not realise that as a child becomes active, walking around exploring his or her environment is far more interesting than eating. A combination of eating smaller amounts, being physically active and a growth in height will obviously result in a thinner child – and for many parents lead to a concern about eating habits.

Presentation of food

One way to encourage children to eat is to present food attractively.

In an early years setting, having the children all sitting together at a meal provides an ideal opportunity for social interaction – talking to each other, asking for things to be passed to them, observing other children eating.

Meal times should be enjoyable. Try not to use them as part of a punishment, for example sitting a child apart because of some previous misdemeanour. Meal times should never be used in this way because, as we have already seen, food can very quickly become an emotional weapon.

Provide appropriate utensils, for example spoons for runny foods such as soups and stews, knives and forks where needed, or chopsticks, etc. If a child has difficulty

Meal times should be an enjoyable experience involving social interaction

with the usual utensils, consider giving alternatives and the appropriate assistance. Specially modified cutlery can be bought for children with physical disabilities affecting their hands. The important point is to remember that ideally everyone should be independent in self-feeding.

Keys to good practice
Presenting food

- Aim to provide small portions, attractively presented, with the appropriate utensils. Most children will eat a serving-spoon-size portion and then return for more, but may be put off eating if they are given a large portion to start with.
- Be sensitive to cultural variations, for example Asian children eating chappattis and other food with their fingers.
- Be sensitive to the impact of eating in a large group. School dining rooms can be very daunting to young children, who may be overwhelmed by the number of people and the noise.

A child should be provided with comfortable facilities for eating

Factors affecting appetite

- Excitement at a forthcoming event such as an outing or holiday.
- Diverting activities such as a new toy, other children playing outside, recent skill acquisition, for example walking.
- Tiredness.
- Stress can have two effects on the appetite: either to 'comfort eat', usually the less healthy types of food, or to depress the appetite. If there are stressful events in a child's life, for example parental rows or divorce, money worries at home, bullying, school phobia, changing schools or nursery, they will often be reflected in a child's eating habits.
- Illness will usually affect a child's appetite. Even having a common cold is enough to stop a child eating. Lack of food will not cause problems for a few days. Once the child is well and active again, the appetite will soon return, and any weight lost will be rapidly regained. It is important to ensure that adequate fluids are drunk – fresh juice, milk and water – to avoid dehydration.

Eating routines

Remember that there will be as many 'ideal' eating routines as there are families. You will work with children who have very different experiences of food and meal times. This could vary from formal three-course meals taken at the table with the whole family, through to snatched TV dinners at different times, or the children eating first, with adults eating alone later. The use of a table and utensils will vary.

It is important to remember that your experiences of food and eating are not the only type of meal time routines. There are variations in terms of:

- the times of meals and the names of meals (lunch, dinner, tea, supper)
- places to eat (table, floor, chair)
- utensils used (chopsticks, fingers, knife and fork).

Keys to good practice
Encouraging good eating habits

- Involve children in choosing, cooking and serving their food as much as possible.
- Introduce changes to diets slowly, one new food at a time.
- Offer small portions of attractively presented food.
- Avoid over-filling a plate.
- Accept a dislike for a food – it may be accepted at a later time.
- Offer different eating experiences – with friends, in a cafe, picnics, etc.
- Set an example by eating healthy foods.
- Keep sweets and snacks for after meals.
- Don't fuss if a child is not hungry.
- Do not use food as a bribe.

Preparing food and using equipment within the health, safety and hygiene requirements of the setting

Food poisoning

Food is an ideal medium for the transmission of infection. It is therefore essential to prepare and store food safely and hygienically. Food poisoning is a notifiable disease that can and does cause a significant number of deaths every year, especially in the frail, elderly and very young children. Symptoms include diarrhoea, vomiting, pain and dehydration.

Bacteria are organisms that can cause disease if they are in the right environment to grow. Bacteria are all around us and in the correct place do not cause harm. Indeed, we need bacteria to keep our bodies healthy – they are part of the complex ecosystem that is the human body and environment. However, problems arise when bacteria from faeces, for example, find their way into food or the food is kept in a warm room, resulting in bacteria multiplying quickly.

A bacterium is a single-cell organism that multiplies by dividing, and can, in the right conditions, multiply into seven billion cells in 12 hours. As there are likely to be several hundred bacteria in a portion of infected food, it does not take much imagination to think of the number that can soon develop. Bacteria produce waste products called **toxins**, and these can also cause food poisoning as well as the bacteria themselves.

The chart below outlines the main bacteria that cause food poisoning, and what you can do to prevent an outbreak.

Bacteria	Source	Symptoms	Onset	Control methods
Salmonella	Intestines of animals and birds Raw chicken and eggs	Abdominal pain, diarrhoea, vomiting, fever Some people become carriers Lasts 1–7 days	12–36 hours	Separate raw and cooked foods in the fridge Cook meat thoroughly – bacteria and toxins are destroyed by cooking at 100°C for 30 minutes Avoid giving raw eggs in any form to children
Staphylococcus aureus	Human nose, throat and mouth, skin, boils, cuts, hair	Abdominal pain, vomiting, prostration Lasts 6–24 hours	1–6 hours	Keep cuts, sores, etc. covered with waterproof dressings Avoid touching nose, mouth, hair. Tie back long hair Do not handle food if you have a cough or cold, boils, etc.
Clostridium perfringens	From the soil via dust, insects, faeces	Pain, diarrhoea. 12–48 hours	12–18 hours	Thorough cooking to the centre of joints of meat, pans of stew, etc. Keep raw and cooked foods separate

Bacteria	Source	Symptoms	Onset	Control methods
Bacillis cereus	Cereal grains – rice (especially cooked rice). Also in flour, potatoes, milk powders	Vomiting, pain, diarrhoea Symptoms from toxins last 12–24 hours from food, up to two days from gut	1–5 hours	Thorough cooking and reheating of dishes with cooked rice and other grains Store food at correct temperature. If in doubt about cooked rice, throw it 'away
E.Coli	Normal bacteria of human digestive tract, transferred from unwashed hands via faeces	Pain, fever, diarrhoea, vomiting Lasts 1–5 days	12–24 hours	E.Coli in food shows poor personal hygiene. Hands must be washed after a visit to the toilet and scrubbed before preparing food
Clostridium botulinum	From soil via animals, fish and vegetables Outbreaks due to cross-contamination	Paralysis of nerves causes problems with swallowing, breathing and vision. Death is common	12–36 hours, but may be longer	Avoid using cans of food that have 'blown' Store frozen foods at correct temperature
Listeria	Cross-contamination from carriers and the environment Infected foods – pre-prepared, chilled	Fever, septicaemia, meningitis Dangerous to young babies and pregnant women. Can cause abortion and death	Long onset	Vulnerable groups of people should avoid soft cheeses and pate and reheated meals Prevent cross-contamination during storage

It is essential to be aware of the importance of the regulations relating to food storage, handling and preparation. Undertaking a course in Basic Food Hygiene is the best way to gain and practise this knowledge. Ask your employer or trainer if this is possible.

As an early years worker, you will be handling food, ranging from helping a child to feed through to preparing food for a child.

Keys to good practice

Preparing and handling food

- Always keep cooked food covered.
- Keep cooked and raw foods separate, even in the fridge.
- All surfaces should be cleaned at least once per day and should be easy to clean.
- Equipment such as can-openers, slicers, food-processors should be regularly cleaned and sterilised.
- Fridges and freezers should be at the required temperatures – below 4°C for fridges, –18°C for freezers – and be regularly defrosted and cleaned.
- All cloths, tea towels, oven gloves must be washed/boiled frequently.
- Disposable towels should be used for drying hands and mopping spills.

- Floor mops should be kept away from food handling areas and kept clean and in good condition.
- All rubbish bins should be well away from food, and be regularly disinfected.
- All kitchen staff must be aware of the causes and prevention of food poisoning.

How many hazards can you spot in this kitchen?

There are laws to protect the public from risks of food poisoning: **The Food Safety Act 1990** and the Food Hygiene Regulations. The Food Safety Act affects all parts of the food chain, from the growing of crops and rearing of animals to the serving of food itself. Under the Act:

- ministers can make regulations for all parts of the food industry, to ensure that food does not harm the people who eat it
- it is an offence to cause illness by preventable contamination of food
- deliberately or knowingly contaminating food is a criminal offence
- premises may be closed, and for those found guilty of contravening the Act there may be large fines and possible imprisonment
- all managers and staff have responsibilities, with anyone who handles or serves food being required to be qualified with a Basic Food Hygiene certificate as a minimum qualification.

Allergies and reactions to food

Children can be allergic to many foodstuffs, producing a range of symptoms and problems if the food is eaten. The chart below lists some common food allergies.

Allergy	Symptoms	Dietary restrictions
Nuts	Respiratory problems; allergic shock – swelling of airways, may result in death	All nuts or foods containing them. Check all food labels, as many processed foods have nuts hidden in the contents
Wheat (gluten)	Coeliac disease – failure to thrive, large bulky stools, weight loss – due to the effect on the small intestine	All foods containing wheat and flour. Includes biscuits, bread. Need to be replaced by rice biscuits, rice cakes and rice bread
Milk and milk products	May cause eczema, asthma or digestive problems	May need to use soya-based products in place of dairy products
Food additives – (colorants and preservatives) – often identified on food labels as E numbers	Behavioural problems – hyperactivity Skin rashes, eczema	Check all labels for additives – some may be names rather than numbers, for example sunset yellow (E102, tartrazine). Avoid highly coloured foods and drinks.

If a child has a food allergy, it is important that he or she still receives a balanced diet. The advice of a dietician should be sought and followed. The child's diet should be carefully screened to ensure that the product he or she is allergic to is not hidden in some foods – labels on foodstuffs need to be carefully checked. You should ask the child's parents for a list of foods that can be tolerated. If a child has several allergies and is under the care of a dietician, it might be useful if you could have a discussion with the dietician to help in your support of the child.

Children with certain diseases and conditions need to follow special diets as some foods can make them ill, for example:

- diabetes (carbohydrate and sugar intake need to be balanced against insulin levels)
- phenylketonuria (protein intake needs monitoring and restricting)
- coeliac disease (see chart above).

With any allergy or illness, always check with the child's parents or medical support if you are unsure about his or her dietary needs. Care needs to be taken when the child is going to other children's homes or on outings from school or nursery, as it may not be so easy to check on the food consumed.

An important point in supporting children with dietary allergies or needs is to help them eat as normal a diet as they can. Wherever possible, find food substitutes that are similar to the popular foods being eaten by other children, so that a child does not feel left out.

Using food and meal times as a learning tool

Meal times should be an enjoyable event in a child's daily routine, and can be used to help young children learn about:

- counting – cutlery, numbers of people, portions, etc.
- colours
- setting a table
- sharing
- using right and left hands
- concepts of division – half, quarter, etc.
- shapes – square cakes, round buns, long thin beans
- solids and liquids
- textures – soft, hard, crunchy
- living with other people
- traditions and customs
- socially acceptable behaviour.

Meal times and food offer scope for informal language development, for example talking about the food, where it comes from, how it is changed (a potato from the raw vegetable into mash, for instance), different favourite foods, differences in eating patterns (home/school) and also general conversation at a time when the children have the full attention of the carer.

Consolidation

Consider the way food is prepared and served in your workplace. Make a note of the points to consider in relation to food, and in making meal times an enjoyable, safe and nutritious experience for the children in your care.

| Element C2.2 | Contribute to children's personal hygiene |

WHAT YOU NEED TO LEARN

- Hygiene routines for bodily elimination and hand washing
- Caring for children's hair, skin and teeth

Hygiene routines for bodily elimination and hand washing

Part of all children's routine is based on attention to their personal hygiene. From birth, a child needs these basic requirements to be attended to. This happens as part of the close interaction with the child's carer, and is an important part of a child's social development. Family routines and attitudes vary, and may be affected by cultural rules as well as by personality. Some families view personal hygiene functions as intensely private, to be carried out only behind locked doors. Other families have a more relaxed approach, with no concern for locks or privacy. You are probably already aware of this – compare your own experiences with those of your colleagues. The attitude that children experience at home in relation to personal hygiene will obviously affect their reaction in day care.

New babies do not need to have a bath every day; they do not have the chance to get very dirty just eating and sleeping! A baby's toilet needs are catered for by the use of nappies. By the time children are two to three years old, the need for bathing is much greater, and they will be starting to deal with their own toilet needs, leading to almost full independence by the age of five or six years.

Part of the socialisation of a young child is the move towards independence in personal hygiene. Many an exasperated parent of a two- or three-year-old has had a vision of the child going to school still in nappies and unable to get washed and dressed alone. This scenario does not happen if a child is developing within normal ranges.

Children cannot become capable of dealing with their own personal hygiene, however, until they have reached the right stage of development.

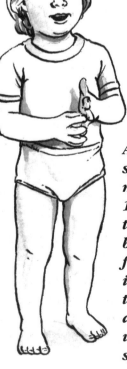

Babies have no control at all over bowel and bladder movements. Both empty automatically when they are partly full, often in response to eating and drinking

As the central nervous system approaches maturity, by the age of 18 months, a child starts to recognise feelings of bladder and bowel fullness, and can start to indicate needs and use the toilet or pot in the daytime. This coincides with the development of speech.

Nappy changing

For the first 18 to 24 months of life, most babies use nappies to collect urine and faeces. Therefore, it is unlikely that you will complete your career in early years care without changing some nappies. There are two types: disposable nappies and terry nappies, which need to be laundered.

Key issues

Advocates of terry nappies claim they are significantly cheaper to use than disposable ones, as well as being environmentally friendly.

Investigate some of the brands and types of nappies that are available and compile a comparative chart of their strengths and weaknesses and the costs of using them. Which are cheaper to use? See if you can gauge opinion among parents about their views on terries versus disposables.

Keys to good practice
Changing a nappy

- Always wash your hands before and after changing a nappy.
- Always gather all your equipment together first.
- Clean the baby's bottom using either water and cottonwool or baby wipes. Always clean from front to back, especially for girls, to avoid transferring bacteria to the genitals.
- Ensure there is a bin, bag or bucket nearby ready to receive the dirty nappy. Immediately after finishing the task, clear rubbish away and then wash your hands thoroughly.
- NEVER leave the baby unattended on a changing table or at any height above the floor.
- Make sure that other children in the area cannot get hold of soiled materials or equipment.

Nappy rash and other problems

Nappy rash appears as a very red, sore area over the buttocks that can, in severe cases, look like chafing. Nappy rash is caused by the urea that is present in urine breaking down and releasing ammonia. Ammonia is a chemical with a very strong smell. If you have changed a nappy that has been on a baby overnight, you will probably have smelt a whiff of ammonia.

To prevent nappy rash, do not allow a baby to spend too long in a wet nappy, and certainly never leave a baby in a wet and dirty nappy.

Applying a barrier cream will also help, and petroleum jelly is a good standby. There are many proprietary creams on the market, all offering different claims of efficiency.

All babies will benefit from having some time each day without a nappy. A warm room and a covered mat on the floor are a suitable place to leave the child for a time without a nappy.

Sometimes a baby can develop thrush on the buttocks. This may be distinguished by small outbreaks of spot-type lesions away from the main red area. Medical advice is needed to deal with a nappy rash involving thrush. Thrush is caused by the fungus monilia, and often occurs if a child has been on antibiotics or his or her resistance is generally low.

Several other problems may be detected at nappy changing time, as outlined in the chart below.

Problem	Description	Cause	Treatment
Sweat rash (milaria)	Rash of small red spots on face, chest	Overheating Immature sweat glands	Cool child down by removing clothes, Use cotton next to skin Avoid overheating with clothes and room heating
Cradle cap	Yellow/brown crusting on the scalp, particularly on anterior fontanelle	Build up of sebum – failure to wash and rinse area properly (often due to unnecessary concern that the 'soft spot' can be damaged)	Soften with olive oil, shampoo and rinse well – special shampoos available
Chafing	Soreness in body creases – neck, groin and armpits	Insufficient washing and drying of skin	Prevent by good skin care Care needed in the neck area due to baby dribbling Apply mild cream, for example zinc and castor oil
Eczema	Sore red rash – may affect face or any of the body, particularly skin folds. Can be very severe, with bleeding and weeping	Usually an allergic response – possibly to cow's milk	Requires medical treatment Avoid soap and using detergents for washing clothes Keep nails short to stop scratching Use emulsifiers in the bath Breast-feeding helps to lessen severity and delay onset
Constipation	Very hard, dry faeces – baby may cry on passing them	Insufficient liquids, especially water Dehydration in warm weather	Try to ensure that the baby drinks enough water or diluted fruit juice
Diarrhoea	Very smelly, loose faeces, at frequent intervals	Over-rich formula feeds Poor hygiene in making feeds Infection	Lots of water to drink If it continues longer than 24 hours, seek medical help
Urine infection	Smelly nappy, even when only wet. Often produces a nappy rash	Infection	Seek medical advice

Toilet training

Toilet training cannot take place until:

- the child's nervous system has matured so that a full bladder or bowel is recognised (from about 18 months to three years)
- the child's communication skills are developed so that he or she can indicate a need for the toilet
- a potty, or toilet seat and step for access and safe use, is available.

Until about the 1950s it was thought that a baby could be toilet trained from birth, by sitting him or her on a potty while feeding. All that happened was that the potty caught the automatic reflex action of the gut and bladder during feeding. By the time the child was about one or two years old and starting to recognise his or her own individuality, there was often rebellion and the training 'failed'.

Approaches to toilet training

As children become physically able to gain control of the bladder and bowel, they are becoming aware of their control over others. Sensitivity is needed to prevent toilet training from becoming a battleground between a child and the carers.

Encouraging recognition of a full bladder and offering the use of a potty or toilet, combined with lots of praise when used, is one approach. Children should never be made to feel they have done something wrong if they wet or soil themselves. Great care should be taken to avoid embarrassing the child in front of others.

If you are involved in the toilet training of a child, as with everything else you must consult and cooperate with the parents. Some parents may have quite fixed views on how they wish to approach the issue, while others may value your advice and support. It is essential to try to be consistent, to avoid confusing the child.

There is a wide range in the age at which a child will become dry during the day and at night. Toilet training is usually a hot topic of conversation among parents of children aged between 18 months and three years. You will always hear of the 'superstar' who was dry day and night within two weeks of reaching 18 months, compared with the child who at the age of three still has accidents, especially when busy playing or at night time. Always remember that both extremes are totally normal. Night-time dryness can take a long time to develop. Many children are still wetting at night at the age of seven years, and can take until their late teens to develop night-time bladder control.

Equipment for toilet training

Good hygiene practices should be encouraged from the very start. Appropriate equipment is essential. Toilets and sinks at the right height for the children are vital, with soft toilet paper, paper towels, soap and water at the right temperature. Care must be taken to ensure a child's privacy, while being on hand to help if needed. Privacy is especially important for a child with special needs who may need more assistance. An older child who is still using nappies, for example, needs very sensitive care routines, to recognise his or her relative maturity.

Children who are wheelchair users should be provided with accessible facilities

Equipment for children who are wheelchair users should be of the right type, with wide doors for easy access and to ensure the child's maximum independence. No child who uses a wheelchair should ever have to be helped to the toilet simply because the toilet cubicle is too small. The Disability Discrimination Act 1998 covers issues such as this.

Active knowledge

Children cope with toilet training far better if they have the right equipment. Has your setting got the following equipment?

- Potties.
- Small toilets – there should be a minimum of one small toilet for ten children, with the same number of sinks. Water should be at 63°C, with germicidal soap and paper towels provided.
- Box steps to help with large toilets.
- Seats to set on top of toilet seats.

Keys to good practice
Toilet training

- Make sure that a child is ready for training – there is a wide variation in the age a child may be ready (14–36 months).
- Make the potty a familiar part of a child's environment and let the child sit on it with a nappy on as part of play.
- Let the child see other children using a potty as much as possible, as an example.
- Try to introduce toilet training in warm weather, when the child can run around without a nappy on.
- Always praise the child when a potty is used appropriately, but do not show disapproval if accidents happen.
- Quickly and quietly clean up accidents without making an issue of them.

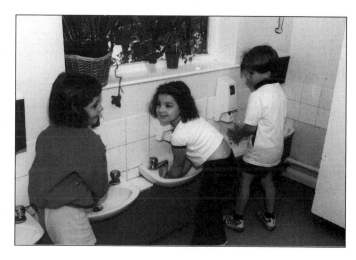

Children need facilities to be at the correct height if they are to become independent

Active knowledge

Ask a selection of parents of children aged approximately three to four years about the toilet training of their children. Did they encounter any problems? If so what, and how did they deal with them? Were there similarities between the different children?

Hand washing and hygiene

The importance of careful handwashing cannot be over-stressed. Even hands that seem clean can have a mass of bacteria on them. Trips to the toilet transfer thousands of potentially harmful bacteria on to the hands, through wiping bottoms, touching toilet handles, etc. A brief handwash without soap will leave most bacteria still on the hands. If those hands subsequently go into a child's mouth, there is a serious risk of infection.

The bowel is full of bacteria called **E.Coli** (see page 12) which help to keep the bowel healthy. However, if E.Coli gets into the upper digestive tract through poor handwashing, it is a different story. Bacterial surveys of open sweet trays in shops, and bowls of peanuts on pub bars, have revealed high levels of E.Coli contamination.

E.Coli can also cause vaginal infections in girls. It is important always to wipe a baby's bottom from front to back to avoid contamination in this way. In addition to correct cleaning of the nappy area when nappy changing, little girls should be taught in this way when being toilet-trained.

Handwashing can be made a game, with competitions for the cleanest hands. For older children, plates for culturing bacteria can be taken of dirty and so-called clean hands to show them the results or poor hygiene.

Dealing with an outbreak of gastroenteritis

Occasionally, early years settings have outbreaks of gastroenteritis, salmonella or dysentery. These illnesses can spread very rapidly in a nursery and require special measures to reduce the spread of infection. It is essential that routines are examined and good practice is meticulously followed, including the careful cleaning of toilet areas, handles and floors at regular intervals. Local public health services may visit and supervise children when they are washing their hands to help to curtail the outbreak. Look at Element C2.1 on food hygiene for some causes of gastroenteritis (diarrhoea and vomiting).

Staff directly involved in changing nappies or helping children at the toilet should wear disposable plastic aprons, and thoroughly wash their own hands. Soiled material should be carefully disposed of in accordance with the policy of the setting.

Germs hate soap and water!

The topic of hygiene can be made into a positive learning experience for children. For example, you could use images of germs, and fighting battles with them, to develop activities. If children understand why hygiene precautions are necessary, they are more likely to follow them. Your local Health Promotion Unit will have posters and leaflets to help with ideas.

Caring for children's hair, skin and teeth

Care of the skin

All children need to be washed or to wash themselves regularly. Failure to keep the skin clean results in sore skin and a smelly child. Skin smells when it is not kept clean because of the action of bacteria on sweat and dead skin cells. Sore areas develop because of the build up of sweat and dead skin rubbing in skin creases and against clothes.

Bath time

- An active, healthy child ideally needs a bath or shower daily. This may not be possible for some families who cannot afford the cost of heating large quantities of water or who may not have access to facilities.
- Bath time should be an enjoyable experience for children, with endless opportunities for older children to learn about floating and sinking, volume, etc.
- It is important to take precautions to prevent accidents, for example non-slip mats in the bath, care when running the bath (cold water in first). Never leave a child unattended in the bath – a child can drown in 3 cm of water.

Keys to good practice
Skin and hair care for children

- Always remember that you are aiming to help a child eventually to become independent in personal care. Whenever possible encourage children to undertake their own care, under supervision.
- As a minimum requirement, children should have their hands and faces washed each morning, after using the toilet and before meals.
- Keep nails short and clean – scrub with a soft nailbrush.
- Wash hair twice a week, and comb daily with a close-toothed comb to remove any headlice that might have been picked up.
- Very curly hair needs care and treatment with conditioners, and should be combed with a wide-toothed comb.
- Every child should have his or her own flannel, toothbrush, comb and brush, which should be cleaned regularly.
- Some skin is more prone to dryness than others and may need massaging with moisturisers, for example black skin has this tendency. Always take care of a child's skin creases.
- Check with parents to ensure that you are not flouting any cultural or personal preferences in the care of their child's skin and hair.

Bathing a baby

It is unlikely that you would be asked to bath a baby in a nursery setting. Older children may possibly need bathing if they have become particularly dirty, but this is not likely with a tiny baby. If you do need to bath a young baby, look at one of the many childcare books available – they all have excellent descriptions of this task.

Care of the teeth

Key issues ✓

Is tooth care a function of day care for children? It could be argued that a child who cleans his or her teeth at home in the morning and at night does not need further cleaning at nursery or school. Ask your colleagues for their views. Maybe your workplace has a view or policy on this. If so, what is it? Should children in day care clean their teeth after snacks and meals? How could the provision and care of toothbrushes be managed?

Consolidation

The parents of 18-month-old Bethany have asked you to help them with her potty training. She is at your nursery from 9 to 5 every weekday. Make a note of the steps you would take, including the equipment that would be needed. How would you plan to meet her general hygiene needs?

Element C2.3   Respond to illness in children

WHAT YOU NEED TO LEARN

- Recognising illness in children
- Appropriate action for minor ailments, and acute illnesses and accidents
- Caring for sick children
- Storing and administering medicines
- Informing parents and other staff of a child's illness
- Record keeping

Recognising illness in children

All children pick up infections and become ill from time to time. The human body is prey to many different types of pathogens (disease-causing organisms) including the following:

- **Bacteria** – microscopic organisms, such as streptococci and staphylococci, many of which live harmlessly on or in the body – cause illness when they grow in the wrong place, and multiply. Bacterial infections can be treated with antibiotics.
- **Viruses** are smaller than bacteria and are capable of mutations to avoid treatment. Viral infections cannot be treated with antibiotics. Some viral infections have effective immunisations, for example flu and measles.
- **Fungal infections** – yeast-type infections that cause candidiasis (thrush), athletes foot – may be treated with antifungal agents.
- **Parasites** – organisms that live on or in the body such as thread worms and lice.

Immunity to infection

Immunity is the ability of the body to resist infections caused by pathogens. We are all in constant contact with bacteria and viruses, but we do not become ill every time because of our immunity. There are several ways that we become immune to pathogens.

- Through **passive immunity** – in the uterus (womb) the unborn child (foetus) gains immunity to all diseases to which the mother has immunity, through the placenta, later, breast milk provides the baby with a similar immunity.
- Through **active immunity** – from birth, immunity is built up as a result of having illnesses such as colds and viral infections, and through immunisations, for example for polio, diphtheria, mumps and whooping cough.

You should be familiar with the immunisation pattern for children. Ask at your GP's surgery or health centre for a leaflet. You will see a chart similar to this:

Age	Immunisation
8 weeks	Diphtheria Tetanus Pertussis (whooping cough) Hib (viral meningitis) Polio } as one injection
12 weeks	As for 8 weeks
16 weeks	As for 8 and 12 weeks
12–18 months	MMR (mumps, measles, rubella) – as one injection
4–5 years	Diphtheria Tetanus Polio } as one injection
10–14 years	Rubella BCG (tuberculosis)
15–18 years	Diphtheria Tetanus Polio } as one injection

Immunisations protect children from diseases that can kill or seriously impair them, such as whooping cough and diphtheria, or are dangerous to others, such as rubella (hazardous to an unborn child where the mother has no immunity). In addition, children travelling overseas may need other immunisations, and parents should be advised to see their GP. A child whose immune system is damaged through suffering from leukaemia may need to be immunised or protected against some other illnesses, such as chickenpox.

Key issues

There is often controversy about the vaccination of young children. Sometimes scare stories appear in the media about children who appear to have been harmed by a certain vaccination. Examples include the Pertussis vaccine in the 1970s, and more recently the joint administration of the MMR vaccine. It is important for you as an early years worker to research the latest information about such issues, so that you remain well informed. When parents ask you for your advice you should always refer them to their GP or health visitor to discuss the situation regarding their child. Usually, any small risk of damage from vaccine is far outweighed by the benefits of vaccination, both to the child concerned and other children.

Recognising the signs and symptoms of illness

Children often present with signs and symptoms of impending illness. Very often the illness will be something very minor, and within a day or two the child will be back to normal. However, you need to be able to recognise when an illness is more serious and requires medical attention.

The spider diagrams below list some common signs of illness and when to call for urgent medical help.

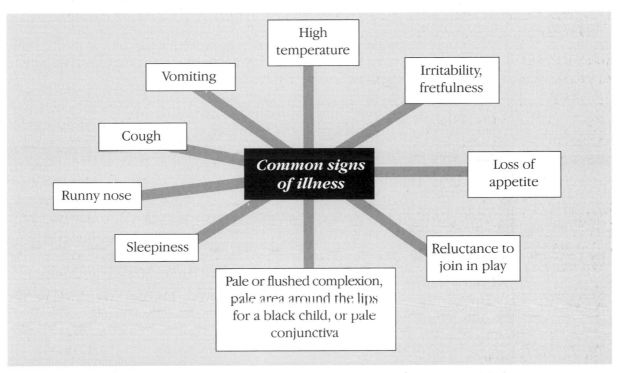

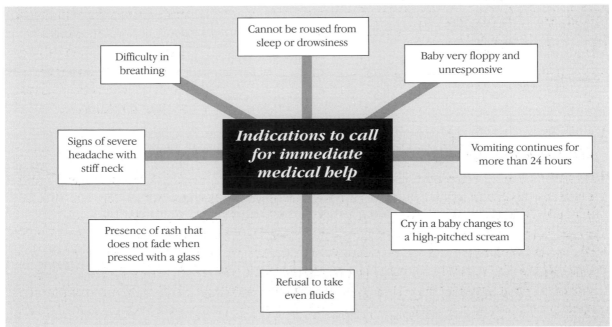

Appropriate action for minor ailments, and acute illnesses and accidents

Common childhood illnesses

Illness	Signs and symptoms	Treatment or action needed	Incubation
Common cold	Sneezing, sore throat, runny nose, headache, temperature, irritability	Treat symptoms with rest, fluids. Encourage child to blow nose to avoid catarrh	1–3 days
Gastroenteritis	Vomiting, diarrhoea, dehydration, which in extreme cases can lead to death	Replace fluids using glucose and salt solution such as Rehydrat. Medical help should be summoned.	1–36 hours
Tonsillitis	Very sore throat, difficulty in swallowing, fever, headache, aches and pains	Rest, fluids, medical attention as antibiotics may be needed if the cause is bacterial	Varies
Scarlet fever	Fever, loss of appetite, sore throat, pale around mouth, 'strawberry tongue', bright pinpoint rash over face and body	Rest, fluids and observe for complications	2–4 days
Dysentery	Vomiting, diarrhoea with blood and mucus, abdominal pain, fever, headache	Medical attention, rest, fluids. Strict hygiene measures, especially in early years settings	1–7 days
Chickenpox	Fever, very itchy rash, with blister-like appearance	Tepid bath containing bicarbonate of soda and calamine lotion applied to skin to stop itching. Try to stop child scratching to avoid scarring	10–14 days
Measles	High fever, runny nose and eyes, later cough, white spots in mouth, blotchy rash on body and face	Rest, fluids, tepid sponging. Medical attention to check for complications	7–15 days
Mumps	Pain and swelling of jaw, painful swallowing, fever	Fluids, (may need a straw to drink through), warmth to swelling, pain relief	14–21 days
Rubella (German measles)	Slight cold, sore throat, swollen glands behind ears, slight pink rash	Rest, treat symptoms. Avoid contact with pregnant women	14–21 days
Pertussis (whooping cough)	Snuffly cold, spasmodic cough with whoop sound, vomiting	Medical attention. Rest, fluids, feed after a coughing attack	7–21 days
Meningitis	Fever, headache, irritability, drowsiness, confusion, dislike of light, very stiff neck. May be small red spots beneath the skin that do not disappear when a glass is pressed against them	Immediate medical attention. Take child to hospital or call an ambulance if the GP cannot be contacted	2–10 days

When is a child infectious?

In nearly all illnesses children are at their most infectious before the symptoms appear. Many illnesses have a cold and/or fever as their first signs. It would not be practicable to exclude all children with these symptoms from nursery, for example, nor would it have much effect on the spread of a disease. Different settings have different rules about excluding children with common illnesses, ranging from excluding all children with symptoms, to exclusion only while the child feels unwell.

Accidents and emergencies

Young children are prone to having accidents and injuring themselves. Even a seemingly simple banging of heads when two children run into each other could be very serious if a carer failed to notice symptoms that something was wrong.

All early years settings must have at least one person qualified in first aid. As an early years worker, it is your responsibility to take a first aid course if your employers do not provide it. You should keep that knowledge up to date. Knowing how to deal with an emergency will help you be far more effective in coping with any future incidents. Everyone working with children should be able to deal calmly with an accident or illness, and decide when it is necessary to call for additional help.

In the event of an accident, before you do anything you must assess the situation. Do not try to deal with an incident if there is any danger to another person. Other children should be moved away from the scene as quickly as possible, and someone should be asked to look after them. Assess the scene for dangers, for example electricity, broken glass, spillages.

Next you must give attention to the casualty's:

A – AIRWAY
B – BREATHING
C – CIRCULATION.

Open the **airway** by gently lifting the child's chin and tilting the head back slightly. Look, listen and feel for breathing. The tilted position lifts the tongue away from the back of the throat so that it does not block the air passage.

If a child is not **breathing** and the airway has been opened, you can breathe for him or her and supply oxygen to the blood by giving artificial ventilation – blowing your own expelled air into his or her lungs. You cannot learn this technique from a book – a good first aid course will teach you the special techniques for babies and children.

You can check for **circulation** by feeling for a pulse in the neck (the carotid pulse). If the heart has stopped, chest compressions can be applied to force blood through the heart and around the body. They must be combined with artificial ventilation so that blood is oxygenated. Once again, a first aid course will teach you the necessary techniques.

The aims of first aid are to:

• preserve life
• stop the condition getting worse
• promote recovery.

In an early years setting where there are other people around, always ask someone to ring for an ambulance while you are dealing with an emergency. The chart below gives examples of common emergencies and how to deal with them until expert help arrives.

Emergency	Action required
Bleeding – severe (no foreign body, glass, etc. in the wound)	Lay child down Cover the wound with a pad or dressing Apply pressure with fingers or hand Raise and support the injured part Call for ambulance Treat for shock
Bleeding – severe (glass or other foreign body in the wound)	Same procedure, but apply pressure on either side of the wound Pad around it
Less serious bleeding, cuts and grazes	Clean with plain water and cover with a clean dressing
Shock – caused by injury, bleeding, upset Casualty will be sweaty and clammy, have a rapid pulse. Will eventually become unconscious, and may die	Lay child down, raise legs and cover Treat any cause such as bleeding Loosen tight clothes Dial 999 for an ambulance
Head injury May cause loss of consciousness, in which case treat as unconscious patient	Control any bleeding by applying pressure with a pad Lay casualty down Take or send to hospital Monitor level of consciousness, vomiting, etc.
Unconsciousness May be the result of any emergency or accident.	Assess child's response by gently shaking shoulders and asking questions Check Airway, Breathing and Circulation (see above) Treat any obvious condition, for example bleeding Place in the recovery position Dial 999 for an ambulance
Convulsions Often due to a high temperature in a child, or the child may have epilepsy	If hot, cool child by removing clothing Protect from injury – clear surrounding objects Sponge with tepid water Place in recovery position Dial 999 for an ambulance
Broken bones	Steady and support the injured part – sling for an arm, etc. Protect with padding Do not move a broken limb unnecessarily Take or send to hospital
Back or neck injury Always suspect after falls from swing, slide, tree, etc.	Do not attempt to move Steady and support neck and head Dial 999 for an ambulance
Swallowed poisons, berries, tablets	Do not try to make child sick. If child is sick, save a sample of the vomit to take to the hospital Check ABC (see above) Dial 999 for an ambulance Try to save a sample of the poisons, etc. to take to hospital

Emergency	Action required
Allergic reaction To stings, medicines – red blotchy skin, swelling of face and neck, problems breathing	Dial 999 for an ambulance Put into comfortable position Monitor condition – check ABC (see above)
Choking	Give five back slaps between shoulders – older child leaning forward; baby over knee face downwards Remove any obvious obstruction from mouth Give five chest thrusts – stand behind child, make a fist against lower breast bone, grasp with other hand, and press sharply into chest; for a baby two fingertips on lower half of breast bone Check ABC (see above) Dial 999 for an ambulance
Asthma attack	Make child comfortable, sitting in position most comfortable for him or her Let child use inhaler – usually a blue reliever Encourage child to breathe slowly If attack does not subside, call for medical help
Burns and scalds	Cool with cold water – place under running tap, or apply wet cloths, for at least ten minutes Remove any constrictions – clothing, watches, bracelets – that are not stuck to the burn Cover with clean cloth Take or send to hospital

In the case of an accident, in addition to the above, you must:

- send for a first aider if you are not qualified in first aid
- call for your supervisor
- calm the other children
- inform the child's parents
- record the incident in the accident book.

Calling an ambulance

When dialling 999, always have ready the details of the accident and injury, the age of the child and, of course, where the injured child is. In serious incidents involving breathing difficulties or severe bleeding, an ambulance should be summoned as soon as possible, preferably while first aid is being given. The prompt arrival of trained paramedics can make all the difference to the end result for the child.

Caring for sick children

You have a role in helping to protect children from illness. For example, careful hand washing, blowing noses, covering coughs and ensuring cleanliness of toilet areas can help to reduce the spread of infection.

You also need to be sensitive to the needs of children who have been ill. Even when they have recovered from the acute illness, they may need activities that are usually more suited to a slightly younger child, or they may need more reassurance, attention and cuddles. Parents may need advice and reassurance on these points as well.

It is not part of the role of an early years worker in nursery or school to look after sick children – an ill child should not be brought to nursery or school. However, many children develop signs of illness during the day and will need your attention.

Taking a child's temperature will help you to check on his or her progress, although observing the child will give you a good indication of how ill he or she is. Some children can have a high temperature and only be mildly ill, and vice versa.

To take a child's temperature you will need to use a thermometer. There are three types currently available and you should familiarise yourself with the one used in your setting.

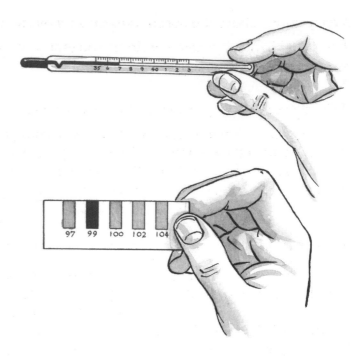

Different types of thermometer

- Fever strip – put the strip on the child's forehead for a few seconds; the strip changes colour and shows the temperature of the child. Although easy to use, the fever strip is not as accurate as a clinical or digital thermometer, but may be the most practical type for nursery or school.
- Clinical thermometer
  - this is made of glass and contains mercury, a poisonous substance, so you will need to use it with care. To take a child's temperature using a clinical thermometer:
  - check that the mercury is at the low point of the thermometer; if it is not, shake the thermometer
  - lift up the child's arm and put the thermometer under the armpit (never in the mouth of the child to avoid the possibility of the child breaking the glass)
  - wait two minutes and then read the temperature
  - sterilise the thermometer before putting it away safely.
- Digital thermometer – easier to read and safer than a clinical thermometer, as it is not made of glass. Put the heat-sensitive end in the child's mouth for one to two minutes. The child's temperature is shown in numbers.

Before using a thermometer, always show it to the child and explain what you are going to do. The normal temperature range for a child is 36.5°C to 37.4°C.

Remember

- When using a clinical thermometer, always place it under the child's armpit (never in the mouth) to avoid the danger of the glass breaking.
- Always put a clinical thermometer away immediately after use – to avoid any hazard from glass or mercury.

A temperature above the normal range is an indication of:

- the child having just eaten or drunk something warm, or
- a recent burst of physical activity, or
- illness.

If illness is the cause, you should do the following:

- remove thick clothing, leaving the child in a cool, covering layer
- cool the air in the room with a fan or by opening a window
- encourage the child to drink diluted juice or water
- at home, paracetamol syrup can be given to help reduce the temperature, but only with parental consent.

Storing and administering medicines

Often after an absence due to illness or a visit to the GP, a child may need to take medicine while at nursery or school. Parents must give written consent for their child to have medicine administered by the nursery nurse or teacher. The medicine must be kept in a safe place and be clearly labelled with the child's name. A record must be kept noting when the medicine has been given, and by whom. Early years workers are not allowed to give medicines to children under any circumstances without this written permission. This includes applying creams, lotions and administering inhalers.

Using an inhaler

Most early years settings have children who require the use of an inhaler for asthma treatment. You should be shown how to support a child who uses an inhaler, and need to be confident that you know how to use the type of inhaler the child is using. Early years settings will vary in their policies on the storage and use of inhalers. The nurse from the GP's surgery that the child attends may be happy to come and talk to staff if needed.

A child old enough to use an asthma inhaler is old enough to keep it on his or her person, or very close at hand. Some settings insist on inhalers being locked away to prevent other children having access to them. But even if another child has a puff of a Ventolin inhaler, no harm will be done, as the drug has little or no effect on someone without asthma.

There are several types of inhaler, as shown in the illustrations.

Newer type of inhaler

Traditional inhaler

If a child has an asthma attack, follow these suggestions:

- stay with the child all the time
- keep the area around the child clear of other children
- remain calm and reassuring
- encourage the child to sit up to increase his or her lung capacity
- try to find out what triggered the attack – an infection, exercise, stress, emotion, weather, allergens.

Active knowledge ✓

Find out about the different types of inhaler used by children at your setting. Your local health clinic should have leaflets describing them. What is your workplace's policy on the storage and use of inhalers?

Creams and lotions

Applying creams and lotions to a child may be necessary if he or she suffers from eczema or other skin conditions.

- Ask the parents to show you what to do.
- Always apply in privacy, to avoid other children gathering around.
- Use plastic gloves or swabs to apply, depending on the instructions – these should be provided along with the lotion or cream.
- Remember that creams and lotions are drugs, just as tablets are – written consent is needed.

Informing parents and other staff of a child's illness

Dealing with the immediate incident in the case of an accident or illness is only part of the procedure for an early years setting. The next important action is to inform the child's parents or carers, and other staff.

Informing parents when their child is ill

The child will have a record card filed in the office with emergency contact numbers. This may not be the child's parents as work commitments may not make it easy for a parent to be contacted. The telephone number may be that of the child's grandparents or aunt, for example – it should be the number of someone who is usually easy to contact, and who in turn can contact the parents.

The person in charge of the setting must call the emergency contact as soon as possible and inform that person of the incident, and where the child is or being taken. Obviously, someone the child knows well should go with him or her to the hospital, until the parents or other carers arrive. This will help to reassure the child, and be a point of contact for the parents when they arrive.

As a student or junior worker, always check procedures with your supervisor. You can provide support to a child who is ill, while the parents are coming to collect him or her, by sitting quietly with the child, perhaps reading a story, and reassuring the child that his or her parents are on their way.

If parents or the emergency contact cannot be reached and the child requires hospital treatment, do not wait to contact the parents. The child should be taken to hospital with a familiar adult, who should stay until a parent arrives.

Parents may ask you for advice about their children when they are ill or appear unwell, as this is very unsettling and worrying for parents. Coverage in the media about meningitis, for example, has quite rightly alerted parents to the risks. However, whenever a child as a fever, it is very easy to be convinced that something serious is starting. Always suggest they should take the child to their GP if they are uncertain what to do. Family doctors prefer to see a child, even if it is only a minor illness, rather than miss a serious problem such as meningitis.

Keys to good practice
In case of illness

- Always try to contact parents as soon as it is evident that a child is ill.
- Ensure that a familiar adult stays with the child at all times until parents arrive.
- Take the child into a quiet room or area of the nursery or school away from other children.
- Provide plenty of reassurance to the child.

Informing parents when a child in the setting has a communicable disease

When a child in the setting has an illness that could spread to the other children, a decision will need to be taken whether to inform all parents.

In many cases with an illness such as chickenpox, parents will usually be aware that it is going around, but would probably appreciate a brief note alerting them to the signs and symptoms.

The issue is more complex with more serious illnesses. For example, meningitis is an illness that has several forms, affects young children particularly under five years old and teenagers, and can be fatal. Meningitis is a notifiable disease, which means it has to be reported to the senior public health officer in the area. Obviously, meningitis is a cause of serious concern to parents, but it is easy for panic to occur. As an early years setting, you should be advised and supported in notifying parents by the Consultant in Communicable Disease and his or her team. Procedures vary depending on the type of meningitis and how many children are affected.

Record keeping

Even with a minor accident that has not needed hospital treatment, an entry should be made in the accident book. Under certain circumstances the accident may need to be reported to the Health and Safety Executive, particularly if a child is seriously injured. A full report is needed, and in any incident the person in charge should examine the details of the case and decide if action is needed to prevent similar occurrences in future.

Social services registration requirements state that an accurate, written report on any significant accident must be made as soon as possible.

Any change in a child's well-being should be noted in the child's records. Some settings keep a 'day book' on each child, with parents jotting down anything that has happened at home to the child, and the nursery doing the same for the day time. These books are useful in ensuring continuity of care. Any illness or other issues of concern should be written in the book.

If a child has to be given any medicines at nursery or school, the parents must give their written consent to this, with clear written instructions as to dose, time, etc. A written record of all doses given in nursery or school must be kept.

Consolidation

A child aged two is suddenly sick in your setting. There have been three cases of 'tummy bugs' in the setting recently. Make notes on what steps you would take in this case. What could your setting do to prevent the outbreak spreading?

Element C2.4 Plan and provide quiet periods for children

WHAT YOU NEED TO LEARN

- Structuring the routine of children to allow for rest and quiet periods
- Providing an appropriate physical environment to promote rest and quiet
- Encouraging and supporting children in preparing for rest periods
- Ensuring children are awakened in an appropriate manner

Structuring the routine of children to allow for rest and quiet periods

Why we need rest and sleep

Rest and sleep are an important part of everyone's life. We all know how we feel if we have had a very late night, or woken very early. Without sleep and rest our bodies become less efficient, and this is no different for children. Very young children will sleep when they need to, and they only need to develop a routine to suit the family. Different families have different ideas about children's sleep patterns. Some families feel that young children should be in bed and asleep in their own room by 6 pm, others that children should go to bed with the adults later in the evening and share a family bed.

Did you know?

A baby could be trained to sleep all day and stay awake all night if the parents worked night duty and wanted this pattern of sleep.

Why do we need to have rest and sleep as part of our everyday routines? This is not quite as obvious as it sounds – your first thought probably was because we get tired. Sleep and rest have several functions, as follows:

- sleep and rest allow the body to recuperate – for muscles and metabolic processes to recover
- growth hormones are released during sleep to produce new bone and red blood cells
- sleep allows the brain and central nervous system to rest, though they do not switch off completely.

If we are deprived of sleep, we begin to suffer memory loss, irritability and even hallucinations. If you think of descriptions of someone who is very tired, 'irritable' will be a key word.

How much sleep do children need?

There is no fixed answer to this question, other than 'as much as they need'! Some babies sleep 18 out of 24 hours, others only 12. Some toddlers can seem to cope on ten hours at night and a nap in the day; others will sleep for 12 hours at night and then need two hours sleep in the afternoon.

Sleep patterns will change with changing routines and events in a child's life.

Case study

Zehra, aged 3, has just started nursery full time. Her mother confides to you that she is worried about her daughter, because she is falling asleep during her evening meal, and is going to bed much earlier than usual.

Do you think this is normal behaviour?

Rest and quiet periods

The body recuperates not only by sleeping – rest has the same function. Very few children will spend all day running around, actively playing, but will sometimes sit down and just 'be', watching the world go by, or ask to hear a story, or watch TV for a short time. These are all resting or quiet periods. Most nurseries and reception classes have a designated 'quiet' time in their daily routine to allow children to recoup their energy. A skilled early years worker will build these times into the children's routine.

When and for how long a setting has a rest or quiet period will depend on the ages of the children. Babies and toddlers will follow their own body clock, and you should discuss the child's routine with parents to find out the usual pattern. There are three levels of quiet period:

- sleep times – especially needed by babies and toddlers, for example in a day nursery
- rest periods – for toddlers and pre-schoolers
- quiet activities – essential for all age groups as a break between other activities and a chance to recuperate. Quiet activities include story time, watching a TV programme or

video and listening to music, all of which should use material that is soothing and not stimulating. Older children may enjoy relaxation exercises.

It is important to try to comply with parent's wishes relating to sleep. A late afternoon nap that results in a child not being ready for sleep until very late in the evening may not be popular with some parents, but others who wish to spend time with their children in the evening might prefer this.

Older children in nursery will usually fit within an overall plan, and you will arrange for changing levels of activity, with a rest or quiet period as appropriate.

Providing an appropriate physical environment to promote rest and quiet

Before children or babies start a rest period, you should follow a routine of preparation that will help them take advantage of the time allocated. This includes the following.

- Plan the routine to allow children time to unwind after vigorous activity, to have a drink and prepare for a rest.
- Attend to children's toilet or nappy needs before settling them to rest.
- Arrange the room and furniture. Check that the room is at an ambient temperature, the position of cots and chairs, and draw the curtains if necessary. Attention to health and safety requirements is essential: cots should conform to BSI requirements; floor space ratios should be complied with (the inspection authorities regulate these). Beds without appropriate barriers should not be used for babies or toddlers.
- Ensure that any comforters such as toys or blankets are ready to hand for the children. You should familiarise yourself with the individual needs of children in your care. Some children like their hair to be stroked as they relax, while others need a cuddle.
- Minimise unnecessary noises and distractions.
- If the quiet time is part of story time make sure books, pictures, etc. are ready by your seat.

Encouraging and supporting children in preparing for rest periods

As an early years worker, it is important that you are in a calm, reassuring mode during quiet time. A child will not rest if you are rushing around in a frenzy of activity. A child in a family setting will probably find it easier to settle for a rest or sleep; children in group settings may find it less easy. It is unusual for all children in a group to be ready to rest at the same time. All children are individuals, and levels of activity, amount of sleep needed, and sleep taken the previous night will all differ. Some children find it very difficult to settle with a group of other children.

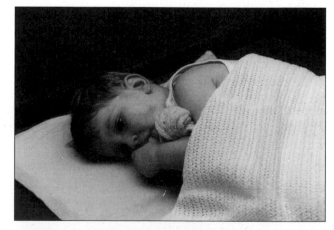

Children need rest and sleep in order to recuperate from active play

You should not insist on a child having a rest if he or she is not ready for one. Instead, offer a quiet activity such as reading a book or doing a puzzle or drawing for an older child. Younger children should be quietly played with in another room if possible. The important point is not to allow a child who is not ready for a rest to disrupt those who are.

Ensuring children are awakened in an appropriate manner

Never expect a child to wake up immediately feeling bright and ready to join in the next activity. Not all children will have relaxed straight away and gone to sleep, and so some may have had only a very brief nap. It should be possible to allow a child to carry on resting. As a child wakes from a sleep, he or she usually needs a visit to the toilet. After using the toilet, as well as washing their hands children will feel more awake if their faces are washed as well. A drink of juice and a gentle introduction to activity such as a puzzle or playing with small toys will prepare them for the next planned activity, and allow all the children to 'catch up'.

Observation

Choose two children of approximately the same age in your setting and make a detailed observation of their sleep and/or rest requirements throughout the day. How do their needs fit into the routine of the setting?

Keys to good practice
Rest and quiet

- Rest/quiet periods should suit the child, not the setting.
- Attention should be given to the child's particular needs, for example a comfort blanket.
- An atmosphere of calm restfulness should be created to encourage relaxation.

Active knowledge

What is the procedure in your care setting to allow children to have adequate rest and quiet periods during the day? Do you think this could be altered? Of so, how?

C2 Unit test

1   List the main components of a balanced diet.
2   What were the main recommendations of the COMA report?
3   What factors can affect a child's appetite?
4   List the common causes of food poisoning.
5   Outline 3 aspects of the Food Safety Act 1990.
6   Give 6 examples of useful things a child can learn from meal times.

7   Give 4 examples of skin problems experienced by young children, and for each describe signs, symptoms and treatment.
8   Give 3 causative agents of illness in children.
9   List 4 common signs of illness in a child.
10 When would you call for emergency medical help for a child in your care?
11 What is the procedure for reporting accidents in your setting?

Unit C3
Promote the physical development of children

This chapter focuses on the importance of promoting physical development in children up to the age of 7 years, 11 months. Emphasis is placed on the need to allow children to explore, discover and experiment at their own pace. We will consider the importance of a safe environment and the equipment needed for activities both indoors and outdoors. You will already know that all areas of development are interconnected, and therefore you will not be surprised to discover in this chapter that when you concentrate on developing a child's physical skills, other areas are also developed.

While children follow recognised patterns of physical development, there are obviously wide variations. Your responsibility as an early years worker will be to facilitate development by encouraging independence and changing the child's environment as appropriate, such as altering the layout of the room or providing suitable equipment and materials. As children develop, they gain control of their bodies and it is essential that adults involved in a child's care and education have some understanding of physical development.

The elements for this unit are:

C3.1 Develop children's confidence in movement
C3.2 Develop children's skills of locomotion and balance
C3.3 Develop children's gross motor skills
C3.4 Develop children's fine motor skills

Element C3.1 Develop children's confidence in movement

WHAT YOU NEED TO LEARN

- Why it is important to encourage a child's physical development
- The stages of physical development
- How to create opportunities to develop children's confidence in movement
- How to communicate with children during physical activity
- Helping children to develop new movements
- Learning aids and how to use them

Why it is important to encourage a child's physical development

Some of the reasons for encouraging physical activity and exercise in children are shown in the spider diagram below.

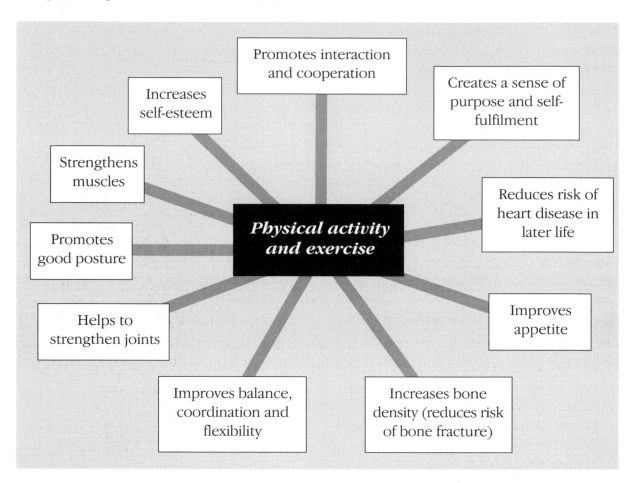

Key issues

More children in developed countries are becoming unfit through lack of physical exercise, largely because of time spent watching television and playing computer games. Being unfit as a child can lead to serious health problems, such as heart disease and obesity (being overweight) in adult life. Find out about fitness indicators in children.

The stages of physical development

It is important to understand some of the basic principles of development. The brain governs the way the body works. It stores information for future reference and helps children to make sense of the world. Children need to practise new skills so that information is reinforced in the brain.

Primitive reflexes – for example, the grasping reflex – will usually disappear by the time a child is three months old. These reflexes are replaced by voluntary control, where a child chooses and wills his or her actions.

Gross motor skills, that is movements of the whole body or a limb, such as walking, jumping, throwing and catching, are developed gradually, starting with the head and working downwards.

Fine motor skills – that is manipulative movements with the hands – begin at the centre and work outwards to the fingers.

The **central nervous system** matures so that it can interpret the messages it receives and send out commands to the muscles. The development of skills can then take place. The central nervous system consists of the brain, spinal cord and nerves. Messages move between the brain and the nerves. The nerves then stimulate the muscles to obey commands. For example, a child sees a ball. A message is sent from the nerves in the eyes to the brain. The brain then sends a message to the muscles in the arm to reach for the ball.

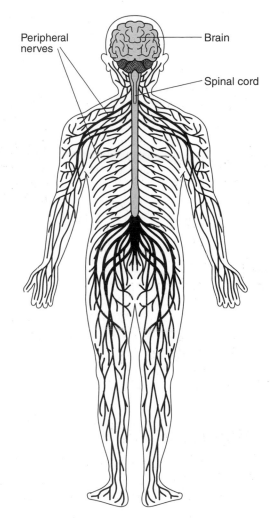

The central nervous system

Physical development in children follows a sequence – for example, a child walks before she can skip or hop. These general sequences are:

- **from head to toe** – for example, head control is acquired before coordination of the spinal muscles, and upper body movement before use of the legs
- **from outer to inner** – for example, children can coordinate their arms to reach before they have the fine manipulative skills to enable them to pick things up
- **from general to specific** – for example, a young child shows pleasure by a massive general response, with eyes widened, legs and arms moving vigorously. Older children show pleasure by smiling or using words or gestures.

Growth and physical development

These are closely linked. Physical skills will not be achieved until the body reaches the stage in growth necessary to support the skills. Growth refers to an increase in physical size.

Growth is measured by:	Growth is determined by:	Growth is affected by:
height	heredity	Antenatal conditions (before birth)
weight	nutrition	Perinatal conditions (during birth)
head circumference	hormones emotional influence	Postnatal conditions (after birth)

Cell division is the basis of physical growth. Life begins with a single cell (the fertilised egg), and cells divide and multiply if they have the right food and materials to do so. The process of differentiation then takes place, as the cells turn into different types such as muscle cells, nerve cells and brain cells. In a growing child cell division takes place in all parts of the body, and as a result the child gets steadily bigger.

Some parts of the body grow and develop more quickly than others, which alters the proportions of the body as the child grows.

Below is a list of all the postnatal factors that affect a child's development.

Diet	Should be healthy and well balanced
Environment	Should be healthy and hygienic
Exercise	Helps to develop bone and muscle
Illness	If severe, may temporarily slow down growth rate
Seasons	Growth is faster in spring and slower in autumn
Hormones	Influence growth and affect body shape
Heredity	Children inherit their parents' physical features
Attitude of carer	Children need to feel loved, secure, wanted and be given praise and encouragement

Developmental norms are a method of assessing a child's development. The method is developed by professionals using observations and research, and estimates the age at which most children can reach certain stages of development. This is an 'average' (rather than a normal) age at which a child may reach specific development. Below is a chart of the expected physical development of children aged from 12 months to 7 years, 11 months.

Age	Fine manipulative skills	Gross motor skills
12 months	• picking up objects with thumb and forefinger • picking up and holding toys such as rattles • pointing to objects • holding cup with help • putting small objects in a container	• mobile – crawling, rolling or shuffling (some children may be walking) • sitting up unsupported for long periods • walking with assistance • trying to crawl upstairs
15 months	• holding and drinking from cup using two hands • building tower of two blocks • making marks with crayons • trying to turn pages in books	• crawling downstairs feet first • walking independently • seating self in small chair

Age	Fine manipulative skills	Gross motor skills
18 months	<ul><li>stringing four large beads</li><li>turning door knobs and handles</li><li>pulling off shoes</li></ul>	<ul><li>bending down from waist to pick up toys</li><li>squatting to look at toys</li><li>rolling and throwing a ball</li><li>walking downstairs with adult help</li><li>pushing and pulling toys while walking</li></ul>
2 years	<ul><li>using a spoon to feed self</li><li>zipping and unzipping large zippers</li><li>placing five rings on a stick</li><li>putting on shoes</li><li>drawing circles and dots</li><li>building a tower of five to six bricks</li><li>beginning to use the preferred hand</li></ul>	<ul><li>kicking a stationary ball</li><li>climbing on furniture</li><li>putting together and pulling apart snap-together toys</li><li>walking up and downstairs confidently</li></ul>
3 years	<ul><li>turning pages in a book one by one</li><li>holding a crayon and drawing a face</li><li>using a spoon without spilling</li><li>washing and drying hands with help</li><li>putting on and taking off coat</li></ul>	<ul><li>walking and running forwards</li><li>walking on tiptoes</li><li>throwing large ball</li><li>kicking ball forward</li><li>jumping from low steps</li><li>peddling and steering a tricycle</li></ul>
4 years	<ul><li>buttoning and unbuttoning own clothing</li><li>cutting out simple shapes</li><li>drawing a person with head, trunk and legs</li><li>putting together 12 piece puzzle</li></ul>	<ul><li>walking on a line</li><li>aiming and throwing ball</li><li>bouncing and catching large ball</li><li>running and changing direction</li><li>hopping on one foot</li><li>pedalling and steering a tricycle confidently</li></ul>
5 years	<ul><li>forming letters, writing own name</li><li>drawing recognisable pictures of trees, houses, people and animals</li><li>colouring in pictures neatly</li><li>dressing and undressing easily</li><li>completing 20-piece puzzles</li><li>cutting out shapes using scissors quite accurately</li><li>drawing around a template</li></ul>	<ul><li>skipping with a rope</li><li>running quickly and avoiding obstacles</li><li>using a variety of large equipment, e.g. swings, slides</li><li>throwing large ball to partner and catching it</li><li>hitting ball with bat or stick</li></ul>
6-8 years	<ul><li>sewing simple stitches</li><li>cutting out shapes accurately and neatly</li><li>handwriting is evenly spaced and may be joined</li><li>drawings are detailed and representative</li><li>making a simple sandwich</li><li>tying and untying laces</li></ul>	<ul><li>riding a bicycle without stabilisers</li><li>running</li><li>chasing and dodging others</li><li>hopping, skipping and jumping confidently</li><li>kicking a ball with direction</li><li>balancing on a beam or wall</li></ul>

You may encounter children who do not develop according to the norms and have special needs. You will need to support their skills according to their capabilities.

How to create opportunities to develop children's confidence in movement

One of the most important roles of an early years worker is to ensure that children enjoy developing physical skills and that they are secure in the activities available to them. The environment you help to create, the activities provided and the communication you have with children all have to be carefully considered in order for them to develop confidence in their movement skills. Close supervision, praise and encouragement will help children to move safely and independently.

Remember

A child of seven may need as much encouragement as a child of eighteen months. Older children can develop a self-conscious attitude towards movement and often feel that they are not as good as other children at certain types of movement, such as running.

Opportunities to help children develop confidence in their movement can occur when children are:

- walking and running
- throwing and catching
- hopping and jumping
- riding trucks and bikes
- skipping
- climbing
- balancing.

Learning to ride a tricycle can help a child to develop confidence in movement

Keys to good practice
Developing children's confidence

- Treat children equally and do not discriminate against them because of their gender or culture. For example, boys can learn to sew as well as girls.
- Build on a child's previous experience – for example, a six-year-old who has learned to walk along a line on the floor can then learn to balance and walk on a wooden bench.
- Encourage children to repeat actions such as throwing the ball in a circle. Skills will develop with practice.
- Understand which particular physical skill a movement is developing, for example a gross motor skill or fine motor skill.

Active knowledge ✔

Study the charts on pages 42–43 and 50 and consider which physical skills the following children would be developing.

- A 15-month-old child building a tower of bricks
- A two-year-old kicking a stationary ball
- A three-year-old drawing with a crayon
- A six-year-old making a sandwich

Opportunities to concentrate on a specific area of development can occur as part of the daily routine or can be set up by the early years team. Opportunities can be found inside or outside, and can include:

- climbing on the climbing frame
- playing with balls
- riding bicycles in the garden
- skipping with ropes
- playing circle games
- dancing to music
- doing a jigsaw
- tying shoelaces
- using a spoon
- turning pages in a book.

Your involvement may be to support an activity that is already taking place, or to set up an activity for the children in order to develop a particular area of physical development.

Active knowledge

It is important to remember that observing children's physical development will help you to assess the type of opportunities you need to provide in order to develop their confidence in movement. This observation may be recorded as part of you setting's record-keeping plans. Ask your supervisor if you can look at a sample record that refers to a child's stage of physical development.

Experimentation

When providing opportunities for children to develop their confidence in movement, remember that they love to experiment and through this they can extend their experience and develop their skills

For example, a floor cushion given to a group of 3 year old children might encourage them to:

- roll the cushion
- push the cushion
- jump on the cushion
- pick up the cushion.

Many everyday pieces of equipment can be used by children to explore, enjoy and have confidence in their movement.

How to communicate with children during physical activity

Communicating with children is extremely important when you are aiming to develop their confidence in a physical skill. One obvious method is to discuss what they are doing as they move. Here are some examples of *verbal communication*:

'We are jumping in the air'
'We are crawling on the floor'
'You are climbing the steps'
'You are building the tower well'
'You are pedalling fast'

By using these phrases, the children will learn the correct words for what they are doing. This labelling of physical activities will encourage children of any age and will develop confidence and understanding of the skill they are using.

Most children develop a physical skill before they know the word for what they are doing, either because their language is not yet developed enough or because they do not have a word, such as 'hopping', in their vocabulary. Here are two examples of how you can encourage them to understand the name for what they are doing, by using non-verbal as well as verbal communication.

- Ask a 10-month-old baby to wave goodbye to you and wave at the same time. The baby will hear you label the action and you can show him or her what the word means by doing the action yourself.
- Ask a group of three- to four-year-olds to crawl slowly around the room in a drama session, and reinforce their understanding by doing it first or with them. You can ask them to crawl quickly, later in the session, to find out if they have understood the original concept of moving slowly.

Case study

Pat was leading an activity session in the garden with a small group of four-year-olds. She wanted to encourage them to jump and hop to develop their gross manipulative skills. She started the session by asking the children to jump as high as they could, doing it with them. After they had thoroughly enjoyed jumping around the garden, she asked them to do small jumps, to see if they had understood her first instruction. Tim continued to do high jumps, and Pat carefully held his hand and did some small jumps with him. Tim was then able to follow Pat's instruction on how to jump. She gave him and the other children a great deal of praise.

1   *How did Pat's actions help Tim to understand what he needed to do?*
2   *Why is it important for adults to talk to children in these situations?*

Developing children's vocabulary

Descriptive words and phrases are important in encouraging children to have the confidence to focus on *how* they move. Examples are:

'crawl like a snail'
'hop like a kangaroo'
'run like a tiger'

The way you express these phrases will help children to develop their vocabulary about movement. You might want to draw out the word 'crawl' and say the word 'hop' quickly.

Remember

Children with limited hearing will need to be positioned in any group activity so that they can easily see your facial expression and body language. If hearing is severely impaired, a child may wear a radio box or communicate with sign language.

When children are developing confidence in movement it is important for you to ensure that they are aware of the way their body moves. Study the points below to understand your role, as the early years worker, in developing a child's bodily awareness.

- Use action songs to draw attention to parts of the body, such as 'Head and shoulders, knees and toes'.
- Encourage children to be aware of *how* and *where* they move – using words such as under, over, up, etc.
- Encourage children to think about where they are in relation to each other, using phrases such as 'next to', 'very close', 'the other side', etc.

Helping children to develop new movements

In order to encourage children to develop physically you will have to help them achieve confidence in their basic skills, such as walking, running and climbing. Allow them to repeat such familiar movements, and then gradually add to them. As an early years worker you will have to provide the following

- praise
- encouragement
- a safe environment
- suitable equipment.

Some of the different types of movements that you can introduce are quick and slow, under and over, big and small, high and low.

Case study

Sheila, an early years worker caring for three- to five-year olds, was outside in the garden supervising a group of three-year-olds who were playing on a wooden climbing frame. She encouraged them to climb under the parts of the frame and over others, ensuring that they were safe and aware of each other. Sheila was careful to describe the children's actions and to praise them. At one stage she said 'Ben, I really like the way you climbed quickly over the rope and them under the pole'. Ben enjoyed the praise and continued to try hard to develop 'under' and 'over' movements.

1 *What other activities could Sheila have implemented to develop children's concepts of moving 'under' and 'over'?*
2 *After the children have developed the confidence to move under and over lower parts of the climbing frame, how could Sheila develop this particular physical skill?*

Equipment is not always necessary to help children develop new movements, but there are many items useful for both indoor and outdoor play in any setting, such as the following:

- push and pull toys
- cushions and other soft play objects
- climbing frames
- slides
- balls, bats, bean bags
- bicycles and trucks
- trampolines (carefully supervised).

Learning aids and how to use them

Audio, visual and tactile aids are all essential when developing children's confidence in movement. They can help to make any experience more creative and enjoyable.

Audio aids

These are aids that can make a noise. Music can encourage children to move, either using their whole bodies through movement and dancing, or moving parts of their bodies to rhymes and songs. You will have seen the pleasure children gain from dancing in a circle and perhaps clapping their hands or stamping their feet. In this way children can have the opportunity to develop their coordination while playing.

Active knowledge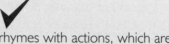

Choose two favourite songs or rhymes with actions, which are enjoyed by the children in your setting. Make a note of ways in which they could be used effectively to develop the children's confidence in movement. You will need to bear in mind the age of the children involved.

Children can be encouraged to use commercially made instruments, such as drums and tambourines, and to record their own sounds on a tape, such as soft and loud sounds and a variety of rhymes. Home-made instruments are a creative and inexpensive audio aid. Plastic bottles can create wonderful shakers using a variety of fillings, such as pebbles and water.

Children can be encouraged to make music to move to

Tactile aids

Tactile aids can be felt, touched and held. They encourage children to develop confidence in their movement through their sense of touch. A large parachute is a wonderful aid for children with special needs, who crawl and jump under its colourful circle of material. Ribbons, streamers and hoops will allow children to enjoy creating new movements, while a tunnel set indoors or outdoors will encourage children to crawl, feeling their way through a limited space.

Visual aids

Bright posters, photographs and instructions (for older children) are a way of encouraging children's confidence in their movements. A poster showing an elephant could be used as inspiration to encourage children to move like elephants, while a large photograph of a soldier might inspire them to march around the room! It is important that a variety of people are portrayed in visual aids, to give children of all abilities the confidence to experiment.

Consolidation

Study the physical development chart on page 13. List a variety of pieces of equipment and describe which age group you would use each item for. Then consider one item in detail, and describe:

- the age of children who would benefit from it
- basic skills the children might already have
- how you would use it to develop the children's movement.

Element C3.2 | Develop children's skills of locomotion and balance

Every child must develop his or her skills of locomotion (moving along) and balance (maintaining an upright posture) in order to reach full potential. These skills are naturally developed through play. Your role as an early years worker is to provide suitable activities and equipment, using your knowledge of the stages of physical development. You will also need to be aware of the importance of enabling children with special needs to take part in any activities you provide.

WHAT YOU NEED TO LEARN

- Providing activities and equipment to develop children's skills of locomotion and balance
- Developing different locomotion skills
- Promoting cooperation among children
- Encouraging children to participate in activities
- Exploring different ways of using equipment in a safe manner
- Developing spontaneous play activities

Providing activities and equipment to develop children's skills of locomotion and balance

Balance develops as children learn to control their muscles and try to overcome the force of gravity and maintain an upright posture. Balance follows this pattern:

Control of head and arms
↓
Control of trunk and arms
↓
Control of legs

Locomotion refers to moving the whole body along. This skill requires balance, muscle control, gross motor skills and self-confidence

Locomotion starts when a baby crawls or shuffles on his or her bottom, pulls himself or herself up and moves off. Walking, hopping, skipping, jumping and running will all gradually follow.

Active knowledge

Study the chart below and note which of the areas of physical development require balance and which are locomotion skills.

Activities and equipment that help to develop children's skills of locomotion and balance vary, of course, according to the developmental age of the child. The chart below provides ideas on activities and equipment for the different developmental stages of locomotion and balance.

Developmental stage	Suggested activities and equipment
12 months – moves around floor by crawling and shuffling. Tries to climb small steps, stands by pulling on furniture, walks holding on to an adult.	Safe space. Push along toys. Empty cardboard boxes.
18 months – stands alone. Walks but can fall easily. Pushes pram or trolley. Climbs on to chairs, stairs etc.	Push and pull-along toys, for example a trolley weighted with bricks. Space to practise steps, with adult nearby. Toys and chairs to climb and sit on.
2 years – walks confidently, runs but falls easily. Pushes and pulls wheeled toys. Climbs more confidently. Walks upstairs with support. May kick a ball.	Toys to push and pull. Space for running and playing with balls. Toys for riding and climbing. Close supervision, but independence encouraged
2 years 6 months – Runs. Jumps with two feet. Kicks a ball. Will sit on tricycle and use feet to push along.	Space to run and suitable equipment to climb. Trips to the park to encourage locomotion and balancing skills. Ride-on toys and ball play.
3 years – Walks forward, sideways and backwards. Walks on tiptoe. Stands on one foot briefly. Kicks a ball hard. Walks upstairs. Uses pedals to ride tricycle.	Space for running, ball games, and ride-on toys. Music, movement, dancing and swimming.
3–5 years – can walk along a line. Walks up and downstairs. Catches, throws and kicks a ball. Confident climber.	Games with hopping and skipping. Opportunities to climb. Space to run and dance. Swimming. Long walks. Bike with adult help or stabilisers.
5–8 years – Can now use most types of equipment. Muscle coordination is good. Has mastered balance. Learns to ride a bike on two wheels.	Climbing equipment, slide, swing, etc. Rope swings, adventure playground. Space for running games. Bat and ball games. Skipping, football. Joins clubs, team sports and games. PE at school.

Equipment

When choosing equipment and activities suitable for developing a child's locomotion and balance, it is better to consider first the needs of the child, rather than the available equipment. For example, a large, growing child may need a large climbing frame, which might not be available in the care setting. In this case the early years worker could arrange a visit to a local playground where a large adventure climbing frame is available for the child to enjoy.

To ensure that equipment is used properly, it should always be supervised and children should be encouraged to use items correctly so that they become aware of the need to act in a safe and responsible manner. Children who are too large for or misuse a piece of equipment will become a danger to themselves and other children who are using it.

Children who are too large for a piece of equipment will become a danger to themselves and others

Listed below is equipment suitable for children developing their skills of locomotion and balance, and how it should be kept safe.

- Climbing frames with slides and safe surfaces – to be installed and regularly checked by a professional.
- Play houses for younger children and log houses with rope ladders and dens for older children – to be safely erected and regularly checked for splinters, loose hinges, etc. Check rope regularly as it can weaken with age. Ensure doors are easily opened.
- Large boxes to climb in and out of – ensure they are free of staples and sharp edges.
- Planks, logs and benches to balance on – ensure they are on a safe surface and free of splinters.
- Large rubber tyres to step in and climb over – ensure they are thoroughly cleaned before first use.
- Tunnels for crawling through – usually made to safety standards, but they must be regularly checked for any sharp edges. Use on safe surfaces.
- Ride-on toys and push-along toys – to be checked when constructed, and regularly checked for rust, loose wheels, bolts, etc.
- Loops, balls and bean bags for throwing, catching and rolling – they must be of a non-toxic material.
- Skipping ropes – to be used under close supervision.
- Bats and balls to encourage running – ensure that the bats are non-toxic and free of splinters.
- Trampolines for jumping, hopping and balance – must be carefully constructed and supervised and regularly checked for any weakening in supports.
- Swings (for balance) – swings must be carefully constructed following manufacturers' instructions and regularly checked.

Keys to good practice
Safety of equipment

All equipment must be made to specific standards and display one of the following symbols:

- the kite mark means that the British Standards Institution (BSI) has checked the manufacturer's claim that the product meets specific standards
- the lion mark is found only on British-made toys and means they have met the safety standards required
- the CE mark means that the product complies with European and British Safety Standards

You can see what these marks look like by turning to Unit E3 (page 272).

Active knowledge

Check the health and safety procedures in your setting and find out how the checking of equipment is carried out. Carefully study any documentation your setting has.

Every setting should have a health and safety policy and procedures for regularly checking equipment used by the children. Registration and inspection officers who regularly inspect provision for the under-eights will want to see detailed evidence of health and safety procedures.

Most equipment can be adapted for children with special needs. If equipment cannot be adapted, alternative equipment may be used. Parents, colleagues and other professionals who work closely with a child with specific needs should be able to advise upon suitable equipment and where it can be purchased.

It is important that children have a positive attitude towards those with specific needs to develop locomotion and balance, and that they play appropriately together. Consider the following case study.

Case study

Patrick is in a primary class of six- to seven-year-olds. He uses a wheelchair and is able to develop locomotive skills only in the upper part of his body. His local education authority follows an inclusion policy, which means that children with special needs are integrated into mainstream schools wherever possible.

The children are playing a game with a ball in a circle. When the children throw the ball to Patrick they are aware they have to throw at his level. Sometimes he wheels his chair to collect the ball if it has been thrown out of the circle – his classmates don't run to collect the ball for him. The teacher encourages Patrick to throw and catch the ball just like the other children, always aware that Patrick cannot move his legs. Whilst his teacher always tries to treat Patrick like his peers, he is aware of the fact that Patrick has limited mobility and must concentrate on developing the locomotion and balance of the upper part of his body.

1   *Why is it important that the other children let Patrick collect the ball himself?*
2   *Why is it important for all the children that Patrick is included in the game?*

Planning activities

Parents and carers may express concerns about the activities their children are involved in. It may be advisable to encourage such parents to attend sessions to find out how activities are planned and supervised. However, some wishes may be religious or cultural and respect must always be shown in such cases, however you feel about the situation.

Opportunities for outdoor and indoor activities will obviously vary according to the setting, but both should be encouraged as much as possible. The amount of space available will affect the choice of activity. It is possible to exercise indoors in a small space such as a living room, where children can climb over cushions and balance during games such as 'Simon Says'. In settings that have more space, play houses, tunnels and indoor slides can be used. Games such as musical statues encourage balance and locomotion, as do songs such as 'Head and shoulders, knees and toes'. Walking with bean bags can help develop posture and balance whilst drawing a chalk line on a floor can develop balancing skills.

Outdoor apparatus should always be an extension of equipment provided indoors to encourage free floor play. However, an outdoor play area often has different surfaces to facilitate a variety of activities, and older children can enjoy surfaces marked for hopscotch, stepping stones, etc.

Developing different locomotion skills

The key movements of locomotion and balance are:

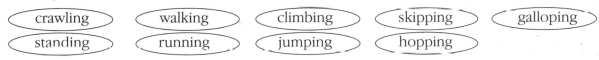

crawling   walking   climbing   skipping   galloping
standing   running   jumping   hopping

Activities and equipment to develop different locomotion skills

- Children who are *crawling* need to find out the meaning of space and distance and need a safe environment to give them the freedom to develop their arm and leg muscles and explore the environment.
- Children who are learning to *stand* are using their arms to pull themselves up and balance. They need stable surfaces and toys, and a soft surface to land on when they first stand alone.
- Children who are learning to *walk* will need toys to push and a hand to hold as they put one foot in front of the other, trying hard to balance. They must be given time to push themselves up by their hands and try again.

There are many ways for children to practise their locomotion and balance skills

- Children who are developing their *running* skills need space to move around while they are learning to control their speed and pace, and develop their leg muscles.
- Children who are learning to *climb* will need safe objects to climb on.

- Children who are learning to *skip* will need space and some guidance to learn to transfer their balance quickly from one leg to another.
- Children who are learning to *hop* will need a safe surface and space to transfer their weight to one leg.
- Children who are learning to *gallop* will need plenty of space and perhaps music to encourage the rhythm of this type of locomotion.

Observation

Observe a child in your care practising a skill in locomotion or balancing. If necessary, facilitate the observation by setting up an activity for the child. In your report discuss how you observed the child's skill using your knowledge of developmental stages. Make a recommendation as to how the child could be further supported in developing this skill.

Children should be encouraged to understand the difference between locomotion skills and activities. This may be done by simply labelling the activity as it is occurring, such as saying 'Tom, you are jumping high,' or by giving children instructions in more structured activity sessions, according to their stage of development. A lesson in primary school might well encourage children not only to use a variety of locomotion skills but also to control the way they start, stop and their speed. They might be asked to start walking with large strides slowly around the room, and stop when told wherever they are. In this way children will become aware of the way they can best use different locomotion skills.

Active knowledge

Consider one of the movements in the above list that a child in your care is developing. Using the knowledge that you have gained, plan an activity with suitable equipment to help develop the child's balance and locomotion.

Promoting cooperation among children

At three years of age, children are beginning to play together, for example on large outdoor apparatus or tricycles, and run around together. Early years workers should encourage activities that promote cooperation among children, allowing them to share, take turns, discuss each other's movements positively, and allow for each other's stage of development. It is important that a child who does not run fast or skip competently is accepted by other children and supported by adults to develop his or her skills. It may be necessary to encourage children to cooperate in smaller groups in order for children to learn to work together and have the confidence to develop to their full potential.

Encouraging children to participate in activities

It is essential that children at every stage in developing locomotion and balance are offered a range of activities both indoors and outdoors. You will need to ensure that all children have equal access. As children mature, they are influenced by the society around them and may begin to show gender preference. For example, boys may not want to skip if they feel it is too feminine, and girls may refuse to play football if they view it is a 'boy's game'. By being a positive role model you can discourage gender preference, and other stereotyping. If a groups of children rarely uses a piece of equipment, such as the climbing frame, it may be advisable to discuss with your team how these children can be given appropriate encouragement.

Keys to good practice
Encouraging children to take part and to cooperate

- *Be a good role model yourself* – join in with the activities and be active; children will enjoy seeing adults playing football or balancing on a bench.
- *Check that the activity chosen is suitable for all the children in the group*, for example, a child in a wheelchair will enjoy playing catch with a ball, but may feel excluded if you choose a moving ball game like football.
- *Choose games that involve sharing and teamwork* – relay races or crawling through tunnels in turn can be great fun, but make sure no-one wins until the whole team has finished.
- *Praise children who share and help each other* – explain clearly why you are giving the praise, so that the children can understand the advantages of being considerate to each other.
- *Talk about games and famous sports people* – you could use famous sports people as good role models, especially in non-gender-specific games like tennis and swimming.

Exploring different ways of using equipment in a safe manner

In order for children to fully develop skills of locomotion and balance and an understanding of how to apply such skills, they must be encouraged to use equipment independently. If a child is not encouraged to consider different ways of exploring a piece of equipment, such as a hoop or bean bag, he or she will not develop sufficient independence or feel a sense of achievement. Close supervision is required to ensure that the children are safe at all times, but you should aim to be discreet.

Keys to good practice
Using equipment safely

- Ensure you can see all children.
- Keep moving around so that the children do not feel watched.
- Check that the children do not become over-excited.
- Ensure that the equipment is used correctly.
- Encourage children to rest when tired.
- Encourage the children to explore further, for example, say 'Now try hopping across the stepping stones on your other foot, Heather.'

The case study below is an example of how an early years worker used an activity in different ways.

Case study

A group of reception class children were enjoying a PE lesson outside in the playground. Their nursery nurse, Katie, was encouraging a group of them to use the white lines on the playground to develop their balance. She asked them to hold their arms out and make small steps along the lines. Then she encouraged them to invent new ways of moving along the lines. 'Try hopping', she said. Then they tried skipping and tried holding hands as they walked along the lines.

The children showed each other their new locomotion and balance skills at the end of the session.

1   *How did Katie involve the children in developing their locomotion and balance skills?*
2   *Can you think of other outside equipment she could have used?*

When developing walking and running skills children can be encouraged to use equipment such as benches and hoops in a variety of ways, while children can develop balance on a tricycle, in their own games and in activities that they do together.

Developing spontaneous play activities

A well-structured curriculum will allow for children to play spontaneously, either within a structured activity or during free play time. Such opportunities may be facilitated by an adult or by the children themselves. If they are provided with a range of safe equipment, children will quickly develop locomotion and balance in play. Some examples of such opportunities are:

- climbing trees
- exploring mountains of cushions
- using empty cardboard boxes
- playing games using balls, bean bags, etc.

Element C3.3   Develop children's gross motor skills

This section focuses on ways in which those working with children under eight months can help them to develop their gross motor skills. These are skills that include the use of the large muscles in the upper arm, legs and torso. These three areas of large muscles can enable a child to:

- throw
- catch
- strike
- kick
- bounce
- whirl
- spin
- pedal.

You will discover that many indoor and outdoor activities can help children develop these skills.

WHAT YOU NEED TO LEARN

- Providing opportunities to practise gross motor skills
- Providing objects to develop gross motor skills
- Safety, supervision and utilising space
- Encouraging children to manipulate objects to extend their gross motor skills
- Developing positive strategies to encourage children to participate in gross motor activities.

Remember

Gross motor skills are developed initially by the control of the head, working downwards.

Providing opportunities to practise gross motor skills

You will need to consider providing activities both indoors and outdoors for the children in your care, taking into consideration:

- the size of the equipment
- the individual needs of the children.

Opportunities can be either planned or spontaneous. Carefully consider the opportunities listed below. Many of these opportunities can be planned indoors if space is available.

Age	Planned opportunities	Spontaneous opportunities
0–12 months	Push and pull toys to encourage standing and walking.	Stable surfaces, stairs to climb (supervised). Objects such as balls to crawl after.
12 months–2 years	Provide ride-on toys to climb on and ride. Roll and throw different balls. Prams, etc., to push. Swimming, encouraging different arm and leg movements. Encourage walking up and downstairs, slides, etc. Simple kicking ball games.	Climb in and out of cardboard boxes from the supermarket. Bath time and the paddling pool, where children will splash with arms and legs. Swings, slide and rocking equipment in park. Walking up and downstairs at home. Riding small tricycles, cars, etc.
2 years–4 years	Running activities. Large outdoor apparatus to climb and crawl through. Throwing and kicking ball games. Bouncing games. Games that include running, hopping and changing direction. Balancing on outdoor equipment. Swimming lessons. Trampolines.	May use objects such as mountains of cushions, etc. to climb and crawl over. Independent play using any large equipment, balls or running in the garden. Playing (supervised) in a large paddling pool.
5 years–8 years	Skipping activities, running, obstacle races. Throwing and hitting games. Hoops, balancing on equipment. May all take place in PE, drama and movement lessons. Swimming lessons. Dancing, tennis lessons, etc.	Bicycles, roller skates, skateboards. Playing ball. Running, dodging and chasing games. Play in the park. Playground games such as hopscotch and skipping.

Children who are developing their gross motor skills must be given the confidence to use their skills. Look at the following case study:

Case study

Andrew was supervising a group of three- and four-year-olds who were playing in the garden of a nursery. They had taken a ball from the equipment box and were running around trying to play football. One of the children, Tarik, aged 3, began to get upset as he didn't often have a chance to kick the ball and when he did he missed it. Andrew gently took him to one side and showed him how to practise kicking another ball forward into a goal. They took it in turns and had great fun!

Andrew was aware that Tarik, like most three-year-olds, is beginning to want to play with his peers, but may only just be competent in kicking a ball forward. Andrew knew about the stages of children's gross motor development and therefore created the right opportunity for Tarik to develop the skill of kicking.

1 *Why was it important for Andrew to intervene in this activity?*
2 *How did Andrew's actions help Tarik?*

Children who are developing their gross motor skills can usually:

- start to *throw* a large ball at the age of three, but not *bounce* and *catch* until the age of four – the skill of aiming to a correct position will not develop before four years of age
- Steer and pedal toys at three years old, but not develop confidence until the age of four.

It is important to ensure in any setting that the space is used appropriately, always remembering that children will benefit from outdoor play opportunities to develop their gross motor skills. If the opportunities for outside access are limited, furniture can be cleared away to give children appropriate opportunities such as catching soft balls, spinning hoops and throwing bean bags.

Observation

Choose an appropriate time indoors or outdoors and observe a child in your care developing gross motor skills during a play opportunity. In your evaluation, consider whether the child followed a broad pattern of gross motor development. What other opportunities would you provide to extend his or her skills? Use research to validate your conclusion.

Providing objects to develop gross motor skills

In order to develop children's gross motor skills, early years workers should provide objects that are safe and appropriate to the children's developmental level. Many useful items are simple and inexpensive; below is a list of objects that could be provided.

Gross motor activity	Possible objects	Large muscle development
Throwing	Bean bags, soft balls, hoops, different sized balls, frisbees	Leg, arm and hand muscles
Catching	Bean bags, soft balls, hoops, different sized balls, frisbees	As above
Striking	Variety of balls, small goal posts, rackets, bats, nets	Leg and arm muscles
Kicking	Variety of balls, small goal posts	Leg muscles
Bouncing	Balls of varied sizes, hoops, trampolines	Arm and hand muscles
Whirling	Banners, streamers	Arm, leg and hand muscles
Swimming	Floats, armbands, rubber rings	Arm and leg muscles
Hopping	Hopscotch, similar floor markings	Leg muscles
Jumping	Trampoline, soft play objects	Leg muscles
Climbing	Soft play objects, climbing frames	Leg, arm and hand muscles
Walking	Bench, balancing bar	Leg muscles
Running	Balls, slopes, soft play cones	Leg muscles

Recording gross motor development

Work settings will often have their own way of recording the development of such skills. Below is an example of an early years worker's record of the gross motor skills of a four-year-old.

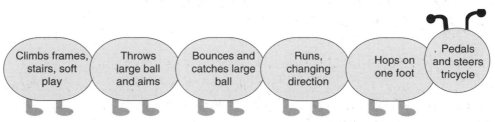

Climbs frames, stairs, soft play | Throws large ball and aims | Bounces and catches large ball | Runs, changing direction | Hops on one foot | Pedals and steers tricycle

The chart is coloured in and dated after the child has been observed completing the task. Some settings use different colour codes. For example:

Confident

Needs assistance

Not yet confident

Active knowledge ✔

Plan a suitable outdoor activity for a group of six three-year-old children. Look at the chart on page 50 and decide what objects will be needed and which muscles will be developed.

Safety, supervision and utilising space

When you are supervising indoor and outdoor activities that develop gross motor skills, it is vital that equipment is of the highest safety standard to avoid any risk of a child being injured. Space must be allowed for children to run, hop, skip, throw, and so on. Space will obviously vary according to availability but no room should be overcrowded. This may mean a setting needs to allow small, supervised groups of children to use a large area to develop their gross motor skills freely and without inhibition.

Active knowledge ✔

Ask your supervisor if you can read the health and safety policy of your setting. Consider how you would refer to it when checking the safety of planned activities to develop gross motor skills.

Keys to good practice

Equipment safety
- Always ensure that objects and equipment are regularly checked for wear and tear, such as fraying ropes and rusting joints.
- Check that equipment is clean and dry, especially slides, steps, etc.

Personal safety
- Ensure that each child has the space to move freely without bumping into other children or objects.
- Ensure that the appropriate adult/child ratios required by your social services department are maintained for adequate supervision.
- Swings and rope ladders should be used by one child at a time. All other children should be discouraged from playing nearby in case they are hurt by a swing or rope.
- All children should be visible to ensure safety.

Safety of the environment

- Check that outdoor areas are free from harmful waste such as dog faeces (which can cause eye damage to young children), broken equipment or litter.
- Ensure that surfaces are soft and safe, to encourage freedom of movement.

While you are maintaining their safety it is important that children are given the freedom to develop their skills, with adult support but not too much intervention.

Encouraging children to manipulate objects to extend their gross motor skills

It is vital to encourage children to play with appropriate objects when they are developing their gross motor skills. Such activities are called gross manipulative activities, and will include the following.

- Balls – throwing, bouncing, catching. Games include football, catch, piggy in the middle, rugby, ball in the swimming pool.
- Bats and rackets – throwing, catching, stretching, bouncing. Games include cricket, short tennis, french cricket, table tennis, badminton.
- Bean bags and frisbees – throwing, catching, circle games, throwing into hoops, team games.
- Hoops – swirling through hoola-hoop, bean bags into hoops, rolling hoops, hoop obstacle races.
- Banners and streamers – running, whirling and pattern games, circle games, playing with a large parachute.

There are children who are naturally able to throw, catch, kick or bounce and will need only the minimum amount of support. However, other children may be less confident, agile or dexterous, and it is the role of the early years worker to ensure that they are given time to develop their gross manipulative skills without feeling daunted by comparisons with their peers.

Case study

Fiona was playing in the garden in two-year-old Freddy's home. He was very unsure about using a ball. Fiona used a large foam ball and took time to encourage Freddy to gently roll the ball to her and throw the ball. They also rolled the ball to Freddy's teddy, who, with Fiona's help, sent the ball back to Freddy!

1 *Which large muscles was Fiona helping Freddy to develop?*
2 *Why was Freddy being encouraged to roll rather than throw the ball?*

Key issues

Play therapists are specially trained professionals who will advise how objects can be adapted for children with special needs, such as cerebral palsy, visual impairment, and so on. Find out about how a play therapist works with children.

Developing positive strategies to encourage children to participate in gross motor activities

As with other activities to promote physical development, the early years worker will need to help children understand what they are doing. Therefore it may be necessary to demonstrate a task in order for children to develop a particular gross motor skill appropriately. It does not matter if you or the demonstrator are not very good at the skill – in fact it can encourage children to see that not everyone is good at everything.

- Play alongside a child – throwing a ball, skipping, etc.
- Show the child how to throw and catch. For example, hold out arms ready to catch a ball.
- Ensure that each child takes a turn or takes a leading role in an activity such as throwing in a circle.
- Encourage both boys and girls to join in all activities, individually and together.
- If a child has a special need you must ensure that the equipment is adapted so that he or she can take part.
- Give plenty of praise and encouragement.

Consolidation

In this section you have discovered how children can develop gross motor skills that involve the use of large muscles in the arm, leg and torso. With the knowledge you have gained, suggest the age when a child might achieve the following skills:

- throwing over-arm
- steering toys
- catching.

- kicking a ball
- peddling

Element C3.4   Develop children's fine motor skills

Fine motor skills, also known as fine manipulative skills, are small and often intricate movements of the limbs, made primarily with the hands. Examples could be:

- turning a page
- drinking from a mug
- drawing a picture
- doing up buttons
- lacing up shoes
- positioning a piece in a puzzle.

- Providing appropriate equipment and activities to develop fine motor skills
- Supervising children appropriately during fine motor skills activities
- Providing activities that develop hand-eye coordination and extend concentration span
- Using relevant opportunities to encourage children to develop their fine motor skills
- Encourage and assist children to use fine manipulative skills

Providing appropriate equipment and activities to develop fine motor skills

Fine motor skills involve the use of hand-to-eye coordination, which includes aspects of vision and fine, delicate movements. The equipment and activities that are provided to develop a child's fine motor skills will generally follow the stages of development. Consider the chart below.

Age	Fine motor skills	Appropriate activities	Equipment
12 months	Picking up objects with thumb and forefinger Picking up and holding toys, such as rattles/teddies Pointing to objects Holding cup and saucer Putting small objects in container	Play alongside child – e.g. make a tower of bricks to knock down, put cuddly toy in truck to push along	Primo Lego, which has rounded corners A variety of wooden bricks of different shapes, colours and textures Hand-held, textured rattles and soft toys Stacking beakers
15 months	Holding a drinking cup using two hands Building tower of blocks Making marks with crayons Trying to turn pages in books	Show child how to use toys Encourage and praise early self-help skills Look at picture books with adult	Primo Lego Wooden bricks Tea sets Chunky crayons Card or fabric picture books
18 months	Stringing large beads Turning door knobs and handles Pulling off shoes	Allow child time to play repetitively, threading beads, dressing toys and opening doors on pop-up toys	Duplo Lego Large wooden beads Activity boards – including knobs, buttons, wheels
2 years	Using a spoon to feed Zipping and unzipping large zippers Placing rings on a stacker Putting on shoes Drawing circles and dots Building a tower of five or six bricks Beginning to use the preferred hand	Take a child to the park to use swings and rocking equipment Praise and encourage child to overcome frustration Sit with child and show how to hold crayons and make shapes Read with child	Super maze Wooden ball sorter Lacing shapes Crayons Duplo Lego Activity boards and toys to encourage use of zips and buttons Children's plates and cutlery

Age	Fine motor skills	Appropriate activities	Equipment
3 years	Turning pages in a book one by one Holding a crayon and drawing a face Using a spoon without spilling Washing and drying hands with help Putting on and taking off coat	Provide stimulating activities so child can develop fine movements, e.g. cooking and painting Provide opportunities to engage in imaginative play Provide opportunities to play with other children Provide new challenges for child to enjoy	Design mosaic Bead pattern sets Lego soft – extra large Lego suitable for groups Suitable crayons A variety of books including 'lift the flap' books Bubbles (for blowing and making shapes) Simple jigsaws (12 pieces)
4 years	Buttoning and unbuttoning own clothing Cutting out simple shapes Drawing a person with head, trunk and legs Putting together puzzle (at least 12 pieces)	Encourage children to become more independent Give children a variety of activities Encourage children to play cooperatively	Clothes with buttons and zips in home corner Computers – use of mouse and keyboard Drawing materials Stickle bricks Octaplay – 8-sided shapes Brio/Mobilo Scissors and coloured paper Water toys for pouring and squeezing Playdough Junk for junk modelling Stencil shapes e.g. for potato prints
5 years	Forming letters, writing own name Drawing recognisable pictures of trees, houses, people, animals, etc. Colouring in shapes, etc. Dressing and undressing Completing jigsaw puzzles (at least 20 pieces) Cutting out shapes using scissors Drawing around a template	Start playing cooperative games e.g. Ludo, snap	Magnetic letters Tracing letters Lego/Mobilo Computers Clothes in home corner Drawing materials Water toys and sand Board games which involve shaking dice and moving objects Puzzles with 20 pieces
6-8 years	Sewing simple stitches Cutting out shapes accurately and neatly Handwriting is evenly spaced and may be joined Drawing detailed and representative pictures Making a simple sandwich Tying and untying laces	Encourage participation in everyday tasks Provide new activities – making models Encourage children to explore own interests, sewing, ceramics, etc. Encourage children who avoid physical activity Provide cooperative games e.g. snakes and ladders	Lego dacta Drawing and writing materials Computer Sewing materials Large needles, colourful and textured threads Appropriate scissors Clay, etc.

When providing any activities or objects for children to develop their fine motor skills, it is important to understand that children develop their manipulative skills in the following order:

- finger play
- attempting to grasp objects
- holding and exploring objects
- palma grasp using whole hand
- more delicate palma grasp using whole hand
- more delicate palma grasp involving the thumb
- primitive pincer grasp using thumb and forefinger
- exploring with index finger
- delicate mature pincer grasp.

Observation ✔

Observe a child in your care playing with a toy or object that involves using a pincer grasp. This could include painting, drawing, sorting, sewing, etc. Is the child at the expected stage of development for his or her age? Note how long he or she concentrates on the task.

The spider diagram below shows some toys and activities that help fine motor skills development.

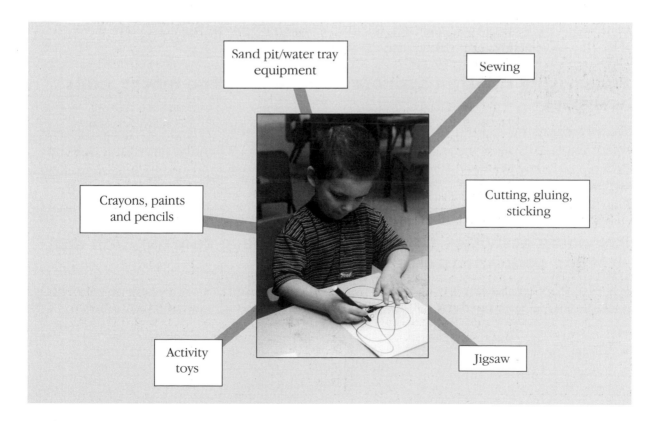

Special needs

Children with special needs must be provided with appropriate activities. It is essential to gain information from parents and other professionals in order to choose the right equipment for children with specific needs. Toys may be textured, highly coloured or perhaps emit vibration as well as sound. For example, a child with a visual impairment using building blocks may need bricks that have velcro backing, in a variety of shapes and sizes. This will allow the child to develop his or her fine motor skills and to gain a sense of achievement. Such provision also allows children to join in the games of their peers.

Key to good practice
Special needs

- It is essential that children with special needs are provided with appropriate equipment and activities so that they can play alongside their peers.
- Remember that all children may want to play with specialised toys; this should be encouraged, and is an integrated approach.

Left or right hand preference

Even as young as six months of age, children can start to show a preference for using one hand rather than the other. 'Handedness' is usually firmly established by the time a child is two years old. However, some children delay this until the age of four or five, and some even change their preference! A few people remain ambidextrous throughout their lives.

A variety of left-handed equipment is available for children, such as scissors. This specific equipment and appropriate guidance will enable children who are left handed to develop their fine motor skills with confidence.

Supervising children appropriately during fine motor skills activities

You will already be aware of your responsibility for supervising children's activities to ensure safety, but also to allow them control in what they are doing. When the fine motor skills are developing, there is a need for constant adult support and the appropriate equipment. Keep sharp objects out of reach of small children and ensure that spills are cleared up from the floor. As with other activities, you will need to refer to your setting's health and safety policy.

Providing activities that develop hand–eye coordination and extends concentration span

It is essential that children develop their manual dexterity so that they are able to concentrate on skills such as writing and drawing. The three main aspects of manual dexterity are:

- hand–eye coordination
- fine motor skills
- concentration span.

Hand–eye coordination

Young babies use their eyes and hands separately and will slowly start to understand that their eyes can see what they do with their hands! This is referred to as hand–eye coordination, and without it children cannot develop their fine motor skills.

Activities that develop hand–eye coordination may include jigsaws, painting with fingers, working with scissors, drawing, threading, sewing, or using playdough.

Fine motor skills

As discussed above, these are skills that require control of the small muscles, in particular in the hands and fingers.

Activities that develop fine motor skills may include dressing dolls, modelling clay or using dough.

Concentration span

This is the period of time a child is able to give complete attention to an activity. A child needs to be able to focus his or her mind on one area, shutting out any distractions. By the time children are three years old they can concentrate for a short time.

Activities to develop concentration span may include jigsaws, cutting, gluing, or board games.

Using relevant opportunities to encourage children to develop their fine motor skills

The development of fine motor skills takes place not always through planned activities; many opportunities for their use will arise from the daily routine. Consider the following:

- doing up and undoing buttons and laces
- washing hands
- activities such as puzzles
- setting out activities
- clearing away activities
- picking up items from the floor
- helping to make sandwiches.

Active knowledge ✔

Consider the routine of your setting and list the opportunities to develop fine motor skills that occur throughout the day.

Encourage and assist children to use fine manipulative skills

It is important to give a great deal of encouragement to children developing fine manipulative skills. Children must be given independence and allowed to carry out activities without feeling hurried; let the children develop their own ideas, select their own materials and retain control.

Case study

Cathy was sitting with Nigel, aged five, who was trying to tie his shoe laces after a PE lesson. Nigel was tired and cross, as it was the end of the day and all the other children were dressed. Cathy let Nigel try to tie the laces and then asked if he would like her to do one lace when he had done the other. She carefully talked Nigel through the process and helped him to complete the task. She praised him and promised him they would try again tomorrow. Cathy also talked to his Mum about practising the task at home.

I *How did Cathy encourage Nigel's fine manipulative skills despite his frustration?*
2 *Why did Cathy discuss the situation with Nigel's mother?*

Remember that when children are frustrated it may be because they are tired, or attempting a task they are not ready for. The role of the early years worker is to give praise and encouragement, and to intervene before the child becomes distressed.

Consolidation

At what age do you think children may develop the following skills?

- finger painting
- threading beads
- cutting with safety scissors
- writing their first name
- doing up and undoing a large zip.

C3 Unit test

I   What is the difference between a fine manipulative skill and a gross motor skill?
2   How would you encourage a two-year-old to climb a slide?
3   Define 'locomotion' and 'balance'.
4   How should any setting ensure that the equipment to develop children's physical skills is safe?
5   Why is spontaneous play important in developing a child's gross motor skills?
6   How would you encourage a visually impaired five-year-old to develop his or her fine motor skills?
7   Name the key movements in locomotion and balance.
8   What are the three groups of large muscles that enable a child to develop gross motor skills?
9   List four pieces of equipment that would encourage a 12-month-old to develop his or her fine motor skills.
10   What is the key role of any early years worker in promoting the physical development of children?

Unit C5

Promote children's social and emotional development

The first five years of life are an important time for emotional and social development. Children are immensely affected by their surroundings and the quality of care that they receive. They are, however, very adaptable and with the support of a consistent carer can overcome negative experiences. Research has shown that we do not complete our emotional and social development at a set age, but continue to develop as adults. This unit will help you to understand how to consider a child's social and emotional development at all times. Children need to feel secure in their daily life and settings to allow them to benefit from experiences designed to help in other aspects of development. A child's self-esteem and confidence can be easily affected by negative experiences. As an early years worker, you have an essential role in ensuring that all experiences are designed to help in the positive development of a child's social and emotional development.

The elements for this unit are:

C5.1 Enable children to adjust to the setting
C5.2 Enable children to relate to others
C5.3 Develop children's self-reliance and self-esteem
C5.4 Enable children to recognise and deal with their feelings
C5.5 Enable children to develop a positive self-image and identity
C5.6 Prepare children to move on to new settings

To start to understand how to support children in their social and emotional development you need to understand the stages in this area of development. This chart should help you as you work through each of the elements in this unit:

Age	Social/emotional development
Birth to 4 weeks	Sleeps for much of the time when not being handled or fed Expression vague, becoming more alert Stops crying when picked up and spoken to Will imitate facial expressions Turns to look at nearby speaker's face Stares at bright shiny objects

Age	Social/emotional development
1 month	Gazes intently at carers
6 weeks	Social smile at carers
4 months	Fixes on carer's face when feeding Smiles and engages with carers Reacts to familiar situations with coos and gurgles Responds well to friendly handling
9 months	Very interested in surroundings Recognises familiar and unfamiliar people Shows stranger anxiety; reserved with strangers from seven months Clings to carer and hides face from strangers Plays peek-a-boo and imitates hand clapping
1 year	Shows definite emotions and is aware of emotions of others Will play on own Likes to be in sight of a familiar adult Shows affection to familiar people Waves bye-bye
15 months	Very curious about other people and objects within own circle Closely dependent on familiar adult's presence
18 months	Stranger shyness; dislikes changes in routine Varies between being clingy with adult and resisting adult's involvement Starts toilet training, recognises need to 'go' Start of tantrums when upset Has separate sense of self Little idea of sharing and strong sense of 'mine'
3 years	Strong sense of gender identity Less anxious about separation Plays alongside others Joins in active make-believe play with other children Shows affection for siblings
4 years	Enjoys cooperative and dramatic play Understands cooperation and competition Responds to reasoning Can take turns Enjoys independence but still needs comfort and reassurance Needs companionship of other children, is alternately cooperative and aggressive with them Shows concern and sympathy for other children
5 years	Will choose own friends and is cooperative with them Understands needs for rules and fairness Comforts others who are upset Enjoys elaborate make-believe play
7 years	Developing stable self-concept Understands differences between social rules, display rules and moral values Becomes engrossed in activities Develops fears of ghosts, 'things' under the bed, etc. Concerned about being disliked

Element C5.1   Enable children to adjust to the setting

Starting somewhere new can be a daunting prospect for anyone, particularly for a young child who may be away from his or her regular carer for the first time. The introduction to a new setting can, if correctly handled, have a positive impact on the way that a child ultimately settles. All early years workers have an important role to play in the preparation and support of young children coming into their place of work. This element provides you with the understanding to provide that support.

WHAT YOU NEED TO LEARN

- Strategies to ensure children feel welcome in their new setting
- Recognising the level of support a child needs
- Allowing children to familiarise themselves at their own pace
- Supporting children in the early stages of the new setting
- Sharing information with children and their parents

Strategies to ensure children feel welcome in their new setting

First days

Think back to your first day at school or nursery – if you can remember that far back! Was it a happy experience, or did you cry and feel abandoned as your parent walked out of the door, leaving you in an alien environment? How did it feel not to know where the toilets were? Was lunchtime pleasant or did it feel overwhelming to have to eat your lunch in a large room with lots of other children?

Now imagine how you might have felt if no one spoke the same language as you and you could not understand any of the instructions you were being given. Trying to settle in a new setting where the language and surroundings are alien to anything you have previously experienced heightens stress and is disruptive for a child.

Everyone has experienced that 'new girl/boy' feeling. You may well still feel it from time to time. Changing jobs or course, even as an adult, summons up those same sensations and reactions – many that can be traced back to those early 'first days' in childhood.

When you have a new child starting in your setting, remind yourself how he or she might be feeling, and you are on exactly the right track to helping the child to adjust to a new setting. Ensure that the child's parents are involved at the start of your partnership, and the task becomes even easier.

Helping a child to adjust to a new setting should begin some time before the first formal day. A new start should be planned well in advance. It is essential that the following key people are involved in the planning:

- the child
- the child's parents or carers

- the key worker in the setting
- other central staff with whom the child will come into contact
- staff from a previous setting that the child may have been attending (see Element 5.6).

The amount of thought and planning involved in the start at a new setting will often be reflected in the ease with which a child adjusts.

Preparation

Whenever possible all children starting in a planned new setting should have visited and spent time there. There should be few, if any, exceptions to this rule, only for example if the admission is an emergency resulting from some family disruption, or the child was prevented from making preliminary visits because of unexpected admission to hospital. With appropriate handling and thought, children can start to form attachments to staff in the new environment before their parents leave them. Familiarity with the physical environment, staff, routines, etc. will in most cases smooth the way for a happy introduction.

Where children experience a change that is on one level, i.e. a change of setting, a certain level of stress is involved. With each additional level of change, the levels of stress rise further, for example moving home, change of town, new step-parent, etc.

Most settings have a policy that encourages initial visits, involving parents, carers from the old setting if appropriate and, of course, the child.

Introductory visits

Ideally, a child starting at a setting should pay several familiarisation visits with his or her parents or carers. The first visit should involve spending a short time looking around to help parents and the child in the decision process as to which is the most appropriate setting. A child's initial reaction can often be an indicator of his or her ultimate response. Interest in the toys and equipment, even if the child remains firmly attached to the parent, is far more encouraging than a refusal even to go in or look at the facilities.

A second visit should be longer with the parent staying throughout, and the child being encouraged to be involved in an activity. The key worker should play alongside, joining in if the child appears comfortable. Liaison with the parent to discover the child's favourite activity, and not forcing it on him or her, can help in the process. Some children will join in without a second thought; others may take some time to feel the appropriate level of confidence. All movement towards joining in must be child led, and never forced. On third and subsequent visits,

The key worker and parent can support the child

the key worker should take a more active role, with the parent leaving the child for a few minutes, having told the child he or she is going.

With time the length of parental absence is increased, as the child builds up an attachment to the key worker and is comfortable without the parent. Eventually, depending on the child, the parent leaves the child at the beginning of the session and returns at the end.

This programme may not be required or possible for all situations. It cannot be over-stressed that the length of time of each stage is totally dependent on the child and the parents. A very timid or insecure child may take far longer to settle than an outgoing one. Parents may not be able to spend a long time in the process – in some cases it may not be possible at all. You should be prepared to respond to the individual circumstances and needs of all children, offering more support to a child who has not had the benefit of a full, gradual introduction.

These early visits are crucial to the quality of the child's response to the setting. Remember, you are hoping that the child will actively want to come to nursery, playgroup, school, etc.

A positive response can be encouraged by:

- making activities attractive, and removing broken toys or games with missing pieces
- presenting activities that are appropriate to the child's age and stage of development
- planning the layout of the room – avoiding cluttered settings, including a quiet corner and displaying familiar items clearly
- inviting the child to join in, but without exerting undue pressure
- allowing the child to stand and observe, from a 'safe' position near the parent or the key worker
- encouraging an atmosphere of calm busyness in the setting
- showing a caring response to children in distress – respecting a child's need or otherwise for cuddles and physical contact
- encouraging other children to invite the child to play, if necessary manipulating the situation.

Keys to good practice
Making children feel welcome

Think about things that make somewhere new seem a friendly place. Now apply these to a child entering a new setting. They should include:

- a warm welcoming smile from staff, without being over-powering
- getting down to the height of the child to speak and explain things, rather than towering above him or her
- welcoming the child by his or her preferred name, previously discovered from the parent or asked for on arrival
- allowing time for the child to respond to questions or not, as he or she prefers
- offering a hand to the child, and respecting the response if it is a refusal
- having a suitable activity to offer to the child, and encouraging him or her to join in if appropriate – but again respecting a refusal to do so
- making it obvious to the child that the accompanying parent is welcome, and can stay for as long as required.

Familiar items

New children should be encouraged to bring a comfort object or familiar toy with them. These items provide a link to home and parents, and can help to provide a sense of security. Children may have one of a wide range of comfort objects and routines including:

- a favoured doll or teddy
- a comfort blanket, old jumper, shirt or even rag
- keeping their outdoor coat on
- thumb sucking or hair twiddling.

Care needs to be taken to avoid any suggestion of ridicule relating to the comforter, and once the child starts to relax and be less dependent on the comforter, you should ensure it is kept safe and that the child takes it home at the end of the day. Avoid any well-intentioned attempt to wash comfort blankets, clothing or soft toys, however grubby – the comfort factor has an integral smell element!

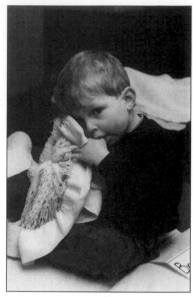

Comfort objects provide a sense of security

Introduction of setting and staff

Although you may feel that the building that you work in is only small, it will not seem so to a child. Even if the child has been shown around the nursery, school, etc. at the initial visit, make a point of repeating the exercise, especially pointing out important things such as the toilets, where lunch is eaten, the way out to the outdoor play area, where coats are kept and so on. You should make sure the new child has a peg for his or her coat, with a suitable label on, before the actual first day – this helps to make a child feel that he or she already belongs there.

Staff in the setting should be introduced to new children, but be careful not to overload them with new faces in the first few days. Anybody directly involved with new children, for instance in the same room or area, must be made known to them, but not others who may only be distant figures in the early days.

Other children in the setting can be invaluable in helping to welcome a new child. If the setting is in the child's home area, it is quite likely that the new child may already know some of the children. This is very helpful and will help to dispel some of the unfamiliarity felt in the first few days and weeks. Even if the child does not know anyone, children are usually very keen to make a new child feel welcome – most of them will remember their feelings on starting in the setting and will invite the newcomer into their games and play.

Whenever possible try to offer children over the age of about 18 months choices. This can help them to feel in control, rather than that they have been taken over. These choices need not be huge ones but could include:

- choosing the symbol on their coat peg
- choice of drink or snack
- whether to join in a game
- choosing the story at their first story time.

These choices will be controlled ones, with probably only two options, but are important in helping to boost children's self-esteem when they may be feeling very small and lost.

Keys to good practice
When children are new to a setting

- Children should always spend time at their new setting before the first 'formal' day. Parents should be involved in this time.
- Make sure new children know where toilets are, who to ask if they need help, etc.
- Full details of new children's likes and dislikes, routines, etc. should be discovered before the first day.
- New children should have a 'key worker' who helps with the settling-in process.
- Never leave new children alone in the first few days to find their own occupation – always help and direct.
- Introduce new children to other children.

Recognising the level of support a child needs

Even with a lot of advance planning some children will still find it difficult to adjust to a new setting. There are some indicators as to which children might find this to be the case:

- Children who have not previously been cared for away from home.
- Children who have experienced upheaval, for example parents separated, hospital admission, in foster care, refugees.
- Children living in isolated settings who have not had contact with many people outside their immediate family.
- Children who have experienced several changes of setting already, possibly in a short space of time.
- Children who have recently moved a considerable distance and so lost friends and a familiar home base.
- Children for whom the language used in the setting is not their first language, and is not used regularly at home.
- Children whose cultural background is very different from that of the majority of children in the setting.

Children will vary in their response to any new situation, depending on their individual personality. The age of the child at the time of starting in a new setting will have an effect on how he or she reacts – look back at the developmental chart on pages 69–70.

- A baby under six months is unlikely to be distressed when left for the first time as he or she has not yet reached the age of thinking that someone who is out of sight has vanished for good. This reaction starts at about eight months and is a part of the process of discovering object permanence.
- Between the ages of one and three years children are most likely to be distressed when they leave their primary carer as they have not enough experience to realise that the carer will return. Any lengthy period of a previous separation will increase this distress.
- Over the age of three years, children who have already experienced being left by a carer for short periods may settle quite easily if other conditions are satisfactory.

It is important not to generalise and to be aware that all children will find the first few days in a new setting stressful and will require a lot of empathetic support and help to overcome this.

Allowing children to familiarise themselves at their own pace

Respecting a child's pace

Children develop at different rates, and may be more advanced in one aspect of development than another. Equally, all children have unique personalities that result in different ways of responding to events. It is very difficult to predict which child will react in which way. Remember to respect each child's individuality, and take pride in finding out his or her different nuances. This will enable you to respond in the best way to each child. This approach applies in all aspects of work with children, but particularly in the early days of a relationship with a child. You should never try to hurry a child's settling-in process – always respect the individual's pace of settling. If a child wants to have one-to-one stories, then do so. A child may be very secure in playing in the sand – again, allow that freedom; equally, another child may never have encountered sand or water play, and may need time to help him or her to learn how to play with that medium.

However, often a child seems to settle very quickly, only to regress several weeks later.

Did you know?

For children starting at primary school, the early days at 'proper school' can seem very exciting, with the newness of it all catching a child's imagination and interest. After a few days or weeks, some children then almost rebel, and declare a wish to stop going to school. This reaction can be quite unnerving to parents who previously thought their child had settled very well.

Some children may never settle in a particular setting – this may be simply that the setting in question is not the best one for the child. This may be a case of the child not being emotionally mature enough, a personality mismatch between the child and proposed key worker, or simply that the setting is not appropriate. This can occur in a large setting when the child may prefer a small, cosy setting or vice versa.

Case study

Andrew, aged two and a half years, started trial visits at the playgroup that his sister Joanne had attended. He had been in the building with his mother to pick up his sister on several occasions. Joanne had now moved on to nursery. His first trial day was not a success. Even with his mother Andrew did not want to join in, and when she tried to leave him for a few minutes, Andrew cried inconsolably. Several more attempts did not improve the situation, and eventually it was decided to leave it. Six months later, Andrew started at a nursery school, without any problems. The trial days were a success and within three days his mother could happily leave him.

What do you think had happened in this case? Had Andrew just become that little bit more emotionally mature and could cope with separation? Do you think that the playgroup was not suited to Andrew? Have you ever experienced a situation of this kind?

Some children enjoy a lot of physical contact, and need the reassurance of cuddles and hugs, especially in the early days as they learn the differences between your role, and that of their main carer. Many staff in reception classes report a child calling them 'mummy' by mistake in the early weeks. You should, within the boundaries of professionalism, respond to that. Some early years settings have restrictions on the amount of physical contact a worker can have with a child. This reflects fears about accusations of abuse. There is a sensitive dividing line between offering children physical comfort after a fall or if they are distressed in the form of a hug, or perhaps a one-to-one story with the child sitting very close, and being over-physical in your contact.

Supporting children in the early stages of the new setting

An earlier section explored the benefits of a lengthy induction phase to a setting. However, not all situations allow for such a settling-in period. A child may have to enter a setting at very short notice due to ill health of a parent or family disruption. It is likely that the child will be upset by the events leading up to the need for him or her to enter the setting; the distress of separation will only add to this. As an early years worker, you will need to use all your skills and knowledge, normally practised over a long introduction period, in a very short time.

Key issues

Recognition of distress

Before the 1970s, most children's hospitals or wards did not allow parents to stay with their children, in the mistaken view that the children's crying when the parents had to go was a sign that the parents were upsetting the children. Stays in hospital tended to be a lot longer than they are today, with more than one week being common for operations that nowadays see a child discharged home within two days. Residential nurseries were common, caring for children if mum was ill or a new baby was due. A husband-and-wife team – the Robertsons – inspired by the work of psychologist John Bowlby, started to study the effects of separation from parents of young children. Their research in the 1950s clearly identified three stages of distress when children were left in an unfamiliar setting by their primary carers. Their work was important in the recognition that children need parents in hospital, resulting in our current policies of a parent staying all the time.

Stages of distress

1 Protest – displayed as anger, loud crying, trying to follow carer, clinging to carer.
2 Despair – shown in a listless stance, no interest in the surroundings or activities.
3 Detachment – the child is withdrawn, plays alone and does not interact with adults or other children.

Children may take several days to progress through the three stages, and a child who has reached the second stage of despair should be a cause for serious concern. The air of detachment indicative of the third stage is almost a self-protection mechanism to prevent future hurt. Most parents and early years workers will be familiar with the protest stage. A well-thought-out process of induction into a new setting should avoid most children having to suffer even the first stage of the distress reaction.

Sharing information with children and their parents

Sharing information with parents

Most parents find the separation from their child as painful, if not more so, as the child does. To parents, handing the care of their child to someone else is a difficult task, especially if it is the first time that the child has been cared for by someone else. If the move to formal care is due to the parent going back to work, guilt at doing this may be an additional factor, and the parents need as much support and help as their child.

Sometimes these feelings may be conveyed to you as mistrust or concern that you will not care for their child as well as them. Some parents may seem aggressive and defensive in their dealings with you initially – recognise this as their response to what may be a very difficult time for them. A sensitive, professional response will help to calm their apprehensions. It is important to understand the reasons for the reactions and ensure that you reassure the parents by your professional behaviour and obvious interest in their child.

Sharing a child's day

Sharing details of the child's time with you with the parents will help to dispel many of their fears. You should report truthfully how the child has been that day. Do not be tempted to tell the parents that their child has been happy if that is not the case – it is amazing how parents can pick up the truth, and the important factor of trust will have been eroded.

Encouraging children to take home pictures they have drawn, models they have done, or showing parents their child's work will help to reassure parents. If possible, introduce parents to the parents of friends that their child has made. For a young child or baby a notebook sharing daily information is useful, especially in terms of food taken, sleep patterns, etc.

Dialogues with parents can be used to find out relevant information about the child at home. A child who appears to you to have settled well may have started bed-wetting at night, may not be sleeping well, etc., and sharing this information can help to start useful discussions to help the child cope in a more positive manner.

A defined handing-over period at the end of the first few days or weeks should be an integral part of the settling-in period. This will establish an effective relationship between the key worker and the parents.

Element C5.2   Enable children to relate to others

The purpose of social development of humans is to help to prepare us for living and working with others. There are few adults who live a life totally separated from other people. We are not born with all our social skills intact. Certain skills may be inborn, but many others are learned from our experiences, and relate to the types of surroundings and settings in which we are brought up. This element explores how you can support a child in developing these important skills.

WHAT YOU NEED TO LEARN

- Encouraging children in their relationships with others
- Intervening and dealing with children's conflicts and anti-social behaviour
- Using play and learning experiences to encourage useful interactions
- Helping children develop the concept of respect for other people

Encouraging children in their relationships with others

One of the reasons that children attend some form of pre-school setting is to help in the development of their social skills, with the aim of developing into well-balanced members of society. Socialisation has two main strands:

- Primary socialisation takes place in the family setting, and involves learning behaviours for living in society from family and immediate carers.
- Secondary socialisation involves children learning about acceptable behaviours in their society from sources outside the family.

Attending playgroup, nursery and school has an important role to play in the secondary socialisation of children. A range of people are important in this socialisation role, including:

- other children attending
- staff working in the setting
- parents of other children.

Children generally have an intense desire to be accepted and liked by everyone – adults and children – and will quickly pick up the cues about acceptable and unacceptable behaviour. Parents are often surprised by changes in the values or attitudes that have been developed at home.

Children are often described as being at various stages of socialisation and play at different ages. Although types of relationships are more common at

Children interact and play together in a variety of ways

different ages, they are not exclusive to that group. From birth children interact in a variety of ways with other children and adults, as follows:

- solitary – alone, without reference to others
- parallel – alongside other children, but with little interest in them or their activity
- associatively – still alongside, but taking an interest in the other child, making contact, showing their game, etc.
- cooperatively – sharing activity, allowing turn-taking.

It is important to recognise that all of these different types of association may be appropriate to a child at different times of the day, week, etc. Although they are developed over the first two or three years of life, each one remains as further social skills are gained.

Observation

Observe a small group of three or four children, aged four years if possible. Try to decide what types of association you see over a period of a day. Time sampling, where the children are observed for five minutes every hour, may be the best method. Do some of the children associate in some styles more than others? Make a report of your observations.

Intervening and dealing with children's conflicts and anti-social behaviour

Children working together in pairs or a group will usually start to quarrel at some stage. It is unusual for an activity to be completed fully without some degree of altercation between two or more children.

Research has shown that quarrelling with each other is an important part of developing social skills. Between three and four years children start to learn from disputes as well as cooperation. Falling out with a friend should, with discreet support from adults, be quickly followed by making up – helping children to recognise that an argument does not mean loss of friendship.

Intervening in arguments between children should be done with care. Immediately stopping a quarrel is not very helpful to children; it prevents them from having the chance to sort out differences and still remain friends. If an adult intervenes, there can be resentment from one side, and a sense of having manipulated the situation from the other. All too often, by the time an adult has seen a quarrel between children, he or she has missed the chance to see where and how it started, and it all too easy to take the wrong side. You should intervene only in the following situations:

- where physical violence or bullying is occurring
- when racist or other discriminatory language is being used as abuse
- where a group of children is ganging up on an individual.

When it is necessary to intervene, it is vital that all the children involved are considered, both victims and aggressors. Apart from the child who appeared to be the victim, try to work out why the other child was so angry. Is it an isolated incident, or part of a pattern?

Remember though, that children will not form positive relationships with everyone they meet. Personality clashes will occur between children and between children and adults. This is normal and should not be a cause for concern. Do you get on equally well with everyone you know?

Observation

Spend some time observing a group of children and note who interacts with whom. Are there any obvious close friendships, or children who avoid each other?

Anti-social behaviour – the influence of children's experiences

Anti-social behaviour should always be challenged and includes:

- bullying – physical, verbal and emotional
- discriminatory language and behaviour
- stealing or destroying other people's property.

All children need to experience what it feels like to matter so as to be able to respond to others in the same way. Unless children experience someone's concern when they are upset and know what it is to be consoled, they will not be able to console someone else. Generally, children have a natural tendency to help and protect other children. Even a very young child will recognise a child in distress, and most children will try to comfort the distressed child –

by a cuddle, or offering a toy. In terms of socialisation skills this is an important step – it shows that a child can and will think of others before his or her own needs. Although you may witness caring behaviour in a child, the next time you observe the same child, he or she may be behaving in the opposite way. Socialisation skills take time to develop, but children who have a well-developed sense of reacting to others' needs are often the most popular children, because of their warmth and friendliness.

Unfortunately, many children see other examples of how to behave – and these may be anti-social examples. A family who verbalises discrimination against other cultural groups or people with disabilities, or voices stereotypical views about men and women, will have passed many of these attitudes on to even tiny children. 'Children learn by how they live' is a popular saying, but one with huge implications.

A child who is bullied may well develop a tendency to become a bully.

Most children will try to comfort another child in distress

Bullying may involve:

- physical violence
- intimidating or threatening behaviour, often by shouting at the victim
- ignoring or laughing at the victim in his or her distress
- belittling the victim
- ignoring efforts.

As children learn their social skills by example, many childcare experts believe that smacking a child only conveys the message that hitting other people who are smaller than you is acceptable. They question how a child may be challenged for smacking a younger sibling when that is precisely how the parents discipline the older child. Likewise ignoring a crying child, calling a child names or laughing at a child's distress presents the child with a very poor example of caring for others.

As an effective early years worker, good behaviour towards children is vital, and apart from showing children your example, you might just give a parent who is struggling pause for thought.

Remember

As an early years worker, it is against the law for you to physically chastise a child in your care.

Keys to good practice

Being a good role model

- Always praise the efforts of a child.
- Shouting at a child will encourage the child to shout back.
- Never belittle a child.
- Behave towards a child as you expect him or her to behave towards other children.
- Anti-social behaviour should always be challenged.

Key issues

There has been a lot of coverage in the press about the attempt by the European Courts to make the smacking of children by a parent punishable under the law. Try to find some recent newspaper or magazine articles and start a file of them, adding to the file as the campaign progresses. This is a topic that causes polarisation of views, even among early years workers – ask your family and colleagues for their views.

Dealing with anti-social behaviour

You may feel that there is little that can be done to counter the influence of a child's family. Luckily, even when children have learned inappropriate attitudes and behaviours from the family, most children still exhibit positive behaviours, for example concern for other children, sharing toys, taking turns. The secret is to praise these positive traits, using them as examples if a child has to be taken to task for an anti-social incident.

As an early years worker, your role involves challenging any child who is being openly anti-social through bullying, or making racist remarks. A simple reprimand such as: 'That was not a kind thing to say... We do not use words like that to other children...' and comforting the child who has been the recipient, is often all that is required to deal with anti-social behaviour.

An isolated incident may be dealt with solely by prompt and appropriate intervention. Repeated incidents may need a wider approach, and a reflection on the policy of the setting. All early years settings should have a few simple, basic rules relating to good practice in terms of equal opportunities and bullying. Parents must be made aware of these rules, and the setting should be run on the basis of them. The rules should cover the basic principles:

- respecting the needs, rights and possessions of others
- understanding basic concepts of right and wrong.

Active knowledge

What are the basic rules of the setting you work in? Find out who developed them, and how they are used in practice. Do you think the staff adhere to all of them? If not, give your reasons why you think some rules are ignored.

Activities in the nursery or school can and should be used to reinforce the rules, using materials that deal sensitively with racial abuse or bullying, for example. Remember that how the staff, including you, behave towards each other and the children will help to reinforce the rules of the setting.

Older children in schools can often help to draw up the rules of the classroom, and, unsurprisingly, they usually come up with the ideas we have already discussed.

Using play and learning experiences to encourage useful interactions

As an effective early years worker, you need to arrange play activities for children appropriate to their age and stage of development. (Look again at the chart on page to help you.)

To children, play is the means by which they learn. Units C5, C10 and C11 look at a wide range of play and experiences to promote different types of development. Any game, activity or experience that involves more than just the child will also be encouraging useful interactions. There are few if any play opportunities that do not have a multi-functional role in the child's development. An activity does not need to be an obvious play activity – helping to set the tables for lunch at nursery, for example, involves working with others, sorting, patterns, and helping you, the carer. All activities provide the opportunity for verbal interaction, learning about turn-taking, considering other, etc.

By the time children are a year old they need lots of opportunities to develop their autonomy, i.e. their ability to do things for themselves within a safe environment. Children at this age are at a stage when their range of skills is rapidly expanding. They are eager to try anything and everything, from climbing on to chairs or up stairs, exploring cupboards, boxes, plugs, fires, shelves, electrical goods, pill bottles, outside the front door, in the garden – in fact anywhere they are allowed to go. These examples should show you that it is an important part of an early years worker's role to ensure that this exploration and development of autonomy are done in a safe manner, yet without stifling children's natural desire to find out for themselves.

Lots of praise for effort at this stage will help to develop children's self-esteem. Avoid criticism by distracting them from potentially dangerous situations without fuss. This will encourage children to look for attention through pleasing adults rather than by being naughty.

Children between the ages of three and four years are perhaps the most easily influenced in terms of their future social development. At this age they are increasingly influenced by each other and will try out being in control and being led by others. Encouraging caring and cooperation with each other is crucial.

Relationships with others

Children have an innate need to relate to others, even from babyhood – this is pro-social behaviour and helps in the development of humans as a social race. There are few, if any, adults who can lead a fulfilling life without some degree of cooperation or relationship with others.

It is important to provide children from a very early age with the opportunity to meet other children and adults. The very nature of most babies makes this easy. There are few adults who can resist the overtures of a baby, secure in the arms of its carer.

Babies enjoy cooperative social behaviour in games such as peek-a-boo, and will smile at and touch each other from as young as six months and, within limits, with other adults as well. From a year or eighteen months toddlers enjoy copying each other and sharing ideas. By two or three years a child needs a wider social circle to be able to choose groups of friends.

Observation

Try to note down the different interactions of two children, say one of approximately nine months and one of two or three years, over a period of time. What are the differences in the interactions?

Activities and games need to relate to the age and stage that a child has reached, with opportunities for interaction increasing as the child grows older.

Games allowing each child in turn to be in control and to be led are important to help them develop skill in both leadership and following others' instructions. Paired and group games can be used to provide a contrast between a very close working relationship with one other person, or the skills required in responding to several people at once.

Play and activities are an ideal medium to introduce children to cultures and languages outside their immediate experience. Involvement of parents/relatives of children from different cultural backgrounds, outside visitors, or visits to other centres can widen children's horizons in their interactions with others.

Role play

Role play is an ideal medium for children to rehearse adult roles, practise new skills and express their feelings. Providing a range of materials to promote role play can help children to develop many social skills. For example:

- Equip the home corner with a range of articles and scenarios from a variety of cultures.
- Include a wide range of costumes and equipment, covering different cultures, genders and occupations, in the dressing-up box.
- Set up a model shop with, for example, salt-dough fruit and vegetables, empty packets, etc. and play (but realistic) money.

Role play in these types of settings can be free of language barriers, and starts to introduce children to other cultures and backgrounds, as they interact with other children. Play in the home corner can be a solitary play experience, but can also allow for parallel or social play.

By offering children the opportunity to meet a variety of people, both adults and children, from outside their own narrow circle, you can encourage them to begin to understand other cultures and backgrounds. Exposure to a whole range of role models will challenge the stereotypes that can start to form at this age.

The home corner can encourage development of many social skills

Make sure that children hear stories about female doctors and car mechanics and male nurses and hairdressers, in contrast to the usual stereotypes. Stories should reflect the cultural diversity of the UK, and introduce the children to other countries as well.

Inclusive education, i.e. children of all educational needs being included in one setting, helps to promote the inclusion of people who have a disability within society in general. If your early years setting includes children who have a disability, make sure that everything you do respects those children as fully participating members of the group.

Consolidation

Consider the children you work with. List some of the activities in which you could involve the children to improve their skills in interacting with other people. What skills would they gain from each activity?

Helping children develop the concept of respect for other people

Early years settings should have few formal rules. A well-run organisation should avoid the need for them. However, children need to believe that their basic rights will be upheld wherever they are cared for, and to ensure this most early years settings have a few rules relating to the moral concepts that order the day-to-day running of the nursery or school. Other settings such as child minder or nanny will usually work along similar, but less formal, lines. Children have to know, however implicitly, that they must:

- respect the needs, rights and possessions of others
- know the difference between right and wrong.

More importantly, children should understand that their rights will be protected if anyone tries to abuse those rights, i.e. that there are sanctions for stealing or spoiling other children's property or being a bully or abusive. Gently correcting very young children when they transgress is usually enough. Many stories, songs and rhymes are concerned with moral concepts, and play a very useful role in helping children to understand the principles. For example, think about two of the most popular fairy stories – Cinderella and Snow White – both involve someone being badly treated, and yet winning through, while the 'villain' gets her just deserts.

Older children at the start of primary school are usually already developing very strong moral values and will relish drawing up their own rules for good behaviour. Many schools have adopted the approach of allowing children to decide the basic principles of community living themselves, with little room for bullying or other anti-social behaviour.

Consolidation

Draw up a charter for social living in an imaginary community. Use only very basic principles that encourage respect and consideration for all concerned.

Element C5.3   Develop children's self-reliance and self-esteem

Element C5.2 looked at enabling children to develop social skills. To participate actively in society a child needs to feel important, that he or she matters, that people are going to want to interact socially with him or her. As children grow older they need to be able to use their social skills by themselves, without relying on adults always being there to support them. Many child care experts would argue that a child who is self-reliant and has a good level of self-esteem is better equipped at the start of his or her formal education than a child who can already read and write.

- Encouraging children to use communication skills effectively
- Encouraging self-help skills and self-reliance
- Avoiding stereotypical assumptions about children's levels of potential achievement in self-reliance
- Supporting parents in promoting children's levels of self-reliance and self-esteem

Encouraging children to use communication skills effectively

Children need to believe that their ideas and contributions are important. While an early years setting obviously requires a basic set of routines and plans to ensure coverage of essential issues such as health and safety and meeting the needs of various controlling bodies, children should be involved in making choices around everyday activities wherever possible. Every time you ask a child for his or her ideas or opinions, and act on them, you give that child's sense of worth a huge boost. Equally, asking for children's opinions and then ignoring them can have a negative effect. This open method of decision-making does need care to ensure fairness to all children, and to ensure that the work of the setting is appropriate.

Case study

Preston Road nursery is a private day nursery with 40 children aged two to five years. The early years workers develop its outline plan of activities for the month at a staff meeting. Suggestions made by the older children and the parents of younger ones are considered and used whenever possible. This month the theme chosen is 'changes', and the older children are told that they will be looking at this topic. In a small group, the children explore the meanings and types of change, through ideas such as dough changing into buns when baked, or bulbs changing into flowers, or babies developing.

Talk about this with your supervisor. Do you think it would be possible to implement this practice in your setting? Imagine how a child might feel to know that he or she is working on something that was his or her idea.

Keys to good practice

- Always listen to a child's ideas and opinions.
- Always take a child's ideas seriously.
- Explain why suggestions cannot be used if that is the case, and help a child to suggest an alternative.
- Make sure that less vocal children have the chance to make themselves heard.

Encouraging the development of self-help skills and self-reliance

Some children seem to relish the process of achieving self-reliance and being independent; others are less keen to do things for themselves. This can depend on several factors:

- the child's place in the family – younger siblings may be used to older ones doing tasks for them
- parents' attitudes to independence
- some factor inhibiting achievement of certain skills, for example physical skill development
- lack of a role model, or the lack of opportunity to develop a skill
- different rates of progress
- interest in other activities.

Self-help skills develop at the child's individual pace

Self-feeding is a skill that children achieve at widely differing ages. Physically, a child should be able to start self-feeding from about twelve months onwards. This coincides with the achievement of independent walking for some children and the chance finally to start exploring all the exciting objects and places previously only viewed from a stationary position. Food may be viewed very functionally by some children, and the time taken to mess around with a spoon, sitting in a chair, can be regarded as a waste of valuable exploring time. A physically active child may be far more self-reliant in reaching desired objects than a child with a big interest in food who can feed himself or herself. Recognition and acceptance of a child's different interests and skills is important. Most children eventually reach self-reliance in all the important areas.

By the time children start formal schooling around the age of five years, most should be able to:

- dress themselves
- go to the toilet alone, clean themselves and wash their hands
- use the appropriate implements to feed themselves, eating a normal diet in relation to the appropriate cultural setting
- know their name and address, and preferably telephone number
- play with other children
- concentrate for short periods of time
- fetch the required materials for some activities on request or instruction.

However, each child should be considered individually and account taken of differences in ability.

Avoiding stereotypical assumptions about children's levels of potential achievement in self-reliance

Self-esteem is a reflection of the way we feel about ourselves, and children develop a sense of self-esteem from birth. Self-esteem is built on the reactions we get from other people, as this is a reflection of the way they see us. Right from birth children need to know that they matter – it is difficult to build positive self-esteem if you do not feel that you are important to anyone. A child who is helped to develop a strong sense of self-esteem from the start will be able to deal with most of the emotions that life throws at him or her. For a child with any form of disability, this can be particularly important. Children who have suffered some form of abuse often have very poor self-esteem, and will need a lot of support from early years workers to alter their view of themselves.

The reactions of other people to a child can depend on outward physical appearance, and a child may be taunted because he or she wears glasses, has a dental brace or is from a visibly different cultural group to the majority. It is important to deal with these issues by offering genuine warmth and support to the child and dealing with the reactions of other children.

Ways to raise self-esteem

Every interaction you have with a child is a potential opportunity to add to that child's self-esteem. Conversely, it is also an opportunity to damage it.

Case study

Imran, aged four, was always in trouble at nursery school, often seeming deliberately to taunt the other children and spoil the work they were doing. The staff tried all sorts of tactics to encourage Imran to join in with the children and make friends with them. There seemed to be very little progress, and a discussion was held with the family health visitor on one of her visits to the nursery. She reported that Imran was the youngest of three brothers – the other two were very clever and bullied their little brother, calling him stupid because he could not dress himself and still wet the bed at night. A meeting with Imran's mother revealed she was very worried about her youngest son as he had been acting in the same way towards his young cousin. A plan to boost Imran's self-esteem, by praise and recognition, and a quiet word with his brothers, soon started to show an improvement in his behaviour.

What do you think had been happening here? How do you think the situation could have been avoided at nursery?

Supporting parents in promoting children's levels of self-reliance and self-esteem

Many parents underestimate the degree of self-reliance their children have developed. Helping a child to become independent is a double-edged sword for some parents, as they may find it difficult to let their child show increasing signs of independence.

You may have observed a parent doing things for a child that you know the child can do for himself or herself, for example putting the child's coat on, taking the child to the toilet, making all the child's choices. As an early years worker, it can be difficult to accept this – it can almost feel as though the work you have done is being devalued, and that the child is losing those small gains towards independence. It is worth giving some consideration to why this happens:

- parents may want to feel that they are still needed by their child
- it may be quicker to do something such as putting a coat on for a child if the parent is in a hurry

- there may be a genuine lack of understanding of a child's abilities at different ages and stages
- the child's independence may be contrary to the parent's cultural and moral values
- parents may hold certain stereotypical views relating to gender, age, etc.

Supporting parents in accepting children's new skills

Careful management of a situation can help to convince parents that their child really is capable of some activity, and at the same time give a big boost to the child's self-esteem. When a parent comes to collect a child from your setting, invite him or her in to show the parent a 'new' skill. Most children will relish the chance to show off whatever move towards self-reliance they have made that day or week, for example, that they can put on their own shoes, that they helped to carry in the snacks, or chose which story to read. It is harder for parents to ignore such developments when shown by their child and early years worker in nursery or school.

Problems can arise if the parents have very low expectations of a child, frequently compare them to an older sibling, or suggest there is a lack of skill due to gender or age. Equally, parents may have over-ambitious expectations of their child, such as expecting their three-year-old to be writing his or her name, or a child with some physical restriction to be winning races on sports day. As an early years worker, it is important that you emphasise the skills and abilities a child does have, however small an achievement these may be. Constantly failing to meet over-ambitious expectations can seriously damage children's self-esteem. In these cases it may be necessary to discuss the issue with the parents – but consult your line manager first.

Case study

Laura, aged three years, had led quite a sheltered life before starting nursery school. Her mother had stayed at home to care for her, and had been determined that Laura should not be pushed into stereotypical female pursuits such as doll play. Indeed, there had been a positive move to encourage her enjoyment of cars, building blocks, etc. and an effort to avoid the pressures of TV adverts for popular toys.

After a week at nursery, Laura's parents were surprised to hear Laura playing doctors and nurses with her toys – Laura being the nurse – and even more surprised at Laura's demands for a doll.

What do you think has happened to Laura? Where have her changed ideas come from? Does your setting actively encourage non-gender-specific activities, or is there an obvious distinction between girls' and boys' games and activities?

Keys to good practice
Being supportive

- Value all children for who and what they are, including the children who appear to be difficult to accept. Even the least appealing children have something worthy of praise, for example the jumper they are wearing, or being first to be ready for a story.

- Provide positive images for all children. You need to ensure that displays, book corners, posters, etc. in the setting offer a wide range of images, for example different cultural groups, gender images, and children with disabilities.
- Make sure that there are enough books, videos and posters to counter negative images that the children may encounter. A child may only ever see gender stereotypes unless you actively overcome that. A child who is from an ethnic minority group may find it difficult to identify with adults in school or nursery.
- Make sure that children have good role models in the adults they work with, and those who come into the setting or are seen at places they visit. Adults representing different groups should be encouraged to come into the setting, and be actively involved to avoid the risk of tokenism.
- Never tell a child he or she is silly or stupid – the child may start to believe it. If a child makes a mistake, give him or her an idea of how to avoid doing so next time.
- Try to help a child to achieve success in activities. To do this you need to have a good understanding of the stage of development a child has reached, and what will help to push the child on to the next stage. Giving children an activity that is too difficult is guaranteed to make them fail. For example, reading books should be sensitively chosen, games should reflect the age and stage a child has reached.
- Never compare, or allow a child to be compared, with an older sibling – every child is an individual, and being the younger brother or sister of a clever, older sibling does not mean the child will be as clever. He or she may be very good at sports, or not shine in any particular activity. This should not mean the child is any less valued.
- Consistency helps children to feel secure, allowing them to develop within secure boundaries. Aim for consistency in:
  - care from the same people (key working will help this)
  - daily care routines, so that children feel their daily needs will be met, within an expected framework
  - boundaries of behaviour (to avoid confusion when different people react in different ways to the same behaviour, for example).
- Allow children choices in their daily lives, for example which activity they are going to do, which story to read, etc. There are many opportunities for this within the bounds of safety considerations, and having a choice in certain things gives children a sense of responsibility and control.
- Encourage children to speak politely to each other, and ensure they have good examples of polite behaviour from staff and parents as far as possible. Respecting other people helps children to develop their own self-respect.
- Help children to deal with their strong feelings of anger, joy, etc., and show that you will support them.
- Make it clear that if a child engages in negative behaviour, it is the behaviour that you do not like, not the child.
- Whenever possible give a child some degree of responsibility. This may involve fetching the book for story time, taking registers to the office, or helping to care for younger children. Pets are an ideal way to give a child some responsibility.

Observation

Make a list at the end of a day of all the actions you have done to boost a child's self-esteem. Are there any actions that may have had the opposite effect? If so, how could you avoid these happening again?

Element C5.4   Enable children to recognise and deal with their feelings

Children's feelings can be extreme – a child can be in deep despair one minute, and overjoyed about something else a few minutes later. Adults can find this swing disturbing if they do not understand the reasons behind a child's sudden mood changes. The level of control of one's emotions is a cultural issue. Different cultures and different families have different levels of expectations of what is appropriate. Knowledge gained by observation of different situations will help you to deal with these differing expectations.

WHAT YOU NEED TO LEARN

- Encouraging the expression of feelings in children in a safe and accepting environment
- Activities to encourage children to explore, recognise and deal with their feelings
- Dealing with the effects of emotional outbursts
- Using learning opportunities to help children develop their understanding of emotions.

Encouraging the expression of feelings in children in a safe and accepting environment

A well-run early years setting should have an atmosphere of openness that actively encourages the expression of feelings by the children, be they positive or negative feelings. Children should feel able to express their feelings within a group, or individually to members of staff, without fear of censure or ridicule.

Most feelings that a child experiences come from natural, acceptable reactions to everyday or life events, such as:

- having to leave playing to go for a meal, bath, etc.
- receiving a new toy
- arrival of a new baby in the family
- running free on a sunny day in the garden
- another child taking a toy
- arrival of a friend or relative.

Repression of feelings can give rise to a build-up of tension and aggression among even very small children. Often, a child may have built up tensions and feelings from events outside the early years setting. As the child may spend large amounts of the day with you, the early years setting is often the place where these feelings emerge, in a safe and secure environment.

Types of feelings

Feelings come in all shapes and forms. In one day a child may feel any of these:

Children's feelings are rarely half-hearted – while an adult might moderate his or her reactions and feelings, a child rarely will. For example, spend time watching a child who is overjoyed – he or she will totally 'light up' and this joy will be reflected in the child's body language, facial expressions, language and movements. Equally, an unhappy child is easily identified by outward signs. Later in this chapter we look at signs of distress.

Observation

Make a list of all the outward signs shown by a child who is very happy. Think about verbal and non-verbal communication. Now make a similar list for an unhappy child.

It is easy to create an environment where the expression of feelings is encouraged, and equally easy to create the opposite – a sense of not being able to express them. Being open and expressing your own emotions is the first step towards producing a positive environment. Show when you are happy or pleased about events, however small; likewise do not brush a child's questions away if you are unhappy one day. Telling children to be brave or smile when they are clearly unhappy will not encourage them to share their feelings. It is far better to comment that they look sad, and ask them whether they would like to share what is causing the feelings. Getting children to describe how they feel helps them to recognise what they are experiencing.

Keys to good practice

Helping children to express feelings

- Encourage the expression of feelings of children in your care.
- Respect children's feelings.
- Respect children's confidence if possible.
- Help children with language difficulties to express themselves through pictures, actions or if necessary use an interpreter.
- Respect cultural differences in the expression of emotions.

Influences on emotional expression

Not all children find it easy to express their emotions. A child's personality will affect whether he or she reacts openly or in a more restrained way. Expression of emotions can be affected by:

- cultural expectations, for example repression of overt emotions among certain sections of society, open expressions of grief from Afro-Caribbean communities
- gender stereotyping, for example being told boys do not cry
- role models in a child's life, for example having an open, sharing family or repressed parents who express little
- examples from peers and the early years setting.

Children who have difficulty expressing their emotions can be helped in this by the example of other children and by activities to stretch their experiences of expressions, for example using the scenario of a story to prompt children to describe how they would feel in a certain situation. Other ways to encourage children to express their emotions include: asking them to describe how they feel when they are sharing news, exploring the variety of words to describe feeling happy, sad, etc., and discussing what they are feeling physically.

Activities to encourage children to explore, recognise and deal with their feelings

Play is one of the best methods of encouraging and facilitating the expression of a child's feelings. Young children may not possess the language skills to explore their feelings fully. With any type of play there will be some possible way of using it for expressing feelings, for example:

Type of play/activity	Possible uses
Physical gross-motor play – running, riding bikes, climbing, trampolining, etc.	Physical release of pent up feelings of rage, frustration. Opportunity to release adrenaline which is produced in stressful situations.
Role-play, for example child in a powerful situation Working through situations that the child has experienced	Can help to redress feelings of inferiority. 'Acting out' real-life situation or imaginary scenarios.
Play with dolls – can be anatomically correct if required in cases of abuse	Helps to work out situations, act out aggression or treatment a child has received.
Painting, drawing	Literal or representative images of events, use of colour to show feelings – bright and sunny for pleasure, dark and gloomy for unhappiness. (Check what colours of paint were available before jumping to conclusions!)
Puppets – manufactured, or the child involved in making them	Type of role play to allow a child to express feelings through a 'third party'.
Dough, plasticine	Allows physical bashing of an inert medium.
Use of stories	Careful selection of related stories could be used to develop ideas with a child, and lead to further group or individual discussion.

Dealing with the effects of emotional outbursts

In providing a supportive environment for the expression of emotions, it is essential to consider the following issues, since an emotional outburst may have an impact on other children in the setting.

- The type of support to give children witnessing another child's outburst so that all children can deal with extreme outbursts in others. Children who experience emotional outbursts may be reserved or quiet, or may witness violent outbursts at home. Other children will need explanations of why an outburst has occurred, and a simplified reason (within the bounds of confidentiality) can help other children to support a distressed child.
- Carefully controlling outbursts without inhibiting the child, to protect other children. If you are alert for the signs in a child who has a tendency to outbursts, it should be possible to divert other children or remove the child from full view and provide the necessary support.
- The possibility that an outburst is indicative of problems that may need liaison with parents and other professionals.
- Whether behaviour is acceptable in terms of stages of development.

When dealing with the effects of emotional outbursts, you must pay due attention to your setting's requirements.

Temper tantrums

Case study

Jolene, aged two years, was happily playing with her new cars when her father came to get her ready for bed. Jolene was not ready to stop her game; her father was waiting to go out and insisted. Within seconds, a previously happy scene – with Jolene singing tunelessly – changed into a full-blown temper tantrum. Jolene's tantrums could be a frightening sight – a whirlwind of exploding emotions, involving foot stamping, screaming and lashing out. Her father waited a few seconds and then calmly sat and held Jolene, gently but firmly, until her outburst had died down. Her screams and shouts eventually turned into sobs, and ended in a comforting cuddle. Jolene then went to choose a book to read after her bath.

Why do you think Jolene reacted so angrily to her father? Think about how you might have dealt with the situation.

Children from the age of eighteen months up to about four years can find it impossible to control their anger. Temper tantrums are usually a result of frustration, when a child is not able to do something that he or she wishes to, either because of personal limitations or the restrictions of carers. Handled well, a tantrum can be over fairly quickly and forgotten about. Tantrums may also involve breath holding, even to the point of the child turning blue, although the body will automatically react to start the breathing again. During a tantrum a child needs a caring adult to help him or her deal with the outburst. Child care experts have in the past suggested a range of different tactics to deal with temper tantrums, such as totally ignoring them until the child settles down, responding sharply or even smacking. The current advice is to hold the child gently during a tantrum. However, this is a skill you need to observe being used by experienced workers, and should be done with a child who is known to the carer.

We often tend to be more concerned about helping children to deal with negative emotions, and as they grow older to express them appropriately. There are many occasions, though, when a child will be 'bursting' with good news, joy and pleasure, and has to release that feeling. Early years workers need to be

Child care experts recommend holding a child gently during a tantrum

alert to creating opportunities for children to share good news and feelings of pleasure, just as much as helping them with negative feelings.

Often a child will come into nursery or the classroom and not be able to find a chance to tell you the news, as you are busy with the other children. Over the course of the session, the impetus to share the news may fade, leaving a child feeling let down and disappointed. The start or end of story time or circle time are good times to give children the opportunity to share news and feelings.

Feelings are not always extreme in children, and with increasing emotional maturity they usually become more restrained. A child may show different levels of emotion in different situations, showing quiet pleasure at the successful completion of a painting or puzzle, for instance. These types of situations, which occur throughout the day in a child's life, need to be responded to in suitable ways, by acknowledgement of the emotions and appropriate praise.

Signs of distress in children

Children may find it very difficult to articulate events or feelings that have caused them distress. Distress may result from many events, ranging from what may seem fairly small things to major, life-changing events.

Potential causes of distress in children
- Losing a favourite toy
- Arrival of a new baby in the family
- Moving house
- Starting a new class at school
- Change from nursery to school
- Illness in the child or a parent
- Mum going back to work
- Change in childminders
- Stay in hospital
- Tension at home
- Falling out with a sibling or parent just before leaving for nursery or school
- Argument with a friend
- Death of a pet
- Death of a grandparent.

The reaction to the above types of events is not always predictable, but there will usually be some degree of reaction. However, if well prepared for, predictable events such as changing class or going to hospital may bring only a small reaction.

Children will show a range of symptoms of distress. It is essential that as an effective early years worker you are alert for them. A child showing overt signs of distress needs your support. Distress involves a change in the behaviour of a child.

Possible signs of distress
- Being withdrawn, or suddenly more demanding
- Reluctance to join in activities
- Clinging to a familiar carer

- Reduction or increase in appetite
- Sleeping problems
- Regression to old comfort habits
- Regression in behaviours, for example wanting a bottle again
- Wetting or soiling – day or night time
- Bullying other children
- Stealing
- Self-harm.

The main feature of a sign of distress is that the behaviour is uncharacteristic for that child. By being alert for changes in behaviour and having an awareness of the events in a child's life, an effective worker can intervene and work with the child to deal with fears and emotions that are being expressed inappropriately.

Some children will need further professional help from social workers or psychologists to help them work through the distress or to help them remove the causes of distress. Referral should always be through the senior person in the early years setting, in partnership with parents, and confidentiality should be respected.

Using learning opportunities to help children develop their understanding of emotions

Even if a child has never personally experienced the full range of emotions, it is possible to consider them in the early years setting. An understanding of other people's feelings is part of the socialisation of a child. A child of two or three years will enjoy stories about simple emotions, such as a puppy finding his mother, or a favourite toy. Older children will relate to more complex emotions, for example dealing with loss, new siblings, etc. An early years worker should be alert to possible learning opportunities, which may appear in the following examples:

- books
- stories in the news
- films a child may have seen
- video recordings
- pictures
- visitors to the setting.

Any of the above examples could be used to promote discussion with the children, either individually or in a group, exploring the types of emotion the participants might feel, and how to describe them.

Children should be encouraged to share emotions with others, especially their carers. Older children need to know and feel that they can share unhappy emotions with carers in a safe environment.

Active knowledge ✓

How does your workplace deal with children who may have outbursts of negative or positive emotions? Do all staff react in the same way? Why do you think this is so?

Element C5.5   Enable children to develop a positive self-image and identity

The world is full of images of highly successful people, where evidence of success is equated with material gain. Many children cannot identify with the popular images shown in the media, and a positive self-image can be difficult for them to achieve. It is important that you should have the aim of developing a child's positive self-image and identity, which may have to work against the input of a child's family, surroundings and the responses of other people.

WHAT YOU NEED TO LEARN

- Supporting children's self-image and identity
- Appropriate positive and non-stereotypical images and role models to promote self-identity
- Recognising and supporting children with a low or negative self-image and identity

Supporting children's self-image and identity

Self-image and identity are about feeling comfortable with yourself in relation to your immediate world, i.e. family and society. To feel comfortable we need to see other people like our family and ourselves, and to see people in the wider community representing identities we aspire to. There are many aspects of experience that can affect a person's self-identity and image, and negative ones can lead to tragic attempts to deny such aspects as

- race
- language
- gender
- disability
- sexuality.

Promoting a child's positive sense of identity and self-image is one of the most important aspects of working with children. Children's self-concept starts to develop during the first year, and every social encounter they are involved in affects it, for better or worse. A sense of identity involves understanding that you exist as a person in your own right, having a positive self-image, liking and respecting yourself, and having the skills to look after yourself.

A baby in his or her first year of life does not know that he or she is a separate being from the main carer. This is a concept that a child develops in the latter half of the first year.

Observation

Try to watch a baby of about three or four months playing with his or her hands and feet. Apart from the fact that these wiggly appendages are interesting, a baby of that age is discovering his or her body, finding out where it starts and finishes.

A six-month-old baby looking at himself or herself in a mirror sees another baby, but as the weeks progress the baby gradually realises that this person is himself or herself. By about eighteen months a child has realised fully that he or she is not an attachment of the carer, but a fully separate being. Hence the egotistical state when 'no' is the answer to every question – all the child is doing is asserting the new-found sense of self.

Many psychologists have developed theories about the development of identity and self-identity, including Sigmund Freud and Erik Erikson. The difficulty with these is that they were built on an understanding of the characteristics of white, middle-class Europeans, and so such theories should not automatically be applied to all nationalities and cultures.

Key issues ✔

Do some research into the work of different psychologists in relation to the development of identity and self-image.

What did Freud mean by the id, ego and superego? What are Erikson's 'eight phases of man'?

Try to find work by psychologists who were not white and middle class. How do their ideas compare to those of Freud and Erikson?

It seems unavoidable that the way a child is treated in infancy will affect that child's view of himself or herself throughout life. Constantly telling a child that he or she is worthless, stupid, ignorant or ugly will soon encourage a belief that it must be true. Conversely, praising a child and showing that he or she is accepted and valued can only help to encourage a positive self-image.

Some children have features that in certain situations may render them more likely to be the subject of negative comments or ridicule. Not all members of society are enlightened, and there is still much stereotyping and prejudice about some people, which can lead to discrimination. Even though a child's self-image may already have been damaged to some extent, an effective early years team can help to reverse some of the effects and turn a poor self-image into a positive one.

When working with children who are wheelchair users, have visible birthmarks, are from a different racial group to the majority of the children, have impaired hearing or present with challenging behaviour, for example, it is essential to ensure there is no hint of different values being attached to them in your setting. Every child must be given similar amounts of love and attention to make him or her feel valued and important.

Key to good practice
Supporting children's self-esteem

- Face your own stereotypes and prejudices, then you can work towards opposing other people's in relation to children.
- Always value and accept children for who they are, not what they do or look like.
- Tell children that you do not like their actions or behaviour, never that you do not like them.
- Regularly praise children.
- Always keep promises made to children.

- Always make sure that children feel safe and secure with you, and that you can be trusted.
- Make sure that there are objects in the early years setting that every child can relate to.
- Provide a wide range of images of different cultural, gender and disability situations in all early years settings.

It is easy to boost the self-identity of outgoing children with an already well-developed sense of their own worth. However, children who have a poorly developed sense of identity can be difficult to help, as you may be faced with behaviours that almost reinforce this poor sense of self-worth.

Stereotyping

Stereotyping can restrict perceptions of a child's overall personality and ability. Stereotyping is about judging someone by a physical characteristic, for example he or she wears glasses or is from a different ethnic group to your own. Remember the child instead as the one who did a beautiful painting, or who enjoys doing number work, or better still as Joanne or Imran.

You may see some early years workers grouping children according to stereotypes, such as all the girls in one line, but you should avoid labelling children according to unchangeable characteristics. It is far better to group children randomly, or by some characteristics that does not suggest skill, character or appearance such as the month of their birthday or the initial of their name.

Children need empowering to try all approaches to activities, for boys to be gentle, girls to be tough, so that they can explore the full range of their own personalities and develop a good sense of their own identity and image.

Activities to promote a positive self-image

Any activity that gives each child a central role will help to produce a positive self-image. All children come to nursery or school with a personal history, both of their own and their families. Value that experience. Even quite young children can take part in many of the following activities:

- circle time – each child in the circle tells the rest about something he or she has done or brings in an object related to the weekend, for example
- treasure tables – displaying important objects from the children's lives
- life story books – with photographs and details of each child's life to date
- display features for the walls – with self-portraits and descriptions of the children by themselves
- special topics on the countries, languages, etc. of children within the group – could include inviting in

Children can share their experiences in circle time

relatives to talk about a topic, asking children to bring in relevant pictures or objects

- holiday features – describing places where children have been, but careful not to rely simply on exotic locations. Encourage information on visits to relatives, days out, etc.

Many of these ideas can be incorporated into the weekly or termly plan for your workplace. A period of time focusing on differences can be useful, for example looking at different heights, show sizes, features, houses, size and type of family – the important point here is 'different' does not mean better or worse. Care is needed to avoid unkind comparisons, but it can be extremely important to foster the acceptance of difference.

Appropriate positive and non-stereotypical images and role models to promote self-identity

Active knowledge ✓

Over the next few weeks, keep a notepad with you and jot down examples of stereotypical images that present themselves to you, in your work situation, at home, with friends, in the media, etc. Also make a note of images that make you stop and look again, because they are not stereotypical.

As you are collecting material for the above activity, think about the impact that the stereotypical images have on people who do not conform to them. Perhaps you do not fit the usual image of an early years worker – perhaps you are male, or have some disability, or are from an ethnic minority that is under-represented in your workplace.

Children are constantly exposed to stereotypical images which may run contrary to their racial or cultural group, or gender. Most early years settings screen learning materials to ensure that stereotypical images do not enter their resources.

Children learn best initially from familiar situations, so it is important, for example, to have reading schemes that the child can relate to, showing familiar images. The child's first language needs to be included, not only to help the child relate to the material, but also to allow all the family to read with the child.

All children have dreams of what they are going to do when they grow up. For many these change on a weekly, if not daily, basis. We base our dreams on images and examples we see – often small children want to be a shopkeeper or a bus driver because they see these examples daily. Familiarity with other experiences and with TV programmes, films, etc. widens children's horizons, for example to include airline pilots, nurses, doctors, firefighters, inventors, business people, and sports people. If children only ever see these job-holders stereotyped on the basis of gender, race, disability or age, it can be difficult for them to maintain their dream. To counter such stereotypes, early years settings should show a wide variety of examples of all sorts of people doing many different types of jobs and activities. Resources and ways to help you do this include:

- posters – ensure that these are up to date and include a range of different images
- books – there are many specialist bookshops that have a wide range of suitable materials available, but also check your local bookshops

- videos – ensure that these are up to date, and check that visual diversity is not spoiled by verbal or non-verbal stereotyping
- invited guests – through business networks, careers centres, personal contacts, etc.
- games
- events such as open days in appropriate places, for example the Houses of Parliament, community centres, independent living centres
- support or pressure groups, for example Disability Alliance, can be sources.

Care is needed to avoid showing examples in such a way that they appear unique or odd. Unusual examples need to be represented as acceptable and something that the children could aspire to, rather than token role models. Examples from public life or TV personalities are particularly useful.

Key issues

Not many years ago, advertisements for would-be nurses showed only women, and suggested that training to be a nurse was a good preparation for marriage. Such an advert would be illegal now, but still the vast majority of trainee nurses are female. Early years work has much the same image. Research the career advice material that is available for young people, looking at all types of jobs and those that have been previously associated with a particular gender or cultural group. What are the images that are being portrayed now, and how is the imbalance of recruits changing, if at all? How can we address such imbalances?

There are some situations where it is particularly important to make sure that children see role models that differ from their own experiences. Children who live in areas of social deprivation are at risk of not expanding their horizons outside their immediate experience. A child from an economically poor environment is less likely to encounter other images due to the cost of going to the cinema, on holiday, books, magazines, etc.

Case study

During his training to be a nursery nurse, Robert was sent to a school in a very poor area of the town where he lived. In the reception class of 32 children, only five children lived in a two-parent household. The majority lived with their single-parent mothers on a 'sink' local authority housing estate. After some initial reservations from some of the children, Robert was a huge success, with the staff and the children alike, as he presented a totally different model of a carer from those most of the children had seen.

What advantages did Robert have in this situation?

Recognising and supporting children with a low or negative self-image and identity

Many early years workers will have the experience of working with a child who lacks a sense of self-identity and self-esteem, and needs to be made to feel valued and supported. Involving other workers, parents and family members will be necessary to provide the warm, supporting network that can boost a child. A close look should be taken at the organisation and the family concerned, to try to avoid further problems.

Case study

Jack, aged five, had become more and more withdrawn in his last year at nursery school, rarely objecting to having his play interrupted by other children, giving his toys away to them, and looking unhappy. Discussions with his mother had been very brief, and she brushed away any suggestion that there was anything wrong.

Eventually, after an incident in the reception class he had just joined, involving Jack trying to stab his arm with some scissors, a joint meeting was called with Jack's health visitor, his parents, his key worker from nursery and the reception teacher. Jack's mother was initially very defensive, but eventually broke down in tears, explaining that her husband had left home twelve months ago to live with someone else who had a son of Jack's age. A new baby had arrived, and the initial contact Jack had had with his father had almost stopped. In addition, Jack's mother was working many hours a week to replace the lost income, and Jack was being left with a range of different people, depending on who would or could have him. At home Jack was the same as at school. In addition, he was disappearing to his bedroom as soon as he arrived home from school, and had started to wet the bed.

The involvement of a social worker helped Jack's mother to sort out her finances, and his father to start to see him again. Jack started staying at the after-school club at his old nursery school, which was attended by several children from his class, and his mother began to spend more time with him. After several months, Jack began to show signs of being his old self again.

What types of feelings could have led Jack to want to harm himself? Describe some ways in which his carers could help to change those feelings.

A child with a very poor self-image can be distressing to work with. Many children have short periods of time when they feel that no one likes them, because they have not been invited to someone's party, or they cannot have the new toy that everyone else has got, but a child with a permanently low self-image is usually easily spotted, especially among a group of children who have normal self-esteem. You will recognise such children by some of the following characteristics.

- They are too eager to please, never arguing or suggesting alternatives.
- They dislike themselves and may express this in various ways.
- They lack any pride in their personal appearance.
- They never demand anything for themselves.
- They deny that their own feelings count.
- They have no interest in what happens to them.
- They do not believe that anyone cares about them.
- They deny their racial origins, for example by trying to wash away evidence of skin colour.
- They attempt to harm themselves.

You may see other examples in your work with children. A child who consistently displays any of these features is in urgent need of help. As an early years worker, you should be showing at all times that you value all the children with whom you work. If you are a key worker for any children, you will have a greater role with those children to provide supportive experiences and activities to boost their self-image. A child with a serious problem needs prompt referral by you to your line manager – it is highly unlikely that you are the only person to notice that there is a problem.

Confidentiality in such cases is vital – investigating why a child has a low self-image may reveal severe family dysfunction, and this is highly confidential to the family concerned. Always make sure that you work within your setting's code of practice relating to confidentiality. The subsequent lines of referral are to a social worker and possibly a clinical psychologist.

- Social workers will work with the child's family and other agencies involved with the child to provide the appropriate support to improve the child's self-image.
- Clinical psychologists have a more in-depth brief to work on a one-to-one or possibly small family group basis, exploring the behaviour patterns that have led to the problem, and helping to discover strategies to improve the situation.

Part of the professional support that a child needs involves investigating the cause of the negative self-identity. Occasionally, the cause may be self-evident, but nonetheless difficult to deal with, for example a child may have a disability. More often, the cause will be complex and there may be evidence of some form of abuse, lack of bonding with a significant carer, etc.

Great care is needed in supporting a child in these circumstances. If the cause of the problem is a severe family dysfunction, possibly involving abuse, the child is at risk of his or her self-image being damaged further – the child may feel responsible for a family break-up, or for someone being arrested for abuse. There is rarely an easy answer to these situations. You may feel in need of support and reassurance from your line manager if you have been involved in this type of case. Never be afraid to ask for support, and always remember that by reporting problems to a senior colleague you acted in the best interests of the child concerned.

Element C5.6   Prepare children to move on to new settings

All children have to move from one setting to another at some stage, even if it is only entering formal education, and then moving through the system. Many children experience several moves during their early years. A great deal of support is needed to make these changes positive moves and minimise the potential disruption. This element links with Element C5.1 (Enable children to adjust to the setting), and is an important aspect of your role as an early years worker.

WHAT YOU NEED TO LEARN

- Liaison with new settings and other appropriate people
- Ways to ensure a smooth move using play and learning opportunities

Liaison with new settings and other appropriate people

Moving to a new environment can be an exciting or frightening prospect for a child. Children need consistency and continuity of care, and although John Bowlby's theories of early years care have been amended (see Key issues below), frequent changes of carers can nevertheless cause psychological distress to a child.

Key issues

In the late 1940s a psychologist, John Bowlby, warned that young children who do not experience a warm and continuing attachment to their mother for the first three years of life would suffer irreparable psychological harm. In fact, Bowlby's research was misinterpreted; his study had been with orphaned children after the Second World War, and the children had undergone other traumas. Michael Rutter, in *Maternal Deprivation*, reassessed and modified Bowlby's ideas, but still stressed the need for a warm and continuing attachment.

Research the issue of bonding and attachment and consider how it might affect your practice with young children and your views on their care in the first three years.

Children can be exposed to several changes of carer in the first years of life, and if the mother returns to work a few weeks after the baby's birth, her child may not have a long period of bonding and attachment with her. Frequent changes of settings may be due to:

- family moves resulting from job relocation
- dysfunctional families, resulting in a child entering the care of the local authority
- breakdown of care arrangements
- changing structure of the family due to divorce, remarriage.

Early years provision

A wide range of care options are open to parents in the UK. A child may experience daily care with someone other than parents from early as a few weeks old, and at various stages has to move within the education system. The chart below outlines the care/education provision available.

Age range	Care/education provision available	Features
0–2 years	**Home based** Family	Can also involve other types of provision, e.g. occasional crèche Informal, may be paid or voluntary, in a child's or carer's home
	Childminder	Regulated by Social Services, paid care, in the childminder's or carer's home. Childminders usually receive some training
	Nanny	Employed by the family, usually in the child's home. May be qualified, but no regulation of nannies
	Care outside the home Private day nursery	May have baby room for children under two. Should be a key worker system. Risk of staff changing. Range of groupings, ages, family groups, etc.
	Social Services day nursery/ family centre	Similar in aims to private sector, but tends to restrict places to children from families with defined needs
3–5 years	**As above plus** Pre-school groups Private nursery schools	Organised by the Pre-school Learning Alliance Private establishments with the emphasis on pre-school education
	State nursery classes	Provided by education and schools authorities. Provision is variable around the country; often only offer half-day sessions
5–8	**Start of formal full-time education** Primary school to age of 7 years, then junior school; or may be first school where middle school system operates After-school clubs	Parents have choice of schools from those available. State schools work to the National Curriculum requirements. Option of privately funded schools depending on parental wishes and income Can be locally funded or private provision – many attached to private time between school finishing and parents finishing work. Also caters for children in school holidays
	Childminders	Provide home-based care after school and in the holidays (see childminders for the under 2s)

There are other changes in care settings that children may experience in addition to the changes involved in their daily care. They may need:

- to go into hospital – this may be planned or an emergency admission
- to stay with relatives or friends if parents are ill or away from home
- to enter foster care in times of family disruption.

Apart from the move required when a child reaches the age of five years and has to attend school, parents may find it difficult to settle with one type of care for their child, and for a range of reasons may subject their children to many moves and changes of carers and care settings.

A child may be exposed to many unsettling changes, therefore. It is important that great care is taken in the handover of children to their new setting, whether it is at the request of the parents or because of the requirements of the education system.

Effects of a change in care setting

Moving from familiar surroundings, routines, friends and adults can produce feelings of grief in a child. Element C5.1 looked at the stages of distress. Children may feel a sense of loss, passing through phases of shock, denial, anger and crying, and often regressing as they adjust to their new surroundings. An early years worker should be expecting some reaction from a child who is moving to a different setting and from a child who has moved into his or her setting from elsewhere. You may see any of the signs of a child in distress (see page 97), and should be ready to help a child to work through his or her anxieties.

Case study

Lisa, aged four years, has just been for her first visit to the primary school where she is to start in September. You have been doing a lot of work with your group about going to school, including reading stories, watching videos and talking about the idea. Most of the children, including Lisa, are going to the same school. You have noticed that Lisa tends to withdraw into herself when the move is discussed. Lisa has been at your nursery for eighteen months. Before that she had been to two other nurseries in a nearby town, before moving to your area when her mother remarried. It took a long time to coax Lisa out of her shell, especially as her father and his new wife had a baby two months after Lisa started with you.

Why do you think Lisa is appearing worried about the move, despite all your efforts? Think about strategies to help her to adjust to the idea of starting school.

A child does not need to have experienced several changes in care settings for the idea of a move to be disconcerting. To a child who has attended the same nursery from, say, 18 months to the age of five years, the prospect of moving to a strange place can be daunting, despite the child's apparent stability. Prospective moves give rise to many worries including:

- whether it will be difficult to find their way around
- where the toilets will be
- what the school meals will be like
- whether the school will be expecting the child
- what the staff will be like
- concern about being the youngest in the class.

Factors affecting the impact of a move

It is impossible to predict how a child will react to a change of setting. Even well-adjusted and well-prepared children may take some time to settle. Several factors can improve the likelihood of a positive experience, including:

- advance planning of the change
- involvement of the child in preparations for the change, through visits, etc.
- full cooperation with parents and the current setting
- absence of family dysfunction
- no major emotional changes affecting the child, for example new sibling, moving house
- child moving along with friends from current setting
- moving along with friends from home environment
- previous happy move to a new setting
- welcoming staff at the new setting
- continuity of contact with staff from old setting
- a child who relates well to others.

Even if many positive factors are involved in the change, a child can still take some time to adjust to a new setting, or conversely a child who is facing negative factors may apparently settle very well.

The ability to relate well to others can have the biggest impact on the move. A shy, withdrawn child, who finds changes in routine and circumstances upsetting, will need a great deal of support from all concerned.

Case study

Jottica, aged three years, was moving house with her family to a large town some miles away. The youngest of four children, Jottica was a very quiet, reserved child, who had taken some time to settle into nursery eighteen months ago, despite the fact that her older sister was attending at the same time. She is still reluctant to join in with other children, preferring to work alongside her key worker or two or three other quiet children. Her parents, concerned about the effect the move of nursery will have on Jottica, have decided not to tell her in advance in case it upsets her.

Think about how you might help the family and Jottica to work through this situation. What do you think the result of following the parents' plan might be?

Ways to help a child make the transition to a new setting

Often the move to a new setting can be anticipated some time in advance. If this is the case, close collaboration can begin with parents, and the majority of nurseries and schools are happy to be involved in the transition. A range of tactics can be used to help the child in the weeks leading up to the move, including:

- visits to the new setting, accompanied by the key worker from the old setting, with increasing lengths of stay
- reading books and watching videos about moves to new settings
- encouraging conversation with the child about his or her feelings relating to the move, and taking the child's concerns seriously
- liaison between the settings to pass on information about the child, his or her levels of development, particular needs, fears, skills, etc. – this may be written or verbal

information, but whichever it is be sure that the information is accurate and based on fact not hearsay or gossip

- liaison to find out details of the new setting's routines, etc., and then possibly incorporating them into the present setting – for example, if at primary school, children are expected to sit still and work for 30 minutes, you should be planning activities for the child that require this level of concentration
- involving the child in preparations – buying uniform, equipment, etc.
- if possible visiting the child after he or she has moved on, to see him or her in the new setting.

Active knowledge ✔

Find out about the routine used in your workplace to help children move on to a new setting. Is there a recognised procedure, or does it simply depend on the staff involved? Are there different procedures depending on whether the move is planned or not?

Involvement of appropriate people

Helping a child to move on requires close liaison between a range of people. Everyone involved in a child's life in relation to his or her care setting can play a part, including:

- parents – to carry on the transition work at home, and to report on concerns they may have
- early years workers in the old setting – to pass on information about the child to the new setting, including details of favourite games, stories, etc.
- early years workers in the new setting – to inform the old setting about the new routines, etc. that the child will be expected to cope with
- any other professional involved with the child, such as speech therapist or physiotherapist – to ensure continuity of treatment if necessary
- any carers such as relatives or childminders – to support the child when he or she comes home.

Ways to ensure a smooth move using play and learning opportunities

Not all changes in care settings are planned, for example emergency admission to hospital. Hospitals, as an unknown entity, can be frightening places for children. As an early years worker, you should include familiarisation with hospitals in the social education of children to help to minimise some of the worries. The topic of hospitals, and the people who work there, provides a good activity base, with potential for stories, films, home corner play, role play, displays and possible visits, all with the aim of raising awareness among children of what goes on in a hospital. It is worth finding out if a play therapist from a local hospital will come and work with the children to familiarise them with his or her work.

Play can raise children's awareness of what happens in hospitals

A planned admission to hospital could in addition involve the use of dolls to show operation sites, visits to the ward, etc.

Using play to help children express fears

Most children will start to open up to their carers when they are actively involved in play. Encouraging the use of painting as an expression of their thoughts, or dough for bashing out their anger can help the early years worker understand children's feelings. You should always be alert to such opportunities, but when there is an impending move or hospital admission, be especially alert for signs that children want to express their fears.

Useful types of play include:

- role play
- home corner play
- doll play
- make-believe play.

As an effective early years worker, you must watch for signs that children are not adjusting well to the impending change, no matter how well you think they are prepared. Such signs include:

- aggressive behaviour; disrupting other children; demanding attention
- becoming very withdrawn
- regression in behaviour, for example return to wanting a bottle or comforter
- starting to wet or soil, during the day or at night
- loss of appetite
- difficulty in sleeping, frequent waking at night.

It is important to maintain regular contact with the parents at this time.

Evidence of any of the above signs needs serious thought about the possible causes. If the problems are related to the impending change, it may be worth considering whether other approaches are available, for example does the move have to happen immediately? If it is a change to a different room within nursery, then possibly not. If a move has to take place, such as moving house and therefore nursery, or a progression to school, then it is vital to provide further support for that child.

Keys to good practice
Helping to ensure a smooth move

- You need to be sensitive to the personality of the children you are supporting in making a change of setting.
- Liaison between settings is the key to helping children adjust to a new setting.
- Make sure that you are familiar with the possible settings that children in your care may move on to.
- Children's fears and concerns about a move should always be taken seriously.
- Use play and other activities to help prepare children for change.
- Always involve parents and other carers in your plans to support children in a move.
- Be sure that information passed on to settings is correct, properly recorded and supplied only to those who need to know.

Observation ✔

From this element and the information and ideas in Element C5.1, you should now be able to plan how to prepare a child to move on to a new setting. Choose a child or small group of children in your workplace who may shortly be moving to the next stage. Develop you plan to help them with the move, and write down. Discuss it with your assessor, and if appropriate put it in to action.

C5 Unit test

1   Give four examples of ways to help a young child in pre-entry visits to a new setting.

2   Why might a child find it difficult to settle into a new setting?

3   Outline the stages of distress in a young child.

4   What are four ways of sharing information with the parents of a child?

5   List three types of interaction between children.

6   When should you intervene in disagreements between children?

7   How does role play help children in their social development?

8   What social skills should a child have before he or she starts school?

9   List some examples of ways to help raise a child's self-esteem.

10 How do children express their feelings? List as many ways as you can think of.

Unit C7

Provide a framework for the management of behaviour

Helping children to learn to show behaviour that is accepted by society is an important role of early years workers. As children grow up, they will need to be able to control their feelings, think of others and behave in a way that is appropriate to the community in which they are living. Learning appropriate behaviour is a gradual learning process and adults working with children will need to guide children through it.

The elements for this unit are:

C7.1 Negotiate and set goals and boundaries for behaviour

C7.2 Promote positive aspects of behaviour

C7.3 Respond to unwanted behaviour

Element C7.1	Negotiate and set goals and boundaries for behaviour

WHAT YOU NEED TO LEARN

- What is appropriate behaviour?
- Why boundaries and goals are important
- The link between stages of development and setting goals
- The importance of behavioural policies
- Involving parents and other carers
- Realistic boundaries and achievable goals within the setting

What is appropriate behaviour?

Encouraging children to show appropriate behaviour is an important part of an early years worker's role. Children who are unable to show behaviour that is appropriate will find that they are not accepted by others in their society. Unfortunately, there are no universal rules about what is and is not acceptable behaviour as attitudes towards these vary from person to person and also from culture to culture. An obvious example of how acceptable behaviour can change from society to society involves food – the way people eat and expectations of table manners are very different across countries and cultures!

Although expectations of appropriate behaviour can vary, most people agree that appropriate behaviour to encourage in children includes: sharing, taking turns, helping others, respecting others and taking responsibility for own actions.

Why boundaries and goals are important

There are many ways of encouraging children to show appropriate behaviour. Some strategies are discussed on pages 121–126. One way in which we can help children show appropriate behaviour is to be clear in our own minds about the type of behaviour we expect from them and also the limits that must be placed on their behaviour. This is often referred to as **boundary and goal setting**.

Understanding the difference between boundaries and goals

The terms boundaries and goals are often referred to in connection with managing behaviour.

A boundary is a limit on behaviour, for example you must not throw sand.
A goal is an expectation of behaviour, for example that children should share and take turns.

Setting boundaries is important for children – it helps them understand what is and is not acceptable behaviour in the setting. Boundaries also keep children safe as most are set in order to prevent accidents in settings, for example not allowing children to hit each other or to put fingers into the hamster's cage! It is important that children understand what the rules of each setting are, as the boundaries on behaviour at home or in different settings will be different. The differences between settings are partly the result of different safety risks and partly because of the different aims of settings. For example, a child in a home setting may go to the toilet without asking, whereas in a large setting this would mean that no one would know where the child was in the event of fire.

Goals have to reflect children's stages of development and understanding. For example, a goal for a three-year-old might be to share toys with others, whereas this would be a difficult goal for a two-year-old.

The link between stages of development and setting goals

It is essential that adults working with children have realistic goals. Learning appropriate behaviour is a gradual process and depends on other areas of a child's development. For example, a child whose language development is impaired will find it hard to express his or her needs and frustrations. This may mean that the child is more aggressive than other children of the same age. Some skills, such as being able to share, are linked to a child's social and cognitive development, and this means that children under three years find it difficult to play alongside other children. The chart below looks at the stages of development and possible goals for behaviour. It is important that this chart is used only as a guide as there are many factors that may influence the development of children's behaviour.

Age	Stages of development	Goals for behaviour	Role of adult
1–2 years	Actively explores environment Imitates adults in simple tasks Repeats actions that gain attention Alternates between clinging and independence Has understanding that toys or other objects may belong to others	To play alongside other children (parallel play) To carry out simple instructions such as 'Can you find your coat?'	**Good supervision**, as children of this age do not understand the dangers around them. **Distraction**, to stop unwanted behaviour as children often forget what they were doing, for example, if a child wants another child's toy, offer him or her another instead. **Praise**, so that children understand how to get an adult's attention in positive ways and to help develop good self-esteem. **Calm and patience**, as children of this age are often persistent at trying to do something, for example a child may keep going back to something that is potentially dangerous. **A good role model**, as children are learning behaviour through imitating those around them.
2–3 years	Wants to be independent but does not always have the skills Becomes frustrated easily and has tantrums Is jealous of attention shown to other children Has no understanding for the need to wait Finds sharing difficult Is active and restless	To wait for needs to be met, for example at meal times To share toy or food with one other child with adult help To play alongside other children To sit and share a story for five minutes To say 'please' and 'thank you' if reminded To follow simple instructions with help, such as 'Wash your hands'.	**Good supervision and anticipation** – the keys to working with this age range. Children are trying to be independent, but lack some of the physical and cognitive skills that they need. This makes them frustrated and angry. Adults need to anticipate possible sources of frustration and support children, either by offering help or by distracting them. For example, a child who is trying to put on a coat may need an adult to make a game of it so that the child does not become frustrated. Where possible, adults should try to provide as many opportunities as possible for children to be independent. **Calm and patience**, as children who are frustrated can trigger off negative feelings in adults. This has the potential to inflame a situation. It is a good idea to allow plenty of time for children to complete day-to-day tasks. Children of this age often forget and need reminding about boundaries and goals. **Praise and encouragement**, to enable children to learn what behaviour adults are expecting from them. Some unwanted behaviour that is not dangerous should be ignored so that children do not repeat it hoping for adult attention. Adults should also provide plenty of love and attention if children have had a tantrum as some children can be frightened by the force of their own emotions.

Age	Stages of development	Goals for behaviour	Role of adult
			Consistency, as children are trying to work out the limits on their behaviour. **A good role model**, as children model their behaviour on others around them. This is especially important at this age as they act out their experiences through play.
3–4 years	Follows simple rules by imitating other children, for example collects aprons before painting Is able to communicate wishes Enjoys activities such as painting Enjoys being with other children Can play cooperatively Enjoys helping adults	To follow rules in games when helped by adult, for example playing lotto To say 'please' and 'thank you' often without reminder To take turns and share equipment To follow instructions of adults most of the time, for example 'Let Simon have a turn' To help tidy away	**Praise and encouragement**, builds children's confidence and makes them more likely to show desirable behaviour. **Explanation**, should be given for rules as children are more likely to remember and understand them. **Patience**, as children will still need reminders about the boundaries and goals for behaviour. **Good supervision**, as although children are able to do many things for themselves, they are still unaware of the dangers around them. Most of the time children will be able to play well together, but squabbles will still break out. **A good role model**, to help children learn the social skills they will need to resolve arguments and express their feelings.
4–5 years	Plays with other children without help from adults Is able to communicate feelings and wishes Understands the needs for rules Can wait for needs to be met	To consider other people's feelings To comfort playmates in distress To say 'please' and 'thank you' without a reminder To ask playmates for permission to use their toys To tidy up after activities	**Providing activities and tasks** that are stimulating and allow children to develop confidence. Children of this age are keen to help adults and enjoy being busy. Tasks such as setting the table or getting objects allow children to feel independent. **Praise and encouragement**, so that children feel good about themselves. This is important because children are often starting school at this time. Children need to feel that they are able to be 'good'. **Explanation**, to help children to remember and understand the need for rules or decisions. **A good role model**, to help children to learn social skills as they are copying what they see.
5–8 years	Is developing strong friendships Will argue back and question decisions Copies behaviour of older children, for example may swear or spit	To apologise to others To listen to others To follow instructions From 6 years onwards: To work independently and quietly in school settings	**Praise**, as children become more aware of others and compare themselves critically, **and encouragement**, means that children do not look for other ways of gaining attention. **Explanation**, so that children can understand the reasons for rules and

Age	Stages of development	Goals for behaviour	Role of adult
	Understands the needs for rules and plays games that have rules Understands the difference between right and wrong Has many self-help skills such as getting dressed, wiping up spills	To be helpful and thoughtful To take responsibility for actions	decisions. Children should also be made to consider the effect of their actions on others. **Set and enforce clear boundaries**, to counter children's tendency to argue back as they become older. **Being a good role model**, still important as children are trying to understand more about the adults they are with. Speech and actions are modelled increasingly on adults whom children admire. **Encourage children to take responsibility for their actions**. Adults can do this by asking children what the boundaries or limits on their behaviour should be. **Provide activities and responsibilities**, to help children to 'mature' as they learn more about their capabilities. Small responsibilities help children to become independent as well as giving them confidence – for example, they may be asked to tidy areas of a setting or pour out drinks for other children

The importance of having realistic expectations

Expectations that are too high may cause children to feel that they are always in trouble. This can potentially cause problems because there seems to be a strong link between self-esteem and behaviour. A child who comes to believe that he or she is 'naughty' will give up trying to be good, feeling that he or she is not able to achieve good behaviour. On the other hand where expectations are too low, children's social development will be hindered. For example, a child who has not been encouraged to share and take turns will find it difficult to make friends.

Making boundaries and goals effective

Most people accept the need for children to have boundaries and goals to help them show appropriate behaviour. The spider diagram on the next page shows the factors that will make a framework for behaviour effective.

The importance of behavioural policies

In order to make boundaries and goals effective, everyone who works in the setting must understand and agree to apply them consistently. This means that children understand that the boundaries are set and do not change day by day. This helps children to feel secure, and most children, once they understand what is and is not acceptable behaviour, tend to conform.

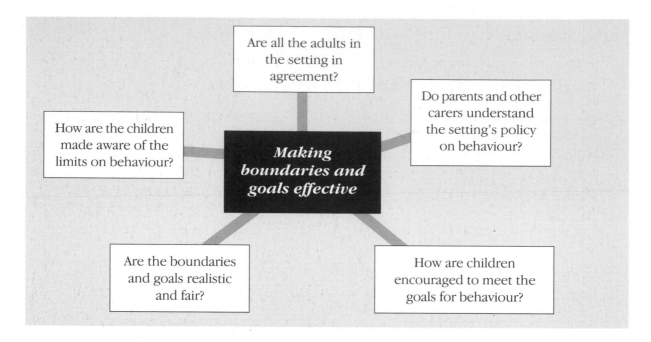

Most settings have developed a policy on behaviour which fits their setting's aims and needs. A good policy will help new staff understand how to manage children's behaviour and what to do if a child shows unwanted behaviour.

Involving parents and other carers

Parents and other people who care for children need also to understand the aims of the setting. Some settings make this part of the admissions procedure to ensure that parents are aware and broadly in agreement. When parents and settings work together in this way, children find it easier to adapt from one environment to another. Discussing behavioural goals and strategies to encourage parents can be particularly helpful where children are showing unwanted behaviour either in the home or in the setting. The case study on the next page is a good illustration of how a child can be helped by early years workers and parents working together.

MAPLEHURST NURSERY
BEHAVIOUR POLICY

Maplehurst Nursery's policy is based on the National Children's Homes principles. As a staff body we are trying to create an environment where children, parents and staff all value, respect and care for each other. We believe the principles listed below will help build a happy and relaxed atmosphere.

1. Always reject the behaviour, not the child. Never label children as bad or naughty either to them or to someone else in their hearing – they will live up to it!
2. Give direction and correction to children in a positive way, e.g. – 'keep the sand in the sand tray' not 'don't drop the sand on the floor.'
3. Give praise as often as possible – notice behaviour you like and remark on it.
4. Set limits. Children need to be secure in knowing you will not let either their behaviour or their feelings get out of control. You will neither let them hurt nor be hurt.

MAPLEHURST NURSERY
BEHAVIOUR POLICY CONTD.

5. Be consistent. The same reaction to the same situation each time gives children a feeling of security. You give them the power to predict the future and an ability to avoid unhappy situations.
6. Do what you have said.
   Do not threaten what you can't do.
   Build up trust.
7. When talking to children about their behaviour be close, calm and at their level.
8. Never force children to say 'sorry'. You may just be teaching them to lie.
9. Make children sensitive to their own feelings and other people's. Feed back how they are feeling, e.g. 'You look angry to me'. Give them different options of how to express or deal with feelings. Get them to be aware that other people have feelings. Point out physical signs – tears, smiles – and ask them to remember how they felt when they did the same.
10. Sometimes there isn't time for reasoning. Children need to recognise an adult's authority and respond to 'No'.

An example of a behaviour policy

Case study

Mark, aged four, is showing unwanted behaviour both at home and in the nursery. His parents and the staff feel that this is probably in response to the birth of his brother. He has had several violent tantrums and has started to throw objects and toys as well. His parents and the key worker have met to talk about ways in which they can help Mark as they realise that a consistent approach might be helpful. Mark's parents have found that they are often giving into his demands rather than risking a tantrum, but this is not helping as Mark is becoming increasingly difficult to manage. The key worker explains how the nursery normally handles tantrums that might be potentially harmful to other children. Together they agree on a strategy whereby Mark is to be praised and have plenty of adult attention, while trying a tactic of giving no eye contact and attention when he is having a tantrum, but praising him once he is behaving more appropriately. They have also decided to keep in close contact about Mark's behaviour and have agreed to meet again in a few day's time.

1   *Why will this joint approach be helpful for Mark?*

2   *Why is it important for the parents and the setting to remain in contact?*

3   *Why is it important for the parents and the setting also to consider ways of encouraging appropriate behaviour?*

Parents who do not share the same aims as the setting

There may be times when parents do not agree with the boundaries and goals of the setting. When this happens, parents may feel upset and angry, believing that their children are being unreasonably treated or are being 'allowed to get away with' something. These situations require sensitive handling as parents will have their own strategies for managing behaviour.

It is always a good idea to listen carefully and find out what the difficulty is – sometimes, you may need to find out more about what has happened before being able to comment on it. In some cases, parents may not understand why a setting has chosen to act in a certain way, but are happy once they have had an explanation. For example, they may feel that their child should have been physically punished, but may not realise that this illegal in settings. Sometimes parents may bring information which shows that a setting needs to adjust its approach towards a child. For example, a child who wet the bed after being told in the afternoon to stop throwing sand and was obviously worried by this and may need to be handled more carefully in the future.

Realistic boundaries and achievable goals within the setting

We have already looked at the link between stages of development and goals for behaviour. In order to make the boundaries of the setting effective, the goals and boundaries must be appropriate for the setting and the activities provided. For example, children will find it very difficult to be quiet when they are playing outdoors and to expect that children will be able to keep their voices down may be unrealistic, although it will be realistic to expect children to come in when they are called!

Active knowledge ✓

Make a list of the main boundaries in your work setting.
How are these explained to the children?
How are children encouraged to keep to the rules?

Helping children to understand the boundaries and goals

Imagine driving a car and not knowing the rules of the road. Working them out would not necessarily be easy and while doing so, you are likely to get into trouble! If boundaries and goals are to be effective, children need to know and understand them.

There are many ways of helping children to understand the rules, limits and expectations of settings, but where possible, it is good practice to explain to children the reason for the boundaries and expectations, for example 'We must not put our fingers in here, because the gerbil might try and bite'. Giving children explanations can help them to remember the expectations and boundaries, and at the same time is a positive approach.

Anticipating

Where possible, early years workers should be able to anticipate potential difficulties and prevent them by telling children in a positive way what is expected of them, for example 'When we go past the baby room, we must be very quiet' or 'Once you have finished the puzzle and *put it away*, you can choose another one if you want'.

Reminding

Very young children find it hard to remember the boundaries and expectations and need to be reminded. Activities that are very exciting and intense can make older children forget the boundaries and so it is important gently to remind them of the boundaries. This can be done in several ways, for example at the start of an activity, 'Who can remember why we must wait before climbing up the slide?' or during an activity 'You won't forget that you are not allowed to go in there, will you?'.

Recording

Older children can be helped to remember the boundaries by having signs put in their environment, for example 'Five children in the home corner'. In some settings, children are asked to write down their own rules and responsibilities.

As an early years worker, you can also encourage children to work out what the boundaries or the expectations are for themselves, for example 'It's very muddy outside. Do you think that there are any areas where you should not play today?'. This is empowering for children as then they do not feel as if the adults around them are always negative. It also helps children to take responsibility and develop independence.

It is not unusual for children who are new to a setting to learn the boundaries and expectations of behaviour by observing and following the lead of children who are already there – a setting which encourages children to get an apron before starting to play in the water, may find that the younger children simply learn to do this by copying the behaviour of older children.

Element C7.2 Promote positive aspects of behaviour

Children need to be encouraged and guided to show wanted behaviour. There are many practical ways in which adults working with children can do this.

WHAT YOU NEED TO LEARN

- The principles of promoting appropriate behaviour
- The role of the early years worker in promoting appropriate behaviour
- The importance of consistency in boundary setting
- Developing children's self-esteem and independence through positive behaviour

The principles of promoting appropriate behaviour

It is useful for early years workers and other adults to understand the psychology behind behaviour management strategies. This means that we are able to use the strategies more effectively. There are several theories about how children learn behaviour, and it is interesting to understand how these can be applied in practice.

Social learning theory

Social learning theory suggests that children learn appropriate as well as unwanted behaviour from imitating others, especially those that are significant in their lives. The idea that children copy others and learn from their actions is quite widely accepted. It means that early years workers and adults working with children will have a lot of influence over the behaviour of children. This is the concept of children having role models.

Research carried out on this theory has also shown that children's behaviour can be influenced by what they have seen on film. This has implications as it would suggest that 'heroic' violence on television or in computer games may be imitated by children.

Using the social learning theory with children

The social learning theory would suggest that anyone working with children will need to be a good role model, i.e. being polite, showing consideration for others, waiting with patience. This theory would also suggest that adults need to keep an eye on the content of television and computer programmes likely to be viewed by children.

Behaviourist theory

Behaviourist theory, first put forward by Burrhus F. Skinner (1904–94), states that we repeat certain types of behaviour if we are rewarded in some way for showing them. For example, a child who says 'Thank you' and is praised for doing so will be more likely to show this behaviour again. Rewards are referred to as **positive reinforcements**. On the other hand, if we show a type of behaviour and either have no reward or are punished in some way, we may not repeat the behaviour. Punishments are referred to as **negative reinforcements**. From the work that psychologists have carried out, it seems that most of us are more influenced by positive reinforcements than by negative reinforcements.

What are positive reinforcers?

Positive reinforcers are anything that acts as a reward, for example you might enjoy the feeling of touching velvet – the sensory touch is a positive reinforcer. This explains why children might continue with behaviour even if they have not had any praise or why children might be tempted to take spoonfuls of sugar even when they know that they should not. The taste of sugar acts as a positive reinforcer!

Common positive reinforcements used by adults with young children are praise, stickers, extra attention, cuddles and maybe food.

Why timing of positive reinforcers is critical

The timing of positive reinforcers is extremely important – where a reward happens quickly after the behaviour, there is a chance of the behaviour being repeated. This is why most people find chocolate and sweets so tempting – we gain the positive reinforcement, i.e. pleasure, almost immediately after putting the food into our mouths. With children, this means that if they receive praise or other positive reinforcements straight away, they are more likely to repeat the behaviour.

Intermittent reinforcement can be particularly effective

We have seen that rewarding children soon after they have shown wanted behaviour is an effective way of encouraging them to repeat the desired behaviour. We might wonder what happens then if children are rewarded only occasionally. The answer is that when positive reinforcement is not automatic but occasional, the behaviour is more likely to persist. It is almost as if we come to an understanding that sometimes we get a reward but at other times we do not, although it is always worth trying just in case a reward follows. This means that children do not need to be praised or positively reinforced for every single action in order that they continue doing it, but that sometimes they will need a positive reinforcement.

Unfortunately, there is a downside to this because children who are **intermittently reinforced** can show persistent and unwanted behaviour. The following example demonstrates this.

Monday:	Jane screams for an ice-cream and is given one.
Tuesday:	Jane screams for an ice-cream, but is not given one.
Wednesday:	Jane screams for an ice-cream, but is not given one.
Thursday:	Jane screams for an ice-cream, but is not given one.
Friday:	Jane screams for an ice-cream and is eventually handed one.

Jane has learnt that it is worth screaming – you might sometimes get what you want. Her unwanted behaviour is harder to break because she has been intermittently reinforced.

Using behaviourist theory with children

This theory means that we must make sure that children have positive reinforcement when they show desired behaviour, for example praise when they are sharing equipment. It also means that we should praise or give some positive reinforcement immediately after children show the behaviour, so that they associate a reward with their behaviour. It is also suggested that we should make sure children understand why they are being rewarded, for example 'Here is a special sticker because I saw how kind you were being to James'.

Behaviourist theory also forms the basis of some specific behavioural modifications programmes.

Why some children repeatedly show unwanted behaviour

The behaviourist theory can also be used to explain why children show unwanted behaviour. In many cases, where children are showing unwanted behaviour they are getting some type of adult attention, even though quite often it will be disapproving. For some children the adult attention that they are getting acts as a positive reinforcer, even though the adult had not intended it to. The example below illustrates this.

> Mary is throwing sand. The supervisor tells her not to throw sand and then moves away to talk to another group of children. Mary continues to play for a minute or so. Mary looks across at the supervisor and throws the sand again. The supervisor leaves the group of children to reprimand her.

In this example, Mary has learnt that by throwing sand she can attract an adult's attention. She has been positively reinforced for throwing sand. The supervisor will not have intended this to happen. This means that sometimes we need to be careful that children do not learn to behave inappropriately so that they can gain our attention. The example below shows how the supervisor might have handled this situation in a different way.

> Mary is throwing sand. The supervisor tells her not to throw sand and then moves away to talk to another group of children. Mary continues to play for a minute or so. The supervisor smiles at Mary and tells her how pleased she is that she is now playing so well.

Self-fulfilling prophecy

This is an interesting theory which suggests that the expectations and attitudes that adults have about children will influence their behaviour. For example, where an adult believes that a child is 'difficult', the child is more likely to behave in this way; whereas an adult who is positive about a child will probably find that the child shows appropriate behaviour. It seems that children can sense the level of behaviour expected from them and will therefore meet these expectations.

Using self-fulfilling prophecy with children

This theory means that we must inwardly feel very positive about the children we are working with. We must show children that we have positive expectations about their behaviour, not negative ones. For example, 'I hope that you won't be silly again this afternoon' is a negative comment because it suggests that we are half expecting the child to show unwanted behaviour.

The self-fulfiling prophecy would also suggest that we must pass on information about children carefully to others, so that they do not have negative expectations of children before they work with them. For example, 'He's a bit of a handful' or 'You need to keep an eye on him' are remarks that can label a child and mean that adults are not positive in their approach.

The role of the early years worker in promoting appropriate behaviour

As an early years worker, you can influence and help children to show wanted behaviour in many ways. The spider diagram below shows some of the main ways.

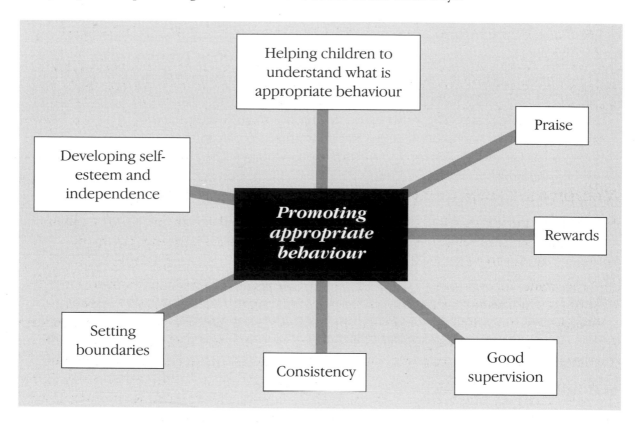

Praise and rewards

Praising and rewarding children links to the behaviourist theory of reinforcing behaviour that we want to be repeated, and although eventually children are expected to develop self-discipline young children need to be praised and rewarded for showing wanted behaviour. Self-discipline is gained gradually and is often linked to confidence and high self-esteem, but firstly children will need to learn the behaviour that is considered acceptable.

Getting the balance between rewards and praise

As an early years worker, you should mostly use praise with children, although when working with children with special needs small rewards might be frequently used to reinforce behaviour.

Rewards do not necessarily need to be large ones – just signals that you are particularly pleased with a child's behaviour, for example being able to choose the story at story time. It is important that getting a reward does not become so important to a child that it is a disappointment when he or she is given only praise. It is also important to avoid rewards in a setting becoming too prominent, to prevent children becoming jealous.

Keys to good practice
Using praise and rewards

- Make sure that children understand why they are being praised and rewarded so that they can repeat the behaviour, for example 'Well done, you tried really hard' or 'You can have an extra turn because you waited patiently'.
- Do not be reticent with praise – frequent praise simply helps children to keep on showing wanted behaviour.
- Aim to give praise alongside a task or as close to the wanted behaviour as possible. For example, 'You are playing together nicely, well done' will probably encourage children to carry on cooperating.
- Choose rewards carefully so that children do not simply show behaviour to gain a large reward. For example, it would be inappropriate to give a child a whole chocolate bar because he or she said 'Thank you'.

The importance of consistency in boundary setting

It is important that children feel very confident about what adults are expecting of them. Clear guidelines are essential, as we have seen on page 117. Children respond well to a consistent approach which means that they know what they can and cannot do.

It is important that early years workers in settings are in agreement about their expectations of children's behaviour so that children do not have to adjust the level of their behaviour depending on who is working with them. In home settings, it is important that the early years worker is in agreement with parents on the boundaries of behaviour and the system of encouraging appropriate behaviour. This prevents situations where children are confused because the rules of behaviour seem to keep changing, for example they are allowed to leave the table once they have finished their meal when they are with the early years worker, but are told that they must wait until everyone has finished by their parents.

Supervising children

Most accidents and serious incidents of unwanted behaviour happen when children are unsupervised or are bored. Wanted behaviour can be encouraged simply through providing interesting activities and by supervising children carefully and being responsive to signs that they are becoming bored or angry. This means that if an adult sees that children are losing interest in an activity, he or she should act quickly to provide another activity or give children additional equipment to make the current activity more interesting.

Signs that adult intervention is required
- Raised voices
- Children beginning to use equipment inappropriately, for example throwing a musical instrument

- Children looking around rather than concentrating on an activity
- Squeals of laughter
- Silence
- Offensive comments

The above signs often show that children are starting to become bored or that they have found something inappropriate to do. By acting immediately, the early years worker may be able to prevent children from learning unwanted behaviour. It should also be explained to children why the adult is intervening. If they understand what is and is not appropriate behaviour, they are more likely to remember in future and feel positive towards the intervention.

Developing children's self-esteem and independence through positive behaviour

As an early years worker, you can help children show appropriate behaviour by making sure that children believe in themselves. Children who feel confident and have high self-esteem are more likely to show appropriate behaviour. A child who feels that he or she is 'only good at being bad' will give up trying to show wanted behaviour. Self-esteem can be raised in children by giving them plenty of praise and also by making sure that they feel that those around them believe in them. In practical terms, this means making sure that tasks and activities are not so demanding that children will fail, while still encouraging children to be as independent as they can.

Children's self-esteem may also be enhanced by making sure that their parents are told of their achievements, for example 'Harvey was so good today, he helped Sarah to find her cuddly rabbit'. On the other hand, if you need to share information with parents that is not positive, you must make sure that children are not around as this may lower their self-esteem.

Consolidation

Why is it important to be a good role model for children?

What types of rewards are used in your setting?

Why is it important not to label children?

Element C7.3   Respond to unwanted behaviour

There are times when children will show unwanted behaviour. As an early years worker, it is important that you have an understanding of why children may show inappropriate behaviour as well as some strategies so that you can intervene in the most sensitive way.

- Factors affecting children's behaviour
- Managing unwanted behaviour
- Managing specific types of behaviour
- Referring concerns about persistent unwanted behaviour

Factors affecting children's behaviour

It is necessary to understand the reasons behind children's unwanted behaviour as these might affect the strategies used to manage it.

There are many factors that might alter the way in which children might behave. Some factors are short term, such as tiredness or hunger, while others are long-term factors that may shape behaviour over a longer period. The common belief that 'children are adaptable' is not altogether true as children react quite significantly to changes in their lives.

Short-term factors

There are many short-term factors that might cause children to show unwanted behaviour such as being aggressive, boisterous and demanding, clingy or attention-seeking. The spider diagram below shows some of the short-term factors that might cause children to alter their normal pattern of behaviour.

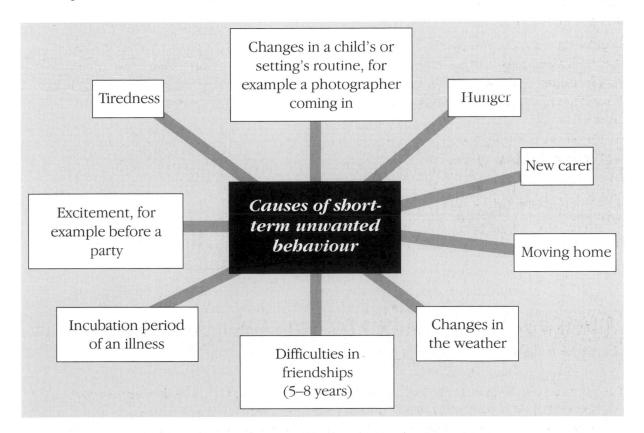

These types of short-term factors will not influence children's behaviour over a long period, but many children will react to feeling unsettled by showing unwanted behaviour. Hunger and tiredness are particularly influential factors and it is a good idea to consider whether a child who is clingy or demanding is actually needing to sleep or eat. Early years workers also notice that the weather can affect children's behaviour, and this means that if children seem boisterous and have not been able to go outside you might consider providing an activity that will encourage some vigorous physical activity.

Where children are reacting to a change in their routine, you will still need to be consistent in setting boundaries. Children who are feeling unsettled need to see that some aspects of their lives have consistency. You can, however, support them during this period by giving them plenty of attention and praise for good behaviour.

Long-term factors

Some children show behaviour that is directly influenced by major events in their lives. This means that you may need to talk and share information with their parents so that you can understand and provide for their needs. The diagram below shows some of the circumstances that may cause children to show unwanted behaviour.

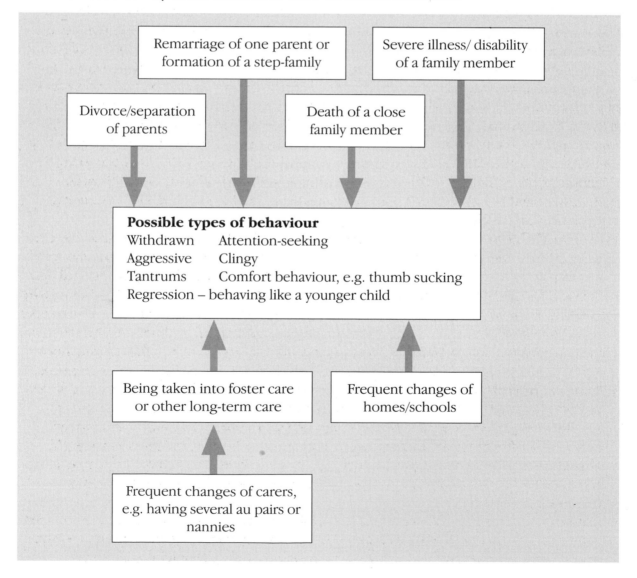

Behaviour patterns

A change in a child's behaviour pattern may indicate an underlying problem or difficulty. This means that early years workers need to be attentive to such changes. In a few cases, a sudden change in behaviour may be a sign that a child is being abused (see Unit C15).

Managing unwanted behaviour

As an early years worker, you should be aiming to use positive preventative strategies to avoid unwanted behaviour rather then have to deal with it. This means anticipating potential sources of conflict or danger and making sure that children are well supervised and have interesting activities. However, there will be times when unwanted behaviour occurs and needs to be managed.

It is important that unwanted behaviour is dealt with sensitively. Intervention needs to be prompt, calm and controlled. There are several ways in which you can intervene, depending on the situation.

- **Through eye contact/facial expression.** Sometimes a simple look will warn children that they are stepping over the boundary and this will be enough to help them remember that their behaviour is not appropriate. Eye contact may need to be held with a child along with an expression of disapproval. Once the child starts to show appropriate behaviour, you should make sure that immediate praise is given. This strategy is particularly useful if you are working in group situations and you do not want to disrupt the activity.
- **Say a determined 'No!'.** Most children respond to this expression and understand its meaning. For this to work, it is important that you use it sparingly. It is also important that children understand that 'no means no', and you do not allow children to continue with inappropriate behaviour. This strategy is particularly effective if combined with facial expression and is useful in situations where children need to be prevented from doing something potentially dangerous.
- **Explain the consequences of children's actions.** It is good practice to make children aware of the consequences of their actions. They may not realise that throwing sand may lead to pain for a child getting sand in the eye. It is also worth explaining to older children what will happen if they continue to show unwanted behaviour – this sets clear boundaries for them. For example, 'If you carry on kicking the ball towards the road, I will have to take it away in case it goes against a car'. Once you have suggested that there will be a sanction, it is essential that you are prepared to carry out the sanction. Do not threaten sanctions that you cannot justify or carry out, otherwise children will not believe you another time.
- **Removal of equipment.** Taking away equipment should be a final measure, but may be necessary if children have either been threatened with this sanction or they are putting themselves or others in danger, for example tying a rope around a child's neck to play horses. This type of activity may be so exciting that even if you warn children about the dangers, they will still be tempted to carry on. If you remove equipment, it is a good idea to give children something else to do so that they do not go from one inappropriate situation into another!
- **Time out.** The idea of time out is not to punish children, but simply to allow them to calm down and step back from the problem. Older children particularly benefit from time out, especially if a sympathetic adult can talk about why they are needing to calm down.

Children should not be made to feel that they are being rejected, but rather that you are helping them to avoid conflict or temptation. Used properly, time out should be a supportive strategy for children.

Managing specific types of behaviour

There are some specific types of behaviour that need careful handling. There may be times when a child regularly showing this type of behaviour may need specific help and the worker passes on his or her concerns to the child's parents and/or the supervisor

Attention-seeking behaviour

Attention-seeking can be a sign of insecurity or, in some cases, that children have become used to having a lot of adult attention. Most children show this type of behaviour at times. It may include answering back, making noises and challenging instructions. Tantrums can also be used by older children as a way of attention-seeking.

Keys to good practice
Managing behaviour

- It is often best to ignore attention-seeking behaviour unless it is dangerous – by challenging it, you may be teaching the children that they can get attention in this way.
- Praise children when they show appropriate behaviour – to teach them that positive behaviour is the best way to gain attention.

Destructive behaviour

This can be a sign of frustration or unhappiness, but it is important that children are not allowed to become out of control, as this is very frightening for them and teaches them that there are no real limits on behaviour. Destructive behaviour might include throwing furniture or toys and hitting out at others.

Keys to good practice
Dealing with aggression

- Stay calm when dealing with children who are aggressive. It is important that they can see that you are in control of the situation.
- Talk quietly but firmly to them. It is often best to take them to a quiet place where they can calm down. (If you are in a large setting, you may need to ask another member of staff for help.)

Attention-seeking behaviour can be a sign of insecurity

- Once children have calmed down, it is important to find out what has upset them and also to make sure that they understand that their behaviour is unacceptable.

Name calling, swearing and other offensive remarks

Children who call names and make offensive remarks are often repeating comments that they have heard. Remarks such as 'fatty' or 'stupid' need to be challenged, but in such a way that children are not blamed for what they have said.

Keys to good practice
Dealing with offensive remarks

- Ask children where they have heard that remark.
- Explain that it is hurtful and why.
- Tell children that these comments are not to be made in the setting.

Ensuring that children's confidence is not undermined

It is important that while intervening in children's unwanted behaviour, you do not create any future problems by damaging children's confidence in themselves, for example letting a child feel 'I am always in trouble, because I'm naughty'.

It is good practice to explain to children why you have intervened and make sure that they understand you are unhappy about the behaviour, not the child. You should also make children feel that you believe in their ability to show appropriate behaviour. You should not remind children about their previous misdemeanours, for example saying 'You were naughty last week, I hope you have learnt to behave' – this will only make the child feel miserable and less likely to be positive about his or her behaviour.

> ## Consolidation
>
> 'You were naughty to push Simon over like that. I will be looking this afternoon to see that you don't do that again'.
>
> 'Pushing Simon over was a silly thing to do. He might have hurt his head. This afternoon, you can show me how well you can really play together.'
>
> Which approach is more likely to make the child feel that he or she can show appropriate behaviour? Why will it be important to praise the child as soon as he or she is playing appropriately?

Physical punishment and restraint

At one time it was considered acceptable to use physical punishment as a way of controlling and disciplining children. This is no longer the case and children's rights are protected under the 1989 Children Act. The message is very clear to those who care for children – physical punishment is not an option, it is an offence!

Physical restraint of children

There are very few occasions when it is acceptable to use physical restraint on children. The prime reasons would be if:

- children are in danger of harming themselves
- children are in danger of harming others.

If restraint is needed, it must be kept to the minimum and must not be used as a way of disciplining or controlling children. Physical restraints such as reins and harnesses should only be used to keep young children safe, e.g. when crossing roads, and in no circumstances should children be punished by being harnessed.

Key issues

In some countries such as Sweden, it is an offence for parents to smack children. In the UK parents can use 'reasonable chastisement'. Smacking is generally considered not to be an effective method of disciplining children as children who have been smacked are more likely to show aggression towards others.

Find out more about the campaign to end all physical punishment, including parental smacking.

Referring concerns about persistent unwanted behaviour

Recording and reporting changes in children's behaviour patterns

A change in the way a child behaves or concerns about the behaviour being inconsistent with the child's development should be reported to your supervisor and passed on to the parents. This may mean either simply mentioning that a child has been unusually tearful or, more formally, keeping a record if the behaviour seems to be more serious or persistent. Records should show the date and time of the incident, what happened and the action taken – an example is shown below. Any written records are confidential and should be stored safely.

Date	Time	Place	Incident	Action taken
12.3.99	10.25 am	Sandpit	Jose bit Alice's arm and snatched the sieve.	Note made in accident book of injury to Alice. Jose was taken away from the sandpit and was asked why he bit Alice. Jose seemed upset and needed some reassurance. He said that Alice had taken the sieve away from him.

Building up a picture of children's behaviour

Where children seem to be persistently showing unwanted behaviour, it is useful to carry out some observations to find out if there is any pattern or trigger to their behaviour. Diaries can be kept that show both negative and positive behaviour. These can be useful as they may give an overall picture of a child's behaviour without focusing on only the negative incidents.

Event samples are also used as a way of recording incidents of behaviour and can sometimes show that children's unwanted behaviour is less frequent than our perception of it (see pages 244–250) for details about how to carry out observations and event samples).

Seeking specialist advice

There may be times when children's behaviour is a reaction to stress or a traumatic event in their lives. In other cases, children may be showing difficult behaviour because they have an underlying medical condition such as eczema or a food allergy. In such cases, seeking specialist advice will be important. In most cases, parents will be responsible for seeking referral via their GP and this is why it is important to share information about their child's behaviour with them. Some parents can be reluctant to seek specialist advice believing that this is in some way a reflection on their parenting skills, and they may need to be provided with some reassurance that seeking advice is a sensible course of action. The diagram below shows some of the specialists who might have a role in helping children and their parents.

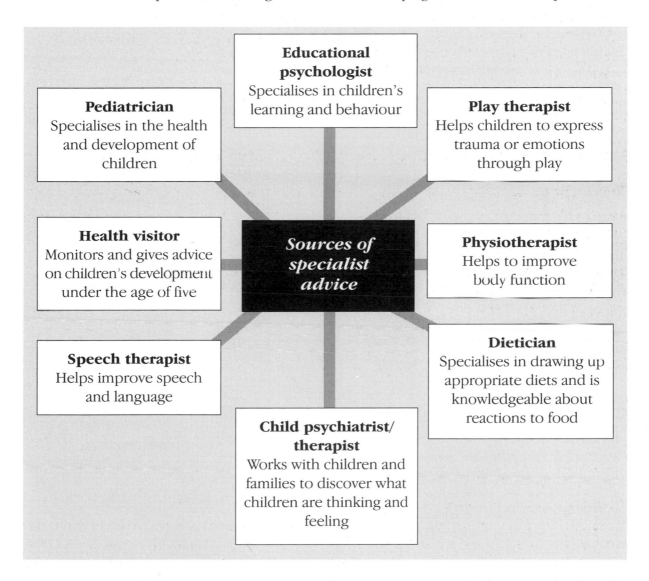

Working with specialists

Once a child has been referred for specialist help, the early years worker might be asked to provide detailed information about a child's behaviour. This is why it is important accurately to record any serious unwanted behaviour. Records need to have dates, times and detailed accounts of the behaviour. Any information that the early years worker passes on or is shared with him or her must be considered confidential.

Sometimes parents and early years workers will be given advice or an action plan to follow to help children show appropriate behaviour. This may refer to the limits that should be put on behaviour, or include advice as to how to deal with specific types of behaviour. It is essential that the advice given is followed and that the early years worker continues to report back to the parents or specialists.

Case study

Mark was four years old when his parents separated. He spends three days each week with his father and the rest of the time with his mother. Since the separation, Mark's behaviour has dramatically changed. He is now very unsettled, has frequent tantrums and is extremely clingy to his key worker. The supervisor has spoken to both parents about her concerns and over the past few weeks they have met to talk about ways of making Mark feel more secure. In order to build up a more accurate picture of his behaviour, the key worker has kept a diary of his behaviour and this shows that Mark's behaviour has not improved, but in many ways is becoming more disruptive. The supervisor has suggested that in view of this, some advice might be sought so that the nursery can make sure that it is handling Mark's behaviour appropriately. After some consideration, Mark's parents have taken him to their GP, who has referred him to a family therapist. An action plan has been drawn up to reward Mark when he is showing appropriate behaviour, and Mark's parents and the nursery are making sure that they are handling incidents of inappropriate behaviour in the same way. Mark's parents are also considering whether their custody arrangements for Mark give him enough stability.

1 *Why might Mark's behaviour be linked to his parents' separation?*
2 *Why was it important that the nursery supervisor involved both parents?*
3 *Why might some parents resist the idea of seeking specialist advice and help?*
4 *What activities might be planned to help Mark express his feelings?*

C7 Unit test

1 Describe some short-term factors that might affect children's behaviour.
2 Give three examples of rewards that might be used with children to reinforce wanted behaviour.
3 How can children's behaviour be encouraged if they see good role models?
4 By what age can most children share and play cooperatively?
5 Why is it important for settings to have a behaviour policy?
6 What is meant by the term 'boundary setting'?
7 Why is it important to talk to parents about children's behaviour?
8 Describe three long-term factors that might affect children's behaviour.
9 Why is it important to report changes in children's behaviour?
10 How can children be helped to remember the boundaries/rules of the setting?

Unit C10

Promote children's sensory and intellectual development

A child's sensory and intellectual (cognitive) development is clearly linked to other developmental areas and the way human thought processes develop. Children develop an awareness and understanding of the world through their senses. Minds are complex structures and in this unit you will learn how children organise their thinking in order to understand and gain the most from their environment. Psychologists such as Piaget have studied the way children think and these studies have contributed much to our understanding of human sensory and intellectual development. However, much more is still to be discovered about the way our brains function.

The elements for this unit are:

C10.1   Develop children's attention span and memory
C10.2   Develop children's awareness and understanding of sensory experiences
C10.3   Develop children's understanding of mathematics and science
C10.4   Develop children's imagination and creativity

Element C10.1   Develop children's attention span and memory

As an early years worker you will have noticed that a child's level of development influences his or her attention span. A child's attention span is developed along with the ability to store information mentally – this helps to build on experiences and learn from them. Memory is the basis of the development of thought.

WHAT YOU NEED TO LEARN

- Planning activities appropriate to children's developmental levels
- Short-term memory and long-term memory
- Theories of how children learn
- Allowing children time to participate in activities within their attention span
- Extending children's attention span and memory

Planning activities appropriate to children's developmental levels

Memory and attention can be greatly improved by planning activities that are appropriate to the developmental level of the child. This will help children to play and learn more effectively, enabling them to complete tasks, which will boost confidence and give a sense of achievement. If you are working with special needs children you must take their particular needs into account when planning activities. In order to plan activities that are appropriate to children's developmental levels, early years workers need to have a clear understanding of the stages of development of memory, concentration and attention.

Babies learn actions through imitation, and do not remember for long

Babies do not remember things for long, but they do imitate people. As they become older they also recall things. This is a simple example of learning from experience.

Short-term memory and long-term memory

Short-term memory allows people to remember things when they need to, and then lose the information – such as a telephone number.

Long-term memory allows people to store information which can then be retrieved in a variety of ways, sometimes by prompting. An example of long-term memory is remembering the stages involved in getting up, washing, dressing and having breakfast.

Attention span and concentration are the power of focusing on certain information. The brain acts as a filter to encourage us to concentrate on what we need, such as when a child is building a tower or painting a picture. Attention and concentration are essential to the learning process – children need to concentrate long enough to store the information they need.

Key issues

Some children suffer from ADHD (Attention Deficit Hyperactivity Disorder). This is a disorder causing children to be unable to concentrate for long periods. Some specialists associate this condition with a diet including artificial additives in foods, whilst others feel that the condition is a result of inappropriate behaviour management.

Theories of how children learn

Before considering the planning of activities for children, you will need to understand how children learn and their developmental needs. There are three theories that form the basis of our understanding of children's learning. It will be helpful for you to study these in order to develop appropriate strategies with children when providing activities for them.

The three theories are:

- social learning
- behaviourist
- constructivist

Social learning theory

The social learning theory was developed by Albert Bandura, who was born in 1925. He suggested that children are influenced by and imitate the behaviour of adults they are with. He carried out a well-known experiment where he showed three groups of children a film of an adult hitting an inflatable doll. Each group saw a different ending to the film.

1 The adult was praised and given sweets. The children who saw this ending were afterwards more aggressive with the doll when they were allowed to play with it.
2 Nothing was said to the adult. Children who saw this ending were also aggressive.
3 The adult was smacked and reprimanded. Children were less aggressive in this case.

Bandura concluded that the children watching the first two versions were more aggressive in their own behaviour because they saw that the adult was not reprimanded, and therefore felt it was acceptable to hit the doll. In other words, children will copy behaviour they see.

How social learning theory affects your role

Your role will be to encourage children to learn from each other and imitate what they observe. It is important to remember that as an adult you have a responsibility as a role model. For example, if children see adults reading books, they are more likely to want to read themselves. This is particularly the case with gender role models – boys are more likely to copy men.

Observation

Observe a child in your care playing in the home corner. Do you feel that the child's play reflects any influence of the adults who care for him or her? Discuss this in your conclusion.

Behaviourist theories

Behaviourists are psychologists who believe that children's learning is formed by direct experiences and that children only repeat experiences that are enjoyable.

Burrhus Skinner (1904 – 1994) discovered that **positive reinforcement** (praising children) would encourage them to repeat the experience and develop their learning. This theory is widely accepted by early years workers as part of behaviour management.

How behaviourist theories affect your role

Ensure that you give children positive reinforcement during and at the end of an activity, such as building a tower, doing a puzzle, etc. Reinforcement can be praise or treats such as allowing a child to choose the book for story time. This will encourage children to persevere with activities that develop their sensory and intellectual skills.

Constructivist theories

These theories suggest that children learn from action and exploring their own environment. The most famous constructivist theorist was probably Jean Piaget (1896–1980). Piaget, who was Swiss, studied children's intellectual development over a period of years. He discovered that children's answers to the intelligence tests that he set followed a logical pattern based on answers drawn from their own experiences. He called their answers schemas. This means that a child assumes something because of his or her own experiences. For example, a young child will believe that everyone has a parent figure, and you will probably have heard a young child ask an adult 'Where is your mummy?' Piaget believed that children adapted their schemas as they learnt new concepts and had new experiences. This is called **assimilation** and **accommodation**.

- Assimilation occurs when a child finds that an existing schema will fit into another situation. For example, a child may think that milk can be drunk from a mug and then discover that juice and water can also be drunk from a mug. He or she has assimilated a new idea (concept) into his or her schema.
- Accommodation occurs when a child develops a new schema because an existing one does not fit. For example, if a child has always had red shoes he or she may believe that all shoes will be red, but discover that there are shoes in other colours.

Piaget felt that children pass through four stages of conceptual development. It will be interesting for you to consider these stages when you are planning activities to develop children's attention span and memory.

Object permanence
Babies learn through their senses. If they cannot see something, they believe it no longer exists. At approximately eight months, babies develop the concept of object permanence – they look for hidden objects or cry if they cannot be seen.

Egocentrism
At this stage children tend to see things only from their own point of view. They are not selfish, but do not have the concepts to understand the views of others.

Animism
Children under the age of six or seven can imagine that objects and animals have the same thoughts and feelings as they do. They will often imagine inanimate objects such as teddy bears to be real people.

Conservation
Piaget suggested that most children under six would not understand that if a material changed shape or form its properties would remain the same. For example, if you pour the same liquid into two differently shaped beakers, it is still the same amount of liquid. Psychologists have subsequently found that younger children are able to understand conservation.

Piaget defined four cognitive stages of learning, as shown in the table below.

Stage	Age	Title	Stage of learning
1	0–18 months/ 2 years	Sensori-motor	Babies learn about their environment from their senses. They are **egocentric** – they see the world from their own point of view only. At around 18 months they start to develop the idea that a person or object they cannot see still exists – **object permanence**. They learn mainly from trial and error methods.
2	2–6/7 years	Pre-operational	Children are using language to express their thoughts. They are starting to use symbols in play, e.g. stick becomes a wand. They are **egocentric** – seeing things from their own viewpoint only. They tend to think that non-living things and animals have the same feelings as they do – **animism**. For example, a child might draw a picture of a worm with a smile. They tend to be taken in by how things appear.
3	7–11	Concrete operations	Children can see things from another's point of view – **decentring**. Children can reason more easily and are less fooled by appearances. They are able to **conserve**. Children can use abstract symbols, e.g. mathematical signs and writing and are developing complex reasoning skills. They still need physical objects to help solve problems, e.g. counters. They understand that non-living objects do not have feelings.
4	11–18+	Formal operations	Children are able to think in the abstract. This means that they can manipulate ideas in their heads, solve sums mentally. Children are more logical and methodical when trying to solve a problem, not using a trial and error approach. Piaget suggested that not everyone would move on to this stage.

Piaget's stages of development have influenced early years workers and are accepted by some psychologists. Children are active in their own development and they use their experiences to develop an understanding of the world around them.

Key issues

There have been criticisms of Piaget's work. Some psychologists consider that the stages of development are inaccurate and that children's learning is on-going. If you would like to find out more about this topic, read *Cognitive Development Today, Piaget and his Critics* by P. Sutherland (1992).

Vygotsky (1896–1934) also believed that children are active in their learning but placed more importance on the role of play. He believed that children could extend their own thinking and move into the next stage of development through free play. He also pointed to the significant role of adults in extending children's thinking by providing stimulating play.

Jerome Bruner, who was born in 1915, built on the ideas of Vygotsky. Rather than thinking that children pass through stages, he felt that they developed different ways of thinking. These are called the three modes of representation. Like Vygotsky he felt that adults played an important part in intellectual development. Whereas Piaget felt that a child would not be able to use symbols until ready to do so despite adult intervention, Bruner felt that adults supported children in increasing their knowledge and reasoning by providing the appropriate guidance and materials, allowing them to solve their own questions.

Bruner's three modes of representation

Mode	Approximate ages (although adults might use all three models)	Description and use
Enactive	0–1	Information is stored according to physical movements. When something has to be remembered, the movement is recreated. Adults may still use the enactive mode to learn physical skills such as icing a cake and wall-papering.
Iconic	1–7	Information is stored using images that may be based on smell, hearing or touch. A smell may trigger a memory.
Symbolic	7 onwards	As not everything can be pictured, we use symbols such as language, musical notation and numbers to store information.

The role of the adult

In order to provide the right activities for children to develop their attention span and memory, it is important that the early years worker also understands developmental needs. The chart below shows some of the different kinds of activities you can offer to different age groups of children. Always aim to offer a balance of:

- **receptive** activities, where the child is **receiving** information – for example, listening to stories, watching a puppet show, looking at patterns or objects.
- **productive** activities, where the child is **producing** something – for example, making a clay figure, painting a picture or doing a scientific experiment.
- **recall** activities, where the child uses skills of **memorising** – for example, showing familiar pictures and asking the child to remember and say what the picture contains.
- **recognition and predictive** activities, where children are encouraged to **predict** what will happen next – for example, asking 'What will happen on your birthday?'

Age	Play and learning development	Activities to develop attention and memory
0–6 months	Watching adults closely Exploring by using the mouth and by touch Playing alone with toys such as rattles and baby gyms	Talking to child Using copying games Treasure baskets
6–12 months	Exploring by using the mouth and by touch Watching and copying adults Repeating movements such as dropping a rattle Enjoying simple games such as peek-a-boo Exploring toys alone	Finger rhymes and actions Treasure basket Rattles
12–18 months	Learning through trial and error – e.g. banging two cubes together and discovering the sound made Repeating actions that have been enjoyed Beginning to play with adults and notice other children Playing and 'talking' alone	Repetitive toys Toys that make a sound Finger rhymes and songs Time to play alone

Age	Play and learning development	Activities to develop attention and memory
18 months– 2 years	Learning through trial and error Imitating other children and adults Exploring things with mouth Possibly carrying out repetitive actions – e.g. putting things in and out of boxes or scribbling on several pages Watching other children but not joining in Enjoying playing with adults as well as by themselves	Tactile toys, such as activity mats Sorting boxes Large crayons and paper Musical toys Building bricks
2–3 years	Beginning to show some reasoning skills – although still learning by trial and error Imitating adults and other children Starting to use symbols in play, e.g. a stick becoming a wand Beginning to play alongside other children Most of play is 'pretend' – e.g. telling off toys	Dolls and teddy bears Dressing up clothes Home corner equipment Building blocks Toy cars and garages Malleable materials Paint and crayons Jigsaw puzzles, musical instruments
3–4 years	Showing more reasoning skills and asking questions such as 'why' Starting to concentrate for longer on play activity that is of interest Recognising shapes and letters Solving jigsaw puzzles through a mixture of reasoning and trial and error Playing cooperatively together and taking turns Playing imaginatively – e.g. playing in the home corner, dressing up	Small world play, e.g. Playmobil, Duplo, dressing up clothes Home corner and equipment Malleable materials Water and sand Construction toys, jigsaw puzzles and musical instruments
4–6 years	Showing more understanding and using reason based on experience Starting to use and understand symbols, e.g. writing and reading Starting to understand simple rules in games Playing cooperatively, taking turns and enjoying table-top games	Recycled modelling Cooking and science activities Malleable materials Jigsaws Home corner and equipment Small world play Simple board games
6–8 years	Enjoying using rules and understanding the need for rules Showing reasoning skills but still using some trial and error Playing in small groups and making up own games which tend to have rules Enjoying playing competitive games but not always coping with losing Tending to play with children of own sex	As above plus modelling, crayons, pieces of card and paper Complex construction toys Books and collections, e.g. stamps and stickers

Allowing children time to participate in activities within their attention span

Whatever children's needs may be, it is essential that they are given the time required to complete the tasks. Consider the following case study.

Case study

Hannah, aged four, was carefully drawing a picture of her family on holiday. She always included lots of detail in her pictures and was halfway through when Jan, the supervisor, told her it was time to finish immediately. She put Hannah's picture in a drawer for Hannah to take home later. Hannah was very distressed.

1   *Why do you think Hannah was upset?*
2   *How could Jan have handled the situation so as to avoid frustration?*

Minimising distractions

It is important to allow children to concentrate in the time span in which they are conducting an activity, so therefore it is important to avoid any distractions. It is also necessary to have realistic expectations of the developmental age of the child and the time needed to complete an appropriate activity.

A number of factors can distract children and break their concentration, for example:

- poor lighting, e.g. too much sunlight
- temperature of room
- noisy environment, e.g. background noise, television and other children
- poor room plan, e.g. activity tables in a thoroughfare, areas not sectioned off
- telephone in the room
- adults talking nearby
- other children interfering in the activity
- visitors.

An early years worker can avoid these distractions by checking before the start of an activity and ensuring that the environment is comfortable and suitable.

Most settings have a time structure to their sessions, so that planned activities can be a suitable length for the needs of the children. Time should be allowed for activities to reach a conclusion if appropriate. Careful preparation of a story can give you a good idea of how long it will take to read, but time must be allowed for questions and for recall. Activities with an end product, such as painting, should allow time for finishing any work that takes longer then anticipated.

Encouraging children to describe past experiences and predict future events

Recall is the ability to describe or demonstrate events or actions that have taken place in the past. As adults we use recall all the time to describe the things done in the past.

Prediction is the anticipation of events in the future. We all use it to plan and prepare. For example, 'Tomorrow I am meeting Kate at the cinema at six o'clock, so I'll need to catch the bus at 5.20'.

Some of the events that early years workers can use for prediction are:

- festivals
- special events
- seasonal activities
- impending visitors

As discussed earlier, young children up to the age of six may remember only things that have happened in the past few days. In order to help them develop attention span and memory, it is important to question children so that their long-term memory builds up information that they can use in their learning. When they start to practise this they may muddle events, but with support from early years workers and other adults they will be able to sequence events (put them in the right order). A four-year-old who has not learnt to sequence might say: 'We went swimming yesterday. It was very late when we came home. I jumped up and down in the water. I went with my friends.' An older child would probably say: 'We went swimming with our friends yesterday. I jumped up and down in the water and it was very late when we came home.' In other words, the events would be recalled in the right order.

To encourage children to learn to sequence their recall, ensure that they have time to talk and give plenty of praise and encouragement. Use prompts, for example: 'And what happened next? Did you see the dog before you went inside or afterwards?' Emotions will often prompt the recall of events, particularly if it was a happy or a sad time, such as a birthday party or the death of a pet animal.

Prediction is a skill that children acquire. They need to see a situation a number of times before they can talk about what may happen next. A young child may enjoy a simple and repetitive game of peek-a-boo or reading a favourite book many times. Such skills develop into the ability to make mathematical and scientific predictions at school.

Key issues

Key Stage 1 of the National Curriculum encourages children's development of mathematical reasoning, to 'recognise simple patterns and relationships and make related predictions about them'. This could involve counting, measuring, sorting, weighing, etc.

When children see something a number of times they begin to recognise it. The time taken depends on their developmental level. Toys and games, and subsequently words and letters in early reading and numbers in early maths, all involve recognition. In order for a child to recognise a letter, such as the first letter of his or her name, concentration and memory are necessary.

Keys to good practice

Developing the skills of recall and prediction

Some children love to talk about themselves and their lives, but this topic needs to be handled sensitively, as other children may be unhappy or be afraid of being teased. You could share information with the children about:

- events that have happened to children you know
- holidays
- pets.

Use your knowledge of the children to talk to them about events in their lives. This can be a good starting point and lead them to recall events such as a birthday, holiday, new pet, etc. Children could be encouraged to keep a diary using words, drawing and photographs.

Active knowledge ✔

Describe at least four activities that would encourage the recall of a child aged 2–3.

Extending children's attention span and memory

Children need to be encouraged to focus upon activities and experiences. When assisting children you should always encourage them to maintain control of their activity, as this will give them confidence in their abilities. Rather than asking children to stop an activity, you could extend the activity to encourage a longer attention span by adding new objects, or asking if you can join in. For example, a group of four-year-old children playing in the water tray, floating and sinking objects, may welcome an adult joining them, discussing the activity and providing them with some new objects to develop their exploration of the topic.

It is also important that unexpected learning opportunities should be used to encourage children to develop their attention span. A three-year-old child who is playing with some play people may use them to re-enact her visit to a new setting. The early years worker could extend the play by encouraging the child to recall the visit.

Praising a child during an activity such as cleaning and tidying may encourage him or her to focus even more on the task and complete it well.

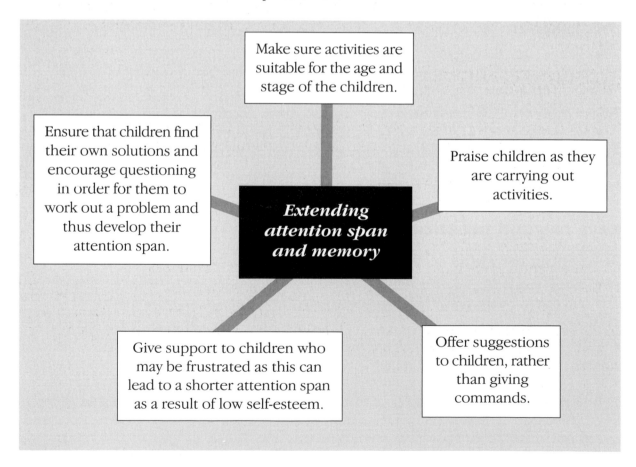

Make sure activities are suitable for the age and stage of the children.

Ensure that children find their own solutions and encourage questioning in order for them to work out a problem and thus develop their attention span.

Extending attention span and memory

Praise children as they are carrying out activities.

Give support to children who may be frustrated as this can lead to a shorter attention span as a result of low self-esteem.

Offer suggestions to children, rather than giving commands.

Element C10.2 Develop children's awareness and understanding of sensory experiences

Children are surrounded by sensory experiences. However, they may not understand them or be able to describe them. This element will help you to plan, share and understand experiences. Some children may have one sense impaired, such as hearing or sight, but they will still experience and enjoy the other senses. Visually impaired or profoundly deaf children in a mainstream setting should have a statement of special needs and an assistant to help them to access the curriculum.

Younger children will rely upon their carers and other professionals working together to help them develop awareness and understanding of sensory experiences. Through exploration, children develop their own sensory awareness and empathy for those with sensory impairments.

WHAT YOU NEED TO LEARN

- What are sensory experiences?
- How to plan suitable and stimulating activities with minimal distractions
- How to use relevant terms to help children name, describe and reflect on their sensory experiences
- How to extend understanding by sharing experiences
- How to adapt activities for children with sensory impairment

What are sensory experiences?

Sensory experiences are those that involve one or more of our five senses.

Activities to promote sensory experiences can take place indoors or outdoors and can be planned or unplanned. As children's senses are very acute, they often react with great excitement to sensory experiences. Think of the effect of a thunderstorm, or the wafting smell of dinner cooking, on young children!

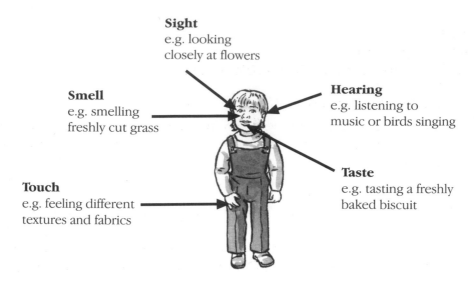

Sight
e.g. looking
closely at flowers

Smell
e.g. smelling
freshly cut grass

Hearing
e.g. listening to
music or birds singing

Touch
e.g. feeling different
textures and fabrics

Taste
e.g. tasting a freshly
baked biscuit

For children who may have one sense impaired, for example children who are deaf, opportunities to explore the other senses are doubly important.

How to plan suitable and stimulating activities with minimal distractions

Children will be encouraged to develop their senses if the activities provided are suitable for their stage of development

Sensory activities with babies

In their first year, babies particularly rely on taste, touch and smell. At a few weeks old, fingers, rattles and other toys are taken into the mouth. We can help babies to learn about their environment by providing activities which stimulate the senses.

Hearing
- gentle music, for example musical mobiles
- singing rhymes and songs
- musical toys

Sight
- mobiles
- brightly coloured toys
- mirrors
- soft books

Taste and smell
- variety of appetising weaning foods – for example vegetables, fruit and cereals with different textures

*Babies' senses are stimulated
by mobiles and tactile toys*

Touch

- 'feely' books
- sensory toys and play mats
- treasure basket – a basket with different objects in it.

Sensory activities with older children

As children get older their senses play a vital part in all areas of their learning, and when planning activities for children you need to ensure that you are using all their senses as part of the development process.

Sight

When planning activities to develop this sense we must consider both children with good sight and those with an impairment. There are a number of ways to encourage children's exploration of sight. Activities can be carried out inside and outside on an individual basis and in a group. You could brainstorm words associated with sight with a group of older children. They may come up with words such as:

wink   blink   iris   tears   eyelash   eyebrow   squint   stare   look   glasses

As part of your work on the theme of sight, you could perhaps borrow a model of a human eye, look at animals' eyes, visit an eye clinic or optician, discuss safety rules for eye care, and discuss aids to sight such as glasses and lenses. Mount a display or create an imaginative play area representing an optician's shop.

Keys to good practice

Working with visual impairment

It is important to encourage children to be aware that others may have a visual impairment. Perhaps you could plan a visit to a setting by a visually impaired person and his or her dog, or blindfold older children and encourage them to try to find their way around a familiar environment.

Art and craft work could include making an eye collage, using pictures of eyes from magazines, or designing elaborate glasses.

Maths work could discuss pairs of eyes, and make a graph of the eye colours of children in your setting.

Language work should develop vocabulary, such as glimpsing, viewing, peering, and so on. Read relevant books and stories, or sing relevant songs. Play games such as Spot the difference, I Spy, and so on.

Active knowledge ✔

Plan an indoor treasure hunt for a group of four, to five-year-olds to develop their visual discrimination skills. Beware of disrupting the other children. Consider:

- what you could use to make this challenging
- how you could make it accessible to all children
- how you could adapt it for other senses.

Hearing

Hearing is essential to speech and language and other areas of development involving talking and listening. Some children will have special needs such as partial hearing, deafness or temporary hearing loss.

A very young baby will be able to discriminate between his or her mother's voice and that of other family members – this is probably the first listening skill that a child will use. To develop a sense of hearing a child must first learn how to listen. Today, many children are brought up in a noisy environment, often with the background noise of television. From an early age they have to learn how to filter out unwanted sound. The skill of focused listening is called **auditory discrimination**. Children with a hearing impairment may find it hard to develop this. As discussed before, it is important during any activity that distractions are kept to a minimum, and this is particularly so for listening activities.

Consider the following activities to develop auditory discrimination.

Music for children does not have to be complicated or hi-tech. A baby will enjoy using a saucepan as a drum, or shaking a plastic bottle containing stones. Listen to pre-recorded or live music. Use circle times to copy clapped rhythms. Even young children will enjoy clapping to their own names.

Play games such as sound lotto, hiding instruments behind a screen. Provide an interest table to include objects that produce sound, for example jars of dried seeds. Provide a listening corner, with or without headphones. There are now many good song and music tapes for children.

Language work could include discussing the ear and how sound waves reach the ears. Invite an audiologist to talk to the children and consider what it might be like to be deaf. Invite someone to demonstrate sign language.

Use vocabulary such as *loud, soft, noisy, shrill,* and so on. Go on a listening walk and encourage children to discuss the sounds they heard.

Case study

Sue was digging in the nursery garden with a group of three- and four-year old children. One of the children thought that she heard a bird singing a nursery rhyme! Sue used this imaginative opportunity to encourage the children to discriminate between different birds' songs, by asking them to work out which other rhymes the birds were singing.

You will notice that Sue used the opportunity to extend the children's listening skills in an imaginative and fun way. The children probably began to listen to birdsong more carefully after that experience, if only to find out which nursery rhymes are sung!

All children enjoy **singing** and being sung to. Action songs will encourage children to listen to the words and follow instructions.

Key issues

The Royal National Institute for the Deaf promotes a standard manual alphabet for sign language which can be used by people working with hearing impaired children.

Taste and smell

The senses of taste and smell are very closely related.

Young children have strong likes and dislikes in taste and smell, and even the texture of food. However, it is important that children are encouraged to discriminate between taste and smell in order to use each sense as a means to fully investigate and explore the world around them.

Remember

During taste and smell activities, it is important to be aware of children's allergies and dietary requirements. For instance, in a sandwich-making activity you should avoid peanut butter as a child with a nut allergy could experience a severe reaction. Before undertaking any smell or taste activities it is advisable to check the children's records for any allergies or special dietary requirements.

A variety of activities can be used to develop children's taste and smell.

- **Food tasting.** From a young age children can taste unfamiliar and familiar foods. This is a good opportunity to include food from other cultures. Children could develop their language by describing the foods and their textures. For example, you could introduce the words 'spicy, juicy, fresh, scrumptious'. Good words to describe texture are 'smooth, lumpy, crisp, crunchy'. Preparing and cooking food also provides an opportunity to distinguish between smell and taste. An avocado pear or aubergine may have no smell, but taste quite strong.
- **Smelling objects.** Children can be introduced to a selection of familiar and unfamiliar smells. These could include coffee, vinegar, lemon, soap, curry powder, cheese or flowers.
- **Discussion.** Older children could be encouraged to discuss their favourite or least favourite smells, or smells associated with places such as hospitals, schools or libraries. They could also discuss smells that warn of danger, such as smoke.
- **Cooking.** Children could cook their own food and share it afterwards.

Touch

The sense of touch is particularly strong in young children. Children are naturally tactile and enjoy the comfort they receive from hugs and cuddles. Often children explore a new environment through touch – think how often you hear parents in shops saying to their children 'don't touch'. Touch overlaps with taste and smell, especially for very young children who handle food before eating and spit out food if they do not like the texture. Some children may not have experimented with food textures, and early years workers should give them the appropriate experiences. Many young children learn that an item is not good to eat by its texture, such as sand.

A variety of activities can be provided to develop experience of touch.

- **Feely bag/boxes**. A cardboard box or a cloth bag is all that is needed to begin this activity. Place a variety of familiar or unfamiliar objects inside the box or bag and encourage children to discuss what they can feel. The items could include natural materials such as shells, stones and fir cones, household items such as spoons and combs, and tactile fabrics. The complexity of the objects provided can be matched to the developmental level of the children involved.

A variety of familiar and unfamiliar items can be used to make up the feely bag

- **Malleable and tactile materials**. Malleable materials are those that change their shape when moulded, such as clay and playdough. Malleable materials are an excellent way to encourage children to explore touch, language and emotions. The activities can be wet or dry.

Wet activities	Dry activities
Clay	Shredded paper
Gloop (soap flakes and water)	Sawdust
Very wet sand	Wood shavings
Ooblick (cornflour and water)	Dry sand
Finger painting	Tea, rice and pasta
Shaving foam	Dry leaves
Compost	Straw
Flour and water	

Case study

Ben, who was working in a nursery school which included some visually impaired children, provided a tactile table with ingredients that allowed creative play. He placed containers of wet sand, playdough and wood shavings so that children could play with them when supervised. All the children were encouraged to discuss the materials and to describe their differences through touching them.

1 *Why was this a particularly good activity for children who are visually impaired?*
2 *Why would the children need to be supervised?*

Sensory-based activities can be planned outside any setting, such as treasure hunts, listening to noises and finding a variety of tactile and natural objects. However, children must never be encouraged to taste or touch anything without permission.

How to use relevant terms to help children name, describe and reflect on their sensory experiences

Language is an essential part of developing children's awareness and understanding of sensory experiences. Carefully consider the language development chart in Unit C11 on page 180. This will help you to use appropriate terms to help children name, describe and reflect on their sensory experiences.

Discussion is essential when helping children describe and understand their experiences. Ask questions such as:

- can you guess the taste?
- what is your favourite smell?
- which part of our hands do we use most for touching?
- what can you hear?
- what can you see?

By labelling events as they occur, you can encourage children to learn new vocabulary and to make sense of their sensory experiences.

Active knowledge ✔

Plan a sensory activity for a group of children in your care. Once you have chosen the activity, consider how you will encourage the children to discuss the activity and their sensory experiences.

How to extend understanding by sharing experiences

Sharing experiences in a positive way with children will result in a valuable learning experience, whatever their age. This can be done only if you are enthusiastic and encouraging. Careful and sensitive intervention is important, but remember that there are no rights or wrongs in experimental play that encourages the development of the senses.

Praise and encouragement

Use praise and encouragement to:

- involve a reluctant child in an unfamiliar experience
- keep a child with an activity for longer to extend his or her learning
- boost a child's confidence and self-esteem
- share ideas with adults and other children.

Constructive commentary and assistance

It is important to be positive. Allow children the freedom to experiment, and intervene only if a child becomes frustrated. Use questions such as 'would you like some help?' 'how could we . . .', 'what would happen if . . . .'

Extend language by introducing simple terms in context. Use correct names, such as for species of birds – pigeon, sparrow, and so on. Encourage children to use descriptive language.

Sharing ideas and concepts

A child with developed language skills will be more easily able to share ideas and concepts. Show the child you value his or her opinion by the way you listen and what you say in reply. All children should be given the opportunity to share their ideas.

Ask children relevant questions, and if they ask you questions to which you don't know the answer, say so.

How to adapt activities for children with sensory impairment

You are likely to work with children with a hearing or visual impairment. You may also meet children who do not have full use of their hands for touching, but are able to handle objects. You will be able to help them explore textures, perhaps by the use of individual attention, extra time, or special equipment.

Key issues

Multi-sensory rooms are becoming increasingly available for children with sensory impairment. They can include special lights, bubble tubes, fibre optics, pictures, different temperatures, a variety of textures, music and smells. They can be beneficial for children with partial sight or hearing, children with behavioural problems, those with brittle bones and those who have a fear of large spaces. Find out as much as you can about the development of multi-sensory equipment for children.

A child with a sensory impairment who is in a mainstream setting may have a trained or named worker to encourage his or her sensory development, but all adults will share in planning and care for the child. Other children in the setting should be made aware of the need to be sensitive to children with a sensory impairment. It is important that children gain maximum benefit from the experiences on offer and that an impaired child is able to develop other senses. You can support and adapt activities for children with the following sensory impairments.

Hearing

- Minimise noise distractions, close windows and doors.
- Have quiet carpeted areas in the room – a carpet helps to deaden background noise.
- Seat the child near an adult and use eye contact.
- Use positive body language.
- Always make activities hands-on.
- If playing a listening game, choose items that allow the child to succeed.
- Provide headphones with independent volume control in the listening corner (be aware of the dangers).

Vision

- Provide clear, bold images.
- Use bright colours.
- Use clear, descriptive language and commentary.

- Keep the main plan of the room consistent.
- Be very safety conscious in general, but especially with taste and smelling.

Touch

- Assist the child's manipulation of items if necessary.
- Use easily distinguished textures.
- Be guided by the child as to how he or she is best able to feel (feet, face, arms).
- Use floor-level activities where the child can use feet if appropriate (foot painting, sand, water, rice, etc.).

Taste and smell

It is common for children of pre-school age to have heavy colds or nasal congestion, and this may temporarily weaken the sense of smell and taste. Children could be helped by being encouraged to blow their noses before starting an activity, and by using strong smells or tastes such as onions or marmite.

If children have been unable to participate in an activity because of illness, try to repeat it as soon as they are better.

Consolidation

Review this section and carry out the following activities:

- make a list of a variety of textured objects that a visually impaired child could easily recognise through touch
- describe how a hearing-impaired child could be supported in listening to a range of sounds.

Element C10.3 Develop children's understanding of mathematics and science

Children are learning mathematical and scientific skills all the time. As an early years worker you can enhance that learning by providing suitable activities to introduce and reinforce concepts. Experiences can be presented to children at any level of ability in an exciting and interesting way. Mathematics is not purely focused upon numeracy – it covers a whole range of concepts and language, including colour, size, sequencing and matching. Many examples can be seen in a child's play environment. Science, too, will be seen in the child's environment in areas such as cooking, leaf rubbing, water and sand play. Children are exposed to scientific experiences every day, and it is the role of the early years worker to point them out and discuss them with the children.

- The key maths and science concepts
- How to use planned and unplanned experiences which promote appropriate science and maths concepts
- How to make activities enjoyable and accessible to all children

The key maths and science concepts

Mathematics

Mathematics in pre-school settings should provide children with an understanding of basic mathematical concepts through everyday activities. Such concepts include the following.

Counting

For many children their first exposure to numbers is through counting. There are many lovely counting rhymes that children learn quickly. Counting introduces children to the idea of numbers, although at first for young children it is just a collection of sounds – counting skills alone do not mean that children have an understanding of numbers. Children often forget numbers or are unable to put out the correct number of objects when asked. To build children's experience in counting, encourage them to count objects as the next step from counting out loud. Counting objects by touching or moving them allows children to understand in a concrete way what is sometimes known as 'one-to-one correspondence'. Many counting activities can be carried out with children during the day. As children also learn by imitation, it is a good idea for adults to demonstrate counting out loud while pointing to objects. When children are counting they should be encouraged to point to or touch each object. It is a good idea to start with fewer then five objects and gradually find opportunities to count larger numbers.

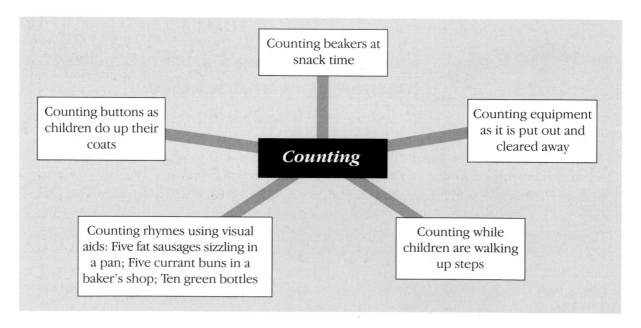

Counting beakers at snack time

Counting buttons as children do up their coats

Counting

Counting equipment as it is put out and cleared away

Counting rhymes using visual aids: Five fat sausages sizzling in a pan; Five currant buns in a baker's shop; Ten green bottles

Counting while children are walking up steps

Matching

Matching is a mathematical skill, although it is one that we tend to take for granted. In order to be able to match, children have to look at an object, compare it to another and decide whether the features are the same. This process leads onto many areas of mathematics, for example in sums, equals (=) means that items are of the same value. There are many activities that can help children match – there are games such as lotto, snap and happy families as well as everyday opportunities to carry out matching.

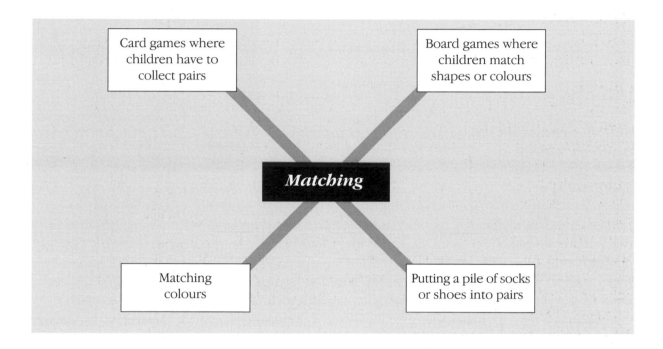

Card games where children have to collect pairs

Board games where children match shapes or colours

Matching

Matching colours

Putting a pile of socks or shoes into pairs

Sorting

Sorting is a process that allows us to compare objects and decide on features that link them together or separate them. This process helps children learn to be selective and logical. Sorting leads into many mathematical areas, for example learning about odd and even numbers, and grouping shapes according to their features. Jigsaws offer children the chance to use sorting skills while allowing them to gain a sense of satisfaction once they have completed the puzzle.

Many everyday opportunities allow children to sort. Tidying up at the end of sessions can be structured so that children are sorting while they are tidying. This can make the process fun – for example, children can be asked to bring all the red pieces of Duplo to a table or put all the cups from the home corner into the cupboard. Groups of small objects can be put into a box for children to sort. Toy jewellery put in a 'treasure box' is a particularly popular activity!

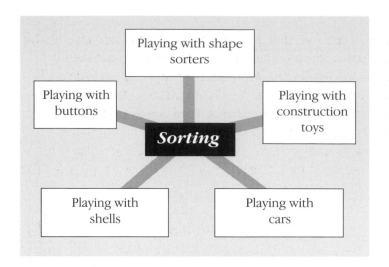

Shape-sorting toys encourage young children to compare objects

Patterns

Recognising and using patterns are important parts of acquiring the concept not only of number, but also shape and measurement. Patterns are all around us, in nature and in man-made materials. A pattern is a logical sequence, and being able to recognise patterns can help children in many ways – for example there is a pattern to multiplication tables. There are many ways of encouraging children to make and recognise patterns. Children can carry out threading activities such as making necklaces, which gives them an end product as well as encouraging their fine manipulative skills. Adults can make patterns for children to recognise, for example setting a table with alternative coloured plates and asking the children to see if they can copy the pattern.

Music and rhythm are also ways of encouraging a sense of pattern. Musical activities that enable children to experience rhythm can be planned, for example children can shake percussion instruments in time to a beat. Songs that have verses and repeated choruses can help children to learn about patterns.

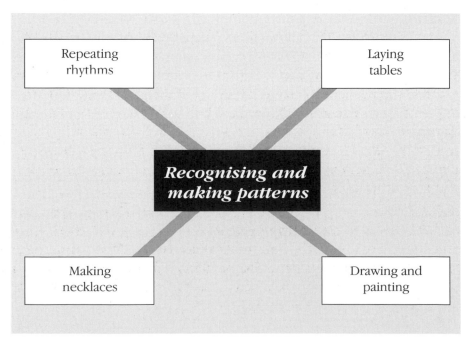

Ordering

Another skill that adults take for granted, although it is a mathematical and logical one, is the process of ordering objects. Sorting objects according to their length requires children to compare an object to another and then decide which is larger. Ordering is an essential skill, as children need to have a firm understanding of the position of numbers in relation to each other. To help children experience ordering, they can be asked to order objects according to their size, such as stacking beakers or arranging teddies according to size. Encouraging children to order objects as part of the tidying up process can also be useful, for example stacking boxes according to size on a shelf. It is important to enrich these experiences for the children by using vocabulary such as 'bigger then', 'shorter than', 'the same as'.

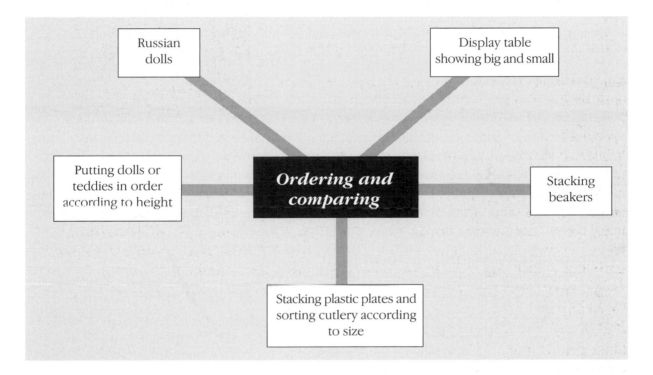

Prediction

Prediction tends to be an area that even older children find difficult, although it is an important mathematical skill. Being able to predict an answer or outcome can mean that an error is spotted. Giving children experiences of prediction helps their confidence as they can learn that it does not matter if your prediction is not the same as the outcome. Rounding up numbers and getting a rough estimate is one way in which prediction fits the broader and mathematical picture.

Helping children to experience prediction is easy to do through everyday situations. For example, children can be asked to guess how many chairs there are around a table and then count them, or how many buttons there are on a coat. It is important that every guess is valued and that praise is given for the guess rather than the correct answer. Counting the objects afterwards is also important, so that children can get a feel for the accuracy of numbers.

Reinforcement of number concepts

Learning the concept of number is a gradual process and children need to experience number in many different ways in order to be completely at ease. Reinforcing number activities means giving children opportunities to repeat them, or find out the same knowledge in a different way. It is important that reinforcement activities are valued, as there is a danger that we can assume children have understood a concept and are ready to go on further when this is not so.

Repeating activities builds confidence and helps children to look for short cuts and patterns. For example, a child who has made a pattern by threading beads may do the same activity but lay out the pattern first to speed up the process.

Children who have counted out the beakers for drinks may be asked to count them back in when all the children have finished. This will teach them that numbers are constant. Later, they could be asked to group them in pairs and then count them.

Recording mathematics

Over the past few years emphasis has been placed on making the learning of mathematics more formal by recording work on worksheets. This brings the danger that children will spend more time writing about than experiencing mathematical concepts. Recognising and being able to write numbers is best seen as a later step in the mathematical process, rather then central to a child's early mathematical experience. It is possible to record a child's work by using photographs of an activity or by asking the child to draw a picture of what he or she has been doing. Some mathematical work can be displayed, for example showing a pattern that a child has made on a display table.

Recognising and writing numbers

There is now a trend to teach children to write and recognise numbers before they go to school. For some children this is quite hard, as a number is a symbol and therefore an abstract concept. Where children have a good understanding of number as a concept they are more likely to use and write numbers confidently, as it is always easier to remember a symbol when you understand its meaning. Practical activities that encourage children to experience number needs to be used first.

Many children learn to recognise numbers without being formally taught them. They do this through playing games that have numbers in them, seeing numbers in wall displays and playing at shops in the home corner. Adults can help children to recognise numbers by writing them down, for example they may count the number of children they are working with and write this number down or write down how many children need aprons.

Where children are ready to be introduced to written numbers, the first step is to help them to recognise numbers. They can be given a card with a number on it and asked to count out objects to match the number on the card. One or two numbers should be introduced at a time, as some children find it hard to discriminate visually between numbers. If children find it difficult to recognise and remember written numbers, it is important not to rush them as some children will not be ready to cope.

Providing experience of measuring

Understanding how to use measure is an important life skill. We measure many things every day, such as time, length, volume and weight. Understanding how to measure is a gradual process and one that we can start in pre-school settings. Young children do not need to learn how to use standard measurement units such as grams and litres, but we should be providing them with an understanding of the need to measure and some idea of how we do measure.

Measuring weight

Children experience weighing in many ways, although cooking is often a favourite! For cooking to be a good measuring activity, it is important that balancing scales are used – this is a simple way for children to see how weight can be measured.

The importance of encouraging prediction skills has already been mentioned. When using cooking as a measuring activity, children should be encouraged to predict. Ask children to guess how many spoonfuls of flour will be needed to make the scales balance, or to feel different weights and guess which is the heavier.

A balancing scale in the home corner can encourage children to incorporate weighing into their play.

Measuring length

Young children do not need to use rulers or standard units of measurement, but they can use their hands and more importantly their eyes to measure length. Once again, prediction skills and developing children's vocabulary are key elements in the experiences. Children can be shown two or three objects at story time and asked to decide which is the tallest or shortest. They can also have fun jumping over lines or trying to make themselves small or large. Children can count how many steps it takes them to reach different places, for example 'how many steps do you need to get from here to the sand tray?'

Measuring volume and capacity

Many adults find it hard to judge the volume and capacity of objects. Have you ever found that the contents of drinks can fit far more easily into a glass than you had thought? Children can experience volume and capacity in the water and sand trays if they are given some simple pouring and spooning equipment and some guidance. Children can be asked to predict how many spoonfuls of sand are needed to fill up a cup or beaker, or whether the water in the beaker will fit into a differently shaped container. Children can also use dry materials such as buttons or beads to measure capacity. They may discover that you can fit more buttons into a container than large wooden beads.

Shape

Young children enjoy using different shapes and are often able to match shapes. There are many creative activities that will allow children to experience shape while at the same time learning the names of basic shapes such as square, rectangle, circle and triangle. The concept of shape fits in well with creating patterns, and children can make pictures or patterns using shapes. There are games that help children recognise shape and colour, for example board games where children have to collect all the shapes in order to finish. Jigsaw puzzles are also good for helping children to develop a sense of shape and spatial awareness.

There is also a strong link between shape and capacity, as children learn that some shapes fit better then others into containers. Adults can help children to learn the names of some of the basic shapes by saying them aloud and pointing them out to children, for example saying 'put your finished plates on the rectangular table over there'.

Time

The measurement of time is a difficult concept for children to understand because you cannot see time. Time is an abstract concept, and it is not until they are in their second year of full-time school that most children begin to understand how it it measured.

In the pre-school setting we can help children to understand the notion of time by referring to events in the day. By the age of four, most children will begin to understand what is meant by today, yesterday and tomorrow, although children will not necessarily be able to recollect accurately what they have done in a week.

An awareness of time can be given to children simply by having some chiming or cuckoo clocks in a setting. Children enjoy hearing chimes and may learn that at certain times a tune may be heard or an action may be seen.

Providing opportunities for science

Many everyday activities can be turned into scientific ones. We often read about the need for young children to explore their environment, and a good science activity does exactly that – it allows children to find out and think more about what they are seeing! The main ingredients of a good science activity include opportunities to:

- predict
- observe
- consider explanations.

Prediction

Children should be encouraged to think about what might happen. For example, during a cooking activity an adult might ask the children what they think would happen if a cake was not put in the oven. This helps children to be scientific as they are questioning the reasons for things, rather than simply accepting the world around them.

It is important that when children are encouraged to predict their thoughts are valued. Children are constantly learning through experience and many of their predictions will be very accurate, although based only on the child's own experiences. For example, a child who has never seen a burnt cake will not know that food often becomes dark brown when over-cooked.

Observation

Observation is a skill that allows children to learn more from what they are seeing. For example, when observing a worm children may notice that it does not have legs, and when observing an egg white being whisked, they may see that it changes colour. Observation allows children to consider changes and differences.

Children need time to observe and will also need an adult to help them focus on things. Adults can use questions to guide observations, for example, 'can you see the lines on the snail's shell?' Young children often observe more easily when they are alone or in very small groups, as they need to talk about what they are seeing.

Considering explanations

The next step from observation is to consider reasons for what has been observed. Young children often come up with simple, correct explanations with the help of the adults around them. Explanations that are incorrect are also valid and should not be dismissed, as the process of considering explanations is of great importance.

In some instances it may be possible to test children's theories, although this next step is more likely to take place within the primary curriculum. Testing theories allows children to check their ideas and see if they work.

Active knowledge

Plan a simple activity for a group of three-year-olds that will promote skills of counting and sorting. Explain how the activity will develop these skills. Give some suggestions for extending the activity.

How to use planned and unplanned experiences which promote appropriate science and maths concepts

Children of pre-school age are required to cover the Early Learning Goals and children of school age are required to cover the National Curriculum.

Key issues

The Early Learning Goals and the National Curriculum are statutory requirements, but are not always followed in independent education.

Early Learning Goals

The Early Learning Goals for pre-school children aged three to five state: 'These goals cover important aspects of mathematical understanding and reflect the key objectives in the National Numeracy Strategy.'

The proposed Early Learning Goals are shown on pages 349–352.

National Curriculum, Key Stage 1

Key Stage 1 of the National Curriculum states the following.

'Developing mathematical language, selecting and using materials and developing reasoning should be set in the context of the other areas of mathematics. Sorting, classifying, making comparisons and searching for patterns should apply to work on number, shape and space and handling data. The use of number should permeate work on measures of handling data.

'Pupils describe simple features of objects, living things and events they observe, communicating their findings in simple ways such as by talking about their walk or through drawings of simple charts.'

Planned activities

Many activities with a mathematical or scientific learning outcome do not use specialised equipment. There are also areas that can be covered without the need for written recording. Suitable specialised maths and science equipment can be provided, however, inside or outside the setting. This can include scales, rulers, tape measures and height charts. Supervised children can use magnifying glasses to examine the properties of natural and man-made materials and living creatures. Magnets can be used to explore the properties of materials.

A well-planned water or sand tray can offer a variety of opportunities for the development of scientific and mathematical concepts. The spider diagram below shows other items that can be used.

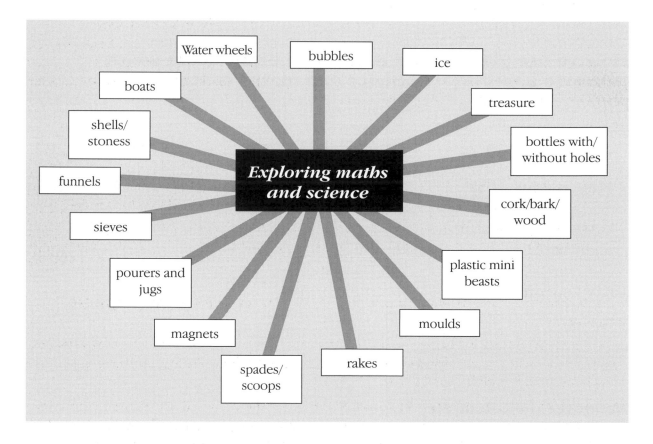

Active knowledge ✔

Which of the Early Learning Goals for children could be developed in the sand and water tray, besides maths and science?

Children love to wash doll's clothes in the water tray – this is exciting for the children and can be carried out at their own level. They can develop language such as hot, warm, cold, dripping, sunshine, pegs, and the activity can be extended using questions. 'Where do the clothes dry more quickly? Why do we rinse clothes? Why do we dry clothes?'

Cooking is a practical and enjoyable way to develop science and maths concepts and children enjoy eating the results. This topic is considered in more detail in the next section.

Construction opportunities encourage scientific exploration about the strength of different types of constructions, the types of materials used for bricks, the maximum height for a tower and types of fixing. Maths can be encouraged by sorting colours, sizing and weighing and discussing number and pattern.

Unplanned activities

Unplanned opportunities can arise for discovering maths and science. These might be connected with the birth of a sibling, the discovery of an injured bird or animal, freak weather, or a child's birthday. When this happens, be careful to extend scientific and mathematical concepts, encourage discussion and allow children time to make discoveries for themselves and understand new concepts.

Case study

Melissa, aged four, brought in some sweets to share with her friends at the nursery. This provided opportunities for sorting, counting, sequencing, and using vocabulary such as more, less and the same.

1   *Suggest some ways in which these opportunities could be used.*
2   *Describe some extension activities to build upon what has been learnt.*

How to introduce and explain terms and concepts using appropriate language

Some concepts that seem natural to an adult may not appear so to a child, but most activities, if well planned, can be matched to a child's level of development. Timing, language and equipment should each be appropriate.

For example, if a young child is at the stage where he or she likes to lick and taste everything, in a cooking activity there would be little time to spend in weighing ingredients. There will be less technical talk, more praise and more hands-on experience. Cooking is one of the easiest and most enjoyable ways for a child to experience maths and science.

The spider diagram below shows some of the concepts that can develop from the activity of baking sponge cakes. Some concepts are mathematical, and some are scientific.

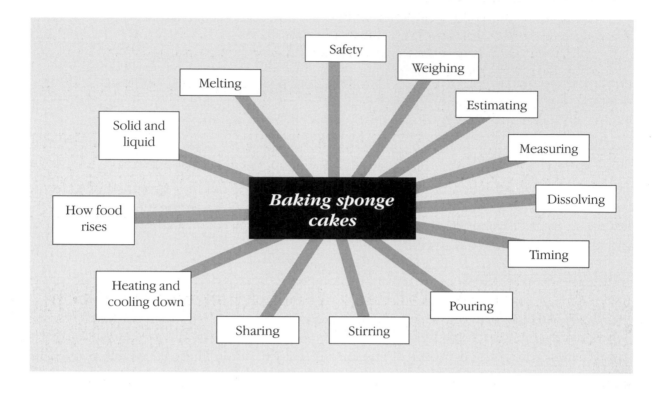

How to make activities enjoyable and accessible to all children

The early years worker has a large responsibility for making activities enjoyable and accessible so that a child's interest is maintained in both the short and long term. If children are encouraged to question and become curious, they will actively seek out concepts related to maths and science. At a later stage they may be able to share their knowledge with others. If a child has been guided and has gained a sense of achievement by discovering something from an activity, he or she is more likely to return to it. Children will then explore and extend their knowledge, becoming problem solvers. Problem solving is an important part of maths and science, and the skills developed will become more useful as children grow older. By using a variety of equipment in a variety of ways, you will retain the interest of a wider range of children.

Case study

Sanka was working in a home looking after two children aged three and four years old. She set up a tea party with four of their dolls, a coloured tea set (one item of each colour) and real food. By doing this she encouraged the children to use one-to-one correspondence, colour recognition and sorting, sharing and estimation.

Allow children to enjoy activities by:

- choosing their own materials where possible
- using appropriate questioning
- using praise to spur children to achieve more
- giving children short-term goals and plenty of praise
- providing special tools to make things easier for children with particular difficulties or needs, such as left-handed scissors
- taking the curriculum outside, such as painting markings that can include number, colour and shape, and organising treasure hunts.

Consolidation

If you were outside with a group of three- to five-year-olds, how could you involve all the children in an activity that would develop their science skills?

Element C10.4 Develop children's imagination and creativity

Imagination and creativity cannot be taught like mathematical and scientific concepts. Children from the youngest age require stimulation and encouragement to develop in these two areas. Creativity can be found in all areas of the curriculum. Imagination is the tool children use to play creatively. Creative play is an important means of encouraging children to experiment and explore the world around them. It helps them discover, through their senses, the properties of different materials. If provided with a wide range of activities children can develop physical, social, emotional and intellectual skills.

WHAT YOU NEED TO LEARN

- The types of creative play
- How to ensure that planned activities are appropriate to the children's developmental levels and needs
- How to use unplanned opportunities effectively
- How to minimise adult intervention
- How to encourage children's enjoyment and involvement in activities
- Health and safety in creative activities

The types of creative play

An exciting range of creative activities can be used to extend children's imaginations and promote their intellectual development. In any early years setting you will see a variety of creative play.

- **Role/fantasy play** gives children the opportunity to explore their environment in an imaginative way. This may take place in the home corner, with small world play, with puppets or in dance and drama.
- **Creative art** activities give children the freedom to explore their world through a variety of textures and media. The role of the early years worker will be to promote appropriate activities for each age group.

How to ensure that planned activities are appropriate to the children's developmental levels and needs

You must ensure that you understand the developmental levels and needs of children when considering the creative activities to be provided for them.

0–3 years
Learn through senses and movement
Can use finger paints, crayons and non-toxic felt tip pens, play dough, water and sand play
Children will become easily frustrated if a task is too difficult
Manipulative skills are developing

3–5 years
Learn through senses
Enjoy exploring different materials
Wet and dry sand
Water – to encourage investigation
Variety of pens, painting activities, cutting and sticking
Construction
Clay and dough
Role play
Manipulative skills are developing

5–8 years
As for 3 – 5 years. Creative activities will be influenced by Key Stage 1 requirements of National Curriculum. Children will be required to use a wide range of materials and techniques to represent their ideas. Will use creative activities to learn about topics. Able to learn specific creative skills and follow instructions. Developed concentration span and manipulative skills.

Many creative activities can be adapted, with a little time and thought, but some children will have specific needs that make it hard for them to express themselves in an imaginative or creative way. In some cases, more concrete skills such as counting and number work may be age appropriate or even advanced. Children who find it hard to play imaginative games should be observed carefully and records should be kept, as a specific learning difficulty such as autism may be indicated.

Home corner and role play

In the earliest stages of development, children's imagination and creativity will be stimulated by what they see around them and their desire to imitate. The home corner is the natural progression for the child who has played with a tea set on the floor while still a toddler. From playing with a simple doll or teddy, the child will progress to playing with a doll with removable clothes, a bed, a name, and later a personality! Remember that both girls and boys may enjoy playing with dolls and teddies.

If there is space, it is an excellent idea to provide a home corner domestic setting with opportunities to cook, wash up, dress and care for dolls. If possible a changeable role play area could also be provided. Where this is not possible, regular changes will be necessary so that role play ideas will appeal to groups of children throughout the session.

Keys to good practice
Encouraging positive attitudes towards gender and culture

- Provide dressing-up clothes from a variety of cultures
- Ensure signs and notes are multi-cultural and non-stereotypical, e.g. if a maximum of four children are

allowed in the home corner 'fire station', you could draw a white male, a white female, a non-white male and a non-white female fire fighter
- Provide cooking and eating utensils from a variety of cultures (woks, chopsticks, etc.)
- Involve an adult in home corner play as a good role model for the children
- Back up the home corner with stories, posters and videos portraying images that break down gender and cultural stereotypes
- Encourage all children to role play in any situation, no matter how gender based it may seem to other adults
- Explain the purpose of the home corner before it is used and stress that it is there for all children to use
- Arrange visits from female fire fighters, male nurses, etc.
- Use empty packets from home to introduce ideas from different cultures
- Provide a role play area without walls to facilitate wheelchair access.

Puppets

Young children will probably first experience puppets at second hand when adults use them as an aid to songs and storytelling. They will later want to follow this example for their own self-expression. Children who are reluctant speakers may be happy to talk through a puppet. Children should have the opportunity to use puppets to:

- act out their own stories
- act out stories from a variety of cultures
- act out stories they are familiar with.

Offer older children the opportunity to make and use puppets.

Active knowledge

Plan an activity using puppets for a child who is unhappy about coming to nursery school for the first time. At the beginning of each session the child is reluctant to leave her mother and is very upset and withdrawn when she goes.

Small world play

From the age of three, children will begin to play with the type of toys that are referred to as 'small world' such as farm animals, railways, dolls' house, etc. These toys become the means of acting out scenarios, with some children electing to identify with one of the characters. In small world play it is possible to offer children the opportunity to talk through a variety of issues.

Playmobil people now come in a variety of skin tones, and Little Tikes have produced a doll's house with a realistic wheelchair and ramp.

Art (including tactile materials)

A young child who has the freedom to handle and explore paper, paint and glue will naturally progress towards self-expression through these and other tactile materials. A child who enters an early years setting at three years of age may be presented with such materials for the first time and may need to explore them at a basic level before moving on to more complex activities.

In the art area children can find many opportunities to express themselves. In a less formal setting, such as the home, many opportunities can still be provided.

Dressing up

Clothes for dressing up will probably be part of the home corner provision. Young children from about a year onwards enjoy wearing hats – at this age, dressing up clothes may be overwhelming but as children develop, handbags, shoes and clothes can be added. Children should be provided with clothes that are the right size to fit over their existing clothes. Provision of clothes such as saris and sarongs will introduce the children to clothes worn in other cultures. Children should be allowed to dress in any clothes they choose, as they are often role playing and exploring their own experiences and environment. As an early years worker you must beware of any teasing by other children and intervene when appropriate.

The clothes provided should have fastenings appropriate to the developmental stage of the children involved.

Drama

Drama is an opportunity for children to explore their imaginations, using their bodies to work independently or as part of a group. They can explore feelings, thoughts, stories, poems and other ideas. Drama is not concerned with performance and children should not be set up to fail by standards labelling actions as correct or incorrect. They should be given the security to develop the confidence necessary to share their thoughts and ideas.

Drama sessions can be used to:

- explore a variety of cultures
- explore cultural festivals and events
- explore familiar stories
- explore feelings
- develop ideas and communication skills.

Case study

Javinder was working with a small group of five-year-olds who had just started school. He led a drama session about feelings. The children were encouraged to move in different ways (angrily, sadly, etc.) and explored ways of showing their emotions through their faces, using music and props. At the end of the session the children played a circle game relating to feelings.

1   Why do you think the children might have enjoyed this session?
2   How did this activity develop their language skills?
3   What other aspects of the National Curriculum Key Stage 1 did this activity relate to?

Dance

Dance is another creative activity in which children can use their imaginations and bodies in a structured, or sometimes more free, environment.

Key issues ✓

Dance is discussed as a means of achieving desirable outcomes in both the Early Learning Goals and Key Stage 1 of the National Curriculum. It can be used to help children's development in all areas. Find out what these two curriculums say about dance.

If children are allowed to dance freely, they will often explore their feelings in the way they move. Cultural issues can also be addressed through dance. For example, the Chinese Dragon Dance is great fun, can involve all children and can be part of an exploration of the Chinese New Year.

Outside areas

A well-planned outside area can include any of the activities offered inside, but could provide additional activities such as those described in the spider diagram below.

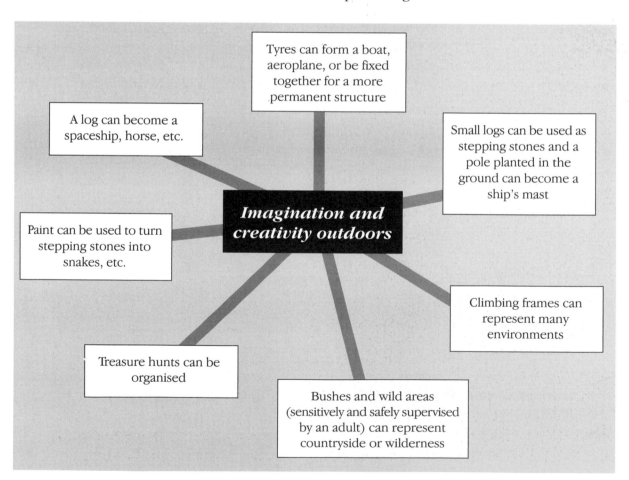

Tyres can form a boat, aeroplane, or be fixed together for a more permanent structure

A log can become a spaceship, horse, etc.

Small logs can be used as stepping stones and a pole planted in the ground can become a ship's mast

Paint can be used to turn stepping stones into snakes, etc.

Imagination and creativity outdoors

Climbing frames can represent many environments

Treasure hunts can be organised

Bushes and wild areas (sensitively and safely supervised by an adult) can represent countryside or wilderness

Music

Another vehicle for self-expression is music. You can encourage children to explore using their imaginations by providing a variety of music, using commercial and home-made instruments. Discuss with children the feelings expressed by different types of music.

Remember

A child with a hearing impairment will have difficulty with certain sounds. Knowledge of the specific nature of the impairment is needed to ensure that the child can participate as fully as possible.

How to use unplanned opportunities effectively

Children must be encouraged to make up their own scenarios and develop their imaginations. There is a worrying trend for children to role play only what they have observed on television, in video or in computer games. Often the type of play that this generates is unacceptable.

When children are making up their own games, the early years worker should provide the resources, information and language needed to extend play.

Climbing frames placed in the garden primarily as an aid to physical development can often become props to imaginative play.

Climbing frames are often used as props in imaginative play

Bikes and trailers become taxis, buses and lorries. Provision of a petrol pump, some road signs and a zebra crossing can greatly enhance the play. Children should also have access to writing materials for making tickets and to dressing up clothes associated with their game.

The sandpit will become a beach, a building site or a treasure island. By observing the children and how they play, workers should be able to provide the resources needed to extend the play.

When children are encouraged in **free art**, their ideas should be developed in the direction their imagination leads them. Early years workers should be prepared to provide opportunities to extend free art, allowing the handling of a variety of tools and materials. Children should also have the facility to mix their own colours and use a variety of paint. With supervision, children can be encouraged to mix their own paint. The more creative you are with the provision of tools and materials, the more scope you will give to the children to develop their imaginations.

Children enjoy bringing adults **items to show**. If a child brings in a music tape, instrument, puppet or toy it can often be used as a starting point for expressive activities. If a child tells of an experience he or she has been through, other children could be encouraged to recall their own experiences. Some of these experiences could be used as a starting point for creative drama.

How to minimise adult intervention

Whenever a new activity is put in place in the setting, an adult should introduce it to the children. An adult can play with the children in the home corner as a role model, but needs to be aware that children play differently when an adult is present – they will often play in the way they think the adult requires and not to their own rules. Much can be learned by observation of the children and how they play. The findings of these observations can be used to influence how an activity is approached next time.

When to intervene

In creative activities it is best if adults avoid intervening unless absolutely necessary. The occasions when it may be necessary to intervene are:

- if the play becomes dangerous
- if the play becomes aggressive
- if the play has gone completely off track
- if the children ask for help.

In children's art activities, adults should intervene

- to teach a new skill
- to moderate behaviour (flicking of paint, etc.)
- for health and safety (to provide aprons, or wipe up spillage on the floor)
- to extend the activity with fresh ideas.

How an adult can extend role play

In, for example, a role-play hairdresser's shop, the adult can ask for a haircut and:

- introduce the idea of an appointments book
- introduce new language
- introduce awareness of what happens in a hairdresser's
- talk about the use of money
- encourage the children to keep the hairdresser's tidy.

The adult should follow the children's lead some of the time.

Case study

Hannah, aged 4 years 11 months, loved to dance and sing. She would ask for music to be played and say 'Can we dance?' Many of the other children would join in. Hannah was very good at interpreting all kinds of music and was a great leader. There was no need for intervention.

How to encourage children's enjoyment and involvement in activities

How much children will enjoy an activity will depend to a certain extent on them, but can be influenced by the adults in the setting. Good planning, enthusiasm and time management can all help.

A full explanation of the function of a role-play area can help the children to enjoy it more. Some children may be reluctant to play in an area they do not understand, and will lose the opportunity to enjoy it. A child who understands how a role-play shop works is more likely to become fully involved in trying out the various aspects.

Observations by an adult, followed by intervention, can ensure that children who may be excluded from the play are included. A major distraction to role play is inappropriate behaviour by some children. Intervention by an adult can keep this to a minimum.

Children should be given a warning before the end of the session so that they have time to finish what they are doing. In some cases those who do not finish can be assured that they can come back at a later stage.

Stressing the process rather than the end product

For an adult a process is a means of reaching a desired outcome and frustration often results when pieces of creative work are not as they were planned to be.

For a child, the process is often more important than the product, and children will often be uninterested in the end result. It is important to avoid asking children what a creative product such as a painting is, but allow them to discuss the picture in their own words.

It is essential to avoid over-directing creative activity – children must always have control over the process.

Health and safety in creative activities

Your setting will have a health and safety policy. It is vital that you are aware of this when carrying out any creative activities. The early years worker will play an essential part in meeting the health and safety requirements of creative play activities and raising the children's awareness of health and safety issues.

When choosing creative materials check:

- can the item be swallowed?
- is the item too sharp or pointed?
- is the item poisonous?
- could the item irritate the skin or damage the eyes?
- can any other damage be caused?

All materials must be non-toxic and carry appropriate safety symbols. Small parts should not be used for children under three in case they swallow them. Seeds, beans and pulses can be dangerous or sometimes poisonous.

Surfaces and floors should be wipeable and stable. Protective coverings must be used when necessary.

Protective clothing is essential for some activities, and children should be provided with overalls to cover their arms and bodies. However, children will still get paint and glue on their clothes. You can help by providing washable materials and asking the parents not to put their children in 'best clothes'. Remember that some hair types will need to be covered when playing with sand, particularly when hair is plaited or oiled. Any parent may prefer a child's head to be covered during sand activities.

Facilities for washing and drying

When children are involved in messy activities, such as painting or clay, they will need to have close access to water, soap and paper towels. When doing messy activities outside, such as foot painting, it is easier to have bowls of water outside for the children to wash their feet.

Hand basins inside should be at the right level and children should be closely supervised if they are to use hot water. Sometimes they may have to be helped to clean the paint from their hands. It is important to remember that areas where soap and water are used should be carefully supervised to avoid floor surfaces becoming slippery.

Access and supervision

There must be plenty of space around each activity for freedom of movement for all children, and particularly for those who may have special needs, such as a child with cerebral palsy or a wheelchair user. Laying out the materials to indicate how many children can take part will help to prevent too many children from joining in at any one time. Numbers should be limited if close supervision is required. If you give children a choice of activities, others may be able to take a turn later in the session.

When the activity is closely supervised you will be able to:

- help children to use materials and equipment appropriately
- make sure they are safe
- support their creativity
- encourage the children to share experiences.

Remember that some activities and materials can be dangerous if not *very* closely supervised. For example:

- bubble blowing can lead to the swallowing of paint
- water play could carry a risk of drowning
- pen tops can cause choking (ensure that they are at least ventilated with a hole)
- ice can burn
- scissors can cut children if they are not correctly used.

Consolidation

Plan a creative play activity for a group of children in your care. You will need to consider:

- the developmental stage of the children
- the needs of the children
- the materials required
- health and safety issues
- adult support required
- equal opportunity issues.

Write notes for the activity, using these as headings.

C10 Unit test

1   What are the differences between short-term and long-term memory?
2   What are the four cognitive stages of learning as defined by Jean Piaget?
3   How can children develop the skills of recall and recognition?
4   How would you encourage a three-year-old child with hearing impairment to develop his or her language?

5 What are children expected to achieve in mathematics and science at the end of Key Stage 1 of the National Curriculum?

6 What is the role of the adult in encouraging creative play?

7 What would you take into account when planning a clay activity for a group of four-year-olds?

8 Explain the following terms with regard to children's attention span and memory:
- receptive
- productive
- recall
- recognition.

9 Why is matching an important mathematical skill?

10 Explain how a jigsaw puzzle could extend a three-year-old's concentration span.

Unit C11

Promote children's language and communication development

This unit will help you promote children's language and communication development. Language and communication are important life skills.

The elements for this unit are:

C11.1   Identify stages of children's language and communication development

C11.2   Provide activities, equipment and materials to extend and reinforce children's language and communication development

C11.3   Share books, stories and rhymes to expand children's language and communication development

C11.4   Provide communication opportunities to enhance and reinforce children's language and communication development

C11.5   Interact with children to promote their language and communication development

Element C11.1   Identify stages of children's language and communication development

WHAT YOU NEED TO LEARN

- Building up a picture of children's language and communication skills
- Monitoring children's language and communication development
- Factors affecting children's language and communication development
- Passing on concerns about children's language and communication development
- Encouraging and supporting children's home language

Building up a picture of children's language and communication skills

How language is used

The desire to communicate starts at birth. Babies learn quickly how to get their needs met by cooing, crying and making eye contact with their primary carers.

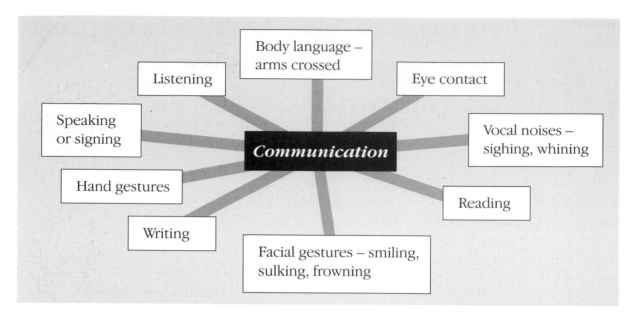

As children get older they become more skilled in communicating – they learn to use facial and hand gestures, ways of responding to others, as well as spoken or sign languages. The spider diagram above shows that communication is more than just language.

By the age of four, children will use many types of communication to show the carer that they want a toy or treat. Later on, at around the age of six or seven, children also learn to use reading and writing as a way of communicating.

Learning to communicate with others is a gradual process. It is interesting to note that babies from around the world appear to learn to communicate and use language in similar ways.

The link between language and other areas of children's development

Language and the ability to communicate can radically affect nearly all areas of a child's development, with perhaps the exception of physical development.

There is a strong link between children's intellectual development (their ability to reason, think and remember) and their language skills. Most child development theorists such as Piaget, Bruner and Vygotsky have come to the conclusion that language is intertwined with intellectual reasoning and learning.

Cognitive development

Language is considered to be the main tool by which we are able to develop our thought processes. Words are often the tool by which we store information. For example, a simple word such as 'snow' may well trigger off a visual memory. Many of us also use words mentally to direct ourselves, for example 'I will make a cup of tea and then I will start looking for that piece of paper'.

In practical terms, this means that children who do not have expressive vocabularies or whose communication skills are impaired may also have difficulties in acquiring concepts and reasoning skills.

Social development

Being able to use a language allows children to express themselves and communicate in a variety of ways and because of this, there is a strong link between children's social skills and their language skills.

Look at the ways shown opposite in which children might often use language.

The need for language and communication skills in everyday life means that in practice, where children have some language delay or communication difficulty, their social development may be affected.

'It's mine'

'I'm a cat and you can be the baby'.

'Can I have a turn now?'

'What's a brolly?'

Case study

Robert was the youngest child in a family of four children. The older children in the family tended to 'baby' him and he quickly learnt to get things simply by pointing at them and making one-word sounds such as 'want'. At three years he had very few words, although his family could understand his needs simply by the expressions he was using. When he started at playgroup, he was very withdrawn and found it hard to cope with play activities that involved language. He spent a lot of time playing in a solitary way, often in the sandpit. The early years workers developed a programme of activities to encourage him to develop his language skills. These included games such as lotto and small group activities such as cooking and gardening.

Why might Robert's family not recognise that his language skills were failing to develop?

Why is it important for early years workers actively to plan activities that encourage language?

Emotional development

Children gradually learn to control their strong feelings, but as a part of this process they need to be able to communicate their feelings and needs to others. A child may tell an adult that he or she is feeling sad because the pet hamster has died, but a child who has no language may simply cry uncontrollably. Being able to use a language also allows children to become independent. They may be able to ask for objects, question a decision or put forward their own ideas. This in turn allows children to become self-reliant and confident.

In practical terms, if you work with children who have limited language and communication skills, you may find that they tend to show more demanding behaviour because they are not able to channel their emotions and needs into words.

Building up a picture of language development

It is important to understand that although most children vary in their rate of development, there seems to be a pattern to the way children learn language and communication skills.

Linguists, who study the language and the way in which we acquire language, have come to the conclusion that children pass through two distinct phases:

- **Pre-linguistic phase.** During this phase, which normally takes the first 12 months, babies seem to learn some of the basic skills of communication. They learn to attract adults, hold eye contact and respond to an adult's facial expressions. In this stage, they seem also to absorb and rehearse some of the sounds of the language they are hearing. It is interesting to note that this pre-linguistic stage seems to be a feature of learning any language. Towards the end of this stage, children are able to understand that words have meaning, with some linguists suggesting that babies of 13 months may have a receptive vocabulary of around 50 words.
- **Linguistic stage.** During this second phase, babies start to use words and eventually learn how to make sentences and use grammar. The language that a child uses is known as 'expressive language'. The second phase is a gradual one, but by the age of five most children are able to use a language fluently.

In order to build up a picture of a child's language development, it is useful to look at the stages of such development. As with any chart showing children's development, the stages and ages should be used only as guides. Some children may be using complex sentences at an early age, while other children do so at a much later age.

Pre-linguistic stage	0–3 months	Cries to show hunger, tiredness and distress Recognises different tones of voices Coos and gurgles when content By three months can recognise carer's voice and is soothed Smiles in response to others' faces
	3–6 months	Still cries to show distress, but is more easily soothed Babbles and coos Babbles consist of short sounds – 'ma ma, da da' Laughs, chuckles and even squeals
	6–12 months	Babbling makes up half of a baby's non-crying sounds Strings vowels and consonants together to make repetitive sounds – 'mememememe, dadadadadada' Babbling becomes more tuneful and inventive and by nine months most of the sounds used are the ones needed for the language being learnt At ten months understands about 17 words such as 'bye bye' Uses gestures to ask for things – points hand and whines to show adult what he or she wants Enjoys games such as pat-a-cake
Linguistic stage	12–18 months	First words appear at around 12 months, although will only be recognisable as a word to carer, for example, 'dede', to mean drink Words are used to mean more than one thing depending on the intonation the baby uses, for example 'dede' used to mean I want a drink, my drink is finished or I want more drink Linguists call these one-word expressions holophrases By 15 months will have about ten words that carers can understand

	18–24 months	Puts two words together, for example 'bye-bye dog' Telegraphic speech appears – uses key words in a grammatical way, for example 'dada come' Vocabulary increases – learns 10–30 words in a month! By two years, most children have 200 words
	2–3 years	New words are quickly learnt Uses plurals, for example dogs Makes errors such as 'sheeps' 'drawed' Starts to use negatives such as 'There no cats' Begins to use questions 'Where cats?'
	3–4 years	Imitates adult speech patterns accurately, for example 'We liked that, didn't we?' Speech is understood by strangers Sentences contain four or more words and are grammatical Vocabulary is large – knows part of the body, names of household objects, animals Errors are still made, especially when using past tenses, for example 'I taked it' Knows and understands nursery rhymes Enjoys asking questions
	4–8 years	From four years, language is developed and refined Mistakes become fewer – starts to enjoy using language as a means of socialising with others, expressing needs and recounting what he or she has done. By five years vocabulary is about 5000 words Uses complex sentences correctly Enjoys telling and hearing jokes Understand that language can be written with symbols By eight years most children are fluent speakers, readers and developing writers of their language

Theories of language development

Psychologists continue to debate whether we are born with skills and abilities or whether we develop them because of our environment. This is often referred to as the nature versus nurture debate. There are several theories of how babies and children acquire language – some are based on the idea that learning a language is an instinct and others that children learn to communicate because they are being exposed to language.

Language is learnt through imitation

Early theories of language were based on the idea that children learn to speak because they repeat language that they hear. B. Skinner, who is also famous for his ideas of how we learn behaviour, believed that adults around a baby would praise or react positively when a baby made sounds that were recognisable and thus the baby would repeat them to gain their attention and approval. This would explain why although babies across the world all start by making similar sounds, by nine months their babbling tends to consist only of the sounds they are listening to.

The theory that language is learnt because children learn through imitation does not explain why children make sentences and words that they have not heard, such as 'daddygone'.

Learning language is instinctive

Noam Chomsky came to the conclusion that the ability to learn a language was in some ways instinctive and that we are born with a cognitive ability to learn a language. Learning a language is more than just learning strings of words. A language has a structure and rules (grammar). Learning the rules of a language is a complex task and this led Chomsky to believe that we are born with some capacity to understand the grammar of languages we are exposed to when young. He called this cognitive structure a 'Language Acquisition Device'.

Chomsky's theory is interesting as it explains how children are able to work out for themselves the rules of grammar without ever being taught them. For example, children quickly learn that 'the dog bit the duck' has a completely different meaning from 'the duck bit the dog', even though the words in the sentence are the same. It also explains why children make mistakes that they would not have heard from adults around them, such as 'I drinked it all'. These types of mistake demonstrate that children have worked out some of the rules of grammar and are trying to use them – in this example, that many past tenses end with 'ed'.

Monitoring children's language and communication development

In order to help children further their language development, some assessment of their language and communication skills is needed. There are many ways of collecting this information, and it is often a good idea to use several methods in order to build up a more accurate picture. Carrying out observations and recordings will enable you to monitor a child's progress.

Ways of gaining information about children's communication skills

Event samples

Event samples (see Unit C16 page 247). can be used to determine the number of interactions children make during a session. When carrying out an event sample, try and record as accurately as possible what the child is saying. If the child's engaged in an activity where this is not possible, try and record the frequency with which hc or she is using language.

The aim of the event sample below was to record the language interaction between three-year-old Curran (C) and the adults (A) in the setting. Concerns had been expressed previously that Curran seemed to be 'shy' with adults.

Event	Time	Situation	Social group	Dialogue
1	9.16 am	Curran is hovering near the painting table	Susan + 2 children	A–C 'Do you want to come and paint a picture too?' C–A nods head
2	9.27 am	Curran is finishing painting	Susan + 2 children	A–C 'Have you finished?' C smiles 'It's a lovely picture. Tell me a little bit about it.' C–A 'It's my mum. Can't take my apron off.' A–C 'Stay still, I'll do it.' Curran hands apron to Susan and runs over to sand area

Event	Time	Situation	Social group	Dialogue
3	10.12 am	Curran is waiting for his drink at snack time	Curran is sitting next to Ahmed. Jo is handing out drinks	A–C 'Milk or squash, Curran?' C–A 'Milk.' A–C 'Can you remember the magic word?' C–A 'Thank you.' A–C 'Good boy.'
4	10.19 am	Curran is putting on his coat in the cloakroom area	Jo + 5 children	C–A 'Can't put coat on.' A–C 'Keep still. There you are. You can go out now.'
5	10.36 am	Curran is waiting for his turn by the slide	Jo + 2 children	A–C 'Good boy. It's your go now.' C smiles. C–A 'I go fast down now.'

Taped observations

Taped observations can help us to listen to children so enabling us to build up a picture of the way in which they are using language. Taped observations have the advantage that you can rewind them and listen to them again. From a taped observation, we can hear the intonation of a child's voice and the richness of vocabulary. As with any other observation, it is a good idea to carry out several recordings so that children are observed in a variety of situations. Try to put the tape recorder as near to the children as possible, but make sure that it is unobtrusive. It is a good idea to write the names of the children on the side of the tape as well as the date, time and activity that the children were engaged in.

Parents as sources of information

Parents are often able to give us information about their child's language and communication skills as they see their child in a variety of different situations. The information that parents are able to provide can be very useful because some children can be quiet in a setting, yet be vocal and boisterous in their own homes! Some settings produce their own checklist or questionnaire as a starting point to use with parents. By working with parents in this way, early years workers are able to identify any potential needs that children might have or areas that may need developing. Any information that parents provide must always be considered as confidential.

It is generally considered good practice for parents to see/hear any assessments that have been carried out. This allows settings and parents to monitor children's progress more effectively.

Case study

An early years worker noticed that James, who was nearly four years old, seemed to be very interested in the book area. He asked James's mother if she had noticed that he was interested in books at home. She said that he had started to sit for long periods looking at his favourite book. The early years worker asked James's mother if she would like to bring in the book next time so that he could share it with James and perhaps use it as a starting point for some pre-reading activities.

Why was it important to involve James' mother?

Suggest ways of working with James' favourite book.

Factors affecting children's language and communication development

There are many factors which might affect children's language and communication development. These are shown below. It is important for early years workers to have some knowledge of them so that they will be able to identify them should they be evident in the children with whom they are working. Most speech therapists who help children with language difficulties find that early detection and support can limit the extent of the language delay or impairment.

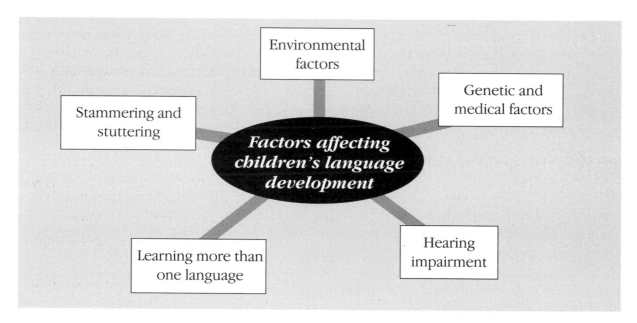

Hearing impairment

Many children during their early years will suffer some type of hearing loss. For most children this hearing loss will be temporary, and this is common when children have had a cold as fluid builds up inside the ear. Some children who frequently have colds or who often have a build-up of fluid may be fitted with a 'grommet' which drains the fluid.

Detecting a hearing impairment

Hearing tests are carried out routinely on babies at around eight months by health professionals. Common signs that babies and very young children are not hearing fully include being difficult to soothe, not making babbling and vocal noises and generally being less smily and alert. Slight hearing impairments in older children are harder to detect, especially when the hearing loss is temporary. Children are still hearing, but the sounds may be muffled, which means they may hear in some situations but not in others. It is easy for parents and early years workers, therefore, to attribute the symptoms of hearing loss to a child's personality – 'He never comes when I call him' or 'she is a bit of a loner and never follows instructions'.

Keys to good practice
Checking for a hearing impairment

- Does the child appear to study a speaker's face intently?
- Is the child withdrawn or appearing to be in his or her own world?
- Is the child's speech muffled or very unclear?
- Does the child mispronounce common words using similar sounds?
- Is the child uninterested in watching television or listening to story tapes?
- Does the child appear to lack concentration in group activities such as story time?
- Does the child find it difficult to follow simple instructions?

Stammering and stuttering

Many children develop a stammer or a stutter when they first start speaking, mainly because their brains are working more quickly than their tongues! This results in them falling over their words. It is important that parents and adults are able to reassure children when this happens and show that they are listening. Interrupting a child or allowing other children to join in may mean that next time the child wants to say something, he or she tries to say it even faster – resulting once again in a stammer.

Genetic and medical factors

Some children may have difficulty in communicating because they have a genetic or medical condition. Children with cleft palate may have difficulties in pronunciation, whereas other children may have a learning difficulty that means they do not seem to be interested in communicating, for example autistic children. Where children are unable to use the spoken language to communicate, they may be taught sign language.

The two common sign languages are Makaton and British Sign Language. If you are working with children who have a language or communication difficulty, you may wish to take a course in one of these languages. It is useful for all early years workers to know some signs.

Environmental factors

There are many environmental factors that may cause children to have language and communication difficulties, as follows.

- Shy children – some children may find it harder to use language in large settings. They may be unsure of talking in front of others, or they may not feel relaxed enough to speak to unfamiliar adults.
- Limited previous language experience – not all children are fortunate enough to be in language-rich environments where adults around them have time to talk and interact with them. This means that some children's language can be delayed because they have not had enough language opportunities.

- Younger children in families – some younger children may be 'babied' by older siblings and parents. This means that their needs are met even if they do not use complete phases. A three-year-old may be able to get his or her needs met simply by using 'holophrases' (one word accompanied by a gesture). As the baby of the family expectations are lowered!

Passing on concerns about children's language and communication development

There are many reasons why children may have language or communication difficulties. It is important that if you suspect a child has some form of language delay or communication difficulty, you pass on your concerns. If you are the key worker or the supervisor, you will need to talk to

If this child constantly has his needs met simply by pointing at objects, his language may not develop

the parents who in turn may be referred via their family doctor to a speech therapist or physchologist. In situations where you do not have overall responsibility for liaising with parents, you should talk to your supervisor about your concerns. It is reassuring for parents to know that most children with minor speech or language problems are able to make rapid progress once they have had specialist help.

Encouraging and supporting children's home language

Learning more than one language

Britain is a culturally diverse society and this means that many children learn more than one language. Being able to use another language is known as being **bilingual**. Someone who can use several languages is said to be **multilingual**.

It is worth remembering that children who are able to use sign language as well as a spoken language are, in effect, bilingual. This often happens where deaf parents have a hearing child – the child learns to use signs as well as spoken language.

Understanding the context in which children may learn more than one language

If you are working with children who have more than one language, it is important to understand the context in which they are learning another language. For example, a child who is learning Spanish from her mother will have different language needs from a child who is hearing only Greek from his parents and grandparents.

Understanding the development of children with more than one language

Children who are learning more than one language may be slightly slower at starting to talk and communicate, probably because they are trying to absorb more than one language system. The delay does not necessarily affect children's overall language development, provided they are given enough support.

Where children are exposed to a second language later on, they will have more success in mastering it if their first language is well-established and secure.

Helping children with more than one language

It is important to understand that young children learn languages by absorption in a natural way. Most young children may not even realise that they are able to use a second language, as they are just using the method of communication that the people around them are using. Difficulties can arise where children confuse language – mixing sentences and words. This usually happens when people around them are moving in and out of languages. This can result in the child not learning to separate languages.

The generally accepted principle for children learning more than one language is that people talking to them should always use the same language. By doing this, children automatically recognise which language is appropriate in the situation. This means that if you speak to the child in English, you should always use English with him or her.

Being aware of gaps in vocabulary

Children who have more than one language will often have some areas of vocabulary missing. For example, a child may not be able to explain to his or her father that the children have played in the sand, if he or she does not know the word 'sand' in the home language. We can help children bridge these gaps in their vocabulary by providing activities such as making a lotto game that has pictures of household items. We can also ask parents if they wish to come into the setting to see for themselves the types of activities in which the children participate.

Celebrating cultural diversity

There is a strong link between children's self-esteem and their achievement if they have more than one language. It is important for children to feel the language they speak at home is valued. By valuing a child's language we are also showing that we value the child as our language is an essential part of us!

Showing children that we value and are interested in their home language has to be handled sensitively. It is important that children are not made to feel like circus performers – asking a child how he or she says 'goodbye' in the language in front of others may make the child feel uncomfortable. A better approach is to realise that by celebrating cultural diversity, we will at the same time be demonstrating that different languages are valued. This may mean having a range of resources that teach all children that there are many different lifestyles, religions and languages.

As an early years worker, you must also be sensitive to children's regional and local accents. It is generally accepted that although children need to hear and be able to use 'standard' English, accents are part of our cultural heritage.

Element C11.2 — Provide activities, equipment and materials to extend and reinforce children's language and communication development

WHAT YOU NEED TO LEARN

- Planning activities to encourage language development
- The role of the adult in promoting language development through activities
- Activities to encourage language development
- Activities that help children to listen
- The role of core activities in promoting language development

Planning activities to encourage language development

We have seen that children need to be able to use language and communication in a variety of ways. In order to learn different language skills, it is important for children to experience a variety of situations when language is used. Early years workers can help children by organising and planning a range of activities and materials that will encourage children to use language.

The spider diagram on the next page shows the factors that need to be taken into consideration when planning activities.

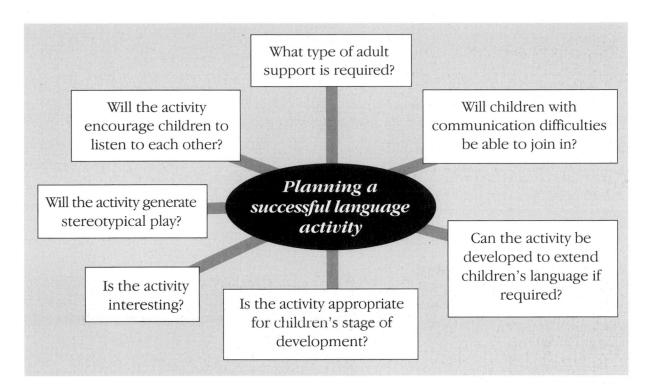

Checking the appropriateness of the activity

It is important to be sure that an activity is suitable for the age and stage of the children you are working with. Planning activities that are too difficult generally end in failure with children becoming frustrated. For example, a game such as picture lotto, which is excellent for helping children to listen to each other and take turns, will not be successful if children have not yet reached the stage of development when they can sit down and concentrate!

The role of the adult in promoting language development through activities

Understanding the type of adult support required

Many activities with young children require some adult input and support, although how much will vary according to the age of children and the activity. Board games with children under four years will require a constant adult presence, whereas an activity where children take part in role play may need less supervision and support. If you are responsible for planning a day's programme, you will need to look carefully at the types of activities and equipment you are putting out to make sure that sufficient adult support will be provided. Adults are needed in the following ways to support activities.

- **Leading an activity.** Some activities will need an adult to lead them and explain what is happening to children. These types of activities are usually the more structured ones, although adults leading them should ensure that children are given plenty of opportunities to ask questions, talk and be active. With older children, adults should be aiming for children to develop such language skills as prediction and description by asking questions and inviting comments such as – 'Why do you think that this has changed colour?'

You should also aim to introduce new and relevant vocabulary during structured activities, for example 'This type of flour is called wholemeal', while making sure that children can follow and understand any explanations.

- **Explaining what to do.** Some activities such as board games or drawing with pastels may require some adult explanation at the start. Even older children who are able to read do not always understand written rules, and adults may be needed to start off a game or an activity. It is important that children are able to understand what they need to do and that the explanation is clear. When introducing a new game or piece of equipment, it is often a good idea to link an explanation with a demonstration, such as 'If it is my turn, I take a card from here and put it over there'. Once children are comfortable with an activity, it is sometimes useful to step back slightly to allow them to take control of the activity, although you should still be available to step in. This, of course, will depend on the age of the children and the type of activity they are doing.

- **Supervising and assisting.**
Activities such as role play, painting and modelling, which provide excellent language opportunities for children, also require adult support and assistance. Children will need adult help if they are having difficulties with equipment, for example if they cannot get a helmet to stay on or if they are finding it hard to share equipment. These types of activities are good for children because often they are a way for children to communicate and listen to each other. An adult presence is essential during these types of activities, but you should see yourself as a facilitator rather than a

For some activities, children require adult support and assistance

leader, allowing children to practice existing language skills. There are times when you may decide to become more active, for example if children have come to a standstill in their game and need an injection of ideas or equipment, or if they are making discriminatory remarks.

- **Adapting activities for children with particular language needs.** Sometimes adults will be needed to adapt activities to allow children with particular language needs to join in. This may mean making a new set of lotto cards to make sure that a child with a different home language may learn some particular new words or joining in with a group of children to play alongside the child who needs more support.

Activities to encourage language development

Choosing activities with potential

Some activities have more learning potential than others. It is important if you are working in a setting with mixed ages or with children who have very different needs that activities are carefully chosen to allow all the children to develop and extend their language. For example, a cutting and sticking activity with a range of different fabrics, pasta, threads and ribbons might help children to learn new words.

This is an example of an activity with plenty of potential – children can talk about what they are seeing, draw the insects and look them up in books

Activities that help children to listen

Part of being able to communicate effectively is to learn to listen to others. Learning this skill is a gradual process, and although there are many activities that can help, it is important to realise that very young children will not be at the stage of development where they can sit and listen to others. This is linked to their cognitive and social development – children under two years old are mostly playing in parallel and it is not until they are around three years of age that they will be able to start playing cooperatively. Children also need to develop concentration skills in order to listen to others, as young children are generally happier when they are being active – a child will concentrate if he or she is involved in a dialogue, but will find it harder if he or she is not. This means that when we plan activities that require children to listen and take turns, we must be sensitive to their stage of development.

The chart on the next page shows some activities that can help children to listen:

Activity	Age range	How to do the activity	Aim of activity
Echo the pattern	4–8 years	An adult or child claps a simple pattern. The other children have to echo it back.	This game encourages children to listen and to work as a group. It develops children's audio discrimination skills.
I went to the shop and bought	4–8 years	One child starts 'I went to the shop and bought a...'., the next child has to say the same thing and add one item of his or her own.	This game helps children listen to each other and develops memory skills.
Feely bag	4–6 years	Children are shown a group of objects. One object is put into a feely bag and a child has to describe to the others what he or she can feel so that they can guess it.	This game develops children's listening skills and their memory. It also helps children's descriptive vocabulary.
Nursery rhyme stop and go game	3–6 years	An adult starts saying or singing a nursery rhyme and the children join in. The adult suddenly stops and the children have to try and stop as well.	This game is fun and allows children to learn their nursery rhymes. It also makes them listen and concentrate.
The lion hunt	3–6 years	The adult leads a 'lion hunt' and the children repeat back the phrases for example, 'Do you want to go on a lion hunt?' 'Do you want to go on a lion hunt?' 'Yes', 'Yes', 'All right off we go....' etc.	A fun activity in which the adult leads the children in search of the lion, using phrases and actions that are repeated back.
Simon says	3–8 years	The adult asks children to carry out a simple action, for example 'Touch your nose'. Children only do the action if 'Simon says', i.e. 'Simon says touch your nose'.	Children learn to listen carefully to what is being said.

The role of core activities in promoting language development

There are some activities and equipment that are found in nearly all early years settings. These are:

- dressing-up and imaginative play areas
- sand
- water
- painting and drawing.

These may be thought of as 'core activities' because they tend to be used or made available to children on a regular basis and are very versatile. This section looks at how these activities can develop children's language.

Dressing-up and imaginative play

From around the age of two years, children enjoy dressing up and taking on roles. Imaginative play, which can also be referred to as **role play**, allows children to create for themselves their own worlds. Dressing-up clothes and other props such as saucepans, tools and furniture enhance this type of play. A good selection of props allows children to explore a variety of different situations and can help them to extend their vocabulary. There are many language benefits to this type of play. Children tend to be very free in their language and talk both to other children and to themselves. It is often thought that role play is a tool by which children practise language that they have heard and also explore the meanings of events that they have seen.

It is good practice to vary the props and even the theme of the dramatic play area so as to encourage children to take on different roles and thereby use a more varied vocabulary.

Dressing up allows children to create their own world

Sand and water

Active knowledge ✓

How is the dramatic play area of your setting organised?

How active are the early years workers in supporting this type of play?

These natural materials can help children's language development if adults are alongside children. Equipment can be put out that particularly encourages children to use language skills such as prediction and description, such as 'The water is bubbling out'. Early years workers can work alongside children and use a range of questions to help children acquire concepts such as floating, volume and capacity, for example 'How many eggcupfuls will I need to fill up this jar?'

Painting and drawing

These activities are the starting point for children to learn what written symbols can convey meaning. Most children are starting to enjoy making marks from around the age of 18 months. At around three years, children start to talk as they draw and comment on what they are doing. It seems as if they are drawing symbols to represent their thoughts. This self-direction gradually disappears as children are able to 'think inside their heads'! Early drawings develop children's fine manipulative skills, which are then needed when they start to write.

The role of the early years worker

Children enjoy mark making and should be given a range of materials to use. Adults can listen to children as they record and use their drawing as a starting point for discussion. Older children can record what they have seen using drawings. Drawings and paintings can be put together into a book for children to talk about.

Observation

Observe a child or small group of children engaged in role play for four to five minutes, either by writing some notes or by taping them.

How are the children using language?

Are children 'rehearsing' adult terms and expressions?

Are the children using props or equipment to help them in their play?

Element C11.3 Share books, stories and rhymes to expand children's language and communication development

WHAT YOU NEED TO LEARN

- The importance of using books and rhymes with children
- Using books to promote an awareness of equal opportunities
- Managing story time
- Helping children to choose their own books
- Making books with children

The importance of using books and rhymes with children

One of the many aims of early years settings should be to encourage children to enjoy looking at and exploring books. An early love of books can help children later as they start to learn to read. The process of sharing books can begin with babies. Babies of six months will start to be interested in pictures and by the age of one year will start to recognise pictures. By about four years, children are handling books confidently and are often able to tell a story from pictures. By seven years, most children have mastered the basics of reading and are starting to become independent readers.

Current thinking on early reading and writing

This is an area of some debate. Most European countries delay teaching the formal skills of reading and writing until children are around six to seven years old. This approach tends to fit in with the theories of cognitive development put forward by Piaget and Bruner. In the UK there has been a move to start concentrating on these skills at a younger age, which has come more from successive governments than from workers in early years. The aim of this is to improve the literacy skills of children by starting children's reading earlier.

Research your setting's approach to reading and writing.

Find out more about the literacy and numeracy hour being used in Key Stage 1.

Types of books available

There is a vast range of books available, from picture books through to factual books. Wherever possible you should try to give children the opportunity to hear and see different styles of books so that they can develop their own tastes and preferences. The variety of books also means that children's vocabulary can be developed, for example factual books might extend a child's knowledge and vocabulary in a specific area.

Picture books

Most pre-school settings have a selection of picture books. Young children need books that have good illustrations so that they can use the books as cues either to remember the storyline or make up their own. Some picture books are designed to be read to children, while others can help children when they first start reading.

Pop-up books

Children enjoy pop-up books because they add in an element of surprise and fun. These books are often more expensive than other types of books, but are usually very popular with children of all ages. Wear and tear on these books has to be expected as they tend to be heavily handled.

Big books

These are very large books that can be used at story time so that all children can see both words and illustrations easily. They are particularly helpful for children who have visual impairments. The main disadvantage with these books are that children find it difficult to handle these books alone. To solve this problem, most settings tend to buy a smaller version of the book as well.

Nursery rhyme and counting books

Most settings have a selection of nursery rhyme and counting books. These are often popular with children because they can recognise the rhyme from looking at the picture.

Joke books

Older children enjoy books that are humorous, and joke books are particularly popular with 6–8 year olds.

Factual books

A good range of factual books is essential in settings to support themes and to give children an opportunity to discuss and learn about the world around them. As children get older, some prefer reading factual books.

Understanding the benefits of story time

Most settings plan a story time into their routine. This is often at the end of a session or at the start of a related activity. In home settings, this may be during a quiet time in the day or just before bedtime. Story time may consist of a short story and some rhymes or simply a story. The benefits of these sessions are wide ranging. The chart below shows the main benefits of story time.

Story time can have many benefits for children

Language benefits	Children learn new vocabulary in a context. Children may learn that letters are used to create words. Children learn how books work, for example which way they open. Story time creates opportunities for discussion and questions.
Emotional benefits	Some stories may encourage children to talk about their feelings. Story time may be part of a routine which is relaxing and enjoyable for children.
Cognitive benefits	Stories may feed children's imaginations. Knowledge may be gained from hearing a story or looking at a book.
Social benefits	Story time is often a social time when children can feel part of a group. Rhymes and songs make children feel united and give them a sense of belonging.
Physical benefits	Story time allows children to rest and relax. These moments are important to prevent young children from becoming overtired.

Using books to promote an awareness of equal opportunities

Books provide an important vehicle for promoting an awareness of equal opportunities. Stories can show strong and positive images of children and adults from a range of cultures. Sometimes the visual images are just as important as the plot to counteract stereotypes.

Children, through experiencing a range of good quality books, can learn that other people may live differently from them. Books that attempt to show a range of lifestyles should be carefully chosen. It is important that there are no hidden messages that may suggest that one lifestyle, religion or custom is superior to another.

The importance of showing children positive images is also discussed in Unit C5.

It is also worth having an alternative book to hand or ideas for some rhymes so that if the story is not appealing to the children, you can swiftly move to something else.

Managing story time

As with many other activities in early years settings, preparation is often the key to success. It is always advisable to read through a story first to get an idea of its length and to see if there are any possible difficulties. For example, you may decide not to use a story involving a fox, if a child's rabbit has recently been killed by one! Familiarity with the book will allow you to adapt it to your audience and will also allow you to show illustrations while you are reading.

In some settings, children may gradually come and sit down at story time, while in others children may all be seated before the story starts. It is important to make sure that all the children are comfortable and can see you so that they can enjoy the session. If you are waiting for children to join you, it is worth starting off the session with some rhymes or finger plays so that children who are waiting do not get bored.

Once all the children are ready, it is a good idea to introduce the book to them and then quickly start off. Maintaining a good pace is important, especially during the first few pages, so that children become involved with the story. Where possible, show children the illustrations while reading to them, and if you are using a book with large text, try also to point to the words as you are reading them.

Involving the children during the story

How much you involve the children during the story will depend on their age and the group size. When you are working with a large group, it is important to keep the interest of all the children and this may mean that you choose to use closed questions which will allow all the children to reply at once, for example 'Do you think that he is happy now?'.

Questions that can be answered by only one child at a time are useful in smaller groups, but it is important that other children do not lose interest in the story. At the end of the story, time should be allowed for some discussion. This discussion can be used to check that children have understood any words or ideas that have come up in the story such as 'What do you think his mother meant when she said "You foolish boy"?', or it might be used so that children can talk about their own experiences.

It is also a good idea to re-read a story that has a repetitive element. This allows children to join in with the words and gives them great pleasure. Many groups of children develop favourite books which they enjoy reading along with the adult. Using big books can allow children to follow the story and look at the words while it is being read. This helps them to understand that each group of letters makes a word.

Managing children's behaviour during story time

It is easy to forget that story time involves asking quite young children to sit still and silently for ten or so minutes. For some children keeping still and quiet during a story session is too demanding. They hear something that triggers off such a powerful thought that they have to shout it out loud, while other children cannot keep their hands still and touch others around them.

There are several approaches to managing children's behaviour during story time, depending on the setting and children you are working with. They include:

- ignoring the behaviour – you may sometimes decide that the behaviour or comments will cease of their own accord once the child becomes more involved with the session
- reminding the child that he or she should be quiet – you may just say the child's name to attract his or her attention and then put your fingers to your lips to remind the child that he or she should be quiet
- moving children – you may, while carrying on reading, stand up and take the hand of the child to move him or her nearer to you or away from the source of the problem.

Whatever the approach used, you should always aim to keep the story session pleasurable for all of the children. Story time is one of the first steps that is needed in order for children to want to learn to read. Being constantly in trouble during story sessions may prevent children from being interested in books.

Keys to good practice
When choosing a book

- Are the illustrations large enough for the group of children to see?
- How long will the story take to read?
- Will the children be able to follow the plot?

Helping children to choose their own books

Learning to choose a book is a skill. Children gradually develop preferences for certain types of books, but it is useful if the confidence and skills required are encouraged early on. Spending time with children who are enjoying browsing and looking at books is very valuable. They gain from the one-to-one attention and learn that books can be pleasurable. Sometimes children may choose books that are unsuitable for their stage of development. Providing that they are happy with their choice and are able to change their mind later if needed, it is best not to interfere. Learning for oneself that some books are more interesting than others is part of becoming a reader!

It is quite common for children to develop favourite books. Children who are reading should never be prevented from re-reading a book they have already read. Re-visiting a book allows readers to gain confidence in their reading and thus enjoyment. Children who are not reading will often gain by looking at their favourite book because they will gradually start to recognise shapes of words or pictures.

Making books with children

Children enjoy having home-made books to look at. Toddlers can have a plastic photo album that contains photos of people and objects that they can recognise, while groups of older children can work together to tell a story in pictures. Making books with individuals or groups of children helps them to understand how books are used. Home-made books can also be used to help with pre-reading and writing skills. Children can draw a picture which is then labelled by the adult using the child's language. This means that they can associate words with what has been written down.

In group settings, books can be made to help children record a theme or topic, for example photos can be taken of children during an activity such as going out on a trip. The book can then be shared with the whole group or looked at by individuals.

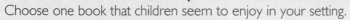

Active knowledge ✓

Choose one book that children seem to enjoy in your setting.

Consider why this book appeals to the children.

Is this book suitable to read aloud to a group of children?

Element C11.4   Provide communication opportunities to enhance and reinforce children's language and communication development

WHAT YOU NEED TO LEARN

- Ways of creating everyday language opportunities
- Helping children communicate
- Correcting children's pronunciation and grammar
- Extending children's vocabulary
- Using questions to develop children's language

Ways of creating everyday language opportunities

Understanding the importance of providing a language-rich environment

Early years workers have an important responsibility for the development of children's language. On page 178 we looked at the ways in which language affects children's other developmental areas. There is also a strong link between children's achievement and behaviour in schools and their language and communication skills. Early years workers need to make sure that children are provided with a rich language environment. The spider diagram on the next page shows the ways in which a child's language must be developed.

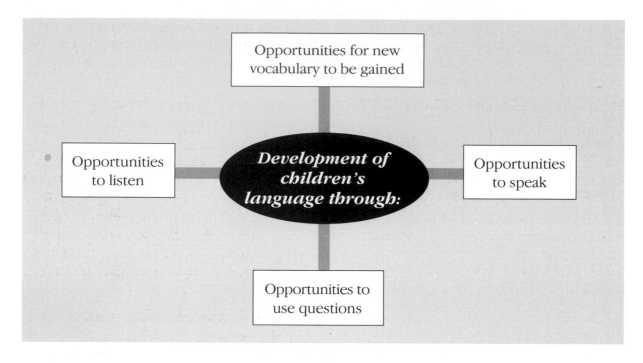

Using everyday opportunities to develop language

There are plenty of opportunities in everyday activities for children's language to be developed, for example during meal times, while waiting for others to join in an activity or on the way to the supermarket. Promoting children's language should not be viewed as happening only during 'planned activities'. Some children can actually feel more relaxed and speak more during an everyday routine event, perhaps because they are feeling more secure.

Here are some examples of how you can use an everyday event to create language opportunities:

Event	Language opportunities
Dressing	Name types of garments; talk about weather and what is suitable to wear; talk about colours of clothes and count buttons, etc.
Meal times	Name types of food; talk about colours and textures in food; talk about favourite foods; discuss where food comes from.
Waiting for a bus	Count cars passing by; talk about what people are doing around you, for example people going to work; look at different buildings.
Washing	Talk about why we need to wash our bodies; consider how animals wash themselves; sing songs about water or rhymes such as Incey, Wincey Spider.

Helping children to gain confidence in speaking and listening

Children need gradually to gain confidence in their ability to communicate. They need to feel that we will listen to them and that we value what they are trying to say to us. There are several ways in which we can show children that we are listening to them:

- by making eye contact
- by getting down to their level so that they can see us

- by smiling or nodding to show encouragement and that we are listening to them
- by recasting their comments to show that we have been listening, for example 'So you liked that type of ice-cream, did you?'.

Helping children communicate

Encouraging children to listen to each other

Very young children will find it difficult to listen to each other and wait for their turn to speak. Language at this age is so linked to thought that children will not be able to think silently! This means that most children under the age of three need to have plenty of adult attention and that activities such as 'circle time', where children have to listen to each other, might not always be appropriate. Between the ages of three and five, children will be able to listen to each other, but only if they are in very small groups and are not expected to remain quiet for very long! Some games such as lotto can act as a first step towards teaching children to wait and listen to each other.

Adults can also help children to listen to each other by focusing questions at particular children, for example 'Mary, do you have a pet?'. This allows children who have not participated in an activity to be drawn in. Sometimes other children will interrupt before a child can answer. It is important to handle this type of situation sensitively. On the one hand, it is important not to crush an eager child, but at the same time, the other child should be given an opportunity to answer. One way of dealing with this is to say to the child who has rushed in, 'That's interesting, but I think that Mary also wants to answer'.

How size of group may affect children's confidence

The size of the group will affect some children's confidence in speaking out loud. Some children are quite happy to share their thoughts with small groups, but will find it harder to talk in large groups. Children who find it difficult to contribute might need to have easy and unthreatening questions directed to them, so that they can feel successful. If you are unsure how to help a child who seems particularly quiet, it may be an idea to talk to the parents, who might be able to give some suggestions and guidance.

Managing negative remarks

Sometimes children may comment negatively about another child while they are speaking. This is rare among pre-school children, but can happen after the age of five years. It is important to intervene firmly, as comments that undermine other children can be the start of other forms of intimidation. Where possible, it is a good idea to intervene as quickly as possible, and in many cases it will be sufficient simply to remind children not to whisper while others are speaking.

Correcting children's pronunciation and grammar

Linguists have noted that an effective way of communicating with young children is to recast sentences. Recasting simply means repeating what the child has said or rephrasing a remark so that the child can absorb it more easily. Recasting helps children with their pronunciation, vocabulary and grammar skills. Look at the following example:

Child:	The marmalade is sad.
Adult:	Yes, the mermaid is sad. She looks unhappy, but then the mermaid finds some treasure.

The child has now heard the word 'mermaid' twice and also heard that the word 'unhappy' can be used to substitute for the word 'sad'. By re-casting, the adult has demonstrated correct pronunciation without making the child feel that she has made a mistake. This subtle way of helping children's language is considered to be good practice. Interrupting children to correct their speech can make them cautious in their speech and may cause some children to lose confidence.

Extending children's vocabulary

Adults need to take an active role in developing children's vocabulary. Children will need to have a wide range of vocabulary in order that they can express themselves fully and also so that they can understand others. The language that we understand but do not necessarily use ourselves is called **receptive language**, while the language that we actively use is called **expressive language**. It is important for adults working with children to make their own speech as rich as possible so that children hear a range of words, for example you might use the word 'fantastic' as well as the word 'wonderful' so that children hear a similar word.

Using objects of interest to extend vocabulary

Interest tables and bringing in objects for children to touch, feel and maybe even draw can enrich children's vocabulary. It allows them to learn new words and also for older children to practice their descriptive skills – 'What does this remind you of?' or 'What colours can you see?'.

Objects do not have to be particularly unusual – for example, children might be interested in looking at a range of pebbles and shells (see also page on setting out interest tables).

It is good practice to put labels and signs on interest tables and also on displays so that children become used to seeing the written word.

Promoting babies' and toddlers' development

It is worth considering the needs of babies and toddlers separately, as their language is still emerging. This means that they need a slightly different style of input from adults around them. Babies and toddlers need to be encouraged to communicate and they also need to hear enough of the language so that they can work out the rules and structure it. This means that when working with babies and young toddlers, early years workers should develop a running commentary style! They will need to be talked to even when they do not have the language to respond. An example of the running commentary style is shown below. In this instance an adult is talking to a nine-month-old baby while changing a nappy.

Adult:	Let's have a little peep at your nappy, shall we?
Baby:	(smiles)
Adult:	Let's start by laying you down here on this mat. Are you enjoying kicking? You'll have to be still for a second...
Baby:	dadadaaaa... bababdadadad
Adult:	I know, you want to be a footballer!

The running commentary style means that the adult is interacting with the baby and encouraging the baby to be part of what's happening. As babies become older, they recognise that the adult is asking them to respond and will enter into a mini-conversation with the adult even though they are just babbling. This teaches them the rules of conversation.

Using questions to develop children's language

Questions can be one effective way of encouraging children to talk and express their thoughts. It is important to understand that there are many ways of using questions with children, depending on their age and the situation.

There are essentially two types of questions:

- **Open questions**, also known as indirect questions, allow a variety of answers. For example, the question 'What did you do today?' can be replied to in several ways.
- **Closed questions**, also known as direct questions, tend to generate single or very short replies. 'What colour is your jumper?' will probably be answered by a single word.

If you listen to someone who you feel is good at talking to and communicating with children, you will probably find that a mix of questions is used.

At first, with babies and young children, closed questions will be one way of promoting a response. Babies learn that the intonation of a question is a cue for them to babble. As the first words appear, questions can then be used to encourage the toddler to use them, such as 'Where's John's teddy?' Such questions also allow the child to communicate and gain self-esteem from being able to answer them, for example 'Where's your hat?' 'What does the duck say?'.

With older children closed questions can encourage them to reflect, and can be used to help a child understand concepts by using a step-by-step approach, as in the following example:

Adult: How many red blocks are there?
Child: 1, 2, 3 – Three
Adult: Good. Will there be more or less if I take one away?
Child: Less.
Adult: Good. Let's take one away... Can you count how many there are now?
Child: 1, 2... Two.

Closed questions can also be helpful to use as a starting point with children who are feeling shy or unsure. They allow a conversation to be started without forcing the child to speak more then he or she wishes. Open questions can then be added which encourage the child to expand more. The example below shows how an early years worker started a conversation with a child who was feeling unsure:

Adult: So how old how you?
Child: Seven.
Adult: I remember that when I was seven I was given a pet for my birthday. It was a hamster called Toby. Do you have any pets?
Child: We have a cat.
Adult: A cat. That's nice. Do you play with him?
Child: He comes into my room.

Adult: What do you do with him?

Child: I stroke him and he rolls over like a dog.

From this you can see that the adult draws the child out gradually. This is quite important as children who are not comfortable may feel under attack if several questions are fired at them. The adult also adds her own thoughts into the conversation, allowing it to flow naturally.

Questions can also help children to reflect upon what they are experiencing, and it is good practice to use questions during an activity to develop children's thoughts. In the example below an adult is working with a group of children making bread rolls...

Adult: Who can tell me what this is? (He shows the group flour.)

Child: It's stuff you put in cakes – flour.

Adult: That's right. Flour is used a lot in cooking all kinds of things. Does anyone else know what flour is put in?

Child: Biscuits.

Adult: Yes, lots of thing, bread, cakes, pizzas. Today we are going to make bread using flour, water and something called yeast. Why do you think that we had to wash our hands before we started cooking?

Child: Because our hands might be dirty.

Adult: Yes, and now we are going to use our hands to knead the bread. I'll give you a piece each and you feel it. What does it remind you of?

In this example the questions were used to check children's knowledge, to involve them in the activity and also to make them use description.

Consolidation

Why are questions used to develop children's language?

Why is it sometimes useful to use closed questions?

What is meant by the term 'expressive language'?

List three everyday opportunities to develop language.

Element C11.5   Interact with children to promote their language and communication development

WHAT YOU NEED TO LEARN

- Communicating with children of different ages
- How to actively listen and communicate
- Factors that can affect interaction
- Encouraging children to communicate

Communicating with children of different ages

Recognising the changing communication needs of children

On pages 180–181 we looked at the stages of children's language development. We saw that babies in their first year are producing sounds and learning the tools of communication, while five-year-olds are starting to recognise written words and to be able to communicate through images and writing. The development of children's speech and other language skills means that early years workers have to adjust their style of communication to suit the developmental needs of the child they are working with.

Communicating with babies

Babies need a lot of language input from the adults around them. Most people talk to babies in a different way than they do with older children. This is natural and quite important. The style in which we need to speak to babies is sometimes called Motherese. This dialogue between babies and adults has several important features as follows:

- simplified language is used
- high-pitched tones are used
- sentences are short
- repetition is used.

Babies need to hear a strong speech pattern and to hear words and phrases repeated. They seem to be drawn to listening to this type of speech. Sometimes the way in which we talk to babies is called a running commentary, as we should be talking constantly. As the months go by, babies start to join in and a dialogue begins to develop, even though it is very one-sided.

Keys to good practice
When working with babies

- Make good eye contact
- Cuddle and play language games such as pat-a-cake
- Respond to a baby's babbling by smiling and talking back
- Use language as much as possible, for example when feeding, changing nappies
- Be expressive when communicating, through facial expression, intonation, etc.

Communicating with toddlers (12–24 months)

Toddlers are starting to learn to use words. At first, one word will be used to mean several things, but during this period, toddlers will learn more and more words. It is estimated that most two-year-olds will have 200 words! Toddlers will only be able to learn new words in this period if they hear them from the adults around them. Pointing

Establishing eye contact is very important when working with young babies

out things to toddlers and naming them is important, for example 'Look, Lisa, look at the *duck*. He's a big *duck*, isn't he?'.

Words also need to be repeated in a dialogue so that the child can absorb the word. During this period, children will mispronounce words, but they should not be corrected. The best way to help is to recast the sentence, slightly stressing the word that is being mispronounced, for example 'Yes, I can see the *duck*' (see also page 201). The running commentary style is still needed to allow children to hear plenty of language.

Keys to good practice
When working with toddlers

- Point out things and name them, for example 'Look at that dog!'
- Use picture books that show objects such as 'my clothes'
- Recast sentences to allow children to hear correct pronunciation
- Use repetition of a word to allow a child to absorb it, for example 'Here's the bus. It's a green bus. It's a big bus, isn't it?'
- Give plenty of praise when a child tries to make sounds of a new word
- Use finger rhymes and nursery rhymes.

Working with children aged 2–4 years

This is an interesting period as children move from making primitive sentences such as 'Daddy gone' to being able to frame whole sentences and questions. Children also start to use drawings to express themselves and to understand the purpose of books. The way in which we communicate with children also starts to change as the running commentary style is no longer so appropriate – it does not allow children the chance to practise their emerging skills. Instead, adults will be talking to children in a more conventional way, using questions, inviting comments and answering questions, for example 'What would you like to do now?' or 'Tell me about your picture'.

Adults also need to develop children's language by varying words and building expressions into a dialogue. This is a change of approach because previously words were repeated and stressed several times. The two dialogues about a cat show the difference in approach.

With a toddler: Look at that cat. He's a black cat. The cat is looking at you.
With a young child: There's a cat. He's a blacky brown colour and quite furry. He's not shy, is he?

As well as extending and developing children's spoken language, adults need to be nurturing the other language skills: listening, reading and writing. This is a gradual process and will occur by providing activities such as painting and drawing, reading stories and encouraging children to look at books and pictures.

Keys to good practice
When working with two- to-four-year-olds

- Make sure that children have opportunities to talk
- Allow children time to answer questions

- Extend children's language by using more elaborate speech
- Provide plenty of interesting activities which allow children to play together
- Encourage children to draw and paint
- Read a variety of stories to children
- Alllow children opportunities to handle books
- Use nursery rhymes and songs with children.

Working with children aged 4–8 years

Children's speech is still developing at this age and they make interesting mistakes, either through not understanding the meaning of words or because they have not fully absorbed the grammar of the language, for example 'He's the baddest of them all'. As an early years worker, you should still be extending children's vocabulary, either by forming sentences that include a new word in context ('It's good news, yes, really *fantastic*') or by taking time to explain a new word ('This is a thermometer. It is used to measure how hot you are').

Children also need to be given plenty of opportunities to use language in different ways, for example reporting back, describing events, predicting outcomes. This means that the role of the adult changes once more, taking on a more passive role by listening and encouraging children to talk.

During this period children will be developing their reading and writing skills. For some children this comes easily, especially if they have had a strong language input in their early

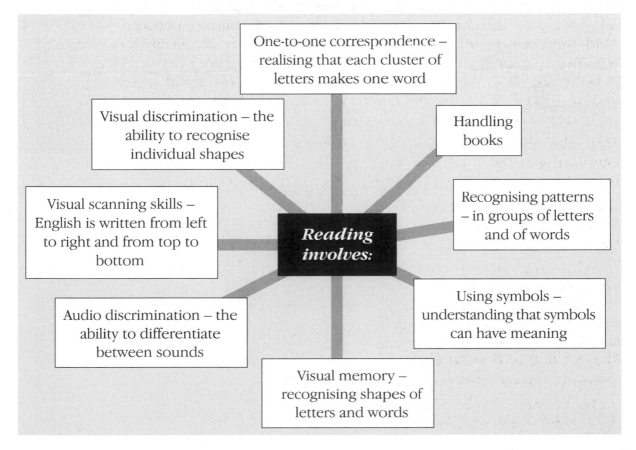

years. The ability to write follows on from being able to read, although children by the age of four can often use drawing to represent their ideas. Learning to read is dependent on children's cognitive development and on acquiring other skills such as the ability to discriminate between sounds. The spider diagram on the previous page shows some of the other skills that are required.

Keys to good practice
When working with four- to eight-year-olds

- Encourage children to develop their ideas through speech
- Extend children's vocabulary by explaining some words and by introducing new ones into the conversation
- Encourage children's visual representations, for example drawing, modelling and painting
- Support children's reading through reading a range of books to them
- Listen actively to children
- Plan activities that ensure children use a range of language skills, for example games such as twenty questions.

How to actively listen and communicate

Encouraging children to talk

Communication is a two-way process. This means that children need to feel that their contribution is valued. A baby may simply babble, but unless an adult responds to the babble, the baby may gradually babble less. In the same way, an older child who tries to talk to an adult but feels that he or she is not being listened to will gradually stop trying.

There are two main ways in which we can encourage children to communicate:

- **By listening and responding to children.** The response that we give children shows them how much we are listening. There are many ways in which we can show them that we are listening:
  - make good eye contact (especially important with babies and toddlers)
  - reflect back ('Mm, a picture for your sister, that's a nice idea')
  - ask questions ('When will you give it to her?').
- **By praising and encouraging.** Children need their efforts at communicating to be rewarded. The best way of doing this is through praise and by giving attention. Smiling and nodding at children as they talk clearly shows them that they are being listened to. Older children should be told that what they have said is interesting. Children who come into the setting with a language impairment or who are learning the setting's language will also need to be reinforced in this way.

As children get older, they associate being listened to with being wanted. This means that if we cannot listen to them because it is an inappropriate time, we must make sure that the child does not feel rejected. There are many ways of doing this, depending on the age of the child and the situation you are in. In all the examples that follow, the children are given a definite time when they can talk and also a reason why they cannot be listened to immediately.

- 'I am sorry, I must see to Jodie. But when I have finished come and find me, so that we can have a proper chat.'
- 'I am sorry, but I must see to Jodie. I know that Mrs Edwards would like to see what you have brought in, would you Mrs Edwards? Take it over to her and when I have finished I'll come and have a look too.
- 'We need to finish our story now because it's home time soon. You can tell me after you have put your coat on.'

Factors that can affect interaction

Adapting communication techniques

In order to be a skilled communicator, you need to be able to appraise the situation you are in and adapt your technique accordingly. This means that if you are working in a loud environment, you may need to make sure that you are making good eye contact with the child in order that he or she can follow you. It also means that if you are working in a situation where another adult is explaining something to a group of children, you are able to talk quietly to an individual child so as not to distract the other children.

You will have to vary your tones and intonations depending on the size of group you are with and the activity you are carrying out. Voices can be powerful tools and, if used carefully, can manage children's behaviour, enthuse children for an activity or soothe them. For example, if you are reading a story, you will need to be animated in order that children can enjoy your story, whereas if you are sorting out an argument between two children, your voice should be particularly soothing and calm.

How environment can affect children's communication

Some children find it hard to communicate in some environments. Children with a hearing impairment may find it hard to concentrate and focus if there is a lot of background noise. They may also need to be able to see clearly the adult or child who is talking to them. In situations where children are finding it hard to concentrate, it may be an idea either to look at ways of reducing background noise or to find an area that is quieter.

In some situations children may find an unfamiliar environment intimidating, for example going into a large hall or into a museum. If this is the case, it can be helpful to allow children the time to settle in and make sure that they are feeling supported, for example holding their hands, quietly talking to them or taking them to a more enclosed area.

Understanding why children may not wish to communicate

In this unit we have looked at the ways in which we can encourage children to communicate. It is also important for adults working with children to understand that there are times when children may not wish to talk and to respect this. Forcing children to talk may in some cases cause children to lose confidence and may make them withdraw further.

Reasons why children may not wish to talk may include shyness, embarrassment or not feeling confident in the setting.

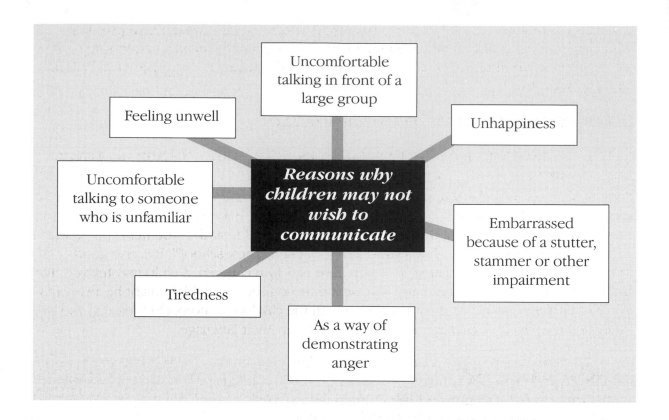

Uncomfortable talking in front of a large group

Feeling unwell

Unhappiness

Uncomfortable talking to someone who is unfamiliar

Reasons why children may not wish to communicate

Embarrassed because of a stutter, stammer or other impairment

Tiredness

As a way of demonstrating anger

Case study

Isabella has moved school twice in six months because of family circumstances. Her father was killed in a road accident and her mother is suffering from depression. She is currently staying with her grandparents. Isabella has become less communicative and at times seems to withdraw. She is uncomfortable speaking in front of large groups of children and never puts her hand up to answer questions, although she is quite happy to sit with children.

Why would it be unwise for early years workers in the setting to ask Isabella direct questions?

What type of activities might help Isabella to talk and communicate more?

How might early years workers recognise that Isabella has gained enough confidence to speak in front of large groups?

When children do not wish to communicate, it is often a good idea to wait until they show signs of wanting to talk. This does not mean ignoring them or leaving them alone, simply accepting that they are not wanting to make a contribution at that time. It is also worth considering if the child needs space and whether your own style and proximity are affecting his or her behaviour. Some children prefer to keep a distance, both physical and mental, when they are in an unfamiliar setting or with an unfamiliar person. Instead of asking them a question, you may decide simply to use a running commentary approach and look for signs of interest. Some children who are withdrawn may find that there is one particular person within a setting with whom they are comfortable. If over a period of time children remain reluctant to communicate, it is worth considering whether specialist help is required, in which case you may wish to talk to your supervisor or directly to the parents. In some cases, a child's lack of communication may signal that he or she is deeply distressed or has some learning difficulty.

Encouraging children to communicate

Using children's personal experiences as a basis for creating language opportunities

Sometimes it can be helpful to use the information that we know about a child's family or lifestyle to help the child to communicate. This background may provide an area of common ground with which to begin a relationship, for example 'So I hear that you help your grandad in his garden sometimes' or 'How's your sister finding her new school?'. It is also good practice to follow up conversations that you have had with children. A child may tell you that he or she is going to a birthday party. The next time you see the child, it might be an idea to ask if he or she enjoyed the party. Using events in the child's life shows children that you are interested in them as well as being helpful in extending their language.

Observation

Plan a series of five activities that will help children's listening skills.

Explain why these activities will develop their listening skills.

Carry out at least two activities with either an individual child or group of children.

Evaluate these activities, explaining your role and what the children gained from carrying them out.

CII Unit test

The following questions may provide some knowledge evidence for your portfolio:

1 List the factors that may affect children's communication and language development.
2 What is meant by the term 'open question'?
3 What is meant by the term 'pre-linguistic phase'?
4 Why is it important to talk to parents about children's language and communication needs?
5 What factors should be taken into consideration when planning a story session?
6 Name four activities that can develop listening skills in children.
7 Why is it important to read though a book before reading it aloud to children?
8 What are the main benefits of story time?
9 What factors may prevent children from wishing to communicate?
10 What are the links between language and other areas of development?

Unit C15

Contribute to the protection of children from abuse

This unit looks at child protection. As an early years worker, you have a substantial amount of contact time with the children in your care, and are therefore in a good position to notice signs of abuse and behaviour changes. Equally, you have contact with children on a one-to-one basis and might have a child telling you about abuse. You therefore need to know what to do (and what not to do!) in this situation. You may also be involved in teaching children how to protect themselves.

The elements for this unit are:

C15.1   Identify signs and symptoms of possible abuse
C15.2   Respond to a child's disclosure of abuse
C15.3   Inform other professionals about suspected abuse
C15.4   Promote children's awareness of personal safety and abuse

Element C15.1 Identify signs and symptoms of possible abuse

As an early years worker, you need to be aware of the signs and symptoms of abuse so that you can help to protect the children in your care.

WHAT YOU NEED TO LEARN

- Recognising the signs and symptoms of possible abuse
- Recording the signs and symptoms or behaviour changes
- Understanding child protection procedures if abuse is suspected

Recognising the signs and symptoms of possible abuse

There are four main types of abuse:

- physical
- emotional
- neglect
- sexual.

Physical abuse

Physical abuse is intentionally causing physical harm to a child. This can include the use of physical force, hitting, biting, burning, shaking, squeezing and kicking a child. It may also include giving a child poisons, alcohol and inappropriate drugs, and attempted drowning or suffocation. It could also mean allowing other children to physically harm a child.

Because children often have minor accidents, and regularly have bruises and grazes, it is important to try to distinguish between accidental and non-accidental injuries. This is often not easy to do, but if a child constantly appears to have physical injuries, these should be recorded. A pattern may develop in the records, which might be suspicious.

Signs and symptoms of physical abuse

Signs and symptoms	Accidental injury	Suspicious signs which may indicate non-accidental injury
Burns and scalds	Often an unclear outline to the burn with possible splash marks Easily explained by a detailed explanation (a **history**) Not recurrent Significant burns are reported and treated	Clear outline of the burn Unusual position, for example buttocks History is unclear or is inconsistent with the burn Recurrent burns Burns are not treated Indicative shapes – the most common being cigarette burns
Fractures (broken bones)	Arms and legs (although these are rare in young children under two years) Very rarely due to brittle bone disease	Recurrent If there is no history of a severe accident: • numerous, especially if at different stages of healing • untreated or unreported accident • inconsistent history
Head injury	History consistent with injury and developmental age of child, for example children who are just walking are more likely to have frequent bruises on the head than older children	History is inconsistent with injury Bleeding and bruised ears Two black eyes with swelling and tenderness of the eyelids, and no bruise on the lower forehead to explain the black eyes Bleeding into the eyes, which could indicate bleeding in the brain caused by shaking
Cuts and other injuries	Minor and superficial Easily explained and properly treated Animal bite mark Young babies often scratch their own faces with their finger nails	Bite marks (although they could be caused by other children) Large, deep scratches or cuts Injuries to the inside of the mouth, especially under the tongue or the inside of the upper lip
Suffocation	SIDS (sudden infant death syndrome)	Other unexplained deaths in the family Previous unexplained disorder or injury to the baby
Bruises	Most children will have a few scattered bruises which form no particular pattern. These are usually	Recurrent, frequent bruises in hidden or unusual places (see below) Indicative patterns:

Signs and symptoms	Accidental injury	Suspicious signs which may indicate non-accidental injury
	over bony prominences, for example knee, chin or elbow Some serious children's illnesses, such as leukaemia, have extensive bruising as one of the first signs Children with haemophilia (a bleeding disorder) and those on steroid drugs will bruise easily A Mongolian blue spot is a birth mark which usually occurs on the buttocks or lower back in 95 per cent of Afro-Caribbean babies. It can also occur in any other ethnic origin (10 per cent of Caucasian babies)	• pinch marks • hand print • strap, lash or belt marks Bizarre shapes which will resemble the object used to inflict injury, for example a shoe
	Any of the signs in this column could be non-accidental, especially if: • **the details of the accident are not compatible with the injury** • **the injury is not compatible with the developmental age of the child**	**It is important to remember that any of the signs in this column could be due to an accident**

Injuries versus developmental age

When considering physical injuries, it is always important to take into account the developmental age of the child and whether the history of the injury is compatible with this. It would not be unusual for toddlers of 18 months to have frequent bruises on their heads, because at this age they often fall over or walk into things. It would, however, be more suspicious if a child of seven had frequent bruises on the head.

Body map

A body map can be used to record the position of a physical injury (see the next page for a body map).

Behavioural or emotional signs of physical abuse

Physical abuse does not always produce physical signs in a child. For example, if a baby is fed forcefully, he or she is more likely to show emotional signs or have feeding difficulties.

Many children who are showing signs of physical abuse also undergo a change in their behaviour. This will vary depending on the age of the child, but may include:

- shying from physical contact
- being withdrawn
- being aggressive with other children
- undergoing sudden behaviour changes
- showing lack of trust
- showing reluctance to undress for PE or swimming
- having feeding/eating difficulties
- being frightened of, or reluctant to be with, the abuser
- showing 'frozen watchfulness' – the child sits and watches others, but will not become involved.

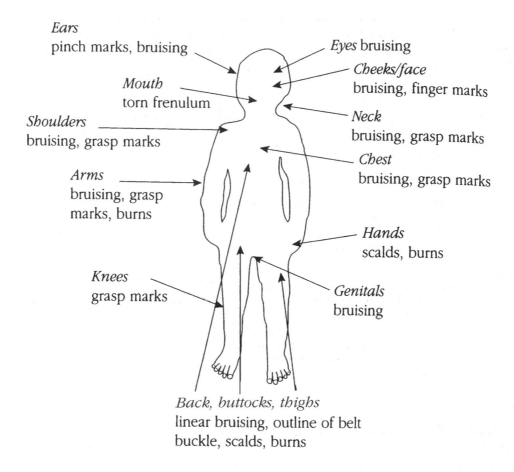

Ears
pinch marks, bruising

Eyes bruising

Mouth
torn frenulum

Cheeks/face
bruising, finger marks

Shoulders
bruising, grasp marks

Neck
bruising, grasp marks

Chest
bruising, grasp marks

Arms
bruising, grasp
marks, burns

Hands
scalds, burns

Knees
grasp marks

Genitals
bruising

Back, buttocks, thighs
linear bruising, outline of belt
buckle, scalds, burns

A body map showing the usual position of injuries in cases of child abuse

Case study

1   Zoe, who is three, arrived at your setting with a large cut and bruise under her chin. She was her normal, cheerful self and very proud of her 'wounds'. Her mother explained that Zoe had been playing with her garden swing; she had pushed it and it had swung back and caught her under the chin. This is the second time that something like this has happened: two weeks ago, Zoe had a large bump on her head after tripping over a rock in the garden and falling.

Is there cause for concern? Explain your reasons.

Would you feel the same if Zoe's mother had said that the child had walked into a door and Zoe appeared to be very clingy and upset that day?

2   Jerome, aged four, regularly seeks the attention of the staff by staying close and wanting reassurance. When you are observing him in the home corner one day, he starts hitting a doll very violently and shouting, 'You're ruining my life' and 'I never want to see you again'. Later in the morning, you find him curled up in the book corner sobbing.

Is there cause for concern? Explain your reasons.

Emotional abuse

Emotional abuse is where there is emotional harm to a child caused by verbal threats, criticism, ridicule, shouting or lack of love, affection and warmth. This is much more difficult to detect than physical abuse because there are no physical signs. However, a child who is constantly deprived of love and affection will often have difficulties making relationships with other adults and children, and therefore may well be bullied at school as well as at home.

Signs of emotional abuse

- Behaviour difficulties such as overactivity, attention seeking, being demanding, aggressive or disobedient
- Tantrums in school-aged children
- Low self-esteem and lack of self-confidence
- Speech disorders, for example stammering, stuttering or delayed speech
- Inability to play or difficulty with playing or having fun
- Stealing or telling lies
- Comfort-seeking behaviour such as thumb sucking, persistent rocking movements or masturbation in school-age children
- Difficulty coping with making mistakes, for example in activities or school work
- Poor concentration and learning difficulties
- Difficulty making and sustaining friendships
- Frequent toileting accidents in children of five years and over
- Self-destructive behaviour, such as head banging
- Intense sensitivity to the parent's moods
- Indiscriminately affectionate – the child will sit on anyone's lap, even strangers'
- Failure to grow or gain weight.

Other causes of these signs in children

Many incidents that happen in normal family life can cause a child to be stressed and to exhibit a complete change of behaviour, which may include the signs above being shown for a short period of time. These incidents could include:

- a new baby in the family
- separation or divorce of parents
- death of someone close to the child or a pet
- moving home or nursery school

These behaviour changes should still be recorded and the parents kept informed, in case the signs persist.

Case study

Abdul's mother has just had her fifth baby, which is the first girl. At first, Abdul was very excited about his new sister and kept drawing pictures of babies and telling all of his friends about her. The baby is now six weeks old. Abdul has become much quieter recently and has started picking fights with his friends. He cannot seem to sit still for very long and has had the occasional tantrum when he has not got his way. He sometimes appears in dirty clothes, and is often picked up by his older brother.

Is there cause for concern? Explain your reasons.

Neglect

Neglect means failing to provide for the basic essential needs of a child. It also includes a lack of adequate stimulation or supervision of the child, failure to protect a child from danger or to look after a child when under the influence of alcohol or drugs.

Neglect is probably the most common type of abuse, but has the fewest convictions in law.

Children's needs	Sign of deprivation	Effect on the child of deprivation
Nutrition	Not enough food Too much junk food	Malnourished or overweight Failure to grow Hunger Vitamin deficiencies Poor development
Clothing and shoes	Dirty and smelly Inappropriate clothing for the weather No school uniform	Bullied at school Vulnerable to infections Small or inappropriate shoes can lead to deformity of the feet
Medical care	No immunisations Failure to seek medical attention or to attend developmental check-ups or the dentist	Chronic infections and prolonged illnesses Poor speech Poor teeth with tooth decay untreated and bad breath Developmental delays are not recognised early and therefore cannot be treated Deafness or visual problems may go unrecognised, causing learning difficulties
Hygiene	Living in an unhygienic environment Inappropriate hygiene for the child	Constantly unwell Food poisoning and gastroenteritis more common Skin infections and infestations Head lice (which are rarely treated) The child may be smelly and therefore be ostracised by his or her peers Poor self-esteem Frequent nappy rashes in babies
Clean air	Smoky atmosphere Dampness causing mould to grow	Respiratory infections and asthma The spores of mould can cause chest infections
Warmth and physical protection	Inadequate clothing or heating	Hypothermia and chest infections
Safe environment	Lack of necessary safety equipment, including in the car	Frequent accidents including falling, scalds, house fires Swallowing poisons Inadequate supervision and too much freedom Poor school attendance and truancy
Stimulation and education	Lack of appropriate toys and books Poor school attendance	Learning difficulties and poor school progress Poor concentration Poor self-esteem and lack of confidence
Moral and social guidance and protection	Lack of love, discipline and boundaries Poor parent–child relationship	Early smoking, alcohol and substance misuse Isolation

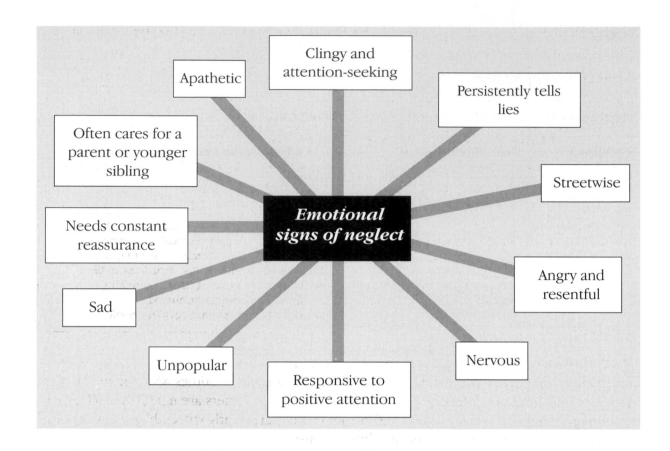

Emotional signs of neglect:
- Apathetic
- Clingy and attention-seeking
- Persistently tells lies
- Often cares for a parent or younger sibling
- Streetwise
- Needs constant reassurance
- Angry and resentful
- Sad
- Unpopular
- Responsive to positive attention
- Nervous

Case study

Tina has been attending the school for about three months. Her family have recently moved to the area following the divorce of her parents. She is living with her mother who works full time at the local college. Tina settled into the school very well, although she finds some of the work hard, and has made several friends. Tina often appears in school without uniform and is frequently a little scruffy. She sometimes forgets her lunch, and never brings in anything to 'show' when the other children do. Her mother sometimes fails to respond to notes sent home, and is occasionally late picking Tina up. However, she always appears to take an interest in Tina's schooling and has attended the recent parents' evening.

Is there cause for concern? Explain your reasons.

Sexual abuse

Sexual abuse is the use of children, both boys and girls, for sexual gratification. It can include exposing children to pornography and unsuitable videos.

The media often highlights cases of paedophilia, but a child is much more likely to be abused by a family member or friend or someone he or she trusts. Sexual abuse can cause life-long emotional damage to the child, leading to difficulties and mistrust in relationships, poor self-esteem and self-confidence, and depressive illnesses. Often, children do not realise that what the adult is doing is wrong, but they may be aware that they have a 'special relationship' with the abuser. The effects of abuse may not manifest themselves until the child becomes an adolescent, or even later.

Signs of sexual abuse

Physical signs	Behavioural signs
Bruises or scratches which are inconsistent with an accidental injury Difficulty in walking or sitting Pain, soreness or itching in the genital area Signs of cystitis such as pain when passing urine Bed-wetting Sleep problems Recurrent stomach pains or headaches Vaginal discharge or bleeding	Sexually precocious (having a knowledge and understanding of sex inappropriate for the age or development of the child) and using seductive behaviour towards adults Use of sexually explicit language Excessive preoccupation with sex, especially in play Drawing and stories may indicate a sexual awareness and interest unusual for the age Feeding or eating problems, which may lead to eating disorders such as anorexia later in life Low self-esteem and lack of self-confidence May appear unhappy or confused May dislike being left with certain people

What makes some children vulnerable to abuse?

Some children are more vulnerable to abuse than others and sometimes within a family, there may be one child who is 'scapegoated' and abused while the others are not. This can be due to the personality of the child, which makes him or her particularly vulnerable in that family. Other factors that make children more vulnerable are:

- being the oldest child
- where there has been separation of the child from the mother soon after birth – this could be due to prematurity
- disability
- being an unwanted child or the child is the 'wrong' gender
- the child doesn't live up to the expectations of the parent
- being 'the loner'
- where children have been abused previously, they are more vulnerable to further abuse, even if this abuse is from a different source.

Recording the signs and symptoms or behaviour changes

Recognising abuse and the role of observations

In order that early years workers can recognise abuse, it is important to be aware of these signs and to be aware of age-appropriate behaviour in children. For example, you would expect a three year old occasionally to wet his or her pants, but not a seven year old.

Observation is a useful tool in the recognition of abuse, because it is a very good way of recording behaviour and play. Regular detailed observations, done in a variety of situations, might give a record of:

- recurring themes in the child's play or language
- incidents that provoke a behaviour change

- how the child interacts with other children and adults – useful in assessing the child's social skills
- how the child reacts with his or her parents or carers
- mood changes, and whether these are associated with a particular event such as home time
- reactions to different routines such as PE or swimming

It is important that the child is not aware you are observing him or her, because this might change the way the child reacts and plays.

How to record signs of abuse

It is very important that if you have any suspicions that a child is being abused in some way you write down this information as soon as possible, before small details are forgotten.

Each workplace has its own guidelines for how and where this will be recorded, but your report will need to contain the following information:

- Name, age and address of child.
- Parents' names.
- Date and time of making the records.
- Are you reporting your own concerns or those of someone else?
- A brief description of what caused your concerns, including incidents leading up to your concern.
- Description of any physical signs – use a body map (see page 215) to indicate where the signs are. It is very important to describe any physical signs accurately without making value judgements as to the cause of the signs. For example, if a child had what appeared to be a cigarette burn, you would need to say: 'The child has a small round burn of approximately 0.5 cm diameter'.
- Description of any behavioural changes.
- If the child has said anything which has caused concern, what **exactly** did he or she say? It is important to try to remember the exact words and record the language the child used, rather than what you think he or she meant.
- Whether the parent has given an explanation for any of your concerns.
- Details of people to whom you passed on the information.

All concerns should be recorded, even if a minor incident.

Confidentiality

Records will normally be kept in a locked filing cabinet or cupboard and be accessible only to those concerned; they will not be available for all staff to read, only those who work closely with the child. Parents have a right to see the records about their children, if they request to do so.

Active knowledge

What are the reporting procedures in your setting if child abuse is suspected?
How is confidentiality maintained?
Where are the records kept and who has access to them?

Understanding child protection procedures if abuse is suspected

Every workplace has its own procedures, and it is important that you are familiar with these, and know to whom you should report concerns about a child. The procedures will be similar to these described in the flow chart below.

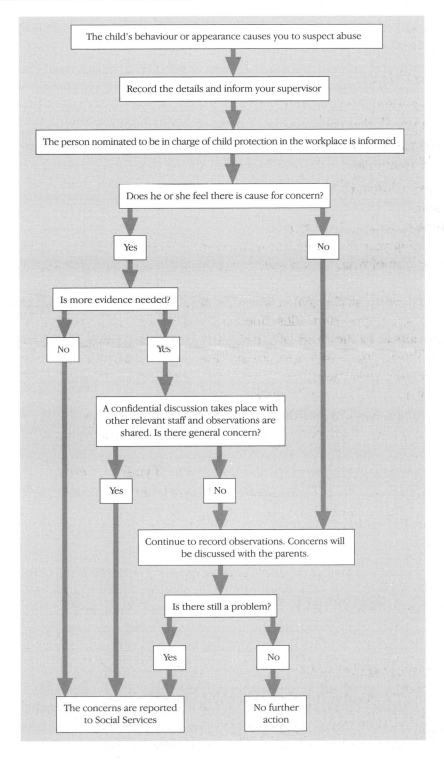

Where concerns are being raised about a child, the parents may be asked if they have noticed the physical signs or behaviour changes, because there might be a very simple explanation for the signs you have noted.

When concerns are being discussed, it is important to remember that there are many other events happening in a child's life which could be causing behaviour changes and regression in some areas, for example in toilet training. These will obviously need to be made known to staff. Confidentiality is extremely important in child protection, and it is important that nothing is discussed with **anyone** who is not directly involved.

If the child has physical injuries, then he or she will need to be taken to hospital or a doctor straight away. The child's parents will need to be informed, and if child abuse is suspected Social Services should be informed too. If the GP or hospital is also concerned, they too will inform Social Services. Any child who attends the accident and emergency department of a hospital as a result of an accident will automatically have his or her name passed on to the health visitor or school nurse for that child. This means that they can keep a record of the types and number of accidents a child has.

Active knowledge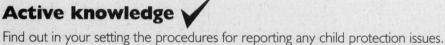

Find out in your setting the procedures for reporting any child protection issues.
Who is responsible for child protection at your workplace?

Element C15.2   Respond to a child's disclosure of abuse

WHAT YOU NEED TO LEARN

- Recognising a disclosure of abuse
- Responding to a child's disclosure
- Recording the disclosure accurately
- Dealing with your own emotional reactions

Recognising a disclosure of abuse

Many adults who have been abused as children can remember times when they tried to tell someone about the abuse, but the person did not listen, did not take the child seriously or did not believe the allegations.

Occasionally, children might tell an early years worker that they are being abused. Children need to be able to trust someone if they are to tell of their abuse, and they need an appropriate moment when there are not many people around. Children may therefore 'hang around' the early years worker and sometimes may exhibit attention-seeking behaviour.

When a child tells someone about abuse it is called a **disclosure**. This may happen in several ways:

- **A full disclosure.** The child relates all of the history of abuse, including names.
- **A partial disclosure.** The child tells only part of the story and may miss out the name of the abuser, or other important details. The child may be testing the early years worker, may suddenly 'back off' and not want to say any more, or the early years worker may get interrupted or the child get distracted.
- **A direct disclosure.** The child tells the early years worker verbally or by using sign language what has happened.
- **An indirect disclosure.** The child might disclose abuse indirectly through play, particularly in the home corner of a nursery, or in pretend play with dolls, farm animals or action figures. Writing stories, painting, drawing and other artwork can also be activities through which the child might express what is happening to him or her and the resulting anxieties and stresses. There are many reasons why children may not want or be able to tell anyone that they are being abused, including the following:
  - children often do not have the right vocabulary to describe what is happening to them
  - they may not know that what is happening is wrong
  - they never get the opportunity to tell anyone
  - they do not think they will be believed
  - talking about what is happening would be too painful
  - they do not want to get the abuser into trouble – children usually will still love the person who is abusing them, but not like what the person is doing to them
  - they are worried that they would be sent away from home if they told
  - they may be worried about the consequences of telling anyone, especially if they have been threatened or told to keep it a secret
  - they are too embarrassed
  - they may think that it is their fault and that they will be punished as a consequence
  - they try and pretend that it is not happening to them, and therefore try to block their memory of the abuse
  - they have tried to tell someone before but the adult did not listen.

Responding to a child's disclosure

Keys to good practice
Responding to disclosure of abuse

If a child tells you, either directly or indirectly, about abuse:

- Stay calm. You may feel shocked, angry or helpless, but these feelings must not be transferred to the child, who needs you to be in control of the situation.
- Maintain eye contact and ensure that your eye level is the same as, or lower than the child's.
- Listen, and allow the child to recall events spontaneously.
- Don't question the child, or ask for details, because the information may become distorted. This may be done later by someone who specialises in interviewing children.
- Reassure the child that he or she has done the right thing in telling you.
- Praise the child for surviving the abuse. Tell the child that he or she did not have any choice and that it was not the child's fault.

- Tell the child that you will need to speak to someone else.
- Don't make any promises and never promise confidentiality. Once you have been informed of abuse, or if you suspect abuse, you are duty-bound to report it.
- Don't make any value judgements about the abuser, because the child may still love or like that person. You can say that what the abuser did was wrong or that he or she has a problem and needs help.
- Show acceptance of what the child says, even if it appears unlikely. Young children rarely lie about abuse. (All allegations of abuse must be taken seriously and reported.)
- Tell the child what you are going to do next and that you will let the child know what happens. Remember to use language that is appropriate.
- Explain that you will always be willing to listen should the child wish to talk.

It is important that all allegations are taken seriously and that issues such as the length of the child's statement, family history, culture or religion, the child's tone of voice or behaviour do not affect the normal reporting procedure. Children may feel ambivalent about telling anyone and may appear unbothered or blase while they are speaking to you. You must still follow the protection procedure (see page 221).

When responding to a child's disclosures, here are a few helpful things to say and some others to avoid.

Helpful things to say	Avoid saying
I believe you. I'm glad that you've told me. It's not your fault.	Why didn't you tell anyone before? Why? When? Who? Where? How? You should have... Don't tell anyone else. Are you sure that this is all true?

Following a child's disclosure, you will need to pass the information on immediately, following the setting's guidelines. This could be to a supervisor or whoever is in charge of child protection issues within the setting. This person will probably inform the parents unless the child has been sexually abused. Social Services would then be informed.

Recording the disclosure accurately

You will need to record everything that was said as soon as possible so that you do not forget any of the details. You will need to record:

- the child's name, age and address
- the date, time and place of the disclosure
- what was happening immediately prior to the child's statement and any incident that prompted the child to tell
- exactly what the child said, using the words that he or she used, including any 'baby' words (children may have unusual names for parts of their bodies so it is important to be as accurate as possible)
- anything you said to the child – it is important to include this, even if you feel that you did not handle the situation particularly well
- who you informed.

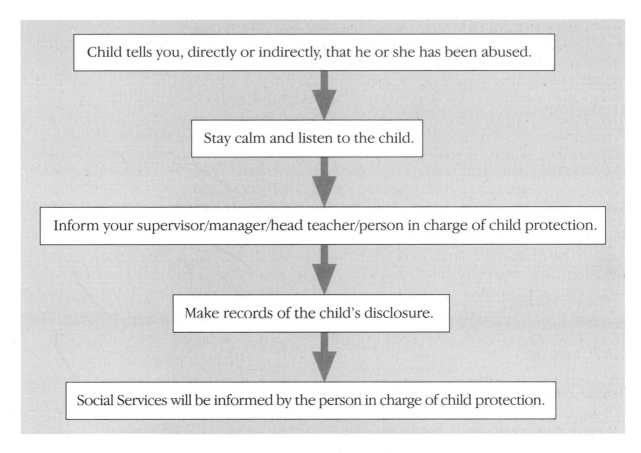

Child tells you, directly or indirectly, that he or she has been abused.

Stay calm and listen to the child.

Inform your supervisor/manager/head teacher/person in charge of child protection.

Make records of the child's disclosure.

Social Services will be informed by the person in charge of child protection.

These records need to be as detailed as possible and may be used as evidence in any child protection proceedings or in court. Try and write them down within an hour, while the information is still fresh in your memory. To be legally admissible, however, they need to be done within 24 hours.

If the child says anything further, then you will need to make a further record.

Confidentiality

Within early years settings information about child protection issues should be shared with other staff only on a 'need-to-know' basis. Records are confidential and should be kept in a locked filing cabinet or cupboard. Access to these records should be only for the staff concerned.

Dealing with your own emotional reactions

It is obviously extremely distressing dealing with any kind of abuse, but it is particularly so when you have been told about it personally by the child. You will need to talk this through with someone, but because of the confidentiality issues involved, it is very important that it is only discussed with those who are involved, and not with all of your colleagues. Gossip can spread very quickly. If you are unsure about who to talk to, discuss the issues with your supervisor.

Talking about your experience of dealing with abuse can help you if you feel angry or upset, but if you are mentioning an incident outside your workplace, you must remember the rules of confidentiality and **never** use names. You must also continue to behave professionally towards a parent or carer whom you suspect of abuse. If at any time you find you are having difficulty coping with your feelings, you must talk to your manager or supervisor, who should be able to help.

Impact of disclosure on the family

A child's disclosure of abuse is going to affect everyone in the family. Parents' immediate reactions are going to be ones of shock, disbelief, anger, helplessness and betrayal. They will also feel immensely guilty that they had not realised what was going on. These feelings will be worse if the abuser was a member of the family, and it may cause a big family rift. The family may need help in coming to terms with what has happened and organisations such as the NSPCC (National Society for the Prevention of Cruelty to Children) can provide counselling. Family centres can also provide counselling to the family.

Case study

While you are doing an activity on 'What makes me happy, what makes me sad', Ola mentions that what makes him sad is when his neighbour babysits for him and hurts him.

What would you do in this situation, and who would you inform?

Two days later, you observe Ola playing with two other children and becoming very aggressive, swearing and using words and phrases that you wouldn't expect a child of his age to know; this is unusual behaviour for him.

What would you do?

Element C15.3   Inform other professionals about suspected abuse

WHAT YOU NEED TO LEARN

- Understanding the roles of professionals involved and your own role
- The legislation on child protection

Understanding the role of professionals involved and your own role

Investigating a report of abuse

Once it has been established that there is a cause for concern about a child, then the person who is responsible for child protection in the setting will inform Social Services. There is an emergency number in each area where a duty social worker can be contacted 24 hours a day.

The police or the NSPCC could also be informed. **Anyone who suspects abuse has a duty to report it and Social Services has a duty to investigate**

Once Social Services has been informed, the department will inform the police and previous records will be checked. Social workers and police will then decide on a course of action, and a joint investigation will be started. In most cases, initial enquiries conclude that there is no cause for concern and the inquiry stops. The investigation involves the following:

- The child's GP, health visitor or school nurse are contacted.
- The child's school, nursery, playgroup, nursery school or after-school club are contacted.
- The alleged abuser is interviewed by the police.
- The child may be interviewed by a police officer or social worker with specialist training in interviewing children. This may be done in a family centre or in a police station with special facilities. A video camera might also record the interview, which should ensure that the child is not interviewed again unnecessarily, and the recording may be used in court.
- If necessary, the child is medically examined by a specialist doctor, usually a pediatrician. The child does have the right to refuse this if he or she is old enough to understand the implications of refusing.
- The family is interviewed and the parents are kept informed of the progress of the investigation.

Throughout the investigations, the welfare of the child is paramount. If the child is considered to be in immediate danger, an alternative place is found where the child can be cared for (see page 232).

If there are still concerns about the child, a case conference will be called in which all of the professionals involved with the child can pool their information.

The case conference

A case conference is normally held within 8–15 working days of the initial inquiry.

The purpose of a case conference is to:

- share information and any concerns about the family
- establish whether the child is at risk and whether the child needs to be placed on the child protection register (see below).
- formulate an action plan for the future protection of the child (a child protection plan).
- nominate a key worker who will be responsible for putting the plan into action.

Those who will be present at the conference might include those shown in the diagram on the next page.

The early years worker's role at the case conference

If you were the person who first had concerns about the child, you might be invited to the case conference. You will need to take all of the records relating to the child and any observations done subsequently. You will be asked to give the facts as you know them. It can be a slightly daunting prospect, but you just need to read the relevant records. It is important that you give facts and not opinions, and identify the sources of the facts.

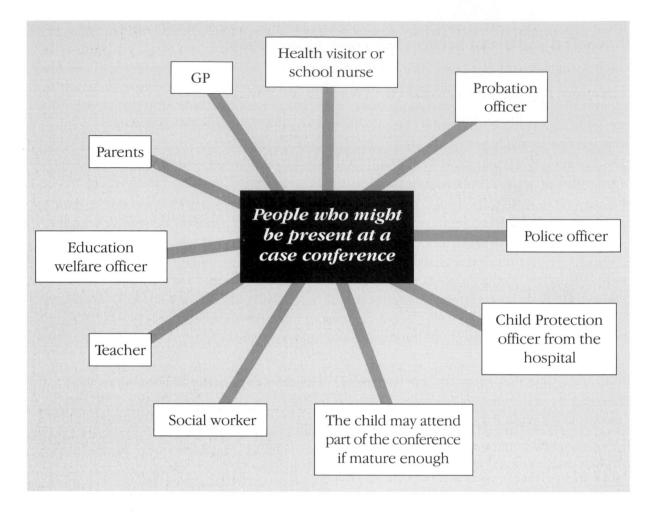

People who might be present at a case conference

- GP
- Health visitor or school nurse
- Probation officer
- Parents
- Police officer
- Education welfare officer
- Child Protection officer from the hospital
- Teacher
- Social worker
- The child may attend part of the conference if mature enough

Child Protection Register

This lists all the children in the county who are considered to be suffering, or at risk of, significant harm.

If the child is placed on the register, there will be a review case conference within three months, and every six months after that until the child is removed from the register.

The child's rights during an investigation

During these proceedings the child has the right:

- to be protected from all harm and abuse
- to have his or her views and wishes taken into consideration
- to be told what is happening and why
- to have his or her views put to the case conference
- to be listened to and to be able to talk about any worries
- to have his or her own solicitor if court action is taken.

The parents' rights during an investigation

The parents' rights during these proceedings are:

- to be informed about the concerns that others have about their child
- to be told what action is being taken to deal with these concerns

- to have their views expressed at a case conference. Sometimes, one or both parents may not be allowed to attend all or part of the conference if it is thought they may prevent the conference from focusing on the needs of the child.

A *summary of the procedures once abuse is suspected*

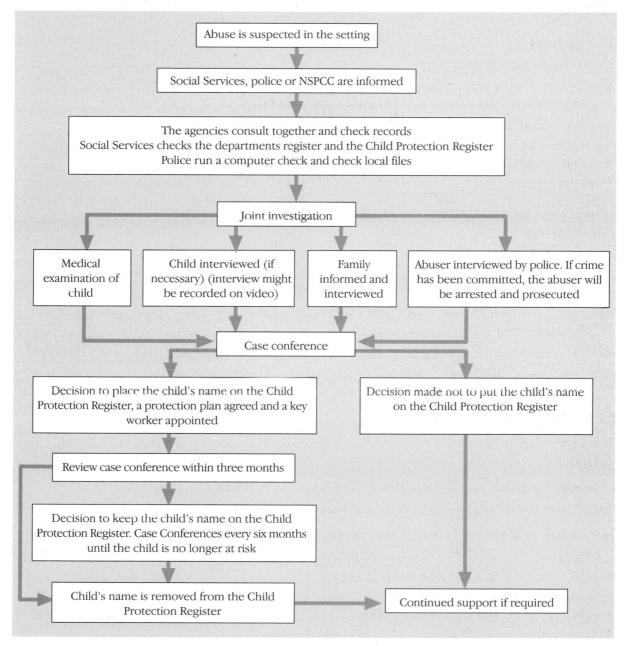

Professionals and organisations involved in child protection

Because there are many different professionals from different agencies involved in child protection, it has been recommended that professionals try to work together more effectively. It is difficult to see the whole picture of what is happening in a child's life if all of the pieces of the puzzle are scattered among different people. This situation is being addressed by the formation of Child Protection Committees, at area and district level, and the formation of Child Protection teams. Child Protection Committees comprise representatives from Social Services, the police, the NSPCC and the local NHS Trust. Child Protection team professionals consist of police officers and social workers who also work with other professionals in all child protection inquiries.

The police

The role of the police is to:

- ensure that the child is protected – they have emergency powers to do this if the child is considered to be at risk of further abuse (see page 232)
- determine whether a criminal offence has been committed
- identify who is responsible
- secure sufficient evidence so that the abuser can be taken to court
- decide whether it is in the best interests of the child and of the public if proceedings are instituted.

Social Services

The role of Social Services is to:

- ensure that the welfare of the child is a priority throughout the inquiries and investigation – this means that the needs of the child have priority over the needs of any adult
- investigate when there is reasonable cause to suspect that a child is suffering or is likely to suffer significant harm
- make enquiries of local agencies who have contact with the child, such as the school and the health visitor or school nurse
- interview the family and possibly the child
- coordinate the case conference
- provide a social worker as a key worker to the child and family and be responsible for the child protection plan.

Social Services provides an emergency number in each area where a duty social worker can be contacted 24 hours a day for advice.

The Education Authority

All those in close contact with children within an early years setting have the responsibility to:

- observe for the signs of abuse, changes in behaviour or failure to develop
- pay particular attention to the attendance and development of children on the Child Protection Register
- raise children's awareness about safety issues and how to protect themselves
- refer concerns to social services, NSPCC or the police.

There needs to be a member of staff who has the responsibility to liaise on child protection issues. Social Services needs to inform the school if children are on the Child Protection Register and when they are removed from the register.

The Health Service

- The local NHS trust has a coordinator for child protection.

- The GP's role is that of identifying family stresses and signs of abuse.
- The health visitor's role in working with the under fives and the school nurse's role with school-age children enables them to detect signs of abuse, poor development, behavioural problems and family stresses. They have a key role in providing support to the family. They will also be informed if a child in their care attends the accident and emergency department with an accident. This will enable them to see if there is a pattern of accidental injuries. They will also monitor all children who are on the Child Protection Register and regularly measure their height and weight.
- Hospital staff in the accident and emergency department and in children's wards are in a good position to detect abuse.

Voluntary organisations

The NSPCC

The National Society for the Prevention of Cruelty to Children (NSPCC) is the only voluntary organisation which has the power to apply for care, supervision and assessment orders (see the next page) in its own right.

Some people prefer to refer suspicions of abuse to the NSPCC rather than to Social Services. If there is cause for concern, the NSPCC will pass the referral to the Social Services.

The NSPCC provides a helpline which people can phone if they have concerns about a child. The organisation provides a counselling service for children and adults. It has its own register and publishes statistics of child abuse. The society regularly runs media campaigns to make the public more aware of child abuse.

The NSPCC helpline number is: 0800 800 500.

Childline

Childline runs a 24-hour helpline for children to telephone about any problem. It is confidential and children can remain anonymous.

Childline listens to approximately 3000 children a day who phone about abuse, bullying, family problems, pregnancy, school and friendship problems.

The Childline helpline number is: 0800 1111.

Kidscape

Kidscape was formed to teach children to protect themselves from bullying and abuse, particularly sexual abuse. The organisation produces many materials, including the Kidscape pack, which is a resource for teachers, and books, videos and training courses. It also runs a bullying helpline.

The Kidscape bullying helpline is: 0170 730 3300 (Monday–Fridays, 10 am–4 pm).

NCH Action for Children

The NCH Action for Children runs over 250 projects nationwide and campaigns to improve children's lives and end child poverty. Its work includes running family and community centres, sexual abuse treatment centres and family counselling sessions.

The NCH Action for Children telephone number is: 0171 226 2033.

The legislation on child protection

In all cases involving children, the 1989 Children Act lays down the following important principles for everyone to follow:

- The child's welfare must be put first. This means that the following need to be taken into account when decisions are made about a child:
  - the child's own wishes
  - the child's physical, emotional and educational needs
  - the child's age, sex, culture and religion
  - any abuse the child has suffered or is likely to suffer
  - how the child might cope with any changes in circumstances
  - how capable the parents are of meeting the child's needs.
- Families matter. The best place for a child is usually within his or her family and therefore the child should be removed from the family only if it is better for the child.
- Delays must be avoided. Any child protection case should be set within a time limit.
- Parental responsibility and rights must be taken into consideration, although the child's rights and needs have precedence.

Child Protection Orders

There are several orders which the local authority and the NSPCC can apply for under the Children Act if a child 'is suffering, or likely to suffer, significant harm'. These are outlined below.

Emergency Protection Order

This is a court order under section 44 of the Children Act. A court will make this order only when the child is in immediate danger. The child will be placed under the protection of the local authority for eight days, with the possibility of an extension for a further seven days. The court will state who is allowed or refused contact with the child.

Supervision Order

This is a court order under section 35 of the Children Act which puts the child under the supervision of a social worker, who befriends and advises the child. It can last for up to one year. The parents do not lose parental responsibility for the child.

Care Order

This is a court order under sections 31 and 33 of the Children Act which places the child in the care of the local authority if a court decides that a child is suffering, or is likely to suffer, significant harm. The local authority will share parental responsibility with the parents, and may continue to do so until the child is 18 years old.

Child Assessment Order

This is a court order under section 43 of the Children Act and is applied for when the parent has not given permission for a child to have a medical or psychiatric assessment. The order lasts for seven days and might mean that a child needs to be kept away from home in order for the assessment to be done. The child may still refuse to have a medical examination if he or she is able to understand the situation. If the assessment shows serious problems, then a Care Order or an Emergency Protection Order may be applied for.

Recovery Order

This is a court order under section 50 of the Children Act and gives the police the right to recover a child who has been abducted or has run away. It can be applied for only if a child is already subject to an Emergency Protection Order or a Care Order.

The guardian ad litem

In all public law cases, the child's interests will be represented by a 'guardian *ad litem*', a social worker who is independent of the local authority. The main role of the guardian *ad litem* is to ensure that the child's views are made known to the court and to ensure that everyone keeps the best interest of the child at the forefront of any decisions. He or she is appointed when the court receives an application for one of the orders above.

Case study

Clara has recently moved house and has started attending your setting. You know that the family have had problems in the past and that they have a social worker. Clara's mother has also just had another baby with Clara's stepfather. Clara has had difficulty in settling into your setting and has not made any friends yet. She is often disruptive and has been seen to hit out at some of the other children. She is often brought and picked up by her stepfather or an older brother and sister, and you rarely see her mother. When she is dropped off one day, you notice that she has a black eye and that her eyelid is very swollen, and she has some bruising on her left wrist. Her stepfather said that she walked into a door.

1   What would you do in this situation?
2   How would you record this incident?
3   How could you monitor the child?
4   What other signs and symptoms might you look for?

The following day, you notice a further bruise on her shin. Clara says that her older brother kicked her accidentally when playing football. Later on, while reading with her and talking about the book, you ask why she thinks the boy in the picture looks sad (he had fallen over and hurt his foot). She replies that he is sad because he does not want to go home as his dad will be cross with him.

5   What would you do about this new information?
6   How would you present this information at a case conference?
7   How could you support Clara in the setting?

Element C15.4   Promote children's awareness of personal safety and abuse

WHAT YOU NEED TO LEARN

- The rights of children
- What children need to learn in order to protect themselves

The rights of children

Although parents and early years workers should be protecting children, they should also be helping children to become independent and responsible for their own safety. There will always be times when a child is not under close supervision of a responsible person; the child needs to have the coping mechanisms for dealing with any situations that he or she has not met before. This means that the early years worker needs to build children's self-confidence and self-esteem and give children the information to help them know what they should do in unfamiliar situations.

In 1959, the United Nations set out the basic rights of a child which include adequate nutrition, housing, medical care, free education, play, recreation and protection.

In the UK the Children Act (1989) came into effect in October 1991. It included recommendations on how children should be cared for and protected and laid down that children have certain rights and should be treated with respect. There was a big change in emphasis over the role of parents – parents were to have responsibility for their children, rather than rights over them.

The Act says that the best interests of the child should be paramount and it gives rights to children to:

- be protected
- be listened to
- be told their rights
- be given the opportunity to talk about any worries they have
- have a chance to have their voice heard in court cases which involve them
- have their own solicitor
- refuse assessment or medical examination (if they understand what this involves)
- have their age, sex, race, culture, language and life experiences considered when decisions are made about them
- have their wishes considered when decisions are made about them and be kept informed of such decisions.

Children need the following in order to protect themselves:

- positive self-esteem
- self-confidence and assertiveness
- knowledge of what to do in certain situations
- trusting relationships with adults in which issues and problems can be discussed.

Ways to improve a child's self-esteem

Children who have poor self-esteem are far more likely to be victims of abuse, and it is therefore part of an early years worker's role to build up children's confidence and self-esteem.

Keys to good practice
Building children's self-confidence

- Treat all children with respect, be fair and give each child some attention.
- Praise children when they accomplish something and behave well.

- Give children responsibility so that they feel valued and important. It is possible to give every child in a class his or her own job to do, with other children or on his or her own.
- Design tasks so they have steps that are achievable – and children experience success. This is particularly important for those children who never appear to achieve anything, or who have behaviour problems.
- If a child misbehaves, the action rather than the child should be criticised. The child needs to get the message that you still like him or her, but it is the behaviour you disapprove of.
- Find something that the child does well and encourage him or her in this.
- Value children's opinions.
- Involve children in decisions.
- Resist the temptation of helping children too much in activities. This means that you should never 'improve' a child's work or make too many suggestions, because this can undermine a child's confidence.

It is also part of the early years worker's role to empower children so that they can protect themselves.

What children need to learn in order to protect themselves

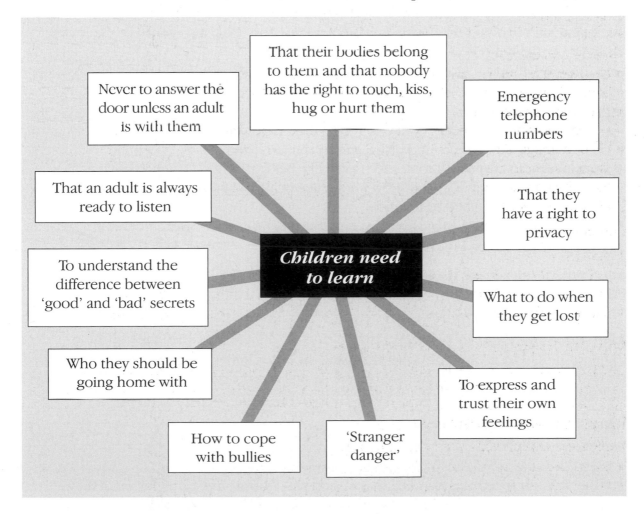

Throughout childhood, children need to be taught about personal safety so that they can gradually be given more independence. This cannot be taught in 'Ten Easy Lessons on Safety' because children would never understand the concepts and they would find the information overwhelming and frightening. It therefore needs to be an ongoing process achieved through the normal routines and activities of the day.

Below is a list of what children need to learn and some ideas on how this information can be incorporated into a setting's routine.

Their bodies belong to them

Children should know:

- that some touches are wrong – if it hurts, is scary, makes them feel uncomfortable or is rude
- that they do not have to hug or kiss anyone if they do not want to
- what personal boundaries are, so that they are aware when their own boundaries have been overstepped.

As an early years worker, you can reinforce this information through your everyday contact with children and through the daily routine of the setting. It is important that you always provide a good role model to children, and ensure that children's views and feelings are always respected. For example, you should always ask a child if he or she would like his or her coat done up, rather than doing it without asking. You could also reinforce the above messages by the following.

- Children's questions should always be answered truthfully, with as much detail as the child would understand.
- It is important to support a child's right to limit adults' and other children's behaviour, for example that the child does not want to be tickled or hugged.
- Games worksheets can be used which enable children to label parts of a body.
- Worksheets can cover such topics as: 'How I like being touched' (for example hug from mum or lick from pet dog) and 'How I don't like being touched' (for example having hair pulled or being scratched by the cat).
- Drawing life-size body outlines on pieces of wallpaper can help children develop a sense of their own self.

Emergency telephone numbers

Playing 'Fireman Sam' or hospitals can introduce young children to dealing with emergency situations in a very low key way.

They have the right to privacy

Children should be allowed privacy when using the toilet, and school-aged children need to know that they cannot be interrupted by anyone opening the door. If children need help, this should be given, allowing the child as much privacy as possible.

What to do when they get lost

Children need to know:

- their full name and address and telephone number
- if they get lost in a shop, that they should stop and look around carefully, and if they

cannot see their carer, go to a shop assistant at a till (many shopping centres have a child safety scheme where the shops have special stickers on the door so that children can go there if lost)

- which adults are safe to approach to ask for help, for example a police officer, a lollipop person or a mother with a child
- they should never go into a house, office or phone box with a stranger, but should wait outside while the parents or the police are contacted.

As an early years worker, you can reinforce the above in day-to-day activities, on trips and through stories such as 'Hansel and Gretel', (which also reinforces the 'stranger danger' message). Using storyboards and playing with puppets can also reinforce what to do, as can a visit from the police.

To express and trust their own feelings

Children need to know that they can express their worries, fears, anxieties and feelings without fear of ridicule. Once again, children should be learning this through the way they are treated by their close contacts.

It is often difficult for young children to talk about feelings because they do not have the words to describe how they feel. This can be done effectively through looking at books with them and talking about how the people in the book might feel and why.

For school-age children, worksheets or discussions on the topic of 'What makes me happy/sad/cross' or 'What makes me frightened' or sharing hopes and fears can start children thinking about their feelings and why they feel how they do.

'Stranger danger'

This needs to include the following.

- Who is a stranger? People are not usually either 'good' or 'bad'. Children need to trust their feelings about people.
- How to deal with approaches from strangers.
- Children should understand that they can run away or break normal rules of good behaviour if they feel that they are in danger. They could therefore shout, scream, kick or punch if they feel threatened.
- If someone a child does not know talks to him or her, the child can pretend that he or she did not hear and walk quickly away.

In the early years setting these could be reinforced by:

- a visit from a police officer
- role play
- books/stories
- videos
- exercise on: what would make a child feel uncomfortable
- giving a child a picture of a hand and asking him or her to write or draw a picture of family and friends and/or professional people on each finger, i.e. people who the child could trust
- ensuring visitors to the setting wear badges, so the children know that the visitor is allowed to be there

- discouraging children from wearing personalised clothing (such as hairbands) showing their names outside of school.

How to cope with bullies

Children should cope with bullies or people who are teasing them by:

- shouting 'No' very loudly
- sticking together with friends
- telling and knowing whom to tell about being bullied.

Most settings have a policy on bullying and it is important that all staff are aware of this so that there is consistency in the way that bullying is dealt with. It is important that all bullying is dealt with promptly. Bully boxes are used in some schools, where information on bullies can be put in a special box – this is less threatening for the children than having to speak to someone.

The Kidscape Keepsafe Code (see the next page) can be taught to children over five years, and role play or puppets can be used to reinforce the 'no bullying' rules.

Who they should be going home with

It is important that early years workers know who the child is to go home with, and that children are **never** allowed to go with anyone other than the parent, unless the parent has informed the setting. This message needs to be reinforced with parents.

Older children can be given a password, so that if there is a change in picking-up arrangements, the child knows that he or she should go only with a person who has the password.

To understand the difference between 'good' and 'bad' secrets

It is often better to use the term 'surprise' rather than 'secret'. Children need to know that it is all right not to tell their carer about a birthday present because it is a happy surprise, but that some other secrets should not be kept, especially if they make them feel uncomfortable. No one should ever ask a child to keep a hug, kiss or a touch secret.

An adult is always ready to listen

If a child has a problem or is uncomfortable with a situation, he or she should be able to turn to an adult for support and advice. Being ready to listen and giving children the opportunity to spend some time on a one-to-one basis can build up the child's trust. This is obviously difficult to do especially in schools, but can be done while reading a school book with the child or other activities.

Rules and code of behaviour for different settings and situations

Although children need to know that normally they should comply with an adult's wishes, they also have the right to say 'No' if they feel uncomfortable about what they have been asked to do. Children can help make up their own class rules in a school setting with guidance from a teacher.

It is always important to keep parents informed when you are doing activities to promote children's awareness of personal safety and abuse, because parents can then reinforce the message at home. Also, by informing the parents, it builds up their awareness of safety issues and informs them about the setting's policies on child protection and bullying. Parents should also be aware of the policy on child protection.

Active knowledge ✓

Your supervisor has asked you to plan how you could incorporate teaching children about personal safety into the curriculum and routines of the setting. Pick one subject area, such as bullying or 'What to do if you get lost', and plan how you could do this. Include ideas for specific activities.

Resources

Some professionals are able to come into the setting to reinforce the safety message, such as a police officer, fire officer, school nurse or health visitor.

Kidscape is an organisation formed in 1986 which aims to teach children to protect themselves through 'The Kidscape Keepsafe Code'. This is suitable for children over five years. It produces teaching aids, courses, videos, books and a Kidscape Kit (containing worksheets and booklets). The NSPCC also produces leaflets, posters and other materials for use with children and parents.

C15 Unit test

1 What are the four main types of abuse?
2 If you suspect a child in your setting had been abused, and Social Services had asked you to look out for, and record, any further signs of abuse, what signs might you be looking for?
3 What information might you include in your records, and why is it important to keep accurate records?
4 What role can observations play in the detection of abuse?
5 Why is it important to maintain confidentiality during child protection procedures?
6 What is an indirect disclosure?
7 What could you say in response to a child's disclosure?
8 What is a case conference, who might be present and what is an early years worker's role at the conference?
9 What are the rights of a child and the parents throughout a child protection investigation?
10 Name three voluntary organisations who have a role in child protection, and explain their role.
11 Under the Children Act, what orders are sometimes used in child protection procedures? Briefly describe their main points.

Unit C16

Observe and assess the development and behaviour of children

Most early years workers observe and assess children informally. They may notice that a child seems tired or particularly excited. Spending time formally observing children allows us to focus on and learn more about the children we are working with. This allows us to consider how we might best meet the needs of individual or groups of children. Observations can also help us to provide more accurate information to other professionals and to parents. This unit considers ways of observing children as well as how the information gained can be used.

The elements for this unit are:

C16.1 Observe children's behaviour and performance
C16.2 Use observation results to inform the children's future care and education

Element C16.1 Observe children's behaviour and performance

This element looks primarily at the reasons why we observe children and how to plan and carry out an observation successfully.

WHAT YOU NEED TO LEARN

- Why observing children is important
- Planning an observation
- Methods of recording
- Carrying out an observation

Why observing children is important

We can learn a lot about the children we are working with simply by stepping back and watching them. This may at first seem to some people to be a waste of time, but if we study the children we are working with, we are more likely to be able to meet their needs. There are many ways in which observations can help us to work more effectively with children. The spider diagram below shows some of the most common ways.

To report to other professionals

There are times when other professionals may need to gain information about how a child behaves or copes in our setting. We may also help other professionals by informing them about a child's progress, for example feeding back to a speech therapist about how a child's language is developing.

To see if children are progressing

Regular assessments of children will help us to see if children are making progress with specific areas of their development.

To check a child's overall development

Carrying out an overall observation of children's development may make us more aware of any areas in which they are not developing as quickly as might be expected. It may also help us to get an overall feel of a child's needs.

Ways in which observations can be used

To report to parents

Observations can help us report more accurately to parents about their child. We may be able to reassure them as a result of an observation or indicate any areas of difficulty.

To learn more about a child's particular needs

Observing individual children can give us the information to help us plan a particular approach to working with them.

To inform planning

Observing children's developmental skills, such as their ability to use scissors, will help us to plan activities that will meet children's needs. This means that we will avoid giving them a task that is too difficult for them to manage. Having an accurate and up-to-date view of a child will also mean that we can plan activities that will encourage areas of development at the child's level.

To evaluate activities, routines or strategies used with children

We can observe a group of children's reactions and behaviour to evaluate whether our routines, strategies or activities are effective. We may be able to determine from the observation how to make changes to the way we work, plan or handle situations in order to meet the children's needs.

To resolve a particular problem

Observing a child more closely may guide us towards understanding a particular type of behaviour or reaction, for example a child who finds it difficult to play with one other child.

Confidentiality and observations

Most parents are happy for their children to be observed, although they probably will not want other parents or people who have no involvement with their child reading such observations! This means that we need to store our observations carefully and make sure that we protect children's identity. There are many ways of protecting children's identity, for example some settings always refer to the subject child A, or refer to a child by his or her first name only, while changing names that are unusually spelt or are uncommon. Children's ages are generally given in terms of their years and months.

The test of whether you have protected a child's identity will be whether someone else who is familiar with the setting can work out the identity from any details you have recorded.

How to store observations will depend on the setting in which you work. Some settings place observations and assessments about the children in their files, whereas in a home setting it is normal to give them to the parent.

Planning an observation

It is important that you plan your observation carefully before starting to record. Careful planning is more likely to result in a successful observation. Several factors need to be taken into consideration when planning.

Gaining permission

Before carrying out any type of recording, you must always seek permission from your supervisor or, where appropriate, the parents. Most settings will have their own procedures and policies relating to observing children. It is not uncommon for some settings to ask parents for permission to carry out observations as part of their admissions procedure. Generally, most parents are happy for their children to be observed, providing that they are able to have access to the records.

This child is being watched to see if she has developed more hand–eye coordination as part of a structured programme

Checking before carrying out an observation also avoids situations where other adults in the setting distract or call for the child because they do not know that you are carrying out an observation.

Methods of recording

Method	Uses
Free description Also known as narrative description and written record	To record the behaviour of a child over a very short period of time, often less than five minutes. The observer notes down what he or she is seeing, which gives a portrait of a child's activity during this time.
Checklists and tick charts	Mostly used to assess children's stage of development. This is one of the methods used by health visitors during routine check-ups. Specific activites are looked for, either during a structured assessment where children are asked to do activities, or by observing children over a period of time.
Time sample	This method is used to look at children's activity over a predetermined length of time, for example over a morning. Children are observed at regular intervals during the recording, say every ten minutes, and the observation is recorded on a prepared sheet.
Event sample	Event samples are often used to look closely at one aspect of a child's development or behaviour, i.e. how frequently the child sucks his or her thumb, or shows aggression towards other children. Every time a child shows the type of behaviour or activity we interested in, it is recorded on a prepared sheet.
Target child	The aim is to record one child's activity over a long period without any gaps in the recording process. Several codes or signs are used during the observation to allow the observer to maintain the recording. A prepared sheet is used to help the observer.

There are several methods of observing and recording children's behaviour and performance. Each method has its advantages and disadvantages and most early years workers find they need to be familiar with several. This allows them to match the recording method to the situation they are observing. The chart on page 242 shows some frequently used recording methods. Guidance on how to use each method is given on pages 244–248.

Matching your recording method to your purpose

With several methods available for use when observing children, it is important to make sure that you choose a method that suits your purpose. For example, the free description method is a good one for examining closely how a child achieves something, but it will not tell you about a child's general activity over a longer period.

For an observation to be successful, you must carefully consider what you are hoping to achieve. This is normally referred to as the aim of an observation. Below are some examples of aims, with the method that was used.

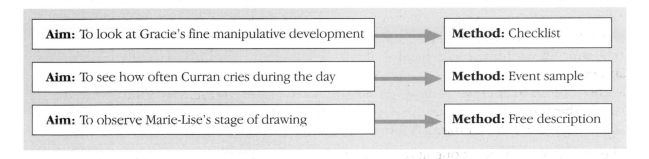

Aim: To look at Gracie's fine manipulative development → **Method:** Checklist

Aim: To see how often Curran cries during the day → **Method:** Event sample

Aim: To observe Marie-Lise's stage of drawing → **Method:** Free description

Being observed can affect children's behaviour and performance

When they know they are being observed, most people find that their performance changes. In some situations being observed means that we try harder, whereas in other situations it makes us nervous and our performance deteriorates. The same is true for children. This means that we must decide, when planning an observation, if we are going to observe children without their being aware of our presence or what we are doing, or if we are going to talk and be part of the recording. The term **non-participant** observer is used when the observer is unobtrusive and does not interact with the children. The term **participant** observer is used when the observer interacts with the child.

Advantages of being a non-participant observer
- Children are more likely to show 'natural' behaviour.
- It is easier to record what happens when you are not actively involved.
- The recording is more likely to be objective.
- Most recording methods can be used as a non-participant observer.

Disadvantages of being a non-participant observer
- It can be difficult to find a place where you are unobtrusive while still able to hear what is said.
- If you are wishing to observe particular activities or behaviour, they might not occur.

- It might take a long time to collect all the information about a child's development if children are not asked to do certain activities.

Advantages of being a participant observer
- You can ask children to carry out tasks or activities rather than waiting for them to happen spontaneously – this is useful when carrying out a checklist on development.
- You can ask children why they are doing something, for example if you observed a child working out a simple mathematical problem, you could ask the child what he or she is doing and why.

Disadvantages of being a participant observer
- Children may feel under pressure because someone is looking at them.
- Children may reply to a question in a different way because they are hoping to please the adult.
- Not all recording methods are compatible with being a participant observer, especially methods where a description of events is required, i.e. free description.
- If an unfamiliar person carries out an observation, the child may feel uncomfortable.

How much of this child's behaviour and performance is as a result of knowing that someone is watching?

Checklist when planning an observation
- Make sure that you have permission to carry out an observation.
- Make sure that other workers in the setting know when and whom you are hoping to observe.
- Decide what you need to observe and have a clear aim.
- Choose your method and consider whether you will need to be a participant or a non-participant observer.

Carrying out an observation

Free description
The aim of free description is to provide a portrait of what a child is doing. This method is useful if you need to observe a situation closely such as the difficulty a child has in doing up his or her coat.

Equipment
Notepad.
Pen.

Method
Free descriptions are generally written in the present tense in the form of a running

commentary. The idea is to provide the reader with a detailed description of the activity and the way in which the child carried it out. This means that you should include details of the child's facial expressions, body posture and any speech that he or she uses. In essence, you should try to note down as much as you possibly can about what you are seeing.

Carrying out a free description is an intensive process and this means that most people can only record for short periods.

Example of a free description

Ravi is standing up in front of Michaela, who is sitting on a chair. Ravi seems to be looking down at Michaela. She is saying 'Shall we dress up?' Michaela nods and smiles, Ravi smiles too and they both walk over to the dressing-up corner. Ravi takes a pink dress, grasping it in her right hand, and places it on the floor. She pulls the back of the dress open with both hands. She steps into the dress using her right foot first and pulls up the dress gradually to a standing position, placing her right arm into the dress and then her left. Ravi walks over to the nursery nurse and looks up. She asks 'Can you do my buttons up?' and turns around.

Checklists and tickcharts

Checklists and tickcharts are quick and easy to use. They are mostly used to record large areas of children's development. They do not usually record how a child achieves a task, simply whether or not he or she is doing it competently.

Equipment

Prepared sheet – some settings have their own formats, although it is possible to devise you own checklist.

Pen.

Method

You can fill in a checklist or tick chart by being a participant observer and asking children to do activities and tasks, or you can note down when children are showing the skills during a session. It is important to use a checklist that is appropriate for the ages and stages of the children you are working with. A good checklist will also have space for comments.

The main disadvantage of checklists and tick charts is that the observer must make a decision as to how competent a child is. This can mean that there is a danger of bias if observers have a strong interest in a child.

Case study

Simon had planned a series of activities to help Sarah, aged four years, learn to count five objects. At the end of the series he thought that he should carry out an observation to see if her skills had improved. On one task, Sarah had miscounted the number of objects. Simon was disappointed because he had previously seen Sarah count up to five in other situations. On his checklist he put a tick in the 'yes' column indicating that Sarah had mastered counting up to five.

Why did Simon act as he did?

Why it is sometimes better for staff who are not involved with particular children to carry out assessments?

An example of part of a checklist designed to look at a three-year-old's fine manipulative skills is shown below.

Child
Child's age _____ Observer _____
Date of observation _____ Time _____

Activity	Yes	No	Comments
Puts together three-piece puzzle			
Snips with scissors			
Paints in circular movements			
Holds crayons with fingers, not fist			
Can thread four large beads			
Turns pages in a book one by one			
Can put on and take off coat			

Time sample

The aim of a time sample is to observe children at evenly spaced intervals during a session or predetermined length of time.

Equipment
Prepared sheet with times when a recording is due to take place.
Pen.
Watch or stopwatch.

Method
The spaces between recordings will depend on the duration of the observation, i.e. if you wish to observe a child over three hours, you might decide to record his or her activity every 15 minutes, whereas if you were to record a child's activity over an hour, you might decide to observe every 10 minutes.

To carry out the observation, you should look to see what the child is doing and record a 'snapshot' of this, in much the same way as a free description. Recordings should indicate what the child is doing and are often written in the present tense.

The disadvantage of time samples is that a significant behaviour might be shown between recording intervals.

Event sample

An event sample records the frequency of behaviours or activities that are being looked for. It may provide clues as to why a child is behaving or reacting in certain ways. It may also show that a perceived problem such as a child being aggressive is not as acute as is thought.

Event samples are normally carried out as non-participant observations, to make sure that an objective account is given.

Equipment
Prepared sheet.
Pen.

Method
The sheet you use for recording will vary according to the purpose of the observation, i.e. if you are wishing to record the frequency in which a baby cries over a day, it will be important to have a column to show what soothes the baby as well as a column to record how long the crying lasted.

Carrying out the observation is relatively straightforward, although if you are wishing to record a particular behaviour or activity over a longer period such as a week, you might need to ask colleagues or parents to fill in parts of the sheet if you are unavailable at certain times.

Below is an example of a prepared sheet which could be used to look at the interaction of Jo with other children over a day.

Event	Time	Activity of child	Social group	Language used	Comments
1	10.03 am	Playing in the sand	Jo, Jacob, Martha and Curran	'Look at me! Look at this, what I've done'	Jo leaned over and said this to Jacob
2	10.07 am	Playing with digger in sand tray	Jo, Jacob, Martha	"Brrrmmm, Brrrmmm, this is my road, out of the way'	Jo was talking to Martha while pushing her toys out of the way

It is important to design your event sample sheet to capture the information you think will be useful. The event sample below was designed to look at how much food a toddler was eating during a day because of concerns that he was not eating enough. Notice how the columns for recording information have been changed from the previous example.

Event	Time	Food eaten	Quantity of food	Setting	Comments
1	18.04–8.09 am	Squares of toast, drink of milk	Equivalent to half a slice of toast and half a beaker of milk	High chair, kitchen	Some squares of toast were dropped on the floor. Joachim sipped milk after eating toast and dropped beaker on the floor. Said 'No more, all gone' and raised arms to be taken out of high chair.
2	9.45–9.47 am	Biscuit	Most of the biscuit	Lounge, standing up	Joachim went up to adult and pointed to her biscuit. Adult gave biscuit.
3	10.15–10.20 am	Biscuit	Half a biscuit	Kitchen, standing up	Joachim pointed to biscuit tin and said 'More, more'. Adult gave biscuit. Some biscuit eaten, rest dropped on floor.

Target child – a precoded observation

This is an observation that is carried out in order to record the activity of one child during a session or predetermined length of time. The aim is to focus on one child. To help the observer keep up with tracking the child, a code has to be used to reduce the number of words needing to be written. This type of observation requires practice and familiarity with the coding system. Target child observations are normally non-participant observations.

Equipment
Prepared sheet.
Pen.

Method
Many settings have their own methods and codes for carrying out target child observations. If your setting does not have a format, you will need to draw up your own sheet and make up your own codes. It is impossible in this type of observation to provide the detail that can be gained from other observations such as free description or time samples. This means that the observer must make some choices about what to observe and what is important during the observation.

Example for target child observation

Individual child-tracking observation

Name of child **Lee**   Observer **Carrie**   Date **24/6/99**

Ages of child **3**   yrs **2** months   No. of adults present **2**   No. of children present **6**

Free play/structured play/directed activity

Time	Description of activity	Language	Grouping	Level of involvement
10.00 am	TC scooping sand using left hand repeated movements	TC →	P	4
10.02	TC burying r. hand, scooping with other	→ TC ←	I	4
10.03	TC nods head. Other child copies TC, TC smiles	C → TC	P	3

Key

Grouping	Language		Level of involvement
WG = Whole group	TC → A	Balanced interaction between adult and child	1 = No activity
SG = Small group	TC → C	Balanced interaction between target child and another child	2 = Frequently distracted
P = Pair			3 = Fairly continuous activity
I = Individual	A → C	Adult interacts with more than one child	
	C → TC	Another child interacts with target child	4 = Absorbed in activity
	→ TC ←	Target child talks to himself/herself	
	TC →	No interaction	

Objectivity in observations

It can be hard to remain objective when observing. Recording methods such as free description rely on noting down as much as is possible, but often so much is happening that some choices have to be made by the observer about what is relevant and important. Two people recording the same activity may produce different observations – for example, one person may decide that a smile is important and record it, while another person may decide not to record it.

Ways to ensure accuracy when observing children

In order to gain accurate information, it is a good idea to carry out several observations on a child using different methods. This allows us to build up a picture of development and should ensure that we are not misled by a single observation into taking a false view of the child. It is also helpful to consider whether some observations should be carried out by colleagues who do not know the child very well, in order to gain an objective view. The single most important thing to remember when recording is to concentrate on what you are seeing, not what you believe or think you know about the child.

Observing children as a non-participant observer

There are some methods such as event samples where, if possible, it is best to be a non-participant observer. This means that you need to be able to observe children as unobtrusively as possible. This is not always easy. If you cannot find a place out of sight of the child you wish to observe, you will need to think of ways in which to work while not drawing attention to yourself. In some cases you may be able to spend some time near the child before starting, which will allow him or her to lose interest in you. If often helps to avoid making eye contact with the child while you are recording, as eye contact can draw attention to what you are doing.

It is also important that other workers in the setting are aware that you are carrying out an observation so that they do not expect you to become involved with the children.

Observing children as a participant observer

If you are actively working with children as you observe them, you will need to be aware that your actions and language may influence their performance. If you are looking at several children, it is important to use similar language and comments to all of the children if you are going to do any comparative work, for example giving all the children the same instructions or praising all the children in the same way. You will need to make sure that the language you use when speaking to children is clear and that they can understand the instruction being given. The way you use instructions will vary according to the age and needs of the children you are working with. For example, a very young child may be best encouraged by making the task part of a game, while children who are shy may need more time to become comfortable before starting the assessment.

We know that being observed can make us feel uncomfortable and so one of the roles of a participant observer is to make the children feel at ease. This might be done by being encouraging, smiling and making eye contact with the children. You may also prompt children or question children in order that they are able to carry out a task if this is appropriate to the type of recording you are undertaking. If you are not meant to support the children in a task, you should make sure that you still praise the children and say things to make them feel supported such as 'Yes, that one is a bit tricky, isn't it. I think we're meant to do it like this...'.

Managing situations where children are not coping with the task

In situations where children are being asked to complete tasks, you will need to make sure that such tasks are not inappropriate for the age or stage of the child. Tasks will need to be within their developmental capability if they are not to feel overwhelmed, i.e. if you are looking at fine manipulative skills and a child is finding it difficult to use a pair of scissors, there is no point in carrying on with the assessment if the child is then required to cut carefully around a shape.

You should note the facial expressions and body language of a child while assessing, to see if he or she is feeling under pressure. If you sense that the child's starting to feel nervous or disappointed in his or her own performance, you should intervene, either by praising the child or by helping him or her to manage the task.

Case study

As part of the setting's observation process, Jack was asked to cut out a shape. He did so quite easily and confidently. When he was asked if he could do a jigsaw puzzle, Jack frowned and started to look worried. He looked at the pieces and it became apparent that this was one task that he was still not able to do. Sandra, who was observing him, put down her sheet and said to him: 'This looks fun, let's do it together, shall we?' When they had finished she praised him for helping her and then carried on with other parts of the assessment. She later recorded that Jack was unable to put together an eight-piece puzzle.

Why was it important that Sandra did not simply carry on with the rest of the assessment?

Why did Sandra praise Jack, even though he had not done it by himself?

Why is it important to notice children's facial expressions and body language while carrying out participant observations?

Element C16.2 Use observation results to inform the children's future care and education

WHAT YOU NEED TO LEARN

- Ensuring observations are informative
- Preparing evaluations and conclusions
- Using observations in the planning process

Ensuring observations are informative

In order for observations to be useful, it is important that you record enough information. Part of this comes with careful planning, for example making sure if you are using prepared sheets that they are suitable for what you wish to observe. Methods such as free description require that you try to write in detail, otherwise you will have difficulty afterwards in producing a useful evaluation.

Active knowledge

Look at the following observations written at the same time:

Observation A

Anne-Marie leans on the table using her left elbow. In her right hand she holds a pencil in an unusual grasp between her thumb and third finger. She puts the pen down to count with her fingers and then brings both hands to her head. She twiddles her hair and scratches her chin. She sucks her pencil and talks out loud. 'One, two, three and that's four' counting the cubes on the table. She picks up the pencil in her right hand and says the answer out loud 'Four'. She quickly writes 'four' on her worksheet. She looks across at her friend and smiles.

Observation B

Anne-Marie is sitting at the table. She counts the cubes 'One, two, three and that's four'. She picks up the pencil and writes the answer on the worksheet. She smiles at her friend.

Which observation is more likely to be useful?

What types of detail make it more useful?

Preparing evaluations and conclusions

Presenting your observations

Once you have carried out observations on a child or children, you will need to present them in a format that will be useful to your setting. Some settings have set ways of recording information and have prepared paperwork. There are some pieces of information that always need to accompany an observation, as follows:

- age of the child in years and months
- date when the observation was carried out
- first name of the child or another way of identifying who was observed, for example child A
- timing of the observation
- setting – where the observation was carried out
- activity that was being recorded
- other children or adults who were present.

These pieces of information are vital in order to be able to evaluate your observation fully. For example, the time of day or the numbers of children around the observed child might have affected the child's concentration.

Evaluating your evidence

Although you will probably learn quite a lot simply from spending some time watching and assessing a child, writing an evaluation will enable you to deepen your understanding of what you have seen.

There are different ways of presenting your evaluations (also known as interpretations) depending on how they are going to be used. For example, most early years courses ask students to research their evaluations quite widely in order to check whether the students have a good understanding of child development. This means that if you are using observation as part of your course of study, you will need to show that you can relate what you have seen to current child development theories. If observations are being carried out in the workplace, there may only be a need to refer to the child's age and stage of development.

There are no set ways in which evaluations need to be written, although the following points should be considered.

- The evaluation should be based on what you have recorded.
- The links between children's actual stage of development and expected stage are noted.
- Supporting evidence is provided for conclusions you are drawing.

Preparing to evaluate an observation

Most people who are carrying out observations, either as part of their coursework or as part of their job, develop their own technique for writing evaluations. Below is a step-by-step approach that some early years workers find helpful.

1   Start by highlighting those parts of an observation that are of particular interest, for example the achievements of children or behaviour that is unusual.
2   Consider what conclusions could be drawn from what you have seen, for example a child smiling and passing a crayon to another child might indicate that he or she is able to socialise and share equipment.
3   Decide whether the behaviour or actions you have seen fit in with the expected stages of development for a child of this age, for example a child of three years old should be starting to share with other children.
4   Show how your conclusions fit in with current theories of child development or early years care practice. (While this step is not always required in workplaces, it is generally required to show knowledge in early years care and education courses such as the NVQ.)

Example of an evaluation

During the observation, I noticed that Alex spent 10 minutes doing jigsaw puzzles. I think this means he enjoys the activity. He is also showing that he can concentrate and play independently. I was able to see that he was favouring his left hand and that his hand–eye co-ordination was well developed. He smiled when he finished the puzzle and looked across at Janie (the staff member). I think this shows that he needed some adult praise and recognition for his work, but also that he is becoming confident.

Alex also showed that he is able to co-operate with other children in the group. I noticed that during his play he passed across an apron to Simon and also went to help Alun when he fell off his chair.

Consolidation

Look at the following snippets of information taken from various observations carried out on children:

A four-year-old can read words from a story book.

A three-year-old observes but does not join in play activities with other children of the same age.

A five-year-old has a tantrum because he is not first in the queue.

Two six-year-olds spend 20 minutes playing cooperatively in the 'shop'.

Consider whether the children are behaving within expected stages of development for their ages.

Using observations in the planning process

It is important to use the information gained from observations to help you plan more effectively. Observations that are carried out and not evaluated are not particularly helpful. Where possible, settings should look at observations carefully and consider how the information gained can help them work with the children more effectively. This means that if you are asked to carry out an observation, you could also include a list of recommendations that your colleagues might consider.

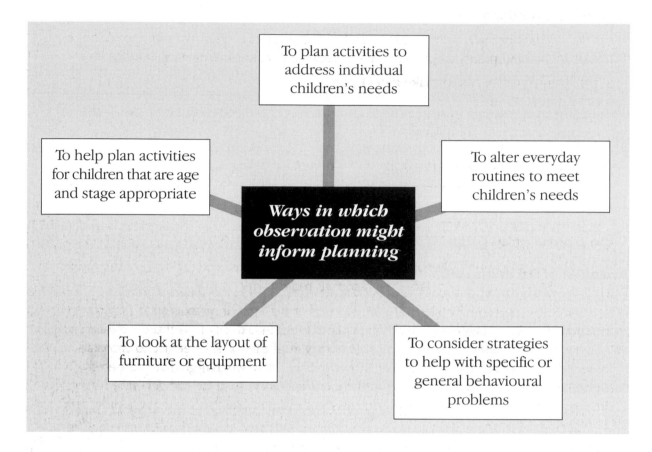

This may mean planning a series of activities to help promote an area of development in a particular child or using the information to change a routine procedure to make it more appropriate for the children you are working with. For example, after carrying out some observations on a group at story time, one setting decided to make story time a little shorter because the observations showed that many children were becoming restless after 12 minutes.

Observations can also be used to help plan strategies where children are showing unwanted behaviour, for example a child who is attention-seeking might be observed and the information gained might help in devising a strategy to manage behaviour. They can also be used by settings wishing to plan a more effective layout, for example a setting might carry out an observation to see which piece of equipment is the least used in the setting.

Below is an example of the type of recommendations you could make.

Recommendations

Ushma needs more activities that require fine manipulative skills. She will need some adult support and plenty of praise as she is lacking in confidence. Suggested activities:

- Threading large beads to make a necklace.
- Large floor puzzle.
- Drawing around farm shapes.
- Sewing cards.

I suggest that Ushma is observed again in a month.

Consolidation

Look at this evaluation of an observation carried out by an early years worker who had been looking at one area of the setting where several minor accidents had occurred:

During the observation I saw that several children were trying to put their coats on at the same time, while some children were trying to make their way to the outside door. I think that the situation may have been made more difficult because children who were already outside seemed to encourage one or two children to hurry up. Several coats were lying on the floor which might have delayed children from getting outside. Some children were also standing in the middle of the corridor while putting on their coats. I think that they stand in the middle of the corridor so that they can talk with their friends as they are getting ready, as some of their friends have coat-pegs on the other side of the corridor.

Write some recommendations that could be made for colleagues to consider.

Why it is important to review and observe everyday routines?

Presenting your recommendations to others

The way in which you present your recommendations will depend on the reasons for carrying out the observations. For example, students working towards gaining a qualification may need to write up their recommendations and then prepare an activity plan to show that they can plan effectively, while workplaces might not always need written outcomes.

Every workplace will have its own ways of using the information gained from observations. In some workplaces recommendations may be talked through or shown to the supervisor or manager, whereas in other settings team meetings might be held to discuss the outcomes of observations. Parents might also be involved in looking at the observations and recommendations, so that they can make suggestions or comments. This means that parents are being kept informed of their child's progress and the ways in which the setting is trying to meet the child's needs.

In some cases other professionals might also be involved in drawing up recommendations. For example, a speech therapist might suggest that a child who is having difficulty in communicating in large groups be given opportunities to communicate in a more structured way such as sharing nursery rhymes in a group situation.

Case study

Jamie was observed because early years workers were concerned that he seemed to be very withdrawn. After speaking to his parents, it was decided that it would be useful to gain some more information about how he interacted with staff and other children in the setting. His key worker decided to carry out three observations at different times of the week using different methods. The aim was to build up a picture of Jamie's language and social development.

At the end of the week, the key worker considered the three observations and, using developmental charts, was able to produce an interesting evaluation and some recommendations. Her main conclusion was that although Jamie was not comfortable when in large groups or with some adults, he played and interacted well with two particular children. On the day when these children were not present in the session, Jamie seemed to be more reserved. A meeting between parents, the key worker and the manager of the setting was held and the key worker outlined her suggestions for helping Jamie. These included making sure that he had plenty of support when his friends were not present and some ideas for structuring activities that would help Jamie interact with other children, for example small group activities such as cooking and gardening. It was also suggested by Jamie's parents that another adult apart from the key worker should also work closely with Jamie so that he learnt to be confident with more than one adult in the setting.

Why was it important to carry out more than one observation on Jamie?

Why is it important to refer to expected stages of development?

How could working with Jamie's parents help meet his needs?

C16 Unit test

1   Give three reasons why observations might be carried out.
2   Why is confidentiality an issue when observing children?
3   What are the advantages of being a non-participant observer?
4   What are the advantages of the free description method of observation?
5   Why are checklists and tickcharts often used to record children's stages of development?
6   Why is it a good idea to carry out several observations on one child?
7   What other pieces of information are needed to accompany an observation?
8   How can observations help evaluate the effectiveness of a layout?
9   How might observations be used to help other professionals?
10   Why is it good practice to involve parents recording children's stages of development?

Unit E3

Plan and equip environments for children

Maintaining a safe and secure environment is the most vital role of early years workers. This unit discusses how to establish and maintain such an environment.

The elements for this unit are:

E3.1   Establish and maintain a safe environment for children
E3.2   Establish and carry out safety and emergency procedures
E3.3   Select furniture and equipment for children
E3.4   Organise and maintain the physical environment for children

Element E3.1   Establish and maintain a safe environment for children

Early years workers have a responsibility to keep children in their care safe. It is a sad fact that more than a million children each year are taken to hospital because of accidents at home and in early years settings. Children and babies are vulnerable to accidents because they are often unaware of the dangers around them and the consequences of their behaviour. This means that early years workers need to be aware of the principles of health and safety and first aid.

This element looks closely at the statutory framework that exists to protect both children and adults in the workplace.

Two main pieces of legislation provide a framework for ensuring children's health and safety while you are working with them: the Health and Safety at Work Act 1974 and the Children Act 1989. By understanding and following these pieces of legislation, early years settings will have the basis for providing a safe and healthy environment for children.

WHAT YOU NEED TO LEARN

- Ensuring children's health and safety – Health and Safety at Work Act 1974
- Ensuring children's health and safety – Children Act 1989
- Caring for animals in accordance with hygiene standards and health and safety requirements

Ensuring children's health and safety – Health and Safety at Work Act 1974

The Health and Safety at Work Act is the main piece of legislation that affects day-to-day provision of health and safety in workplaces. The Act was designed to protect employees, and additional regulations have been added to it since its introduction. The legislation is fairly comprehensive, so settings that implement the legislation carefully will be sure they are providing a safe environment for both employees and children.

If you are responsible for the health and safety procedures of your setting, you will need to make sure that you keep up to date. To check the current regulations, you can contact the government agency responsible: Health and Safety Executive, Information Centre, Broad Lane, Sheffield S3 7HQ (information line 0541 545500; web site http://www.open.gov.uk/hse/ hsehome.htm).

The main features of the Health and Safety at Work Act affect both employers and employees.

Duty of employers

There are important duties for employers under the Act. Essentially, the Act requires employers to ensure, so far is reasonably practicable, the health, safety and welfare at work of all employees. In practice, this is done by providing safety equipment, training and by writing and implementing safety procedures.

Employers with more than five employees also need to carry out a risk assessment on their workplace and to write a safety policy showing how risks are to be minimised.

Duty of employees

Under the Act, employees must make sure that their actions do not harm themselves or others. They have a duty to comply with their employer's safety procedures and to use the equipment provided, and to act with due regard for their own and others' safety.

Health and safety regulations

Since the original legislation, the Health and Safety Executive has also added regulations that employers must follow. It is important for supervisors and managers to understand the principles of these regulations.

Control of Substances Hazardous to Health Regulations 1994 (COSHH)

Most settings use cleaning products or have other materials that potentially could be hazardous. In addition, while caring for children, early years workers may have to handle nappies or clean up after toileting or other accidents. The COSHH Regulations make settings consider how they can limit the risks from these activities. This might mean that all cleaning materials are stored carefully in a locked cupboard. It might also mean that disposable gloves are provided to prevent infections such as hepatitis or HIV being passed on. It is important to remember that as an employee, you will have a duty to use any protection that is provided and also to follow the guidelines of the setting.

The chart below shows how settings might minimise risks.

Potential hazard/ procedure	Dangers of hazard	Methods of reducing risk
Cleaning materials	Accidental poisoning Fire risk Unstable if mixed together Skin irritant	Lock all cleaning products in a kitchen cupboard Ensure all products are labelled Follow manufacturer's instructions Wear protective gloves Do not use products near children
Changing nappies, toileting	Infection	Wear disposable gloves and aprons when changing nappies or assisting children with toileting Put soiled nappies into bags provided and dispose of in separate bin Clean changing areas after use Wash hands before and after nappy changing or assisting children with toileting
First aid treatment	Infection	Record all accidents in accident report book Keep separate books for staff and for children in office Use disposable gloves Dispose of items used during treatment in bags provided

Keys to good practice
Hazardous substances

- Use separate bins and bags for human waste and ordinary waste.
- Use disposable gloves and aprons when handling bodily fluids and cleaning materials.
- Carefully store chemicals in a locked cupboard.
- Always follow manufacturers' instructions.

Reporting of Injuries, Diseases and Dangerous Occurrences Regulations 1995 (RIDDOR)

As part of these Regulations, workplaces must provide an accident report book – in practice, most settings keep separate books for employees and children. All accidents should be recorded, and some types of accident have to be reported to the Health and Safety Executive. Any injuries to employees that mean they cannot work for three or more days must be reported.

Keys to good practice
Reporting accidents

- Maintain separate accident report books for staff and children.
- Keep accident report books in a central place.
- Ensure accident report books are kept up to date.
- Report serious accidents to the Health and Safety Executive; also report when a staff member has been off work for three or more days because of an injury sustained at work.

WAVERLEY NURSERY STAFF ACCIDENT REPORT FORM

Report of an accident or injury to a person at work or on duty

This form must be completed in all cases of accident, injury or dangerous occurrence and submitted to the Health and Safety Officer

Name of injured person

Date of birth

Position held in organisation

Date and time of accident

Particulars of injury/accident

Activity at time of injury/accident

Place of injury/accident

Details of injury/accident

First aid treatment (if any) given

Was the injured person taken to hospital? If so, where?

Names and positions of persons present when the accident occurred

Signature of person reporting incident

A form for reporting accidents involving staff

Fire Precautions (Workplace) Regulations 1997

It is important that all settings have plans and procedures for action in the event of a fire. This means that most settings have regular fire drills and equipment such as fire extinguishers and smoke detectors, and fire alarms are tested regularly. Records of fire drills and tests should be kept, and signs showing what to do in the event of a fire should be placed in every room. Fire officers can also give advice about evacuation procedures and it is good practice in early years settings to make sure that these are rehearsed with the children. In some settings, doors and windows may have to be locked to ensure children's safety. In such cases, it is important that they can be opened easily and quickly by an adult in the event of an emergency.

Keys to good practice
Fire precautions

- Fire exits must be kept unlocked and unobstructed at all times.
- Fire exits must be easily accessible.
- Regular checks should be carried out to make sure that fire alarms and extinguishers are working.
- Rehearse evacuation procedures regularly with the children.
- Advice about evacuation procedures should be obtained from a fire officer.

Settings have to be aware of changes in regulations. The running men signs have replaced text-only 'fire exit' signs

Health and Safety (First Aid) Regulations 1981

First aid skills are always important when working with children, but there is a legal duty for employers to keep a first aid box and appoint at least one person to be responsible in the event of an accident. Most early years settings also need at least one trained first aider. It is important to remember that first aid qualifications need to be updated and that it is sensible to have several staff trained in first aid.

Keys to good practice
First aid

- Ensure several members of staff have first aid training.
- Keep first aid boxes out of reach of children, but still accessible to staff.
- Take first aid boxes on outings.
- Check first aid boxes regularly to see if contents are complete and that items are not out of date.
- Display signs to show where the nearest first aid box is kept.

Suggested contents of a first aid box

There are no specific requirements as to what should be in a first aid box, as the quantity and the contents will depend on the needs of individual settings. It is however essential that contents of first aid boxes are regularly checked to make sure that items are not missing or are out of date. Below is a contents list for a first aid box suggested by the Health and Safety Executive:

- a leaflet giving general guidance on first aid
- 20 individually wrapped sterile adhesive dressings (assorted sizes)
- two sterile eye pads
- four individually wrapped triangular bandages (preferably sterile)
- six safety pins
- six medium-sized (approximately 12 cm × 12 cm) individually wrapped sterile unmedicated wound dressings
- two large (approximately 18 cm × 18 cm) sterile individually wrapped unmedicated wound dressings
- one pair of disposable gloves.

In addition, most first aid kits also contain scissors.

Maintaining safety equipment

Many items of equipment are used to keep children safe in early years settings. Regular checks on all safety equipment should be carried out, and manufacturer's instructions should be closely followed, especially if items need maintaining or cleaning. In general, it is considered good practice to buy new equipment to be sure that it conforms with the latest safety regulations. Second-hand or older equipment needs to be carefully checked as some items can become less effective through wear and tear. The chart below shows some of the common equipment used, and the reasons for its use.

Equipment	Purpose
Staircases	Prevent babies and children from falling downstairs or from having access to certain areas
Reins and harnesses	Prevent children from straying into a road or dangerous area when they are outside. Also used in pushchairs and highchairs to prevent children from falling out.
Electric plug covers	Prevent children from putting their fingers or objects into plug sockets
Highchairs	Help young children to sit safely at mealtimes. Harnesses to strap children in
Bath mats	Prevent children and babies from slipping in the bath
Window and cupboard door locks	Prevent children from opening cupboards and windows
Corner protectors	Protect children from sharp edges on furniture
Cooker guards	In home situations, it might not be possible to prevent children from being in the kitchen. A cooker guard prevents children from tipping over pans.
Car seat/booster cushion	Helps to protect children and babies if a car suddenly brakes or is involved in an accident. Car seats have to be correctly fitted and must not be bought second hand. Seats must be correct for the age of the baby or child
Fire guards	Used to put around heaters and radiators to prevent children from being burnt

Ensuring children's health and safety – Children Act 1989

Within the Children Act, several requirements directly relate to health and safety. Checking that these requirements are met is part of the local authority's duties, and is carried out by inspection units.

Annual registration

Under the Children Act, settings that provide care for more than two hours for children under the age of eight years must be registered with the local authority. Registration has to be renewed each year and the setting must be inspected as part of the registration process. The aim of registration is to make sure that settings are safe environments for children and that staff can provide the necessary care. This means that staff qualifications are checked and that procedures and policies relating to the care and safety of children are examined.

Adult:child ratios

There are now guidelines which early years settings need to follow in relation to the number of children that adults can supervise. Inspectors check whether settings are meeting these requirements. The adult:child ratios vary according to the age of the children being cared for the type of setting. They reflect the fact that very young children need more adult supervision and attention than older children.

Adult:child ratios can vary from region to region as each inspection unit has to satisfy itself that ratios in settings are appropriate. This means that you need to find out the requirements in your area.

The chart opposite gives an indication of the types of adult:child ratios that are commonly found, although you must remember *there are regional variations*.

Age of children	Number of staff or adult helpers to children
0–1	1:2
1–2	1:3
2–3	1:4
3–5	1:6

An example of adult:child ratios from one area

Caring for animals in accordance with hygiene standards and health and safety requirements

Any setting that cares for animals will have to pay particular attention to health and safety. While children can learn a lot from and enjoy contact with animals, care has to be taken with hygiene and safety. Some diseases are associated with animals and it is important before introducing a new pet to make sure that you are aware of any risks. For example, a risk of caring for cats and dogs is the danger that children can become infected with one of the worms that can be present in these animals' faeces.

Keys to good practice
Minimising the risk of infection when caring for animals

- Ensure that children wash their hands thoroughly after handling any animal.
- Feed animals away from kitchen areas.
- Use separate utensils for feeding animals.
- Make sure that animals are not allowed near children's food or sleeping areas.
- Follow recommended care routines for animals, for example vaccinations, worming, flea control measures.
- Regularly clean animals' cages or areas.

In addition, children have to be taught that animals are not playthings. This means that an adult should closely supervise all contacts between animals and children so that the animals are treated with respect. Good supervision should prevent children from being bitten or scratched by distressed or irritated pets.

In the same way that you must ensure the safety of children when dealing with pets, you must also be vigilant outside the setting. Children should be encouraged to watch, but not get near wildlife, and some conservationists would prefer that tadpoles and other small creatures are not taken out of their habitat for study.

An adult should closely supervise children handling animals

For further advice about caring for pets or looking at wildlife, you can contact various animal charities and conservation groups, such as the RSPCA's Enquiry Service, Causeway, Horsham, West Sussex RH12 1ZA. Visit the RSPCA's website at http://www.rspca.org.uk for further information about their services.

Active knowledge

Find out when your workplace was last inspected.

How many children is your setting registered for?

Contact your inspection unit and ask for a copy of its registration standards.

Element E3.2   Establish and carry out safety and emergency procedures

As part of the 1974 Health and Safety at Work Act and its Regulations, settings with five or more employees must have a safety policy. The policy should cover emergency procedures in the event of a fire, accident or other emergency. This element looks at the approaches normally taken to make sure that emergencies can be dealt with.

WHAT YOU NEED TO LEARN

- Evacuation procedures
- Responding to accidents

- Informing parents of an accident to their child
- Recording accidents and incidents

Evacuation procedures

There are many reasons why a building may need to be evacuated, for example in the event of a fire, gas leak or poisonous substance being identified. In order for a building to be emptied quickly, all staff members need to know what to do. In most settings, one member of staff is responsible for these procedures and will need to make sure that all staff are aware of the evacuation procedures. This means that practices need to be held regularly and that signs and notices must be kept in place. Drills and practices should always be taken seriously so that any difficulties can be reviewed. Procedures vary according to the needs and risks of a setting – in some settings the registers are kept centrally and are brought out by one person, whereas in other settings individual registers are taken out by each member of staff.

If you are responsible for devising an evacuation procedure, you must think about the following points:

- How is the alarm to be raised?
- Who is to contact the emergency services?
- Who is to take out the registers and check them?
- What are the safest exit points?
- Where is the assembly point to be?

IN CASE OF FIRE

First consideration must be the safety of the children.

Close doors and windows and try to get the children out of the premises by normal routes.

Do not leave the children unattended.

Do not stop to put out the fire (unles very small).

CALL THE FIRE BRIGADE BY EXCHANGE TELEPHONE AS SOON AS POSSIBLE AS FOLLOWS:

1. Lift the receiver and dial '999'.

2. Give operator your telephone number and ask for FIRE.

3. When the brigade replies give the call distinctly 'FIRE AT 464 BEXHILL ROAD, ST LEONARDS ON SEA, EAST SUSSEX, TN38 8AU, SITUATED BETWEEN THE GARDEN CENTRE AND GLYNE GAP'

DO NOT REPLACE THE RECEIVER UNTIL ADDRESS HAS BEEN REPEATED BY FIRE OPERATOR.

A notice showing procedures in case of fire

Practising evacuation procedures

Most settings carry out a practice every three months. If a practice shows that there are some problems with the procedures, it may be necessary to repeat a practice or seek advice from a fire officer. Rehearsing procedures helps staff become more competent and can help children to be more confident in the event of a real emergency. It is important to reassure children during a practice by staying calm and explaining what is happening. Some children dislike the noise of an alarm and will need adults to reassure them by, for example, holding their hands or by making the practice into a game. After a practice, some children may show signs of distress either by becoming withdrawn or by showing excited behaviour. It is a good idea to praise children and thank them for their help in carrying out the evacuation. Providing an absorbing activity such as reading a story or playing a game should help children to settle down quickly.

Active knowledge ✔

What are the fire procedures in your setting?
Who is responsible for organising evacuation practices?
How often are evacuation practices rehearsed?
How are visitors to the setting made aware of evacuation procedures?
How are children reassured during evacuation practices?

Responding to accidents

However carefully you supervise children and keep their environment safe, early years workers must still know the basics of first aid. It is recommended that you take a course in first aid so that you have some practical experience. Procedures in case of accidents and emergencies are described in Unit C2, pages 28–29. When responding to accidents, it is important to keep a clear head and consider whether there is a likelihood of any further danger to either the child or others.

Assessing injuries

It is important to know when to call in the emergency services.

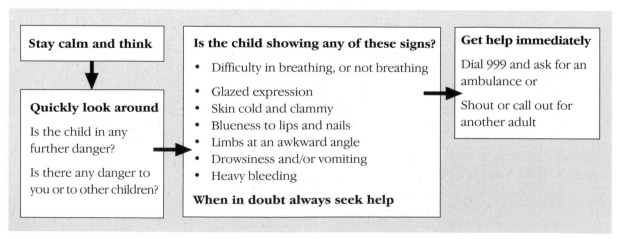

Stay calm and think	Is the child showing any of these signs?	Get help immediately
↓	• Difficulty in breathing, or not breathing	Dial 999 and ask for an ambulance or
Quickly look around	• Glazed expression	Shout or call out for another adult
Is the child in any further danger?	• Skin cold and clammy	
	• Blueness to lips and nails	
Is there any danger to you or to other children?	• Limbs at an awkward angle	
	• Drowsiness and/or vomiting	
	• Heavy bleeding	
	When in doubt always seek help	

Getting emergency help

In an emergency, it is important that you are able to keep calm and get help quickly. You may need to dial 999 and request an ambulance in which case the operator will ask you a series of questions. This information helps the emergency services to send out the appropriate help. You will need to tell the operator:

- your name and the telephone number from which you are calling
- the location of the accident – (think carefully and give as much information as possible so that the ambulance can find you)
- the type of accident – this helps the ambulance crew know what they need to do when they arrive
- the age and sex of the casualty
- details about the injury, and what you have done so far to treat it.

If the child is seriously injured, the operator may give you some advice while the ambulance is on its way.

Dealing with a child who is unconscious

If you think a child is unconscious, you must shout for help. Follow the ABC procedure (see Unit C2, page 27) and, if appropriate, place the child in the recovery position as illustrated below.

Put 2 fingers under the child's chin and 1 hand on the forehead.

Gently tilt the head well back. Straighten limbs. Bend the arm nearest to you so it is at right angles to the body.

Bring the other arm across the child's chest. Place the hand against the child's cheek – with palm outwards. Pull up the child's far leg, just above the knee, using your other hand.

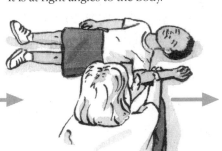

Pull on the far leg and roll the child towards you, still pressing the hand against the cheek – until the child is lying on his side.

To stop the child rolling too far, use your knees as support. Bend the upper leg so that it is at a right angle from the body.

Make sure the upper arm is supporting the head.

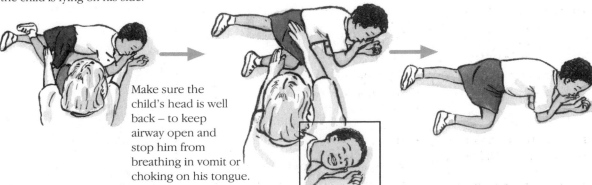

Make sure the child's head is well back – to keep airway open and stop him from breathing in vomit or choking on his tongue.

The recovery position

Emergency first aid treatment

To be able to follow the points in the chart below more effectively, it is important to take a practical first aid course.

Emergency treatment is discussed in Unit C2, but the following is a summary of the key points.

General points

- **Call or shout for help**
- Stop any treatment and follow ABC if a child stops breathing or becomes unconscious (see Unit C2, page 27)
- Do not give food or drink to child who has had a major accident
- Remain calm and reassuring

Burns and scalds

1. **Cool the affected area immediately using cold water or any harmless liquid such as milk if you are not near water**
2. Do this for at least ten minutes
3. Keep talking to the child and explain what you are doing
4. Do not remove clothes that have stuck to the skin or put on creams of any kind
5. Cover the area with a clean cloth such as a linen teatowel. Do not use anything fluffly such as a towel

Choking

1. **Hold the child so that his or her head is downwards. This can be over your knees. Slap firmly five times between the shoulder blades**
2. Repeat if necessary

Cuts and wounds

1. **Direct pressure needs to be applied to the wound with a clean pad. If it is a large wound try and press the edges together**
2. Do not remove anything from a deep wound as you may cause more bleeding
3. Tie a bandage around the pad, firmly but not too tightly
4. If blood comes through, apply another pad and bandage over the top
5. Keep applying pressure for about 15 minutes
6. Lie the child down and raise the injured part so that it is higher than the heart

Fractures, dislocations and sprains

It is not always easy to spot that a child has a fracture although signs may include:

- loss of movement and power
- swelling
- awkward angle of limb.

Keep the child still and get a first aider to come and help you. If a leg is thought to be broken, tie bandages around both legs above and below the fracture to keep the leg still. Use a scarf or bandage to make a sling to keep an arm still

Poisoning

(Child may not look well, begin vomiting or you may see what has been taken)
1. Ask the child what he or she has eaten or drunk if this is possible
2. Watch for signs of losing consciousness
3. Do not make the child vomit or give any drinks
4. **Take the suspected poison with you to the hospital so that medical staff can give the appropriate treatment**

Dealing with minor injuries

Fortunately, most early years workers are likely to have to treat only simple and minor injuries. It is important to encourage children to stay lying down or sitting up to assess the extent of their injuries. With some small bumps and knocks a cuddle and some adult attention are all that is needed to help children feel better.

The chart below gives the treatments required for common minor injuries. Always observe a child following a minor injury in case the injury is more serious than at first appeared.

Injury	Treatment	Check for complications
Bump to the head, e.g. falling over or running into a child	Apply cotton wool squeezed in cold water If the bump is a bad one, apply wrapped crushed ice	Drowsiness, vomiting or headaches could indicate concussion
Nose bleed	Tip the head forward Pinch the soft part of the nose just below the bridge Wrapped crushed ice can be put on to the nose if needed	Seek medical attention if the bleeding continues for more than half an hour or if it is mixed with clear fluid
Grazed skin	Rinse the wound with clean water Allow to heal in the air	
Bruises and trapped fingers	Apply cotton wool squeezed in cold water or wrapped crushed ice	Run your hand gently over the limb to check that nothing feels lumpy, which might indicate a fracture
Vomiting	Do not leave the child Reassure him or her Offer a sip of water to take away the sour taste	If a child vomits after a head injury, seek medical attention as this can be a sign of concussion Seek medical attention if vomit is mixed with blood
Insect stings	Reassure the child Do not squeeze the sting If you have had training, try to scrape out the sting with the back of a knife Use a wrapped ice pack to reduce the swelling	Urgent medical help is needed if the sting is in the mouth or if the child is starting to look ill or have difficulty breathing – some children are allergic to stings

Informing parents of an accident to their child

All accidents, whether major or minor, will need to be reported to parents. Minor injuries can sometimes be more serious than they look, especially head injuries. It is good practice to send a slip or note home which indicates that a minor accident has taken place. Slips should include the following information:

- name of the child
- how the injury occured
- time and date of the injury
- how the injury was dealt with
- who dealt with the injury
- signature of the person who recorded the injury.

Talking to parents about minor incidents shows them you make a child's welfare your top priority

It is a good idea to talk to parents directly, as well as giving them a slip, if they are collecting the child. This allows them to ask any further questions about the incident and shows them that you are genuinely concerned for the child's welfare.

Making contact with parents

When children have serious accidents or feel unwell, they tend to want their parents with them. This is a natural reaction and you should try to contact the parents as soon as possible. As part of the admissions procedure, parents should complete a form that gives information about where they can be contacted in the event of an emergency. The form will also indicate the name and address of their GP and any medical conditions that might affect emergency treatment.

It is important that settings establish who is responsible for contacting parents. In many cases it will be the manager or supervisor of the setting or the child's key worker. When parents are contacted, clear information must be passed on so that parents understand exactly what has happened, how the child is being cared for and what is expected of them, for example that the child is on the way to hospital or that the child is currently being looked after in the setting.

As parents will have varying reactions to an emergency phone call, it is essential that the early years worker is able to stay calm. It may be a good idea to remind parents of the setting's phone number, as well as giving them information about where the child has been taken to be treated, in case they need to contact you.

Recording accidents and incidents

Accidents or incidents such as one child hurting another need to be recorded accurately in a setting's accident report book. Parents should also receive a slip with information. Accident report books should be kept in a central place. Most contain the following information.

- full name of the child
- time and place of the accident/incident
- nature of the injuries
- details of treatment given
- name and signature of the person who dealt with the accident/incident.

Case study

Gracie and Curran have collided in the outdoor play area. Gracie is crying and has scraped her knee. Curran seems fine, but has a bump on his head. The other children are gathering around to see what has happened.

1 *Explain how you would deal with this situation.*
2 *Produce an accident slip for both children.*
3 *Why will it be important to keep a close eye on Curran in the next few hours?*
4 *If Curran begins vomiting, what should you do?*

Element E3.3   Select furniture and equipment for children

WHAT YOU NEED TO LEARN

- The principles involved in selecting furniture and equipment

The principles involved in selecting furniture and equipment

Whether you work in a setting that is well-equipped and established, or in a new setting, it is important that you understand the principles involved in choosing equipment and furniture.

The spider diagram opposite shows these principles.

Safety

Any equipment, furniture or furnishings in the setting must be safe. To help protect consumers there are now stringent safety regulations that cover most products. For

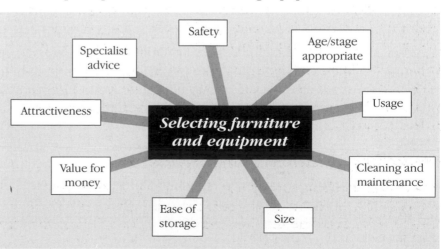

example, new sofas must conform to fire regulations. This means that when you buy a new product, you should be looking for labels that indicate the product conforms to the safety regulations for its class. If you are unsure what a label means, you can contact your local trading standards officer who should be able to advise you about the labelling of a product. Examples of safety signs are shown below.

BSI Kitemark   **BSI Safety Mark**   **The lion mark**   **The CE mark**

Active knowledge ✔

Find out the address and phone number of your local trading standards officer (through your local council). Find out (by contacting this officer if necessary) the meaning of each of the above safety marks.

It is also important to read the manufacturer's instructions carefully and to follow them. A folder can be kept for instructions and guarantees, which will allow other adults in the setting access to information should they need to maintain or clean a product.

Age/stage appropriateness

Equipment and furniture can be potentially unsafe if they are used by children for whom they were not designed. This means that when an early years setting chooses equipment or furniture, staff must be sure that it is suitable for the age and stage of the children who are to use it. Most people understand this when it comes to toys, but it is also important when looking at furniture. Chairs, for example, that are too high for children will cause them to lean forward, whereas older children's backs can suffer if they are sitting at tables at the wrong height.

It is also important to consider the weight of children in your care. Equipment such as tricycles and swings can suffer from metal fatigue and become dangerous if the children using them are too heavy. This might mean that specialist equipment such as tricycles and pushchairs may need to be ordered to meet the play and mobility needs of some special needs children.

Usage

Most settings have very tight budgets. This means that any equipment or furniture that is chosen must be well used. Having under-used toys and equipment is not cost effective. It is a good idea to consider the questions below before choosing toys or equipment. Considering the versatility and adaptability of equipment will be especially important if there are children with special needs in the setting.

- What play needs will be met?
- Is there already similar equipment meeting these play needs?
- Which children will benefit from this equipment?
- How versatile and attractive to children is the equipment?
- How much setting up is required?
- How adaptable is the equipment, for example is the height adjustable?

Cleaning and maintenance

Most equipment will need some form of cleaning and maintenance. Items that are difficult to clean should be avoided and it is always a good idea to find out about an item's maintenance needs before buying it. Most items in early years settings are used heavily and so will have a higher maintenance requirement than items used in the home. It is also useful to find out if spare parts or extras are available, particularly for items with small parts such as games, jigsaws and bricks.

Size

It often happens that an item seen in a shop, when placed in its intended surroundings is a much larger (or smaller) piece of equipment or apparatus than originally thought! This means that it is important to consider the size of any equipment such as slides or furniture. It is often a good idea to take down the measurements of an item and work out how large it is in proportion to the setting.

It is also important that if an item, such as a sandpit, is to be used by several children, it is big enough for them to play around. Photos and images in catalogues may be deceptive

Ease of storage

Some items of equipment may not be used all the time. It is important therefore to consider how and where items are to be stored. Where items can be dismantled, you may wish to see how easy it is to do this.

When choosing furniture that is to provide storage facilities, you should make sure that it offers the amount of storage and shelving required. Since it is good practice to make some toys and equipment accessible to children, you may need to consider how easy children would find the furniture to use.

If you are involved in setting up a new early years setting, make sure that you plan plenty of storage areas. Good storage helps settings to be more organised, children to be more independent and should prevent accidents caused by untidiness.

Value for money

It is always a good idea to compare prices and products, especially if expensive items are to be purchased. Recommendations from other early years settings can be useful when choosing between products, and sometimes more expensive products do not necessarily give better durability. Most settings find that there is never enough money and hard choices have to be made between quantity and durability. Never be tempted to buy products that do not conform to safety standards, even if they appear much cheaper. Safety always has to be a primary consideration.

Attractiveness

Equipment and furniture that is attractive will help create a more pleasant environment for everyone. Furniture, especially soft furnishings, can help an environment look homely and comfortable for children. This is especially important as they can affect mood, and some settings ask for specialist help when designing their colour schemes! It is also considered to be good practice to choose items that reflect children's cultures.

You should always remember that soft furnishings should be checked to see if they have been treated with fire retardants.

Specialist advice

There will be times when it will be important to obtain specialist advice before bringing in pieces of equipment. Choosing equipment for a child with special needs may best be done by parents or other professionals working with that child. They will probably have a better awareness of the types of equipment available. In some areas, equipment can be borrowed from toy libraries, which means that you can check whether an item is useful or not.

Active knowledge ✔

Using catalogues or by visiting retail outlets, choose five pieces of equipment that will help promote three-to-five-year-olds' physical development.

Cost these items and explain why you have chosen them. How do they meet the play needs of the children?

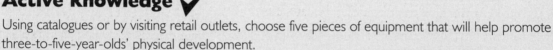

| Element E3.4 | Organise and maintain the physical environment for children |

WHAT YOU NEED TO LEARN

- Ensuring heating, lighting and ventilation are adequate
- Maintaining cleanliness and health and safety
- Planning the layout of a room
- Adapting the environment to help children with special needs
- Using outside areas with children
- What needs to be done at the end of sessions
- Maintaining stock levels

Before children come to a session, a certain amount of preparation is needed to make sure that the environment is safe and will meet children's needs. Taking time to prepare carefully should help sessions to run smoothly. The spider diagram below shows some of the tasks that need to be carried out before the start of a session.

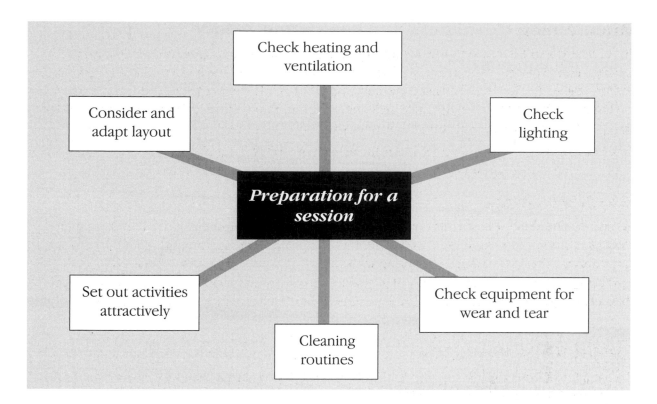

Check heating and ventilation

Consider and adapt layout

Check lighting

Preparation for a session

Set out activities attractively

Check equipment for wear and tear

Cleaning routines

Ensuring heating, lighting and ventilation are adequate

These physical aspects of an environment are important and should be part of a daily check at the start of the day. It will also be necessary to check on the physical conditions during the day as the outside weather will affect conditions inside the setting.

Lighting

Poor light can give children and early years workers headaches as a result of eye strain. Light can also affect mood. This means that before a session begins, an evaluation of the lighting conditions needs to be carried out. It is always preferable for settings to have as much natural light as possible, but on grey, cloudy days, electric lighting will be required. Over the years, there has been more awareness of how to light indoor premises and you should consider whether your lighting system is still effective.

Heating and ventilation

A comfortable temperature for early years settings is 18–21°C, and careful monitoring of the temperature during the day is important. Children who are hot tend to be more irritable and will find it harder to concentrate. It is also a good idea to keep a window open, unless it is very cold, to ensure that fresh air is allowed into the building. Good ventilation can prevent airborne infections from spreading.

The heating system needs to be regularly maintained by professionals, and any gas appliances must be situated where there is adequate ventilation. Never be tempted to block air vents as they are designed to prevent a build up of carbon monoxide. This potentially lethal gas is odourless and can be difficult to detect as the signs of gas poisoning resemble flu-like symptoms.

Maintaining cleanliness and health and safety

Checking equipment

Most settings have a policy of cleaning equipment as it is put away, although it is still important to check equipment for signs of wear and tear before a session starts. These checks are particularly useful if equipment has not been used for a while, for example outdoor apparatus, as well as equipment that has moving parts such as tricycles. Most equipment eventually wears out. The chart below shows how the main materials used in making equipment may wear.

Type of material	Look out for	Examples of equipment
Plastic	Cracking Fading colours Sharp edges	Chairs, sit-and-ride, seats of tricycles
Metal	Signs of rust Flaking paint Metal fatigue	Climbing frames, tricycles, see-saws, pushchairs, highchairs, swings
Wooden	Rough edges Splinters Flaking paint	Chairs, bookcases, wooden blocks, jigsaw puzzles

Cleaning routines

Some settings employ cleaners and caretakers, while in others early years workers are responsible for the day-to-day cleaning of the setting. Most settings carry out cleaning at the end of the session, although checking that the setting is clean will need to be done as part of the preparation.

There are some specific areas of settings where hygiene is particularly important. Kitchens, areas where children eat, toilets and washbasins are all examples of areas where good hygiene procedures can prevent the spread of infections. This means that early years workers must monitor them during the sessions and, if necessary, be prepared to clean them.

The chart below shows the equipment and main areas of a setting that need regular cleaning.

Item/area	Why it needs to be cleaned	Method
Toys and play equipment	Items tend to be well-handled and very young children will put objects in their mouths	Sterilise plastic items in hyperchlorite solution Wipe down items using a cloth impregnated with anti-bacterial agent
Feeding equipment	Bacteria on feeding equipment can cause cross infections	Wash all items thoroughly, and rinse carefully Sterilise items for babies under 12 months
Worktops and surfaces	Food may be prepared on or eaten off these surfaces	Clean surfaces regularly with a clean cloth and a disinfectant solution

Item/area	Why it needs to be cleaned	Method
Tables	Children tend to put items on tables that may have been handled or put in their mouths	Wipe down with a clean cloth and disinfect at the end of each session
Toilets, handbasins, sinks	These are areas where bacteria can be found and in damp conditions can breed	Clean regularly with a bleach solution Check the toilets frequently
Bins	Bins are areas that can attract bacteria	Dispose of items containing any human waste separately Wrap food waste carefully Use plastic bags or sacks to line bins Wash out bins regularly with disinfectant
Floors	Young children will sit and lie on floors during their play	Wash floors after each session Thoroughly clean carpets and wash from time to time

Planning the layout of a room

The way in which furniture and activities are laid out affects the activities that can be carried out and even the mood of the children. A good room layout will allow the children to move from one area to another easily, while helping them to feel secure. Some items of furniture cannot be moved, but tables and other equipment can be changed according to the types of activities that are to take place.

Sometimes the weather may affect room layout, as children who have been unable to go out will benefit from some kind of physical exercise and movement indoors.

Changing the room layout periodically can also help to stimulate children's interest in activities and can mean that some equipment that is under-used becomes more valued by children. If you decide to change a room's layout, make sure that you liaise with colleagues and lift and handle furniture safely.

There are several basic principles that you should consider when planning a room, including:

- making sure that doors and fire exits are unobstructed
- allowing sufficient space around tables for children to move around safely
- making sure that staff have good visibility so that they can supervise children easily
- having one area where children can sit or lie down
- making sure that 'messy' activities are situated near washbasins and on suitable flooring
- ensuring that free-standing furniture, such as cupboards, cannot topple over on to children.

Laying out activities attractively

An important part of preparation is to lay out materials, equipment and toys attractively. Children will then be more interested in them. Making the environment welcoming and attractive is particularly important for children who are starting in a new setting or for children who find it difficult to start playing. In some cases this may mean starting off an activity to give children an idea of how to use the material or toy. For example, a floor puzzle or collage may be begun.

The chart below gives some ideas of the routine tasks involved in preparing for sessions.

Activity	Preparation
Painting table or easels	Put out fresh paint, a variety of brushes, printing equipment, paper and a pencil to write children's names on their work. Prepare an area to receive wet paintings. Children will also need aprons.
Water tray	Make sure that toys such as boats, jugs and cups are clean before putting out. Children will need aprons. A cloth and towel may also be put nearby. Water must be changed at least once a day.
Sand area	If outside, check that the sand has been covered to prevent animals from soiling it. Rake sand and check that toys are clean. Put a dustpan and brush near the area, as sand on floors can be slippery.
Home corner/dressing-up area	Make sure that clothes are clean and arrange them in an inviting way. Dress dolls, lay out home equipment such as the table. Make sure that there are enough props. Consider changing the props in this area from time to time to stimulate different roles, for example a shop.
Book corner	Sort through books, removing any that need repairing. Present books attractively by standing them up. Check that cushions and seating are clean. Consider choosing books about a current theme for display.
Jigsaws/construction area	Check that jigsaws are complete. Remove any where parts are missing. Set out construction toys and attract children's interest by beginning to build something.
Dough	Make up enough fresh dough for the numbers of children who are likely to choose this activity. Check that boards and tools are clean.

Adapting the environment to help children with special needs

Where settings are working with children who have special needs, some adaptations may be necessary to the environment because it is now accepted that children should not suffer discrimination in their care and education because of a disability. The types of adaptations will depend on the individual needs of children. For example, a child who has a hearing impairment will benefit from being in a quiet environment where background noises are reduced. This might mean carpeting, using mats on tables and fixing rubber to the base of legs, so as to reduce incidental noise. Before making any changes to an environment, it will be important to talk to parents and other professionals about how best to adapt the environment, as each child will have different needs.

If a child cannot access the sandpit, consider taking the sand to the child

Early years staff can also help children by thinking creatively of how to enable them to take part in activities. In some cases helping a child with special needs is an exercise in problem-solving. For example, rather then struggling to take a child to an activity, the activity could be taken to the child! This might mean putting construction toys on a table rather than having them on the floor, or taking some of the sand out of the sandpit and putting it into a tray so that the child does not have to stand.

Using outdoor areas with children

Wherever possible, children should be encouraged to go outdoors during the day. Fresh air and exercise help children's development in many ways, for example encouraging circulation, muscle growth and appetite. Most early years workers notice a definite change in children after they have been outside!

As part of the preparation for an outdoor session, you should carry out the following checks to ensure that the outdoor setting is safe:

- **Equipment** – large apparatus such as swings and slides should be wiped down and checked for any signs of wear and tear.
- **Access and fencing** – outdoor areas should be fenced off to prevent children from wandering away and also to make sure that strangers or animals do not have access. Fences and gates should be checked before allowing children outside.
- **Plants and animals** – some plants are poisonous and others such as nettles and thistles can sting or scratch children. Regular checks on the plants in the area are important. You should also look out for any signs of animal droppings including cats' and dogs' facccs. Disinfect any area that has been soiled and do not allow children into sandpits, if they are contaminated, until the sand has been changed.
- **Dustbins** – some outdoor settings can be close to bins and dustbins. It is important that lids are kept on bins and wherever possible they should be moved out of reach of children. In summer there is also the added danger of wasps and other insects hovering around them.
- **Sun protection** – children will need adequate protection from the sun. Hats and sunscreen should be used in very sunny weather.

What needs to be done at the end of sessions

At the end of each session, there is a lot of valuable work to be carried out to ensure that the next session will be successful. It is important that, however tired you feel, resources and equipment are cleaned and stored carefully. Resentment can quickly build up in teams if other staff find that equipment they were planning to use needs washing or is incomplete. In some settings, children help to tidy away, which is good because they learn to take responsibility for their environment, but they should still be supervised to make sure that equipment is put away safely. The main aim at the end of a session is to leave everything in good order so that the next session is easy to prepare. In many settings, activities are put out for the next day, whereas in other settings everything has to be cleared away because the room is used for other groups.

It can be helpful to have a checklist so that staff new to working in the setting know what needs to be done at the end of each session. Design a checklist that can be used in your setting. An example of a checklist is given below.

Tasks	Tick when completed
Sift sand through; throw away dirty sand	
Put lid on sand tray	
Wash sand toys, store in bucket underneath	
Wash, dry and put away utensils in kitchen	
Put towels and teatowels in laundry bin	
Close and secure windows	
Sweep floors	

Maintaining stock levels

As part of the smooth running of any setting, it is important that there is a constant supply of consumables such as paint, glue and paper. In many settings, one person is responsible for ordering resources, but he or she often relies on other staff members telling him or her that stock is running low or that a piece of equipment is broken. If you are responsible for ordering and maintaining stock levels, you will need to carry out regular checks and complete order forms in good time. You may also find that at certain times of the year, such as near festivals, parents evenings or carnivals, more consumables are needed, or that staff have particular requirements such as glitter or shiny paper. Staff find it very frustrating if they cannot carry out their planned activities because of a lack of stock.

Active knowledge ✔

On page 269 you prepared a guide for students or parent helpers who come in to work with children. Add to your guide information that covers:

- how they can help in preparing for a session
- the roles and responsibilities of key people within the setting, for example the person who is responsible for health and safety.

E3 Unit test

1 What is COSHH?
2 Why is it important to rehearse evacuation procedures regularly?
3 How often does a playgroup have to be registered?
4 List four pieces of safety equipment that are commonly found in nurseries.
5 Explain what you would do if you suspected that a child has been poisoned.
6 Describe four factors that you would take into consideration when buying a piece of outdoor equipment.
7 Why should air vents never be blocked up?
8 What is considered to be a good temperature for an early years setting?
9 Why is it important to lay out activities attractively?
10 Why is it important to wear disposable gloves when changing nappies or attending to a cut knee?

Unit M7

Plan, implement and evaluate learning activities and experiences

It is generally accepted that children gain from having a balance of activities and learning experiences – this helps to stimulate their overall development. To provide for a range and balance of activities, most settings have a planning process. This chapter looks at aspects of planning, carrying out and evaluating the activities and learning experiences in settings.

The elements for this unit are:

M7.1 Plan a curriculum to facilitate children's learning and development
M7.2 Develop individual learning programmes for children
M7.3 Implement planned learning activities and experiences
M7.4 Evaluate planned learning activities and experiences

Element M7.1 Plan a curriculum to facilitate children's learning and development

It is now understood that children gain from being in settings that have a planned approach to delivering care and education. Planning activities carefully allows early years workers to be confident that they are not neglecting any area of children's development and that they are providing children with a balance of learning experiences.

WHAT YOU NEED TO LEARN

- Designing a curriculum plan
- Tailoring the curriculum plan to meet children's developmental needs
- Planning the use of resources and equipment
- Developing a positive, anti-discriminatory curriculum
- Using the wider environment when planning
- Ensuring health and safety

Designing a curriculum plan

There are many different approaches to setting up activities for children and settings vary in the way they plan. Some settings produce weekly plans, whereas others may plan for a term at a time. If you are responsible for organising the planning in your setting, you might find it useful to look at many different approaches to producing plans, until you find a system that meets your settings needs. The term 'curriculum plan' is increasingly common, although 'outline plan' may also be used. In essence, a curriculum plan can be thought of as a programme of activities. This means that the content of a curriculum plan will vary according to its objectives – a curriculum plan with the overall objective of helping children to develop their fine manipulative skills may look very different from a curriculum plan that concentrates on delivering the early learning goals for a week.

The design process

There is no single way of designing a curriculum plan, although there is a process through which a plan can be designed.

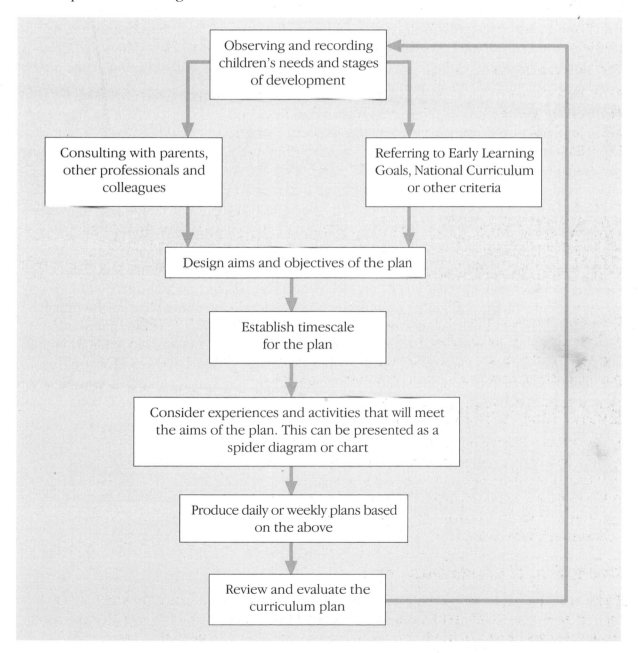

Establishing the aims of curriculum plans

To plan effectively we need to have a clear idea about what we are hoping to achieve in order to develop the aim of the curriculum plan. Therefore we must establish the developmental needs of the children we are working with. There is no point in producing a programme of activities that the children find too difficult or are undemanding. Carrying out observations and talking to parents and other professionals will help us to gather reliable and relevant information about children's needs.

Using observations as a planning tool

In Unit C16 we looked at methods of carrying out observations on children. The results or evaluations of these observations should be considered when planning. For example, an observation on a group of children might show that they are becoming less interested in using one area of the setting, such as the painting table. As a result of this observation, we might consider planning a programme of activities using different types of paints and painting techniques. Checklists might be used with individuals and groups of children to gauge their development in certain areas, such as their acquisition of physical skills.

Gathering information from other sources

Although direct observations are extremely important when designing the aims of a curriculum plan, we need also to use information from other sources. It is good practice for parents to be part of the planning process. Parents see the capabilities and needs of their children in different situations, and are often able to help us in establishing aims. Where we are caring for children in a home setting, this will be particularly important as parents might be establishing their own goals for their child, for example being able to dress himself or herself independently, and we should try to plan activities alongside them.

Other sources of information that can be used include developmental guides and curriculum information such as Early Learning Goals (see page 349) and the National Curriculum. Developmental charts and guides can give us overall information about what most children are able to achieve at certain ages. This is useful if we do not know the children well and have to plan a programme of activities – for example, if we work in a creche or are arranging a holiday play scheme. Documents such as the Early Learning Goals or the National Curriculum will help us to understand the general direction in which children's learning should be proceeding.

Examples of aims for curriculum plans include:

- introducing children to colours
- helping a baby to wean
- looking at the theme of 'growing'
- encouraging children to develop their fine manipulative skills.

Monday	Catching large soft balls Wellie throwing
Tuesday	Throwing bean bags into hoops Catching bean bags from very small distance
Wednesday	Hula hoops Catching bean bags from 5 paces away
Thursday	Skittles Catching small soft balls
Friday	Bouncing footballs Catching bean bags

Weekly curriculum plan to promote children's throwing and catching skills

Tailoring the curriculum plan to meet children's developmental needs

Once we have decided on an overall aim for the curriculum plan we are preparing, it will be important to consider how best to meet children's specific needs. This means focussing on patterns of children's development to consider how much time or practice they will need in order to be competent at a skill or to master a concept. Considering children's development is important, as a curriculum plan must be realistic. Expecting a group of children to learn their colours in a week is unrealistic, for example, so a curriculum plan might be designed to introduce the concept of colours, but the theme of colours would need to be re-visited frequently in other curriculum plans. To help you take into account the normal patterns of development when planning, this book contains several development charts:

Unit C2, page 2: Eating and drinking
Unit C3, page 42: Fine manipulative skills and gross motor skills
Unit C3, page 50: Locomotion and balance
Unit C5, page 69: Social and emotional development
Unit C7, page 115: Goals for behaviour
Unit C11, page 180: Language development

Covering overall areas of development or areas of curriculum

In home settings, early years workers will be able to design curriculum plans that focus either on one area of development or on a care objective, but most early years settings must develop overall approaches for groups of children. Most settings therefore develop plans that cover overall areas of children's development or the curriculum.

It is possible to introduce a themed approach to planning a series of activities. Activities for each developmental or curriculum area can then follow on from each other. On the next page are two examples of curriculum plans, one showing a themed approach linked to the Early Learning Goals, and the other a themed approach linked to children's developmental areas.

Providing a range of learning experiences

A good curriculum plan will give children the opportunity to develop a range of skills and also provide them with a mix of enjoyable learning experiences. Enjoyment is vital, as children will gain more from activities if they are fun. Where possible, early years workers

Language and literacy
Read stories about rainy days
'Rain, rain go away', 'Incey wincey spider'
Discussion about why rain is important

Personal, social and emotional development
Talk about storms and things that may frighten us
Share equipment in activities
Look at countries that have rainy seasons

Mathematics
Making a gauge to measure rain
Ways of measuring puddles

Rain

Creative development
Making hats for rainy days
Experiencing water colours on wet paper

Knowledge and understanding of the world
Look to see what happens to puddles
Nature walk after rain to look at creatures who come out in the rain

Physical development
Movement to music
Vigorous outdoor play

A week's curriculum plan linked to the Early Learning Goals

Physical development
Music and movement – seeds growing
Vigorous outdoor play
Fine manipulative skills developed through activities

Emotional development
Helping create Jack and the Beanstalk frieze
Enjoyment of planting seeds
Confidence and independence through planting own seeds

Seeds

Language development
Discussion about planting beans
Jack and the Beanstalk story
Working in pairs to plant different types of seeds

Cognitive/intellectual development
Planting different types of seeds
Looking at fruits with seeds in them
Sorting activity – seeds, nuts and beans

Social development
Visit of gardener
Sharing of equipment with others

A day's curriculum plan showing areas of development

should aim to deliver learning experiences through play and activities that also allow children to explore and develop their creativity and independence.

Activities and play experiences should obviously reflect the needs of the children we care for. This means that activities used in one setting may not be appropriate for another – for example, a setting that is caring for refugee children may emphasise the development of language and social and emotional development, whereas a creche may organise a series of short activities that children can join or leave easily.

Planning the use of resources and equipment

The type and quantity of necessary resources and equipment should also be considered carefully when designing a curriculum plan. Some settings use a planning format that requires staff to itemise the equipment and resources needed. This is especially important in larger settings, where negotiation may have to take place if certain pieces of equipment or areas are in demand, such as shared outdoor play areas, halls or apparatus.

Daily planning sheet		Monday 22 June	Morning
Activity	**Main learning goals**	**Area/equipment/resources**	**Group size**
Paper weaving	Physical development – fine manipulative skills Creative development	Sugar paper, various colours Scissors Stapler Paper cutter required for preparation	Six
Obstacle course	Physical development – gross motor skills	Hall Bollards and cones Indoor slide Mats Plastic hoops	Eight
Painting	Creative development Personal and social development	Primary colour, ready-mixed paints Painting easels Newspaper/cloth Pencils Aprons Sugar paper	Maximum of four

Wherever possible, make sure that equipment is well used and that the best use is made of the setting's resources and physical space. A plan that considers resources, layout and staffing will help settings ensure that facilities such as libraries, book corners, messy play areas and large apparatus are used to best effect.

When planning, remember that creative play such as painting can often be messy

Developing a positive, anti-discriminatory curriculum

For a number of years, it has been recognised that early years workers should promote equal opportunities through their practices. This means an active approach should be taken when planning. Activities that positively promote a world view and that help children to value each other and respect differences between people should be a priority when planning. It is important that activities are not added to curriculum plans just to 'do equal opportunities'. The idea behind promoting equality of opportunity is that it should be central to everything we do. It is a good idea, however, to look at a draft plan and consider whether we have integrated the promotion of equal opportunities.

Active knowledge ✔

Add to the checklist below to assess whether a curriculum plan is promoting positive play experiences for all children and encouraging an awareness of equal opportunities.

	Yes	No
Do activities encourage gender stereotyping?	☐	☐
Will activities be accessible for all of the children?	☐	☐
Do activities help children to learn about and respect other people?	☐	☐

Using the wider environment when planning

It is always a good idea to consider what is happening outside the setting when drawing up curriculum plans. Planning in isolation may mean that wonderful learning opportunities are missed – for example a local carnival may provide excellent starting points for work in the setting, as children may be able to take part in or watch the carnival. In the same way, settings can ask local people such as the police, dentists and opticians to help children learn about the wider world. It is a good idea to foster links with the local community so that children can benefit from local people's expertise. We should also consider seasonal and climatic changes when curriculum planning. Snow, frost and changes in plant and animal activity can become the basis of many activities, such as making bird food or discussing clothes we wear.

Active knowledge ✔

Look at the bubbles below. Choose two themes and consider five activities that could be based on each of these themes.

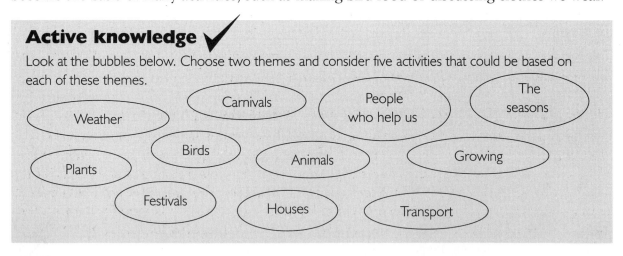

Weather   Carnivals   People who help us   The seasons
Plants   Birds   Animals   Growing
Festivals   Houses   Transport

Language

Describing their observations.
Woodland stories – write letters to the characters who live in the woods, e.g. 3 bears, Red Riding Hood, etc.
Make a list of things they observe on a tree.
Sorting using their own criteria.
Continuation of correct letter formation.
Blending phonic sounds to aid reading unfamiliar words.

Music

Tapping rhythms.
Playing wooden instruments.
'The Three Singing Pigs' musical performance.

Maths

Continue correct number formation.
Matching objects with the correct number.
Reinforcing the idea of more and fewer/less with the correct signs $>$ $<$.
Number stories to 8.
Simple addition (for those who are ready).
Recording by mapping.
Work with calculators – looking at digital numbers.
Measuring length – longer/shorter – comparing lengths leading to measuring with non-standard units.

Art

What colour are trees?
Look carefully at bark and leaf colours and match and mix with paint and pastels.
Layer paintings of woods.
Observational drawings of wooden objects.
Sculptures with wood.
Plaster cast of a tree.
Drawing with charcoal.
Paper making.

PE

Skills with small equipment, e.g. throwing and catching.
Simple partner work leading to partner work.

Wood

Science

Make a collection of things made of wood.
Identify and name parts of a tree.
'Hug a tree' – using senses to describe what they see and feel.
Comparing bark on different trees – rough/smooth.
Comparing wood that is rotting, sawn, planed, carved, drift wood, can they make a rough piece of wood smooth?
Noting similarities and differences between trees.
Sorting wood from other materials, eg plastic, metal.
Paper – sorting different kinds.

Geography

Explore the garden and make plans to show where the trees are.

History

Look at uses of wood – old toys, boats, houses.
Walks through the Old Town to look at the use of wood in old houses and shops.
Look at the circles in wood and count to find out the age.

An example of a school's curriculum plan for five-year-olds

Building flexibility and creativity into curriculum plans

It is a common misconception to think that curriculum plans will prevent children from having time to play and create their own activities. Most early years workers recognise that children need a balance of adult-led activities and free play. This means that some activities and time must be planned for children to be able to explore materials or equipment freely. In settings where very young children are cared for, time must also be planned for them to rest, sleep and relax. Relaxing may mean that children want to look at books quietly or play in a repetitive way. Giving children opportunities to play in their own way and at their own pace allows them to develop independence and self-reliance. In themselves these are excellent learning outcomes, even though they may be achieved simply by a child choosing to lie on a mat and do the same jigsaw three times.

The balance between the number of structured, adult-led activities and spontaneous, child-led activities will vary from setting to setting, depending on the aims of the setting.

Ensuring that curriculum plans are realistic

Good planning is not carried out in isolation. Planning in large settings will work only if other members of staff are consulted, and are happy about the programme and timing of activities. Parents also need to be aware of plans, especially in smaller settings or where an early years worker is caring for children in their own homes. Working with parents when planning will help us to ensure that the plans meet children's needs. This is especially important if we are working with individual children.

In general, it is good practice to make sure that parents are informed of the work we are doing with their children. This allows them to talk to their children about what they have been doing and to reinforce concepts. Sending home an outline of what children will be doing can also be a way of encouraging parents to take an active role in the life of a setting, as they may have materials, resources or skills that they are happy to share.

Ensuring health and safety

Health and safety is also a major consideration if plans are to be realistic. Activities must be planned with group sizes and staff ratios in mind. In larger settings, where there may be several activities going on at once, this may mean planning some activities that require intense adult support alongside activities where children can work or play in larger groups – for example a cooking activity requiring adult support could be scheduled alongside a role-play activity where children need to be supervised rather than directed.

The type of equipment to be used in each activity will also influence the timings of a plan. When some equipment, such as scissors and climbing frames, is in use there is a need for constant adult supervision in order for the activity to remain safe.

Active knowledge

Design a curriculum plan that could be used in your setting. Make sure that the length of the plan is clearly shown and that learning goals are identified.

Give a written explanation of how you designed the plan and how the activities might meet the learning goals.

This task may be used as evidence in your portfolio.

Element M7.2 Develop individual learning programmes for children

There are many reasons why individual learning programmes may be used with children. In some cases, plans are drawn up because one area of a child's development needs to be promoted. Sometimes these plans may be devised with other professionals such as speech therapists in order to help the child in specific ways. Learning programmes can also be developed to build on children's areas of strengths, especially if these are different from those of other children in the setting – for example, a child who is beginning to read may need to have some opportunities to share books and reading materials with adults.

Individual learning programmes do not necessarily consist of adult-directed activities, but can include opportunities for children to play and use materials in their own fashion. For example, a child which has come into a setting with little English may benefit from playing alongside others in the home corner, as well as from adult-led activities such as picture lotto.

WHAT YOU NEED TO LEARN

- Developing an individual learning plan
- Working with others on learning plans
- Recording individual learning programmes
- Ensuring individual learning plans are flexible
- Discussing learning programmes with children

Developing an individual learning plan

Individual learning programmes normally work well when the areas of development that need to be promoted have been specifically identified. This can be done in a variety of ways. A child's parents may have concerns about a child's progress, or a setting may have noticed through carrying out observations that a child would benefit from specific work in one or more areas. In some cases, other professionals such as speech therapists or physiotherapists will request that activities concentrated on specific areas are planned for the child.

Setting aims and objectives

Individual learning plans will identify goals for the child, and then activities will be planned that will help the child achieve these aims. It is important that the aims and objectives are realistic, otherwise children may be expected to carry out tasks that are not appropriate to their needs or stage of development. Developmental charts or milestones can be used to ensure that expectations are not too high, as sometimes a child may appear to be lagging behind when his or her development is within normal ranges for child development. Observations can also be carried out to identify the child's stage of development (see Unit C16). It is often useful to carry out more than one observation on a child, so that an overall picture can be gained. It can also be helpful to carry out observations at various points during the programme of activities, in order to judge whether the activities are having a positive effect and to see if the child is making some progress.

PLAY PLAN

Name of child

Keyworker   Date

Ideas for activities to promote areas of development in the next month

Social and self help skills	Language and communication skills

Creative development	Cognitive development

Fine manipulative and motor skills	Gross motor skills

An outline form to record an individual learning programme

Case study

Toby is three years old. His parents and key worker have become concerned that Toby's language development is poor for his age. Toby's key worker followed up an initial meeting by carrying out an observation on Toby, and suggests that he would benefit from a series of one-to-one activities with an adult as well as opportunities to use language with other children in free play situations. His key worker has drawn up some ideas for language activities to discuss with his parents and her colleagues. Once these ideas have been discussed, she will programme them into a weekly plan for Toby.

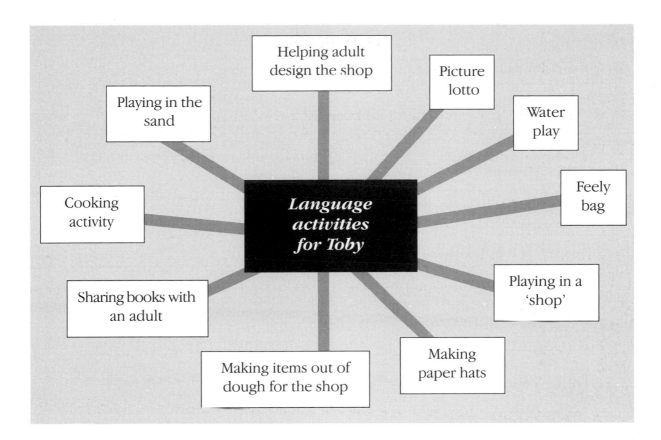

Language activities for Toby

- Helping adult design the shop
- Picture lotto
- Water play
- Feely bag
- Playing in a 'shop'
- Making paper hats
- Making items out of dough for the shop
- Sharing books with an adult
- Cooking activity
- Playing in the sand

Individual learning programmes as part of the overall curriculum plan

When drawing up a learning plan for an individual child, thought needs to be given to fitting it in with the overall curriculum plan for the setting. This is particularly important in large settings where use of equipment, staffing and resources needs to be planned ahead, and organising several different activities and themes within a group would be impracticable. In practice this means designing an individual learning plan that will complement the overall curriculum plan, planning activities that can be adapted to meet a child's individual needs.

The following case study shows how a child's individual learning plan can be drawn up alongside an overall curriculum plan.

Case study

Tom is four years old and finds it hard to play alongside and with other children. His language skills are also slightly underdeveloped for his age. His key worker is designing an individual learning plan that will encourage Tom's social development as well as giving him opportunities to use language. She has looked at the nursery's overall curriculum plan for the week and has picked out a few activities each day that will provide Tom with opportunities to meet his particular needs. She has also chosen some activities to do with Tom which will complement the plan. The theme for the overall curriculum plan is 'growing', and this week the children are looking at plants and seeds. The key worker has chosen some particular activities from Monday's plan to use as a basis for Tom's individual learning plan for that day.

Monday – Adult-led activities	Monday – Other activities
Knowledge and understanding of the world/ Personal and social development Plant runner beans **Language and literacy** Jack and the Beanstalk – story **Creative development** Draw and paint leaves for Jack and the Beanstalk display **Physical development** Pencil control exercise sheet – following the stalk **Mathematics** One-to-one matching with beans	Free painting Sand play Outdoor play with slides, tricycles Home corner Water play Jigsaws, duplo and farm animals Train set and cars

Tom's individual learning plan – Monday

Activity	Learning goals
Planting runner beans	Tom to share equipment with one other child Tom to make eye contact with one other child Tom to re-tell what he has done
Preparing feely bag, an activity for the other children to use the next day.	Help Tom feel responsible and confident Encourage Tom to describe the feel of the different beans, leaves and nuts Help Tom to learn the names of the items for the feely bag Help Tom work with one other child
Draw and paint beanstalk leaves	Tom to share equipment with one other child Encourage Tom to re-tell the story of Jack and the Beanstalk
Free choice activities, e.g. sand play	Tom to share equipment Encourage Tom to talk about what he is doing

Working with others on learning plans

It is good practice to involve parents and colleagues when devising an individual learning plan for a child. In some cases other professionals will also be involved, depending on the reason why a plan is needed. Parents should be informed as they may wish to reinforce skills that are being developed and they may also be able to provide a clearer picture of the child's behaviour and development. Colleagues within a setting should be aware of the plan, because they may be carrying out some activities with the child and will need to reinforce the approach that is being taken. For example, if a goal for a four-year-old is to be able to identify the colour blue, when they work with that child staff will know that every opportunity should be taken to reinforce recognition of this colour.

Recording individual learning programmes

It is a good idea to keep records of individual learning programmes, because this allows early years workers and parents to focus more accurately on the child's needs and to agree an approach. It also provides a record to consult in the future.

Individual learning programme

Name of child **Alice**   Date of birth **12/9/96**

Length of programme   **4 weeks**   Date of review   **14th April 1999**

Target	Strategy/activities	Progress/outcome
To sit and listen to a story for 10 minutes	Nursery assistant to sit with Alice during story time. Alice to choose a rhyme when she is showing expected behaviour.	
To take turns in a small group	Nursery assistant and to run small group games 1 x 5 days	

Name of child   **Jamie**   Key worker   **Judith**   Week beginning   **21/4/99**

Target	Mon	Tues	Wed	Thurs	Fri	Outcomes
To be able to sit as part of a group or class and listen without disruption **Strategy** Reward Jamie with stickers	✓	✓	✓		✓	Much improved, Jamie was pleased to gain stickers
To take turns in games **Strategy** Lotto, snakes and ladders and other games to be played with key worker	✓	✓	✓	✓	✓	Jamie enjoyed different types of games, but snakes and ladders was very successful

Comments

Jamie seems to be more settled this week. General behaviour has been more co-operative. He has shown an interest in games with dice. May be ready to start playing games with more children.

Two examples of records for individual learning programmes

Just as there is more than one way of recording curriculum plans, methods vary for individual learning programmes. If you are responsible for designing a layout, you should try to make it as simple and as effective as possible. Consider what details are required in order to record the programme effectively. In some cases you may have a sheet that covers the aims and objectives of the learning plan with details of reviews, and have individual sheets on which weekly or daily activities are planned.

Whatever the design of the programme, the following information should be noted:

- name of the child
- age of the child
- aim of the learning programme and/or identified areas for development
- length of the learning programme
- names of people responsible for planning or implementing the programme
- ways in which the programme is to be monitored and reviewed
- the programme of activities.

Ensuring individual learning plans are flexible

Most individual learning programmes are monitored and added to frequently, as the needs of children are reviewed and their progress is considered. In some cases, individual learning plans are drawn up on a weekly basis. This means that early years workers can review the child's progress over the week and devise the following week's plan accordingly. For example, a child who is learning to ride a bicycle may need more practice in using the brakes and steering before the stabilisers are removed, so the learning plan would need to include time and opportunities for the child to practise these skills.

There will also be times when individual learning plans need to be adapted because of a change of circumstance either in the setting or in the child's life. For example, a plan may have been drawn up to encourage a toddler to drink from a beaker rather than a bottle, but the plan might have to be altered if the toddler is feeling poorly and needs the comfort of the familiar bottle. Special events in the setting might also mean that plans need to be changed, or activities in a learning plan might have to be altered if it starts to snow so that the child can benefit from experiencing and learning about snow.

Parents may provide information that makes staff reconsider and change the learning plan, especially if the parents are reinforcing activities or strategies at home. They may report that the child is making very good progress, which may mean that activities that will extend the child can be added to the plan.

Case study

Jessica is three and a half and goes to a local playgroup four mornings a week. Her mother finds Jessica's behaviour difficult and challenging, because she often has tantrums and resists carrying out simple self-help tasks such as dressing, tidying up and feeding herself. Her mother has blamed Jessica's behaviour on the arrival of the new baby, a year ago, but is now concerned that Jessica's behaviour is not improving.

The playgroup leader has approached Jessica's mother and together they have decided to work on Jessica's self-help skills and general behaviour. They have decided to meet weekly to set some targets and agree on strategies. The playgroup leader suggests that they should focus on particular skills each week, while at the same time using strategies to help Jessica show wanted behaviour. The first week's plan is below.

Week 1

Goals: To encourage Jessica to dress herself
            To encourage Jessica to show more cooperative behaviour

Activities – home	Activities – playgroup
Dress up in mother's clothes	Dressing up corner
Jessica to be given some choice of clothing in the morning	Stories and books about clothes
Making up games and songs when dressing	Picture lotto – things we wear
Help dress baby	Wash doll's and teddy's clothes
	Matching and sorting buttons

Behaviour strategy

- Stickers to reward Jessica when she attempts to dress herself at home.
- Praise when Jessica is playing and cooperating in a group.
- Praise and adult attention at home when Jessica is showing wanted behaviour.
- No attention or eye contact if Jessica refuses to put on a coat or dress herself.

Jessica's mother and the playgroup leader exchange information at the end of each session. After the second session, Jessica's mother identified that Jessica was not very good at managing buttons. The playgroup leader then added to the plan an activity for the next session, which would help Jessica learn how to do buttons.

1 *Why was it important for the playgroup leader and the parent to work together?*
2 *Why did they need to exchange information at the end of each session?*
3 *Suggest another goal for Jessica to achieve in the following week.*

Discussing learning programmes with children

It can be very useful to talk with children about their learning programmes. Telling children what we are hoping they can achieve will help them understand the goals. If it is decided that it is appropriate to talk to children, this should be handled carefully so as not to make them feel under pressure. Simply say to a child that you are going to help him or her learn a new skill, and explain how the activity will do this. Sometimes children can be involved more fully in the process of drawing up a programme, and asked for ideas and suggestions. This approach may work particularly well with older children, who will gain confidence and the feeling of taking on responsibility.

There will be times when it is not appropriate to tell children about their individual learning programmes, however, particularly when children are very young.

Element M7.3   Implement planned learning activities and experiences

Children who are given a range of interesting experiences and opportunities are more likely to enjoy learning and to gain many developmental skills. Planning individual activities and working successfully with children require good organisational skills. This section looks at the process of taking the ideas for activities stated in curriculum plans and individual learning programmes, and implementing them in settings. Supervisors in early years settings will often have overall responsibility for checking that planned activities are being carried out, and that children are offered a range of responsibilities.

WHAT YOU NEED TO LEARN

- Using weekly or daily planners
- Preparing detailed plans
- Encouraging children to be creative
- Actively supporting children

Using weekly or daily planners

Overall curriculum plans and individual learning programmes generally outline the type of activities that are to be carried out in a setting. The next step is to look at the suggested activities and consider how these can fit into the routine of the setting. Some settings use daily or weekly planners so that everyone in the setting knows the activities and experiences that are to be provided and who will be responsible for them. Links to the early years curriculum or to learning goals can also be shown. An example is given below.

Monday	Activity	Resources	Staff	Learning goals
Morning Green room	Growing seeds	Cress seeds Egg boxes Watering can Aprons Soil or peat	Jo	To understand what seeds need to make them grow To share and use equipment To describe seeds – small, tiny, black To consider how long the seeds will take to grow
Both sessions – free play Messy area	Free painting – greens and yellow	Sponges Selection of brushes Paints, various shades of green and yellow Aprons Pencils	Carly	To enjoy texture and feel of using paints To be free to create own pictures and images To develop independence and self-reliance To select and use own tools To develop fine manipulative skills
Both sessions – free play Messy area	Sand tray	Selection of sand toys	Carly	To enjoy texture and feel of sand To be free to explore sand To share equipment with other children
Morning Book corner	Jack and the Beanstalk – story	Big book	Jo	To listen and concentrate To develop imagination To develop scanning from left to right
Afternoon Book area	Musical instruments – growing loud	Shakers, rattles	Emma	To explore sounds To produce crescendos To develop imagination

Most children greatly enjoy making music as a way of exploring sounds

Preparing detailed plans

There are times when a detailed plan might be written for an activity. Most settings do not write a detailed plan for each activity that is planned, because this would be a lengthy process. However, detailed plans can be useful to show knowledge and understanding of

Detailed plan

Activity   Tray painting

Number of children   4   **Age of children**   3 years

Setting   Messy area   **Preparation time** 10 minutes   **Activity time** 10 – 15 minutes

Resources	Rationale
4 trays ready mixed paint – red, green 4 aprons thin card and A4 paper large brush pencil plastic covering for table	This is a popular activity with this age of children. The end result can be displayed, but there is no right or wrong way of producing a pattern. The children should be able to do most of this activity unaided and it should encourage language.

Learning intentions

Knowledge and understanding of the world	Physical development
• Discover printing and links to books and other printed materials	• Develop coordination and control through placing paper onto tray, drawing pattern and brushing paint

Mathematics	Language and literacy
• Find out about patterns • Count out pencils and aprons	• Talk about feel of paint • Listen to others • Develop emergent writing skills

Creative development	Personal and social development
• Discover feel and texture of paint • Design own patterns and expressing through paint • Use paint in a new way	• Share, take turns • Work as part of a group • Concentrate on the activity • Gain confidence in own achievements

Specific language to be developed: descriptive words about the feel of the paint: sticky, wet, cold, tickly, as well as encouraging children to describe afterwards what they have done.

Implementation
1 Ask the children to put on their aprons.
2 Show the children a pattern that has already been made.
3 Talk to the children about printing.
4 Spread the paint thinly but evenly across the tray with a large paintbrush.
5 Ask one of the children to draw a pattern in the paint with a finger.
6 Place a sheet of A4 paper onto the tray and ask one of the children to smooth it gently down.
7 Lift up the paper and show the children.
8 Ask the children what they think has happened.
9 Put another piece of paper over the tray to see if the pattern can be printed again.
10 Ask each child if he or she would like a turn.
11 Repeat the activity if the children are still interested.
12 Make sure that children wash their hands thoroughly after the activity.
13 Mount and display the work.

A detailed plan for a tray painting activity

how to plan for and implement an activity. Many childcare courses ask that students provide detailed plans as evidence.

Detailed plans may be needed if you wish an activity to be carried out in a certain way by another staff member. It is also a good idea to write up a few detailed plans so that they can be used if a staff member is absent and an idea for an activity is needed.

In some ways, detailed plans are similar to recipes in that they will allow someone else to follow through an activity. Detailed plans can be written up using the following headings:

- Activity
- Rationale (reason for this activity)
- Group size
- Age of children
- Preparation time required
- Activity time
- Resources/equipment
- Learning outcomes
- Implementation (how the activity needs to be carried out)

Preparing for activities and experiences

Good organisation is often the key to successful activities and learning opportunities. If you are working as a supervisor you may have responsibility for ensuring that learning activities and experiences are carried out effectively. The spider diagram below shows some of the points that need to be considered when managing activities.

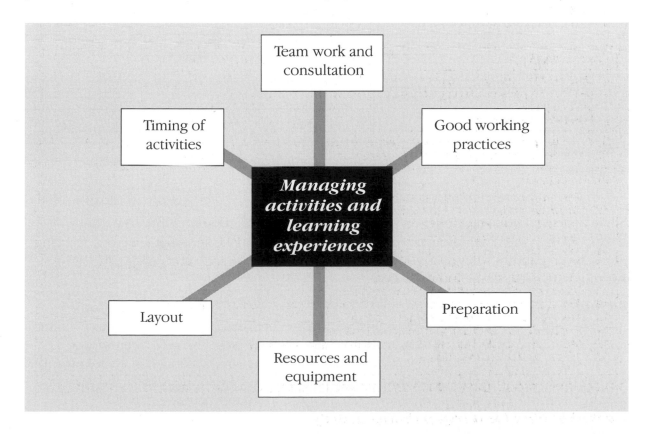

Preparation

Good preparation is one of the most important factors in carrying out activities and organising learning experiences with children. Staff should be encouraged to try out any new practical ideas themselves, such as cooking activities or paint techniques, before implementing them with a group of children.

Time should be allowed in the planning of the day for preparation – for example, paper may need to be cut to size, or tables to be covered. As a working guide, many activities will require 10 minutes of preparation.

Events such as celebrating a festival or going on an outing will require significant amounts of preparation. It can be helpful to use a checklist when preparing for these types of events – an example is given below.

Task	Comments	Tick when achieved
Phone venue to ask for prices		
Find out transport prices and times		
Arrange provisional insurance		
Book provisional date with venue		
Book provisional date with transport providers		
Work out cost per child		
Write letter to parents/carers		
Collate returns		
Confirm venue, insurance and transport		
Ask for volunteers		
Send out reminder to parents, and details about clothing, packed lunches, etc.		
Organise groups and arrange for registers		
Collect float money, first aid kit, sick bucket, etc.		
Brief volunteers and staff members		

Supervisors can help inexperienced staff and helpers by making sure they know what resources they will need for an activity. It is a good idea to make sure that everyone working in the setting knows where resources are kept – this means that if extra paper, glue or toys are required, they can be found easily.

Layout

Activities and learning experiences can become less effective and less interesting to children if they are badly positioned. A quiet activity, where children may wish to concentrate or where an adult needs to work alongside a child, will need to be positioned in an area with as few distractions as possible. Activities such as dressing up or exploring musical instruments will, by contrast, require more space and children will inevitably be noisy if they are benefiting from the activity. When planning activities over the week or day, thought has to be given to their layout and position.

Resources and equipment

Most activities require some equipment and resources. It is important that the resources required for activities are carefully considered, as sometimes particular resources such as paints, toys and tools may be needed. If you are supervising staff, you should keep an eye on stock levels and keep consulting the overall curriculum plan to check that sufficient materials are available.

In Unit E3 we looked at the checks needed to make sure that the environment, equipment and resources meet basic health and safety requirements. Time must be allowed at the beginning of each session for these basic checks to be carried out.

Active knowledge ✔

To help an inexperienced staff member or helper, produce a checklist of resources for each of the following core activities.

- Dough
- Paint
- Home corner
- Sand
- Water tray
- Collage

Timing of activities

There are some times of the day when children will be more responsive to activities. This will depend largely on the ages of the children you are working with. Most children are fresh in the morning, and so will respond well at that time to activities that challenge and stimulate them. Towards the end of the afternoon, many children are feeling tired and need to be offered opportunities to relax rather than to concentrate. This means that many settings where children attend all day will choose to programme more child-led activities and experiences, as well as story times, towards the end of the session.

The length of activities can also have an impact on how well children respond. It is a common mistake for inexperienced staff to misjudge the amount of time required to carry out some activities, such as cooking or making models. Children can be left feeling frustrated if they wanted to play for longer, or if they have not had enough time to have another try. It is a good idea to encourage helpers and inexperienced members of staff to allow plenty of time for practical activities, particularly if the children have not experienced them before. We also need to be aware that expecting children to concentrate for longer than is appropriate is not effective, and may even cause the children to show unwanted behaviour. It is an important role of supervisors to encourage adults working with children to be flexible in their approach, so that if they see that a child is beginning to lose enthusiasm, they can finish or adapt the activity.

Signs that children are losing interest in an activity include:

- yawning
- rubbing eyes
- using equipment inappropriately

- being distracted by other children, looking around
- putting head down on table or head in hands
- distracting other children
- showing inappropriate behaviour.

Teamwork and consultation

It is important for all the staff in the setting to understand what is going on and their particular responsibility. Most settings hold planning meetings where everyone can contribute ideas for activities and be aware of future plans. It is important that planning sessions are used to consider whether curriculum plans or individual programmes are meeting their goals. If you are responsible for drawing up curriculum plans in the setting, it is a good idea to make sure that everyone knows in advance which activities or groups of children they will be responsible for. This allows staff to plan in more detail how they will carry out the activity, and give them time for any preparation that might be needed.

If students or volunteers are helping in a setting, they should be invited to see the planning sheet or given ideas of what they need to do. Some settings prepare notes for helpers to make sure that they understand the learning goals for an activity and how they can help the children.

Monday

Blue group – Sophie, Rajeet, Anya and Tom

Activity – Planting seeds

Learning intentions – finding more about seeds and how they grow

– planting seeds and watering them

– developing drawing and writing skills

Activity The table will already be laid out for you. Cheryl has some spare pots and seeds if you need them.

1 Talk to the children about the size and shape of the seeds and what type of plants they think they will grow into.

2 Ask the children to choose a pot.

3 Using sticky labels, ask the children to have a go at writing their names (Anya may need to get her name card). They can also draw a pattern or picture to decorate the label.

4 Plant the seeds – ask the children what they think the seeds need to grow well.

5 Water the seeds. You might like to ask one of the children to fill up a jug of water and bring it to the table.

6 Encourage the children to talk about what will happen if the seeds do not get enough water. Introduce also the word 'drought', and mention that some countries have very dry periods.

An example of notes for volunteers or helpers

Good working practices

For children to gain the most from the learning experiences planned for them, the people working with them must maintain a good standard of practice. Inexperienced staff or helpers may need some guidance to help them work effectively with children, and if you are acting as a supervisor you may need to provide that guidance. You may also encourage staff to produce detailed plans themselves, to help them think through the activities they are preparing.

The spider diagram below shows some of the elements of good practice that can help to make an activity successful.

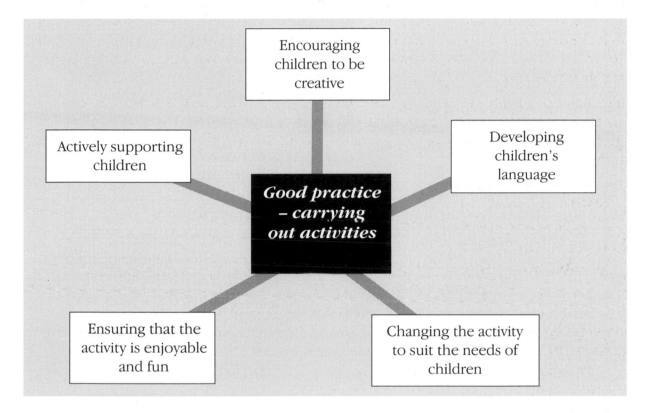

Encouraging children to be creative

Many inexperienced staff find it threatening or worrying if children use the equipment or resources in a different way from the way they had expected. For example, children may decide to stick feathers onto a sheet in an entirely different way from the one planned. It is good practice, however, to encourage children to show creativity and learn spontaneously, and this means that where possible activities should include elements of creativity. Sometimes children will use equipment and resources in a way that has not been planned for, and this type of spontaneous activity should be supported unless children are likely to damage equipment or injure themselves or others. If you are a supervisor, you may need to reassure inexperienced staff and helpers that his type of learning is valid.

Developing children's language

In young children, language is directly linked to their thought processes. This means that most children need to express their thoughts through learning, and that connections have to be verbalised or communicated by adults so that children learn concepts. For example, an adult may need to say to a child 'Where do you think the water has gone?' in order for the child to think about the concept of water turning into ice.

It is important for children to be in a language-rich environment, and this means that adults working with children must gauge when to interact with children. Unless a child is completely engrossed in an activity and needing time to concentrate, it is good practice to spend time talking and listening to the child.

It is good practice to interact with a child when appropriate during an activity

Ensuring that activities and experiences are enjoyable

Children learn when they are relaxed and when activities are fun and stimulating. Forcing a child to participate in an activity does not normally result in the child achieving many of the intended learning outcomes, so very young children should not be compelled to carry out activities. Presenting activities in a lively and interesting way may, however, attract some reluctant children to try them. This may mean turning an activity such as learning to write into a game, or something that seems purposeful for a child – for example, a child may like to try making a shopping list or writing inside a greeting card.

Children need to feel that they can succeed at any activity, and while activities should be stimulating, it is also important that they are appropriate to children's stage of development so that children are not attempting to do things that are too hard for them. Unwanted behaviour is often a result of children feeling bored or disenchanted with an activity.

Actively supporting children

Adults working with children must support them as they carry out activities and have learning experiences. The amount of support and the role of the adult will vary according to the age of the children and the type of activity. Older children using equipment outdoors may need an adult to supervise them only to ensure that their play remains safe, whereas younger children in the same situation may need an adult to take a more active role – for example, standing behind them as they climb. Inexperienced staff may need to learn that sometimes their role is to act as a facilitator, which means giving children the encouragement and resources to develop games and ideas in their own way. If you are acting as a supervisor, you may need to make sure that staff understand that children learn many skills when adults act as facilitators – for example concentration, independence and creativity. Standing back and watching children play is sometimes more valuable than directing children, although staff members must be confident enough to do this.

Where activities are adult-directed, it is good practice to make sure that all the children are benefiting from the activity. This may mean making sure that children are not waiting for too long before they have their turn, or that questions are directed to and answered by different children. If you are responsible for supervising inexperienced staff or helpers, you may need to consider the size of group they are to work with – generally, it is easier to involve and engage children in small groups.

Changing the activity to suit the needs of children

There will be times when it will be evident that a planned activity is not meeting the needs of the children. It may be a little too demanding or too simple. Adults working with children must feel that they can either stop the activity or adapt it in some way. If you are responsible for planning or monitoring activities, you may need to remind staff that it is good practice to do this when necessary. Inexperienced staff, in particular, may need to gain confidence to change activities and if you are monitoring you may need to work alongside them to show them how an activity can be adapted.

Case study

Juliette is a student in her first year at the college. She has written a detailed plan for her activity – she is planning to encourage two-year-olds to carry out a tray painting activity. The plan seems fine, but during the activity you notice that the children are finding it hard to wait for her turn and that one or two of the children are putting their hands in the paint. Juliette is starting to become flustered, and the children are beginning to sense this.

1 *How can the activity be adapted so that children are not waiting for so long?*
2 *How can you support Juliette in adapting the activity, without making her feel that she has failed?*
3 *What other activities could you ask Juliette to try with children, to give her more experience of running creative activities?*

Element M7.4   Evaluate planned learning activities and experiences

It is good practice to consider carefully and systematically how successful we are in meeting children's needs. Evaluating the work we are doing with children can help us plan more effectively in the future, and help us to decide how future curriculum plans should be drawn up. This section looks at the variety of ways in which learning activities and experiences can be evaluated.

- Observing children
- Using reinforcement and extension activities
- Listening and responding to children
- Involving parents
- Evaluating your own performance
- Producing written evaluations

Observing children

One way in which we can evaluate the activities and experiences that we have planned is by observing children. This can be done formally, by recording the observation using one of the methods outlined in Unit C16, or informally by watching children's reactions and participation. Formal observations may be needed to support other professionals, especially if an individual learning programme is involved, and recorded observations may also be useful to determine a child's skills.

Observing children completes the planning cycle, as through observations we may decide on the needs of the children or the activities and experiences that might act as extension activities.

Remaining objective when evaluating

It can be hard to remain objective when considering whether an activity is successful or not, especially if much time and preparation have been involved. It is important, however, to aim to be as objective as possible so that we can learn from our work. Most activities do meet the learning and social needs of children, but by evaluating them carefully you may be able to see more effective ways of working or realise that certain children need reinforcement activities or extension activities.

It is a good idea to have a list of questions that can guide staff members through the evaluation process. Below is a suggested list.

Note that the word activity is used in its broadest sense and can include free-play activities, adult-led activities and other learning experiences.

Overall

Did the children show signs of enjoying themselves?
Did the children concentrate on the activity, or were they easily distracted?
Did children have longer or shorter concentration spans than they normally do?
Did the activity stimulate language opportunities?
Did all the children participate fully? If not, why not?
What opportunities for spontaneous learning occurred?
In what ways did the activity fit the planned learning outcomes?
Were there any children who did not benefit from this activity? If so, why?

Practical aspects

Was the preparation time adequate for this activity?
Were all the materials and resources available?
Were these the best resources for this activity?

Did the activity last the intended time?
How easy was the activity to supervise, direct or support?
Was the activity appropriate for the time of day, and the routine of the setting?

Reinforcement activities
How could this activity be developed further?
Were there any children who seemed to be particularly interested in this activity?
Were there any children who would benefit by repeating this type of activity?
Were there any children who did not respond or were unable to cope?

Using reinforcement and extension activities

It is always good practice to consider follow-on activities for children, or ways of making an activity more stimulating. Often, children will need to keep on practising a skill such as using scissors, but will become bored if the same activity is offered repeatedly. Reinforcement activities can be used to practise a skill in a different way. Reinforcement activities are especially necessary when children are beginning to gain concepts of number or literacy.

Sometimes it will be apparent that an activity has been very popular with children, and they will benefit from further developing some aspect of it – for example, children who have put out food for birds and watched the birds could follow this up by making seed cakes for them. Extension activities help children to develop skills or knowledge further.

Listening and responding to children

It is increasingly realised that very young children are able to express their preferences and voice their ideas. Listening to children and allowing them preferences will help you to find out which activities they find enjoyable. This can help in designing individual learning programmes. If a child who enjoys playing in the sand is given activities that link with this, he or she is more likely to enjoy the activities and benefit from them.

Case study

Marc is three years old and has not really settled at nursery. His key worker has noticed that he seems to enjoy playing in the sand whenever he is given the chance. She has planned a series of activities that centre around the sandpit and that will encourage Marc to talk to her and to other children. These activities included asking Marc to choose the sand toys with her, organising a 'buried treasure' hunt in the sand pit, and making sand castles.

Gradually, over a week, Marc seems to be more responsive. His key worker carries out an event sample in which she records the number of times he initiated conversation with either herself or other children during a morning session, and compares it to one she had done earlier in the month.

1   Why was it important to observe what Marc enjoyed?
2   Why was it a good idea for his key worker to record an event sample?

Asking children for their views

An interesting technique has been developed to help very young children express their preferences. It involves taking a teddy into a setting and asking children what they think the teddy would like best about the setting if he were to stay for a day. This method encourages children to think through what they like most, and use the teddy as an intermediary. The method has been used on children as young as two and a half.

We can ask older children directly about their favourite activities, and also about activities that have not held their interest. In some cases, we may find that a strong indicator as to whether children are enjoying themselves is their friendships! This may mean planning some activities and experiences so as to allow children to work and play alongside children with whom they have an affinity.

Older children may give us ideas about extension activities. Most settings that take the time to ask for children's views find that it is rewarding and that children are pleased to be given the opportunity to talk about what they are doing.

Involving parents

Parents can provide us with valuable feedback, because often children will talk to them about what they have done and enjoyed. Children who are quiet in settings are sometimes talkative with their parents. Listening to parents' views may reveal which activities are particularly popular. Some parents may also be able to provide materials that will extend activities – items for the interest table, books or objects that have been discussed.

Evaluating your own performance

If you are in a situation where you are managing others, it is important that you are able to demonstrate good practice yourself, and this means that you have to be able to evaluate your own performance. This process can feel uncomfortable, but it is valuable and necessary, especially if you lead others. Good practitioners aim to improve their own performance, but also think about different approaches to working with children. Below is a series of

Statement	Score (1 high – 5 low)
I was well prepared for this activity	1 2 3 4 5
The activity was appropriate for the age/stage of the children	1 2 3 4 5
I made sure that all the children were able to participate fully	1 2 3 4 5
I gave children opportunities for language development	1 2 3 4 5
I listened actively to children as they spoke to me	1 2 3 4 5
I allowed children to take ownership of the play/activity	1 2 3 4 5
I was warm, calm and reassuring to all the children	1 2 3 4 5
I encouraged children who were losing concentration	1 2 3 4 5
I adapted the activity to suit the needs of children	1 2 3 4 5
I praised children for their efforts as well as for their achievements	1 2 3 4 5
I created a harmonious and pleasant atmosphere	1 2 3 4 5
I handled unwanted behaviour effectively, but not aggressively	1 2 3 4 5
I encouraged children to respect each other	1 2 3 4 5
I made sure that children were safe during the activity	1 2 3 4 5

statements that might help you consider your own style and approach when working with children. You might wish to complete this assessment after you have done an activity with children.

It is unlikely that you will be able to give yourself high scores on all of these statements, but they might help you to reflect on your own performance. You can also benefit from watching other people at work and considering their strengths.

Using evaluations to shape future planning

Staff in most settings meet regularly to prepare plans and to keep in touch with what is happening. In large settings this might be done in teams, while in smaller settings the whole staff may meet. If you are acting as a supervisor, you should use this opportunity to encourage staff to look at current plans and consider whether any adaptions are needed. It is important that the evaluation process is seen as a chance to improve current plans and not as an opportunity to blame or criticise others. A positive atmosphere is needed to allow everyone in the team the opportunity to contribute and to talk frankly. Sometimes new activities or approaches might not have worked as intended, but it is important that criticism is constructive as a negative atmosphere will discourage staff from trying out new ideas.

It is a good idea to keep a detailed record of ideas or activities that have been extremely successful, so they can be re-used at some time in the future. This record can be kept in the form of a resource file and used for reference at planning meetings.

If curriculum or weekly plans are changed, it is important that everyone who is involved in these plans is informed about the changes. This may mean making sure that a list is kept of staff members not present at the meeting, and also of people who come into the settings to help, such as students and volunteers. In the same way, changes to individual learning programmes may need to be discussed with other professionals and parents, as they may have ideas and information which will make the new plan more effective.

Producing written evaluations

As part of their coursework, many students will need to produce written evaluations on activities they have planned. The aim of these written evaluations is to encourage students to reflect on the organisation of the activity and on their performance.

It can be helpful to write up the evaluation in three parts:

1 Review of activity
This part of the evaluation can be descriptive – essentially it gives a brief account of how the activity went.

2 Learning outcomes and responses of the children
This section should look at what the children gained from the activity. Were the planned learning outcomes achieved?

As children's reactions vary, it can be a good idea to focus on particular children's learning outcomes. How did they react? What parts of the activity did they enjoy? How did they use the materials?

It is also a good idea to consider whether any individual children needed extra support and to consider what type of activities they would benefit from in the future.

3 Learning outcomes for the student

This section should concentrate on the student's performance and what he or she has learnt from carrying out the activity. What has been learnt about the children the student is working with? How might this activity be improved?

When activities are successful, students need to think about the reasons why they were successful.

EVALUATION OF ACTIVITY

Review of activity

When Elliott was given the choice of the type of puppets he would like to make, he produced a lovely coloured drawing of the film *Toy Story* from his drawer. He told me that he had been at his grandfather's house the previous weekend and that they had watched the film on video together. After watching the video his grandfather had helped Elliott to draw the picture to represent the film. Elliott then said that he would like to make his puppets of the characters from the film. He was very absorbed and creative when drawing the characters on the card. He needed no help from me but responded well to praise and encouragement. The activity seemed to bring to mind the pleasant day spent with his grandfather and it calmed him after his crying bouts. He seemed contented and happy while doing the activity.

When presented with the challenge of making a stage for the puppets, Elliott was able to calculate the means of doing so out of the white card on his own, with no assistance. During the activity several of his classmates came over to admire his work. I felt that this was a help to him in social relationships with his peers.

I noticed that Elliott's drawings were extremely carefully done and were intricate, colourful and detailed. I was able to praise him a lot for his ability.

Elliott's enthusiasm in describing the Toy Story characters helped him to forget his distress for the afternoon. He became very animated and communicative.

Learning outcomes for the child

I felt that Elliott was given confidence by his success with the activity – by the praise I was able to give him and by the positive response of his classmates. He was affirmed in his artistic abilities and was able to take home the puppets to show his mother. He was shown that creativity can provide a respite from an upset period in his life.

Learning outcomes for me

I learned the advantage of art and creative activities for a child who is emotionally upset – that it can create a basis for positive conversation with a child. I was shown how such an activity can relax and calm a child.

An example of a student's evaluation

Active knowledge ✔

You can produce evidence for this unit by producing two written evaluations of activities you have carried out with the children. These will need to show that you can evaluate your own performance and that you were aware of the children's responses during the activity.

M7 Unit test

1   What is meant by the term 'curriculum plan'?
2   Why is it important to look at children's stages of development before producing a curriculum plan?
3   List three factors that should be taken into account when drawing up a curriculum plan.
4   Why is it helpful to work with parents when drawing up an individual learning programme?
5   How can talking to children about their individual learning programmes be useful?
6   Why is it important that others in a setting should be informed about the aims of an individual learning programme?
7   Why is it important that adults working with children are prepared to adapt planned activities, if necessary?
8   How can the timing of an activity affect children's participation and enjoyment?
9   List four aspects of good practice when carrying out an activity with children.
10 Give two methods by which you can evaluate the effectiveness of an activity.

Unit P2

Establish and maintain relationships with parents

In your role as an early years worker, it is essential that you are able to build and maintain good relationships with parents and carers. This is because you will be working in partnership with them in their child's best interest. It is important to remember that they are trusting you, in their absence, to look after their children. Many early years settings now stress in their literature how important it is for workers and parents to work in partnership and it is common to read such phrases as 'linking home and school' and 'parental involvement'.

In this unit the term 'parents' is taken to mean those people who have full parental responsibility for children. This could be a relative, for example a grandparent, or other carers such as foster carers or step-parents.

The elements for this unit are:

P2.1   Develop relationships with parents new to the setting
P2.2   Plan settling-in arrangements with parents
P2.3   Exchange information with parents about their children
P2.4   Share the care and management of children with their parents

Element P2.1   Develop relationships with parents new to the setting

A generation ago, parents of early years children may have been seen waiting at the school gate at the end of the day. This is not a common sight today and most nurseries and early years classrooms adopt an 'open door' policy to make sure that parents feel welcome to come into the setting. Parents are encouraged to feel free to voice any concerns or worries immediately, as they are familiar with staff and their child's daily environment. In the same way, frequent contact makes it easier for early years workers to bring up difficult subjects with parents, such as inappropriate behaviour by the child.

WHAT YOU NEED TO LEARN

- Welcoming parents into the setting
- Communicating with parents

- Finding opportunities to talk with parents
- Valuing parents
- Passing on information to parents
- Referring parents to other staff within the setting
- Maintaining confidentiality
- Passing on comments made by parents to colleagues

Welcoming parents into the setting

When a child is first brought into a new setting, parents may have a number of concerns. It could be that they have not been in any educational environment since they themselves left school, and are not comfortable in the setting. There may also be other factors, for example:

- the child may have a particular special need or disability
- the parent may be returning to work and feeling guilty about leaving the child
- the parent or child may speak English as a second language.

You should always make sure that you are approachable and friendly towards all parents so that they are happy about leaving their children with you.

Keys to good practice
Ways to make parents feel comfortable

- Make sure you greet the parents correctly – this means calling people by their preferred names, for example, 'Mrs Patel'. If you are unsure what someone would like to be called, ask him or her directly.
- Smile and say hello – this makes a big difference.
- Talk to the child as he or she comes in – admire a new coat or point out some toys in the setting.
- Always be approachable and willing to help wherever you can.
- Make sure you mention children's achievements to parents to reinforce positive behaviour.
- Encourage parents to come in at any time.

Case study

Mr Allen is a single parent whose only son Jake is just starting nursery. It is Jake's first day and Mr Allen is the only Dad bringing a child in.

How might Mr Allen be feeling? What could you do to make him feel more comfortable?

There should be plenty of opportunity for the parent to speak to early years staff both before the child starts and when he or she is attending regularly. Some nurseries and playgroups arrange to visit children at home before they start. This allows staff to meet children informally in their own surroundings and to alleviate any fears that anxious parents may have. Visits to the setting are also encouraged – this gives both parents and children an idea of what to expect on the first day. Settings offer different admissions procedures. These may include some or all of those detailed below.

Information given	Admissions procedure
Initial visit	Gives both parents and children a chance to look around the setting and meet staff. Any questions they have may be answered
Prospectus or brochure	Gives information about the setting such as its aims, curriculum and different policies
Home visits	To meet parent and child. Parents may feel more comfortable about asking any questions. Children may settle more quickly if they have met staff
Admission forms	May be quite detailed and include information about the child including medical history, development and emergency contact numbers
New parents afternoon/evening	Parents can find out further information and meet other new parents. Evening meetings are particularly valuable as this makes it possible for working parents to attend

Settings need to make sure that any information they have about the child is kept up to date, such as emergency numbers and changes of address. Parents need to be reminded of this and it may be useful to have a reminder prominently displayed on a noticeboard.

Addressing parents

From the first time that parents visit the setting, it is important that they feel valued by staff and comfortable in the situation. This is because parents and early years workers need to make communications between home and the setting flow as easily as possible. It may be that parents wish to be addressed in a particular way – remember that there are now many more one-parent families than in the past, so do not assume that all women with children should be referred to as 'Mrs'. You should find out and use the parent's preferred name at all times, remembering that not all couples with children share the same surname.

Parents should be encouraged to visit the setting to see children's work

Communicating with parents

There may be times when you are faced with a communication problem with a parent who has a particular difficulty such as deafness, or who speaks English as a second language. You must take special care, as you would with a child with a similar difficulty, to make sure that the parent does not feel isolated in the setting and withdraw as a result. This may have repercussions for the individual on a social and personal level, and therefore also have an impact on the child.

Keys to good practice
Involving parents when there are communication difficulties

- Learn a few signs if appropriate.
- Find an interpreter or arrange for one to come into the setting, particularly if there are several families with English as a second language.
- Involve the child where appropriate to help with communication (but not if the subject matter concerns the child).
- Spend time with the parent – perhaps encourage him or her to become involved in the setting itself by helping in a practical way.

All of the above give the parent the opportunity to make more contact with his or her child's setting, and any contact on a regular basis will help to build the parent's confidence and break down any barriers.

With an 'open door' policy, you may find that some parents are too eager to come into the setting, and this can be a problem if it becomes a regular occurrence. The child will find it harder to settle each day and join in with activities. If this happens, you may need to discuss the problem with colleagues, and later speak to the parent about it.

Sources of information for communication difficulties

Many sources of information can be found listed in local telephone directories – you may need to speak to the national head office of an organisation but these are also listed locally. Local newspapers also often carry advertisements from community groups, which may be helpful.

Source	Type of information
Citizen's Advice Bureau	These are centres where people can get free advice about many subjects, and appointments are not always necessary.
Local adult education centres	These centres may be able to help with advice and suggestions for those who speak English as a second language.
Local library	These may be able to give advice and help, e.g. on local groups for those speaking specific languages.

Case study

Miss Roberts is very pleased that her daughter Jessica has started nursery and is keen for her to make new friends. She wants to make sure that Jessica is happy every day before she leaves her, and if Jessica looks at all worried, she immediately says to you that she feels she ought to stay.

What would you say to Miss Roberts? How could you reassure her about Jessica? Why could this become a problem if it goes on for too long?

Finding opportunities to talk with parents

It is important that you make full use of any times that exist for communicating with parents. Even if you only have time to smile and say 'Hello' at the beginning or end of the day, you are acknowledging them and reinforcing the relationship. As well as the drop-off and pick-up times, when the parent would feel comfortable about voicing any concerns or worries, there should also be occasions within the term when parents are able to come into the setting and see their child at work. This will help the child, who will sense that those who look after him or her, are working together. It will also give the child the opportunity to show his or her work and feel that it is valued.

The setting will usually have a timetable run on a yearly cycle, which may include a variety of events for parents to attend, both formal and social. Some common ways in which an early years setting may encourage contact with parents include the following.

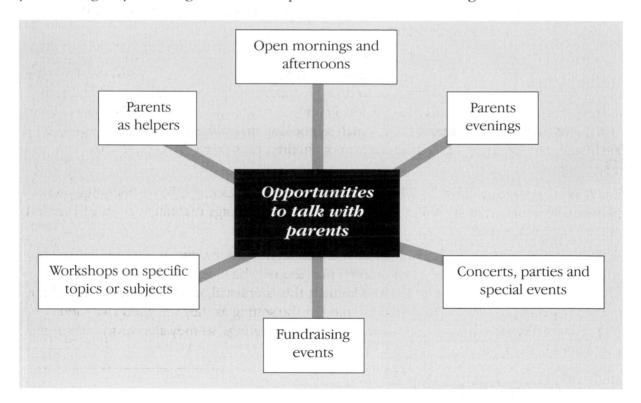

Open mornings and afternoons. These are opportunities for parents to come into the setting to see what is happening. Children are able to show their parents around and let them see examples of their work. Parents will also have the time and opportunity to talk to each other and early years workers, which they may not be able to do on a daily basis.

Parents evenings. These are held by all schools and most early years settings to allow staff and parents to discuss the progress of their children. Parents are given individual appointments so that they are able to discuss their child confidentially. The times when these are held may vary – some settings offer a parents evening early in the year to discuss 'settling in', while others may wait until later.

Concerts, parties and special events. Most early years settings will invite parents to come and watch their children perform, for example in a Christmas concert. Parents may also be involved in other special events in which they can participate with their child. These events are beneficial since they bring people together informally and are enjoyable for everyone.

Fundraising events. These are normally organised by parents who have formed committees to raise money for the school or nursery. They may organise an Easter egg hunt or summer fair, for example, and parents will usually ask staff for some support or involvement. It is important to give this as it encourages parents to feel they are contributing, and also will reinforce the parent–staff relationship.

Workshops on specific topics or subjects. These may help parents who feel out of touch with what is happening in the early years setting. Early years workers will be able to explain the work that they are doing with the children. Talks and discussions on topics such as reading, or early stages of maths, are always useful. Usually these will be held in the evening so that parents who work in the daytime are able to come.

Parents as helpers. Most early years settings have opportunities for parents to come in and help. They may have a variety of useful skills that can be passed on to children. The types of activities which parents may be able to do with children range from helping a child in a nursery with a painting, to hearing individual children read in an early years classroom. There may also be facilities for other activities such as cooking or sewing, and some parents who have artistic talents may like to take a group of children outside to do some simple observational drawing.

It may be that parents are able to help in a practical way, for example by washing out paint pots or taking a child to the toilet – these are the types of things that take up time when you may be busy elsewhere.

If the children are going on a trip or visit, you will need to ask parents for help to ensure that adult:child ratios conform to legal requirements. You may be lucky enough to have some fathers who are able to come and help. Although this is unusual, it is not unheard of and it is particularly positive for young boys to see men in the setting as they are good role models. They should also be encouraged to come and help on outings, as they are particularly useful when boys need to be taken to the toilet!

Keys to good practice
Activities suitable for parent helpers

- Looking at/reading books with children.
- Helping with 'messy' activities to keep the children on task (for example painting, Plasticine).
- Supervising children working on a 'structured' activity.
- Helping to prepare for an activity, for example by cutting paper, mixing paints, collecting junk materials.
- Everyday tasks such as sharpening pencils or putting out the milk.

The above list is not exhaustive, and many parents do not mind how they help. However, sometimes with the more messy activities it may be a good idea to check or give them some warning, so that they can wear old clothes if necessary.

Valuing parents

Although they may not always realise it, parents are their child's first great teachers. Simply by being with their parents in the first few years, children are learning many important skills that will stay with them throughout their lives. Parents are their first role models, and it is by looking at what they do and how they behave that children will start to work out their own personalities. For example, a parent who is involved in a theatre group may find that his or her child grows up to have a similar interest. People who grow up with pets in the house will often have pets of their own as adults. On the minus side, a child whose parent is always late may grow up with the same unawareness of the importance of being on time. Families have their own ways of doing things and all of them pass on a variety of skills, attitudes and beliefs to their children. As early years workers, we must remember that these are just as important to the child as those learnt in educational settings.

Parents may not always be aware of the fact that they are educating their children at home in so many ways even before they come into a setting, or that they learn so much in their early years. It may be up to the early years worker to draw their attention to certain points. Here are some ideas to pass on to parents:

- Be a good role model – let your child see you reading and writing for pleasure.
- Develop talking and listening skills with your child – encourage conversation and give your child the opportunity to express himself or herself.
- Look at numbers in the environment – draw attention to times when we look at numbers for information, for example kitchen scales, bus numbers.
- Look at a book with your child – simply running your finger along the text will establish that we read from left to right and then go back to the beginning of the next line.
- Help your child to dress and undress himself or herself, wash after using the toilet, and generally to increase his or her independence.

Active knowledge

Some of the staff have been asked to produce a booklet as a guide for parents of children starting at the setting. The booklet should give ideas for parents to help children with practical and other activities which they might like to do with their child before coming into the setting.

What type of things might you include?

Why is it important for settings to provide this kind of information for parents?

Parents must also be aware that what they can tell the early years worker is valuable – they are most knowledgeable about their child and you should listen carefully to what they say.

Passing on information to parents

As a general rule, the younger the child, the more likely it is that information will be passed on orally, since in the early years the child is likely to be taken to and collected from the setting. As children grow older, it may become appropriate for them to take certain information home from school, for example to tell parents that they need to bring in a particular item. In this way, they are being encouraged to take responsibility for passing on information. It may not always be appropriate, however, for the child to pass on information, and you will need to be able to deal with both written and spoken communications with parents.

Speaking to parents is the quickest and easiest way of exchanging information and usually happens when the child is being brought to or collected from the setting. It is important for the child to see early years workers and parents exchanging information in this way, since it reinforces positive relationships between the setting and the home environment. It is also a good opportunity for you to tell parents about the particular achievements of the child during the session. Parents who are anxious about leaving their child may be reassured by talking about what has happened, even if they have only a few minutes to talk.

If parents ask you to refer information to another person, it is a good idea to pass on the information as soon as possible, or if you need to wait before you can do this, to write it down so that you remember the details.

Written communication may be used when there is detailed information to be passed on and remembered, for example term dates or details of a visit. It may also be used when parents are unable to come to the setting on a regular basis – this could be for a number of reasons, for example work commitments. You will not need to write formal reports or letters, but you should be able to compose simple written information for parents. If you need to do this, you should always ask someone else to look over it before it is sent out to check that it is clear and gives the information correctly.

Where a class of children are all taking home the same letter, it is worth writing the child's name on each one since they can be dropped or left behind by the child. Also make a note of any child who is absent and write his or her name on a letter to take home at a later date. Remember that if you are handed any written information by a parent, it should immediately be given to the relevant person.

Some schools and nurseries may elect representatives to pass on information from parents to staff, or to help with specific requests such as finding helpers for the Christmas party.

The chart on the next page shows the various types of written information that may be passed between parents and the setting.

From September 1999 all children of school age are required to have a Home-School agreement (see below, page 336).

Communication	Content
Letters	For information, for example a school trip or concert
Headlines or news	Gives parents details about what is happening during the term. May include plans for a topic
Book or reading record	Usually gives details about the child's 'take home' book and whether he or she has read or discussed it
Accident slips	Usually filled in if the child has had an accident such as a bump on the head or has wet himself or herself
Noticeboards	For general items such as term dates, and reminders about returning tear-off slips and notifying the setting of changes in emergency contact numbers or home address

Referring parents to other staff within the setting

It is vital when starting to work in a new setting that you are able to recognise and name other members of staff and understand exactly what their responsibilities are. This is because you may be asked to pass on information or to call on a particular area of expertise that they may have. It may be that you are presented with a situation for which you do not feel you have been prepared, or you are uncomfortable dealing with. For example, a parent may ask for advice on a child's medical condition. In this situation you must always involve another member of staff, either by referring the parent or by asking the other staff member to join the discussion. When in doubt you should always ask for help or pass the matter on.

You may also find that because of your situation in the workplace, parents may confide in you or ask you for personal help or advice. You may need to listen and sympathise as far as possible, but you should not pass on information – better to refer the parent to the appropriate advice bureau or other authority. There will usually be a list of useful numbers in the local phone book or at the library, and it may be a good idea to have some of these to hand in case you need them. When you have been approached for advice or help, you should respect the confidentiality of the situation and wherever possible, after helping the parent, keep the matter to yourself.

Case study

Maria is a young single parent with a boisterous four-year-old. She is clearly having trouble coping with him. She comes into the school one day in tears because her housing benefit cheque has not come through and her landlord is demanding his rent.

What could you do to help Maria? What authorities could you advise Maria to go to?

Active knowledge ✓

Find out as much as you can about:

- the Child Support Agency
- Income Support
- chicken pox
- immunisation.

Maintaining confidentiality

This is a difficult area, but it is most important to respect confidentiality if you are to gain and keep the respect of other adults and parents in the setting. You must recognise the dangers of telling others about what has been communicated to you in confidence. A parent or other member of staff may report something to you and it is vital that you keep it to yourself. A betrayal of confidence may have serious repercussions for more than one person.

Case study

Shaheen, a classroom assistant, has recently been told some confidential news by a parent whose child, John, has just been diagnosed as autistic. The parent was worried by the news and Shaheen has had to reassure him and give him the name of a local help group.

Shaheen is in the bakery across the road from the school and mentions this news to another member of staff. Behind them in the queue is John's neighbour, who goes home and immediately speaks to John's father about what she has just heard.

1 How do you think John's father will feel about Shaheen's breach of confidentiality?
2 What are the likely consequences of this situation?
3 As Shaheen's supervisor, is there anything you could do to repair the damage caused?

It may be that sometimes you need to speak to a parent about a confidential matter – you should be careful and if necessary take the parent to another room, or away from the child, if possible. This is because the parent will not want personal matters spoken about in front of others.

Keys to good practice
Confidentiality

- Make sure you have read your setting's policy on confidentiality.
- Remember that any information about others in the workplace should be treated as confidential.
- If you are in any doubt about repeating information, you should ask a superior.

Passing on comments made by parents to colleagues

It may be that you are speaking to a parent who is unhappy about something that has happened in the setting. You should be careful in this situation not to be judgmental about the parent or to react in an unprofessional way. Remember that the parent may have been upset or worried about his or her child when he or she spoke to you. Pass on the information to the relevant colleagues as the parent would have expected you to.

Case study

Mrs Andrews has picked up her son from the nursery and has discovered that he had been playing outside without a coat on when it started to rain. Although the children were brought in straight away, his clothes are slightly damp and she is not happy about the situation. Your supervisor is busy talking to another parent, and so Mrs Andrews asks you to tell her about it.

1 *How might you be feeling?*
2 *How might Mrs Andrews be feeling?*
3 *What would you say to her to reassure her about what has happened?*

In a similar way, a parent may ask you to pass on information or opinions that you may not agree with to a colleague or supervisor. You should pass on only what you have been asked to say, without adding your own opinions. This is neither professional nor necessary.

Consolidation

Mrs Kahn is bringing Akram, aged three, to the early years setting for the first time. She speaks only a little English and is clearly anxious about Akram. Describe three things you could do to reassure her and make her feel welcome.

Element P2.2	Plan settling-in arrangements with parents

WHAT YOU NEED TO LEARN

- Settling-in policies
- Working with parents to meet the child's needs

Settling-in policies

When children are starting in a new setting, it is important for everyone concerned that they are happy and settled as soon as possible. This is because they will be spending a considerable amount of time in their new surroundings and will need to be settled in before they can start to develop to their full potential. Some children will feel comfortable straight away, while others may take longer to get used to their new environment. In a nursery or playgroup, parents may be encouraged to come in with their child for a few mornings to help the child to adjust. In most reception classes, children will be given a few half days before starting full time, as a school day can seem very long to such young children. You may still notice that because of the length of time they are apart from their parents, some children can find this separation difficult and distressing.

Attachment theory

For the first part of the young child's life, he or she will have been with a primary carer, whether this is a parent or other person, for most of the time. One theory about children's earliest relationships and how they affect the child's development is called the **attachment theory**. This looks at the importance of a strong relationship between the child and the primary carers. It is now widely accepted that the child's secure attachment with primary carers is linked to the ability to go on and form wider relationships. The characteristics of attachment behaviour are that the child:

- is more easily upset when separated from the primary carer than from anyone else
- is not worried when in unfamiliar surroundings if accompanied by the primary carer
- is clearly happier when the primary carer makes contact with or moves towards him or her.

Research by Kagan (*The Nature of the Child*, 1984) has shown that children who are restricted more and kept at home by their parents will show more attachment behaviour than those who attend pre-school groups or nurseries. The child will become more nervous and anxious about new environments and hold on to the person who represents security. In this way, even children who come from severely deprived backgrounds or who may have been neglected will form very strong links with their parents.

It may be that the child has close attachments to several carers or relations, and it is only when the primary carer is not available and no substitute attachment is formed with another that emotional harm can be done.

One of the best known theorists who studied children's need to be with their primary carer is John Bowlby (1907–1990). His theory comprises three aspects.

- Children who have been separated from their parents are more likely to suffer from psychological problems later in life.
- Babies form attachments instinctively. They must form an attachment before the age of 12 months.
- Babies and young children's fear of strangers is instinctive. In nature, animals stay close to their mother in order to prevent them from being attacked by other animals.

This theory about children's needs for attachment in the early years has changed the way in which we care for them throughout childcare settings, for example parents now spend the night with a child who has been admitted to hospital. Parents are more welcome in educational and other settings and are encouraged to come in and spend time forming a partnership with early years staff.

Although children pass through many stages in their social and emotional development, each child is an individual and may reach each stage at a different age. The ease with which children will leave their primary carer and be able to play cooperatively with other children will vary considerably from child to child, depending on individual maturity and experience.

Starting in a new setting

Although each setting will have its own settling-in policy to encourage children to feel comfortable, many of them are quite similar. In a nursery or playgroup there is usually a period in which parents may stay for a time to make sure that their child is comfortable. In a childminding situation, the parent may leave the child for longer and longer spells of time, if necessary. Some parents, however, may not be able to spend this time with their child due to work or other commitments. As an early years worker, you should be able to work with them to find a suitable way of gently easing the child into the setting. In such cases, you will need to be flexible.

Keys to good practice
Settling in

- Ensure essential information such as food likes and dislikes, medical details, contact phone numbers etc. has been obtained and recorded (see page 334).
- Establish routines quickly so that the child begins to feel confident about his or her setting.
- Make sure parents come in whenever needed.
- Speak to the child using his or her name to help him or her to feel settled.
- Reassure any child who is feeling anxious and try to take his or her mind off it.
- Give the child a key worker or someone who is familiar each day so that the child gets to know a familiar face.

When a child starts primary school, several letters will usually be sent out before the term starts to request information. These may include a declaration of health form, notes on absence from school, school meals and so on. (This information is covered in detail later in the unit.) Information packs will answer many of the questions parents may have at this time, and also enable them to pass on information to their children.

As well as the child making a preliminary visit to the school, parents will usually accompany their child on the first day, either for the morning session or at a staggered starting time so that the teacher can greet each child individually. This may go on for three or four days or until the child has settled, so the schools can take into account each child's needs.

Children will be encouraged to be as independent as possible and this will be pointed out to parents. For example, children should be able to:

- dress and undress themselves for PE
- do up their shoes – velcro fasteners are useful until children can tie laces or do up buckles
- put on and take off their coats
- use the toilet independently and wash their hands afterwards
- (once settled) be taken indoors in the mornings with their teacher.

How age and experience affect separation

A considerable range of experience will be brought to the setting by the children when they first come in. Their experience may be very wide or limited to the home. You should be aware of the differences that these experiences will have made for each child.

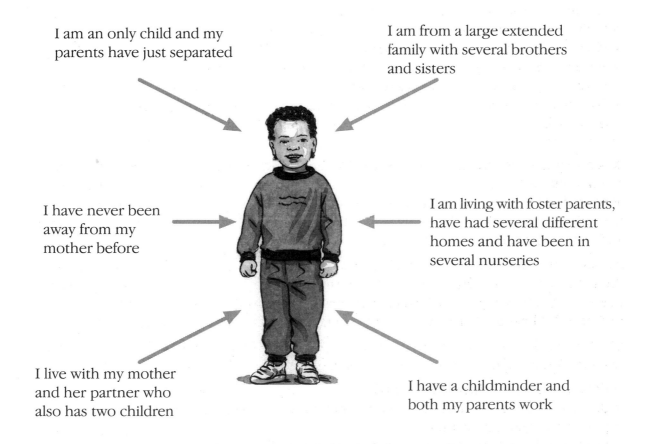

I am an only child and my parents have just separated

I am from a large extended family with several brothers and sisters

I have never been away from my mother before

I am living with foster parents, have had several different homes and have been in several nurseries

I live with my mother and her partner who also has two children

I have a childminder and both my parents work

Some children will settle in easily, while others may take a considerable time. You will need to be flexible and allow time where necessary, for example allocating one member of staff to the child full time.

Separation from carers may also be difficult if the child has experienced many changes or early years settings. The reasons for this could include the following:

- several changes in domestic arrangements due to the break up of a family or a remarriage
- children may have moved several times due to parents' employment
- parents may have had problems with childcare arrangements and had several different carers.

It is important to be aware when children have experienced many different settings, because they will almost certainly be affected by it. This could take the form of behavioural problems or forms of regression such as wetting their pants. You must always be patient with these children, and try to involve them with other children so that they can settle more quickly.

How parents may react to separation

Parents may also have mixed emotions when leaving their children for the first time.

- They may feel a sense of loss because they are used to having their child with them.
- They may feel guilty because they are leaving their child in someone else's care for the first time, or because they are having to return to work.
- They may feel threatened by their child's new relationship with the early years worker.
- This may be their youngest child and therefore the last to start at school, so they may feel isolated and unsure of their role.

Sometimes you may need to help parents at this time if they are having difficulties coming to terms with their child's growing independence. You may have to listen to their feelings, reassure them that their child still needs them and emphasise the importance of their role.

You can involve parents in many ways, as seen earlier in the unit, and should remember that this relationship is ongoing and therefore needs to be nurtured. Parents and carers should feel that they are able to check on their child at any time by visiting or writing to you with their concerns. In this way there will be no barriers between the home environment and the setting.

Working with parents to meet the child's needs

By placing their child in your care, parents have given you the authority to act in their place. This means that you must work in partnership with parents and have the same expectations, routines and boundaries of behaviour. It is essential that parents understand the importance of this and share the same basic views. Otherwise, children will not have a clear understanding of what is expected of them.

Behaviour

This is one of the key issues which needs to be addressed by both parents and early years staff. You must make sure that all parents have either had a copy of the school's policy, or if it is a childminding situation, are aware of the measures taken to deal with inappropriate behaviour. Parents and early years workers need to work together and establish an environment in which problems are less likely to occur. This is achieved in many instances through a pattern of positive behaviour based on high expectations and mutual respect.

Case study

Ben is five years old and has been in reception for six months. He has been in trouble at school for hitting and kicking another boy in the playground. When spoken to about this, Ben replies that the other boy hit him first, and that his parents always tell him to fight back if anyone hurts him.

1 *What should Ben's parents have said to him about playground incidents?*
2 *How will Ben feel if given two conflicting rules for action?*
3 *What would you say to Ben in this situation?*

Parents may seek advice from you about coping with behavioural problems in their child. You may wish to involve another member of staff, either by asking a colleague to join the discussion or by referring the parent to someone more senior.

Routines

Routines and everyday experiences play a central role in children's lives, as it is through repetition and expectation of what will happen next that they increase in confidence. Parents may not realise it, but children's lives at home will already have patterns and routines, for example a child recording a typical day's activities will pick out getting up, cleaning teeth and washing, eating breakfast and so on. Children need to have security, not only in their home surroundings but also in their new setting, as this will help them to settle in and make friends. Look at the example of a reception class's daily routine below.

Dunverton Infant School – Reception daily routine

9.00 am Children come into the classroom and the register is taken. There may be a short discussion time on the carpet where children may show things brought from home.

9.15 am Whole-school assembly.

9.45 am Children are split into various groups and taken to different activities, which are pre-planned and take account of the Desirable Learning Outcomes.

10.30 am Outdoor playtime.

10.50 am Children may have a drink and a story, and perhaps sing some songs and nursery rhymes.

11.20 am Children are not required to have a literacy or numeracy hour at this age, but may undertake some word work or numeracy work, such as simple handwriting skills or number games.

12.00 noon Lunch, followed by playtime.

1.15 pm Time-tabled activities such as PE or singing practice.

2 pm Structured activities, again with the Desirable Outcomes and children's needs in mind.

2.30 pm Children and staff tidy up and prepare for story time.

2.45 pm Story and short sharing time.

3.15 pm Home.

While the above routine will change slightly from day to day, playtimes, story and drink and assembly times will remain the same so that the child will know what to expect at certain times. (For example, after playtime each day it will be time for a drink.)

It is also important that you emphasise to parents that they should always be punctual, both when bringing their child to the setting and collecting at the end of a session. This is because children, particularly in a new setting, will easily become distressed and feel abandoned if a parent does not arrive with everyone else's, or at the expected time. This may also make them reluctant to return to the setting. Similarly, if children are always late to a session, they may feel uncomfortable about attending and unhappy about returning. The parent is also giving a subconscious message that being late does not matter.

It must also be made clear to parents that they should always keep to the agreed arrangements for collecting their child; if these need to be changed, they must always telephone first. In some early years settings there may be a book for the parent to write in if an adult other than the normal carer is to collect the child that day. Most parents will understand that these kinds of rules are to protect their child and that the safety of the children is of paramount importance.

Case study

Mr and Mrs Da Silva are separated. There have been some problems over custody of their twins and at present they are living with their mother. One Friday afternoon Mr Da Silva comes to collect the children, although this does not usually happen. He says that his wife has given him permission to take them away for the weekend. You have not been told about the situation at home and are about to let Mr Da Silva take the children when his wife comes to the door. There is a big argument and Mrs Da Silva complains that you should not have let her husband near the children.

1 *How could this breakdown in communication have been avoided?*
2 *What could be done to ensure that this kind of situation does not happen again?*
3 *How could Mrs Da Silva be reassured that her children will be safe?*

Active knowledge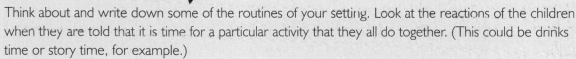

Think about and write down some of the routines of your setting. Look at the reactions of the children when they are told that it is time for a particular activity that they all do together. (This could be drinks time or story time, for example.)

Other factors to consider

You may find that some parents do not agree with all of the values supported by the early years setting. This could be due to different cultural or religious ideas, for example, or because a parent does not understand the value of play within the setting. It is vital to discuss with parents any areas they are not happy with, and to reassure them by explaining why things are done in a particular way. You may be faced with the following problems in the setting.

- parents may be rude or abrupt
- parents may be critical of strategies used by the setting
- parents may be angry with the early years worker or child
- parents may be dismissive of the child's requests
- parents may question the child's well-being to excess.

If, for any reason, parents entering the setting are upset or agitated, always listen to them and be sympathetic as far as possible. You may find that you do not feel able to deal with the situation and must seek help from your colleagues or external professionals. If the setting is based in your home, you may need to sit down and try to discuss the problem rationally.

Remember that parents may have their own problems outside the setting that they may not wish to discuss with you, but which may affect their feelings and behaviour.

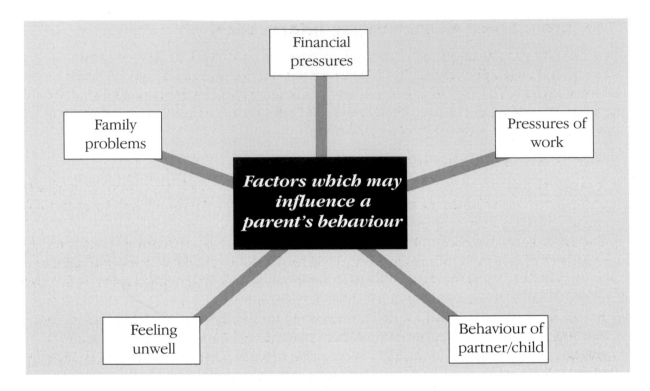

Case study

Luke has spent some of the morning painting a picture of a bus. He has worked very hard and at the end of the morning you have told him he can ask his carer in to come and look at it. When she comes to pick him up, he asks her in but she tells him they have to rush home.

1 *How do you think Luke feels?*
2 *What could you say to him the next day about what has happened?*
3 *What might you say to Luke's carer about it?*

Element P2.3   Exchange information with parents about their children

WHAT YOU NEED TO LEARN

- The importance of exchanging information
- Information provided by the setting

- Encouraging parents to seek information about the setting
- Information about the nature and purpose of children's activities

The importance of exchanging information

When a child starts to attend a new setting, parents and early years workers will naturally begin to exchange information. This will involve not only a formal exchange but also an informal exchange of information in a variety of situations. It is the beginning of what should be a continuous partnership throughout the child's education, and the more information passed between the setting and home, the better.

Benefits of exchanging information

1 **For the child.** It is important for each child that parents and early years workers regularly exchange as much information as they can. In this way, the children will see their main role models forming a positive relationship.

2 **For early years workers.** Members of staff in different settings will benefit from the maximum exchange of information as this will help them to build up an accurate picture of each child. It is also important for them to communicate regularly with parents so that they are aware of any concerns or problems that families may have.

3 **For parents.** Some parents may be anxious when their child starts to attend the setting and it can be a point of reassurance for them that the staff have as much information as possible about the child. Exchanging information regularly with parents will encourage them to feel that the setting is in close contact with their needs.

Information requested from parents

You will find that even before children start to attend the setting, you are exchanging information with parents about them. As already mentioned, the admissions procedure will have involved some detailed information about the child for record-keeping purposes. This kind of medical, dietary or other information will remain with children for as long as they are in the setting and will be available to different members of staff. An example of a declaration of health form is shown below.

There may also be other forms that will ask questions about siblings, any hospital treatments the child may have had and the child's degree of independence. The Department for Education and Employment (DfEE) also requires that local education authorities (LEAs) collect information about the ethnic origins of pupils in schools, their religion and the language spoken at home. This is so that LEAs can ensure that the education provided in schools meets the needs of the pupils attending them. For example, if a school had a class with a large proportion of children from a particular cultural background, the school may be better able to prepare for them given prior knowledge.

All these confidential pieces of information will enable the nursery or school to get to know each child more quickly and accurately, and to make children feel at home. Most settings will then keep a file on each child so that any information that is needed quickly, such as emergency numbers, can be accessed.

Parents may also pass on information verbally, but this is not advisable since early years

Maplewood Primary School

Declaration of Health Form

Child's surname _____ Date of birth _____

First names _____

Address _____

_____ Tel no _____

Parent/carer's work telephone numbers:

Mother _____ Father _____

Name and address of GP_____

_____ Tel no _____

Health details:
Does your child have:

Asthma	YES/NO	Eczema	YES/NO
Epilepsy	YES/NO	Diabetes	YES/NO

Any allergies _____

Details of medication _____

Is there any other information you feel we should know about your child?

_____

_____

workers may become distracted and then forget to record it accurately. If this happens, you should ask parents to put the information in writing. Do not be worried about asking them for it again – it may be of vital use in the future.

Some parents may also wish to give you specific information about family circumstances or factors in their child's life that they feel may be relevant to the setting, for example particular practices the family may undertake for religious reasons, or the need for their child to have certain religious holidays out of the setting.

Emergency procedures

Parents will need to be aware of what will happen in the event of an emergency, and contact telephone numbers should be checked at regular intervals. If you are informed that a child is moving home, you should always ask whether the telephone number is to be changed as well. If a parent cannot be contacted quickly in case of emergency, the setting should have a policy or guidelines for how it should act and who is able to take responsibility. (See also sharing care and management of children, page 341.)

Information provided by the setting

At the time that their child starts in the early years setting, parents will be given some information about the procedures, philosophies and rules that are to be observed. The prospectus will give parents some idea of the philosophy of the setting.

Red Lodge Pre-school Prospectus

Welcome to Red Lodge Pre-school group. Our aim is to prepare the children for full-time education at primary school and to encourage their independence away from the home environment. We seek to promote and enhance the children's physical, intellectual, language, social and emotional development within a secure and stimulating setting.

The prospectus may list some of the different procedures that are in place for behaviour, sickness, absences and safety measures. These should also be pointed out at the open evening or in any verbal contact you have with parents, as it is not always guaranteed that items sent home will have been read. The importance of emphasising procedures cannot be over-stressed, as parents need to be aware of what their children are expected to do. Most early years settings will have some system of rules which the children are made aware of and need to remember. They will usually be in the form of positive reinforcement, rather than a 'Don't do...' list.

Rainbow Nursery Golden Rules

1 Always walk quietly in the nursery.

2 Play fair and friendly games with other children.

3 Treat others and their belongings as you would like to be treated.

Remember that these rules are here to help you.

Children will be expected to know, understand and keep to the rules of the setting, irrespective of any particular problems an individual may have. They should be discussed frequently and parents should reinforce them in any way that they can. In this way, the children will make the link that the setting and home have the same set of rules. Parents also need to know about sanctions that are applied if an individual consistently disregards the rules. Some examples are given in the chart below.

Types of sanctions that may be applied	Purpose
Time out away from the activity	Remove child from situation to 'cool off'
Miss playtime	To deny child 'fun time'
Letter of apology	To encourage child to think about behaviour
Send to work with another member of staff	To remove child from situation altogether

Home–School agreements

Since September 1999, all state schools have been required to have a written 'Home–School agreement'. This document, drawn up by the school with the involvement of parents, aims to ensure that parents are aware of the crucial nature of the partnership they should have with their child's educational setting. At the time of writing, nurseries do not need such a formal document but could follow some of the guidelines which have been introduced as a basis for their own partnership with parents.

The Home–School agreement consists of a statement by the school of its aims and values, the responsibilities of the school towards its pupils, the responsibilities of parents and what the school expects of its pupils. The agreement covers punctuality, discipline and behaviour, and the ethos of the school. Parents are not compelled to sign it, but it should be made clear to them that pupils will still be expected to follow the rules of the setting. Some parents who are not supportive of the school generally may decide not to sign the form, and you will find that for the most part parents who do will already be doing their best for their child. An example of a Home–School agreement is given on the next page.

It may be that some parents are not supportive of the procedures and rules observed by the setting; this can be a sensitive area for parents and staff alike, and you should be aware that these issues can confuse children's lives. If a child has a background with a different set of values, these rules may seem difficult to uphold. It will be impossible for the child to carry the values of home into the setting, and vice versa. If this happens, you should discuss the situation with other members of staff to decide the best form of action to take with the individual child.

Parents' rights under the Home–School agreement

Parents are issued with a booklet by the DfEE explaining how agreements are set up. It also emphasises the importance of home/school cooperation for the benefit of children.

Expectations of parents are listed and explained – for example, under 'regular attendance' it states:

Annot Hill Primary School

Home–School agreement

1   The Parents

I/We shall try to:

- see that my child goes to school on time each day and attends regularly
- support the ethos and rules of the school
- attend parents evenings and discuss my child's progress
- support my child in any homework and other opportunities for home learning
- support the school's policies and guidelines on behaviour
- recognise and support the school's aims and values.

2   The School

The school will:

- contact parents if there are any problems with attendance or punctuality
- let parents know about any problems or concerns that affect their child's work or behaviour
- arrange parents evenings to discuss progress
- send home an annual report
- set and monitor homework
- keep parents informed about schools activities through regular letters, notices and information sheets.

- by law children must be educated between the ages of 5 and 16
- children must attend school on time
- parents must tell the school if the child cannot attend
- if attendance problems develop, the school will expect the parents to help both staff and the welfare service to solve them
- holidays are not a right in term time – the school's permission must be given beforehand.

Some parents will not be asked to sign agreements – for example if the parent has been guilty of abusing the child, or if the parent is seriously ill.

If parents or children break the agreement, staff from the setting may wish to discuss the matter with them. No child will be excluded for breaking the agreement, unless there is a regular problem with discipline. If parents feel that a school is not keeping to its side of the agreement, they should speak to the headteacher or governing body.

Parents are encouraged to make sure they are clear that the agreement sets out what the school will do and how they can help.

Case study

Christopher is a lively five-year-old who can sometimes become over-excited and very demanding of adult attention. He is an only child who has learnt that he can interrupt adults if they are speaking to one another, and he has trouble waiting his turn if you are asking all the children a question.

1 *What should you say to Christopher?*
2 *How could you explain to him that this is not acceptable?*
3 *What strategies could you use to promote positive behaviour in Christopher?*

Sharing information with parents

You may be surprised by the amount of literature your setting sends home to parents, not only about their child but also about events and activities. Records and other data will be kept within the early years setting, although parents are told that they can come in and look at this at any time: information concerning their child should not be hidden. Any other information about their children's work can be shared with parents. This must be clear to parents at all times, as clear and consistent lines of communication will always be beneficial.

There may be times when you have problems with a particular child in the setting and do not often see the parent. You will need to make an appointment with the parent, preferably by telephone since he or she may not wish the person who takes and collects the child to know about it. In cases such as these you will need to be positive with the parent and be able to suggest strategies for dealing with the child's behaviour (see sanctions on page 336).

Case study

Jasmine is a new pupil in the reception class but missed the first term. Many of the children have formed friendship groups and Jasmine is finding it difficult to make friends. She has been asking children to play with her, but if they refuse, she has turned on them and been spiteful. This has been going on for a few weeks when you find out through another parent, who has complained.

1 *What would you say to the parent who complained?*
2 *What would you do to help Jasmine?*
3 *Would you tell Jasmine's parents about the situation? Give your reasons.*

Encouraging parents to seek information about the setting

Parents who come regularly to the setting will be aware of its importance as a point of contact for exchanging information about their child. Those who send their children with others will need to make sure that they are known by early years workers by coming into the setting when they can. In this way, they will be recognised at open afternoons and other times when the setting is open to parents.

Parents may need to be encouraged to come into the setting, particularly if there are barriers between the setting and home situation, such as a lack of communication so far, or if the parent perceives a problem but has not talked about it. In this situation, it may be difficult to gain the parents' interest. Remember, there may be different reasons for this. Always be courteous and friendly to parents in order to encourage the same from them.

Keys to good practice
Encouraging parents into the setting

- Hold a meeting for new parents so that they get to know one another.
- Hold special events and fundraising events.
- Invite parents to the setting if their child has achieved well.
- Invite parents to give their own ideas.
- If there is a group of parents from a particular cultural background, hold a special event so that they can meet each other.

It may be appropriate for you to invite parents into the setting to tell them about the particular achievements of their child. This is good for both child and parent as it will boost the confidence of both, enabling children to feel proud of their work, and parents to feel proud of their children. Some settings give certificates and stickers to celebrate children's achievements or to reward particularly good behaviour. It is a good idea to tell parents about positive reinforcement and how it is used in the setting.

Positive reinforcement

Positive reinforcement is a way of promoting desirable behaviour in children. Psychologists who accept the behaviourist theory suggest that behaviour is repeated if children receive some kind of reward. This may be in the form of praise, enjoyment or other kinds of gratification. Children need to feel recognised and have the attention of adults. If they gain this attention by being praised for good behaviour, they will be more likely to repeat it. Children may also show undesirable behaviour to gain attention. You should give as little attention as possible to undesirable behaviour so that the child does not repeat it. In this way, children will see that you value the efforts they are making. It is very important that you give positive responses to children's actions.

Suggestions for positive reinforcement of children's work
- Give a sticker or rosette each day to a child who has worked particularly hard.
- Put stickers or printed stamps on a child's work if it is good.
- Keep a star chart for each child – when the child reaches five stars, he or she receives a certificate.
- Keep a 'Happy Book' with the supervisor. The child's name will be put in the book if he or she behaves well or works hard. After three entries, the child will receive a certificate; after five entries, he or she will receive a small prize.

Keys to good practice
Promoting positive behaviour

- Give praise and encouragement to children who show desirable behaviour.
- Make sure children understand what they can and cannot do.

- Be a good role model for children – show that you behave in the way that you expect them to behave.
- Ensure that activities and experiences you provide for the children are stimulating and enjoyable.
- Have clear expectations of the children – make sure that their expected behaviour is appropriate to their age and stage of development.
- Try not to give attention to children showing undesirable behaviour.

Case study

Mrs Dhillon has had some problems with her son Ranjid's behaviour at home. He has been quite aggressive with his younger brother, and she asks you for advice about coping with him.

1 *What advice would you give Mrs Dhillon?*
2 *What could you do in the setting with Ranjid, to encourage positive behaviour?*

Information about the nature and purpose of children's activities

Most settings provide parents with a plan or details about what the child is expected to do while in the setting. This will help parents who wish to carry themes through to the home or to discuss with children what they are doing. The children may, for example, be doing a topic on 'growing', and parents may wish to have details about the kinds of vocabulary to use with their child or particular things to focus on. It may be that the children are working on a particular area in which a parent has expertise and may like to contribute – this type of involvement is always welcome in early years settings.

On the next page is an example of a topic web.

Parents should always be encouraged to come into the setting and enquire about their child's experiences and to discuss any concerns. They may be unsure about particular work their child is doing, or whether their child is happy and settled. It is important that you give support by listening and doing what you can to help.

Active knowledge ✔

Find some different kinds of information that your workplace offers to new parents. What information are parents given about:

- the setting's policy on managing unwanted behaviour
- absences
- safety measures?

Can you think of anything you might like to know about but which is not mentioned?

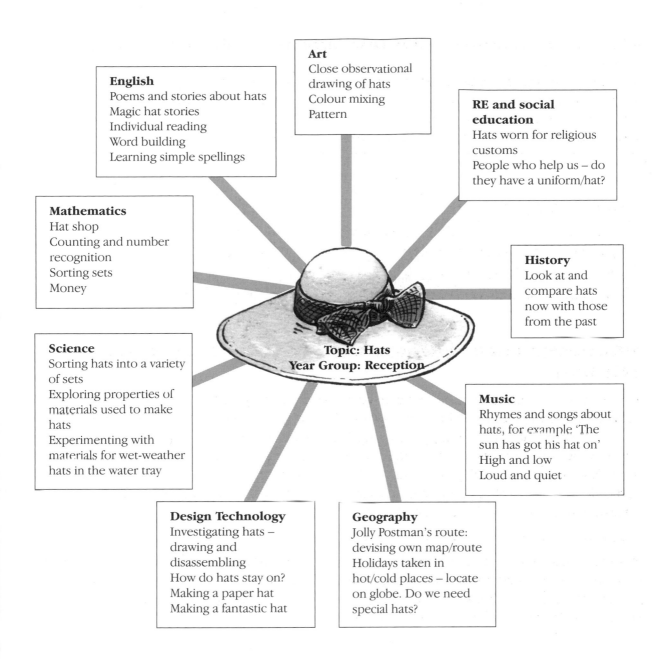

Art
Close observational drawing of hats
Colour mixing
Pattern

English
Poems and stories about hats
Magic hat stories
Individual reading
Word building
Learning simple spellings

RE and social education
Hats worn for religious customs
People who help us – do they have a uniform/hat?

Mathematics
Hat shop
Counting and number recognition
Sorting sets
Money

History
Look at and compare hats now with those from the past

Science
Sorting hats into a variety of sets
Exploring properties of materials used to make hats
Experimenting with materials for wet-weather hats in the water tray

Topic: Hats
Year Group: Reception

Music
Rhymes and songs about hats, for example 'The sun has got his hat on'
High and low
Loud and quiet

Design Technology
Investigating hats – drawing and disassembling
How do hats stay on?
Making a paper hat
Making a fantastic hat

Geography
Jolly Postman's route: devising own map/route
Holidays taken in hot/cold places – locate on globe. Do we need special hats?

Element P2.4 Share the care and management of children with their parents

When children are left in the care of early years workers, parents are effectively trusting them to act *in loco parentis*, that is, in place of a parent. This means that early years workers will have to care for the children in the same way as a parent would. In some settings, parents are asked to sign a form to say that should they be needed and cannot be reached, the staff may act in their place. This will usually be in case of emergency; but on a day-to-day basis, those who work with very young children are often in the role of a parent, since care and education are so closely linked.

As discussed in Element P2.2, parents will have visited the setting and had several opportunities to speak to staff before the child starts. They will have seen early years workers with children and been able to get a 'feel' for the place. They will also have been given information about the setting and its philosophies and childcare methods. It is important for the child that parents are familiar with these. Where parents are unfamiliar with the setting's strategies and methods, the partnership of shared responsibility and care will be more difficult to sustain.

WHAT YOU NEED TO LEARN

- Caring for children in ways that reflect their families' values and practices
- Explaining emergency procedures to parents
- Interactions with children when their parents are present
- Help and advice which early years workers may need to give to parents
- The early years worker's role in establishing and maintaining relationships with parents

Caring for children in ways that reflect their families' values and practices

Children should be cared for in a way that reflects families values and practices, and the way in which parents would wish. It is through constant discussion with parents that early years workers are able to carry out their wishes in the best possible way for the child.

Keys to good practice
Sharing ideas with parents

- Parents and early years staff should share the same ideas on discipline and behaviour. You should always explain to parents and children the strategies used in the setting (see Element P2.3).
- Parents should be aware of the routines and structure of the child's day.
- Parents should have some ideas about the expectations and activities in which their child will be expected to participate.
- Early years workers need to be aware of the differing needs of each child. For example, Hindu children celebrating Diwali could help to teach other children about the festival by sharing their experiences.
- Early years workers need to make sure that they carry out parents' wishes in case of emergency.

Although for the most part parents will be fully supportive, there will always be some instances where a parent does not share the philosophy and childcare methods used by the setting. You may need to discuss each individual case with colleagues.

Case study

Aysha has been playing in the home corner with another child and has not been sharing the play equipment. She keeps it to herself and throws a tantrum rather than let the other child play with it. This has been a repeated problem with Aysha and you finally decide to speak to her parents. When they come into the setting, they tell you that they have told her that if she is playing with something, other children will have to wait.

1 *How would you tackle this situation?*
2 *What would you say to Aysha's parents if they still did not see the setting's point of view?*

You should also be aware that children who share the same cultural or other grouping may still vary in their family practices and values. People are not all the same and cannot be categorised. Each family should be treated as individual, as parents all have their own style of parenting and are influenced by a number of factors.

Factors that may influence parenting style

- Parents' own upbringing. This could have been a loving environment, but may also have been strict or authoritarian.
- Social factors. Parents may have particular pressures on them, such as low income or poor housing, which will put an extra strain on all their resources.
- Family structure. Nowadays there are many different kinds of family as well as the traditional, for example single parents, foster parents, etc.

Explaining emergency procedures to parents

Every early years setting has its own policy on health and safety, and different measures that need to be applied in various circumstances. Parents should be aware of procedures that could affect their child in the setting, for example measures taken in the setting concerning safety, and also accidents and illness.

Under the Health and Safety at Work Act 1974, employers have a primary duty to ensure, as far as is reasonable, the health, safety and welfare of all their employees. As an extension of this, in an early years setting employees need to do all they can to maintain safe conditions for themselves, the children and other staff. Parents should be aware of some of the emergency procedures used in the setting. These include:

- how often fire drills are carried out in the setting and what they involve for the children
- what will happen if parents are unable to collect their child from the setting
- the name of the qualified first aider
- procedures for administering medicines
- what will happen if their child is involved in an accident or becomes ill while at the setting.

Parents should also know that all members of staff are committed to maintaining the safest possible environment for their children by remaining vigilant.

When you first start work in a new setting, you should make sure that you are aware of safety procedures yourself so that you are able to pass on information to parents. You will need to know when and how to contact parents in case of emergency and where telephone numbers are kept.

When you should contact a parent

- If the child has had a bad knock to the head.
- If the child has been involved in an accident that needs medical attention.
- If the child becomes ill and is distressed, or has a raised temperature.

Sometimes children do not want to attend the setting and will say that they do not feel well. It is not a good idea to call parents immediately on these occasions, as often the child will 'forget' that he or she was feeling poorly once settled. You will notice that it is usually the same children who have these disappearing bouts of sickness!

Identifying hazards

Many of the accidents that happen to very young children are avoidable and you need to make sure that proper safety equipment is always used where necessary. You should also be constantly alert for hazards such as trailing electrical cables or broken toys with sharp points or edges, which could cause an accident.

Below are some of the hazards that could be encountered in a setting. There may be others of which you will need to be aware. Make sure that you go over these from time to time, as it is easy to become complacent.

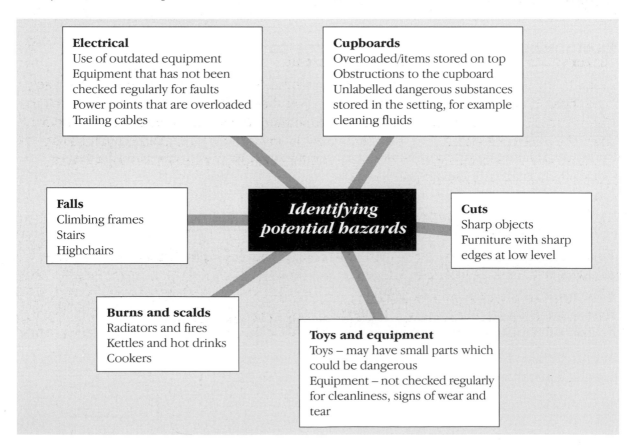

Electrical
Use of outdated equipment
Equipment that has not been checked regularly for faults
Power points that are overloaded
Trailing cables

Cupboards
Overloaded/items stored on top
Obstructions to the cupboard
Unlabelled dangerous substances stored in the setting, for example cleaning fluids

Falls
Climbing frames
Stairs
Highchairs

Identifying potential hazards

Cuts
Sharp objects
Furniture with sharp edges at low level

Burns and scalds
Radiators and fires
Kettles and hot drinks
Cookers

Toys and equipment
Toys – may have small parts which could be dangerous
Equipment – not checked regularly for cleanliness, signs of wear and tear

Interactions with children when their parents are present

Children will usually have several adults in their lives they know well and who exert an influence over them. As an early years worker, you are in a responsible position as you care for and discipline children in a similar role to a parent. You must remember, however, that although the role is similar, it is not the same. Parents have the final say in all matters concerning their child. Although you must take responsibility when parents are absent, if you speak to a child when the parents are present, you should always make it clear that they play the central role. This is beneficial for parents who may be unclear about their role, and can give them more confidence.

Case study

Richard is being collected form the nursery by his mother. He has just put on his coat and is coming out of the door when he knocks against another child and bumps his head against the doorway. He bursts into tears. His mother is somewhere near the back of the line of parents, but you can see her.

Think about what you would do in this situation.

Interventions when parents are present

Sometimes you may be involved in a situation where children are behaving inappropriately and their parents are present. In this situation you should always look to the parent first to intervene. This is because parents, even at the setting, should be the first line of authority over their own children. If, however, the parent is unaware that the child is misbehaving because he or she is talking to another parent, for example, you may need to intervene, particularly if there is any danger involved.

Case study

Sam's mother has come to your home to collect him. You both go into the front room to find Sam playing with some items that belong to you.

1 *What would you do in this situation?*
2 *What would you do if Sam's mother did not intervene? Give your reasons.*

Help and advice which early years workers may need to give to parents

We have already looked at some of the different anxieties parents may have when first bringing their child into the setting. Some parents might feel that they are not 'good parents' and ask for advice and help if they are going through a difficult time. It could be that they feel they are not spending enough time with their child due to other pressures, or that they are having problems disciplining their child. The most important thing you can do is to listen and reassure the parent: most parents are not perfect, but they are the best people for their child to be with. If they need further specific advice or help, they should be referred to a suitable authority. Many of those listed in the phone book are voluntary organisations, and most give excellent support.

Some organisations may be useful to parents are shown in the chart below.

Organisation	Type of work	Address
Parentline	Provides helplines for parents having any kind of problems with a child. Also local groups	Endway House, The Endway, Hadleigh, Essex SS7 2ANN
National Council for One-Parent Families	Gives advice on financial, housing and legal issues	225 Kentish Town, London NW4 2LX
National Childbirth Trust (NCT)	Gives support and information to all parents and parents-to-be	Alexander House, Oldham Terrace, Acton, London W3 6NH

Help groups give various specialist types of support, which could range from help for parents of twins, to marriage guidance and counselling. They are non-profit-making organisations and often work with local authorities, as they can provide expertise, advice and practical support.

Children with special educational needs

There may be occasions when you need to refer parents to another member of staff or other professionals, because you notice a child's behaviour is unlike that of other children in the setting and feel that he or she needs specific help, for example with speech and language. This kind of problem is often picked up in a nursery situation as it becomes apparent that the child has very little vocabulary for his or her age. There may also be behavioural difficulties or a medical condition that impedes the child's progress, and you may be involved in making provision for children who have special educational needs.

The chart below identifies the signs to look for when referring children for observation.

Type of problem	Signs to looks for
Emotional and/or behavioural difficulties	Child may be withdrawn, obsessional or disruptive
Visual or hearing difficulties	Child may be unable to follow instructions and have problems concentrating
Speech and language difficulties	Discrepancy between child's development and that of others the same age
Medical conditions	May prevent the child from participating fully in the setting
Physical disabilities	May prevent the child from participating fully in the setting

To enable the setting to provide a child with additional help and support, the child will usually need to have a Statement of Special Educational Needs. Following an assessment by the local authority, the setting will draw up a plan to monitor the child's progress and state when it is to be reviewed. Parents will be involved in this, and in the case of children under five, are encouraged to participate in the assessment process.

The early years worker's role in establishing and maintaining relationships with parents

Remember that the amount of information an early years worker exchanges with parents will depend upon the worker's position in the setting. For example parents will not usually seek advice from or give information to a student. You should be aware of lines of management and if you are at all unsure about your role, seek advice from a supervisor.

- **Students** are not members of staff and if parents seek information from them, the matter should be referred to a staff member. They need to work under the direction of a supervisor.
- **New members of staff** need to form relationships with parents. They need to learn about routines and check information with other members of staff to make sure they are correct. They should refer parents to their supervisors if they need to find out about specific issues.
- **Teachers or key workers** need to form close relationships with children and parents. They need to keep up-to-date records and show a good knowledge of each child. The information they discuss with parents will be confidential to them and their supervisor.
- **Supervisors** need to know all the children and parents in the setting well. They need to be aware of any incidents that happen on a daily basis, so that they can discuss them with a parent if necessary. They will have access to all information about each child.

Through your work with children, you will automatically be forming a close partnership with their parents. Most parents want to be involved in all aspects of their children's lives and are keen to share views and knowledge of their children. Young children need the long-term care and love that their parents provide, and which they turn to in times of need. Although you may form close relationships with children, and act as parent in their absence, you will not have the same relationship as a parent would. This does not mean that you are not important to the child, but you are important in a different way. By sharing knowledge and information with parents, you enable children to learn and to feel settled so that they will gain the maximum benefit from the setting.

P2 Unit test

Quick quiz

Choose a, b, or c to answer the following questions:

1 Why should parents and children visit the setting before the child starts?
   a So that they will know where to go.
   b So that they will be prepared and know what to expect.
   c Because the child might like to see his or her surroundings.

2 There is a computer club after school and a parent asks you to take his child as he is unable to get there and the club starts only ten minutes after school ends. Do you:
   a Agree on condition that it is just this once?
   b Tell the parent politely that it is not part of your job?
   c Suggest to the parent that perhaps another parent with a child at computer club may be able to help him?

3 Why do children need to know what behaviour is acceptable?
   a So that they have a clear understanding of what is expected of them.
   b So that they will work harder.
   c To enable them to settle in more quickly.

4 Why should early years workers try to find out as much as possible about each child both before and after the child is introduced into the setting?
   a So that they gain maximum background information to enable them to build up an accurate picture of each child.
   b So that they can be sympathetic to the child's needs.
   c So that they can support both parent and child.

5 One of the parents who comes into the setting to help has been assisting the children a little too much with their tasks. How would you handle this?
   a Speak to the parent and explain that the children need to attempt the task themselves.
   b Ask your supervisor to speak to the parent.
   c Ignore it and hope that it does not happen again.

Short-answer questions

6 Why should you be careful with any confidential information given to you?
7 Can you think of some ways of encouraging a reluctant child into the setting?
8 What should you do if you need to pass on written information to parents?
9 Why are fathers especially valuable sources of help in early years settings?
10 How could you thank parents for all the support they give to the setting over the year?

Appendix

Curriculum guidance for the Foundation stage – the Early Learning Goals

The Early Learning Goals establish expectations for most children to reach by the end of the Foundation Stage, but are not a curriculum in themselves. They are organised into the six areas as the curriculum and provide the basis for planning throughout the Foundation Stage, so laying secure foundations for future learning. By the end of the Foundation Stage, some children will have exceeded the goals. Other children will be working towards some or all of the goals – particularly younger children, those children who have not had high-quality early years experience, those with special educational needs and those learning English as an additional language.

Personal, social and emotional development

Successful personal, social and emotional development is critical for very young children in all aspects of their lives and gives them the best opportunity for success in all other areas of learning. It is crucial that settings provide the experiences and support to enable children to develop a positive sense of themselves.

By the end of the reception year, most children should:

- Continue to be interested, excited and motivated to learn
- Be confident to try new activities, initiate ideas and speak in a familiar group
- Maintain attention, concentrate, and sit quietly when appropriate
- Respond to significant experiences, showing a range of feelings when appropriate
- Have a developing awareness of their own needs, views and feelings and be sensitive to the needs, views and feelings of others
- Have a developing respect for their own cultures and beliefs and those of other people
- Form good relationships with adults and peers
- Work as part of a group or class, taking turns and sharing fairly, understanding that there needs to be agreed values and codes of behaviour for groups of people, including adults and children, to work together harmoniously
- Understand what is right, what is wrong, and why
- Consider the consequences of their words and actions for themselves and others
- Dress and undress independently and manage their own personal hygiene
- Select and use activities and resources independently
- Understand that people have different needs, views, cultures and beliefs, that need to be treated with respect
- Understand that they can expect others to treat their needs, views, cultures and beliefs with respect

Communication, language and literacy

Communication, language and literacy depend on learning and being competent in a number of key skills, together with having the confidence, opportunity, encouragement, support and disposition to use them. This area of learning includes communication, speaking and listening in different situations and for different purposes, being read a wide range of books and reading simple texts and writing for a variety of purposes.

By the end of the reception year, most children should:

- Interact with others, negotiating plans and activities and taking turns in conversation
- Enjoy listening to and using spoken and written language, and readily turn to it in their play and learning
- Sustain attentive listening, responding to what they have heard by relevant comments, questions or actions
- Listen with enjoyment, and respond to stories, songs and other music, rhymes and poems and make up their own stories, songs, rhymes and poems
- Extend their vocabulary, exploring the meanings and sounds of new words
- Speak clearly and audibly with confidence and show awareness of the listener, for example by their use of conventions such as greetings, 'please' and 'thank you'
- Use language to imagine and recreate roles and experiences
- Use talk to organise, sequence and clarify thinking, ideas, feelings and events
- Hear and say initial and final sounds in words, and short vowel sounds within words

- Link sounds to letters, naming and sounding the letters of the alphabet
- Use their phonic knowledge to write simple regular words and make phonetically plausible attempts at more complex words
- Explore and experiment with sounds, words and texts
- Retell narratives in the correct sequence, drawing on language patterns of stories
- Read a range of familiar and common words and simple sentences independently
- Know that print carries meaning and, in English, is read from left to right and top to bottom
- Show an understanding of the elements of stories, such as main character, sequence of events, and openings, and how information can be found in non-fiction texts to answer questions about where, who, why and how
- Attempt writing for different purposes, using features of different forms such as lists, stories and instructions
- Write their own names and other things such as labels and captions and begin to form simple sentences, sometimes using punctuation
- Use a pencil and hold it effectively to form recognisable letters, most of which are correctly formed.

Mathematical development

Mathematical development depends on becoming confident and competent in learning and using key skills. This area of learning includes counting, sorting, matching, seeking patterns, making connections, recognising relationships and working with numbers, shapes, space and measures. Mathematical understanding should be developed through stories, songs, games and imaginative play, so that children enjoy using and experimenting with numbers, including numbers larger than 10.

By the end of the reception year, most children should:

- Say and use number names in order in familiar contexts
- Count reliably up to 10 everyday objects
- Recognise numerals 1 to 9
- Use developing mathematical ideas and methods to solve practical problems
- In practical activities and discussion begin to use the vocabulary involved in adding and subtracting
- Use language such as 'more' or 'less' to compare two numbers
- Find one more or one less than a number from one to 10
- Begin to relate addition to combining two groups of objects and subtraction to 'taking away'
- Use language such as 'greater', 'smaller', 'heavier' or 'lighter' to compare quantities
- Talk about, recognise and recreate simple patterns
- Use language such as 'circle' or 'bigger' to describe the shape and size of solids and flat shapes
- Use everyday words to describe position
- Use developing mathematical ideas and methods to solve practical problems.

Knowledge and understanding of the world

In this area of learning, children are developing the crucial knowledge, skills and understanding that help them to make sense of the world. This forms the foundation for later work in science, design and technology, history, geography, and information and communication technology (ICT).

By the end of the reception year, most children should:

- Investigate objects and materials by using all of their senses as appropriate
- Find out about, and identify, some features of living things, objects and events they observe
- Look closely at similarities, differences, patterns and change
- Ask questions about why things happen and how things work
- Build and construct with a wide range of objects, selecting appropriate resources, and adapting their work where necessary
- Select the tools and techniques they need to shape, assemble and join materials they are using
- Find out about and identify the uses of everyday technology and use information and communication technology and programmable toys to support their learning
- Find out about past and present events in their own lives, and in those of their families and other people they know
- Observe, find out about and identify features in the place they live and the natural world
- Find out about their environment, and talk about those features they like and dislike
- Begin to know about their own cultures and beliefs and those of other people.

Physical development

Physical development in the foundation stage is about improving skills of coordination, control, manipulation and movement. Physical development has two other very important aspects. It helps children gain confidence in what they can do and enables them to feel the positive benefits of being healthy and active. Effective physical development helps children develop a positive sense of well-being.

By the end of the reception year, most children should:

- Move with confidence, imagination and in safety
- Move with control and coordination
- Travel around, under, over and through balancing and climbing equipment
- Show awareness of space, of themselves and of others
- Recognise the importance of keeping healthy and those things which contribute to this
- Recognise the changes that happen to their bodies when they are active
- Use a range of small and large equipment
- Handle tools, objects, construction and malleable materials, safely and with increasing control.

Creative development

Creativity is fundamental to successful learning. Being creative enables children to make connections between one area of learning and another and so extend their understanding. This area of learning includes art, music, dance, role play and imaginative play.

By the end of the reception year, most children should:

- Explore colour, texture, shape, form and space in two or three dimensions
- Recognise and explore how sounds can be changed, sing simple songs from memory, recognise repeated sounds and sound patterns and match movements to music
- Use their imagination in art and design, music, dance, imaginative and role play and stories
- Respond in a variety of ways to what they see, hear, smell, touch and feel
- Express and communicate their ideas, thoughts and feelings by using a widening range of materials, suitable tools, imaginative and role play, movement, designing and making, and a variety of songs and musical instruments.

Glossary of terms

Abusive behaviour:	– behaviour which hurts feelings or insults another child or causes physical harm.
Anti-social behaviour:	– behaviour which causes physical pain, destroys or removes the property of others, or hurts the feelings of other children or adults.
Boundaries:	– the limits beyond which we should not go (in behaviour, in taking responsibility).
Carer:	– the individual looking after a child at any point.
Cold cooking:	– could include making sandwiches, milk shakes, instant whip, marzipan sweets, decorated biscuits.
Colleagues:	– others working in the setting or providing advice/support to the setting.
Communication aids:	– could include concept keyboards, touch talkers, tactile calenders, Makaton sign system, phonic packs.
Communication difficulties:	– hearing problems, home language and culture not that of the setting, or any circumstances which create difficulties in sharing information either verbally or non-verbally.
Community:	– area surrounding a setting and those living in the area.
Confidentiality regulations:	– the rules on which the setting has decided to control the spread of information which it is inappropriate to disseminate or share.
Cooperation:	– sharing, taking turns, helping one another, respecting the needs, rights and possessions of others, carrying out tasks assigned within the group.
Creativity:	– bringing into existence something original.
Culture:	– way of life and patterns of behaviour and beliefs which are shared within particular social groups, relating not only to festivals and special occasions, but also to everyday living.
Cultural diversity:	– the wide variety of such patterns that exist.
Cultural requirements:	– what people need to do to keep the 'rules' of or follow the tradition of the cultural group to which they belong.
Curriculum:	– all the activities and experiences which enable children to learn, both those planned with specific learning aims and unexpected events which are turned into opportunities for learning.
Curriculum plans:	– what is to be done in the long, medium and short term so that children will achieve the learning outcomes set (usually written down).
Directly challenging behaviour:	– refusing to obey instructions, verbal or physical aggression directed at adult, tantrums.
Discrimination:	– the practice of treating one person or group of people less fairly than other people or groups.
Emotional development:	– a child's development which enables him/her to understand and cope with emotions and feelings, and to develop a sense of security and a positive self-image.
Environment:	– surroundings, including equipment and people.
Equality of access and opportunity:	– offering ways of ensuring that individuals have opportunities to benefit from services to the same extent; some may need additional or different support to ensure equality of opportunity.
Evaluate:	– to consider the value of an activity, whether it has achieved what it set out to do.
Familiarisation programme:	– activities undertaken to help a child to settle in the setting
Family:	– the group of people (relatives and friends) who are significant to a child.
Fine manipulative skills:	– small and often intricate operations made primarily with the hands (fine motor skills).
Gross motor skills:	– could include throwing, catching, striking, kicking, bouncing, whirling, spinning, walking, jumping (large motor skills).
Information given to parents:	– about the setting: prospectus, policies, newsletters, memos, staff list, emergency procedures; about community facilities; about other issues, e.g. benefits, health-related issues.
Information provided	– medical history/condition, family difficulties, vocabulary

by parents:	specific to child, child's likes and dislikes, new factors in the child's life, the family's cultural and religious practices and their implications for the care of the child.
Information about children and family:	– could include children's full names, addresses and dates of birth, health and immunisation record, contact phone numbers, information of children's special needs or family circumstances.
Information about the group:	– venue, times of opening, any age restrictions, charges, availability of refreshments.
Intervention strategies:	– procedures for adults involving themselves in children's activities to redirect them.
Key worker:	– the person who has prime responsibility for observation of, records of and planning for an individual child and liaising with her/his parents. This person may also have primary care for most of her/his time spent in the setting especially for babies and toddlers.
Large-scale construction toys:	– could include hollow blocks, Quadro, Duplo.
Learning outcomes:	– what children learn as a result of their activity or experience.
Management:	– person/group responsible for the administration of the setting.
Mathematical concepts:	– could include understanding of number, weight, volume, shape, space; order, counting, matching, equals, more than/less than, the same as (conservation).
Milestones:	– key stages in a child's development.
Moral concepts:	– understanding ideas of right and wrong, good and bad, helping others, sharing and fairness.
Multi-disciplinary networks:	– could include under-eight liaison/co-ordination groups and forums, joint training networks.
Musical activities:	– songs, rhymes, tapping out rhythms, humming, moving to music, dancing, playing instruments, listening to tapes etc., clapping, responding to songs and rhymes with actions.
Non-cooperative families:	– families who do not adhere to the agreed practices of the setting.
Non-gender stereotypical:	– not making assumptions about what children can or should do by virtue of the fact that they are male or female.
Open-ended questions:	– questions that necessitate other then yes/no response e.g. What do you think? Why did that happen? How did you manage that?
Organisational constraints:	– the restrictions of space, finance, staffing etc. which have to be taken into consideration by the organisation in its planning.
Organisational objectives:	– what the organisation is aiming to achieve.
Organisational policies:	– the agreed principles on the basis of which the organisation decides its procedures.
Organisational procedures:	– the ways in which the organisation operates.
Other professionals:	– could include health visitors, day-care advisers, medical practitioners, speech therapists, paediatricians, physiotherapists.
Parent:	– birth mother and birth father, or a person who has been awarded parental responsibility by court order (as under the Children Act 1989), or members of a family or other carers who undertake the parenting role.
Patterns of care:	– practices relating to discipline, regular routines, toilet training, management of behaviour, promotion of development.
Planned programme:	– activities/events organised in advance, usually cooperatively and with set objectives in mind.
Planned routines:	– activities which take place regularly and which have been organised and planned cooperatively.
Policy:	– protocols, procedures and requirements to which it has been agreed to adhere within the setting.
Positive behaviour:	– could include playing cooperatively, helping others, remaining on task or concentrating for extended periods, responding to requests from carers, contributing creative ideas, expressing himself or herself effectively.
Positive images:	– those which counter common negative stereotypes, e.g. girls in active and leadership roles; boys in caring roles; black people in positions of authority and responsibility; people with disabilities taking part in active pursuits.
Positive reinforcement:	– praise and other confirmatory actions endorsing an achievement with the objective of making the achievement a part of regular activity.

Prediction aspect of memory:	– anticipation of regular events or features of the environment, the ability to think about, plan for and remember facts associated with futures events (e.g. festivals and seasonal activities, special events of the coming of visitors).
Prejudice:	– opinion or attitude about another individual or group, usually unfavourable, which is not based on accurate information, and which may be upheld even when shown to be justified.
Pre-verbal communication:	– the coos, gurgles and grunts by which babies communicate, prior to the acquisition of speech.
Procedures of the setting:	– the agreed methods of operating of the organisation.
Recall memory:	– description or demonstration of events, actions and emotions previously observed or experienced, with or without assistance.
Receptive activities:	– could include listening, watching or in other ways taking in information.
Recognition memory:	– ability to recognise from visual (such as photographs or drawings), aural, smell, taste, written or tactile cues, things that have been experienced or observed in the past.
Reward systems:	– could include charts for good behaviour, choice of favourite activity, sweets, tokens or other tangible reward.
Routine activities:	– could include eating, dressing, washing, toileting, rest and sleeping, play and exercise.
Scientific/physical concepts:	– physical properties of objects such as colour and shape; growth, life and other properties of living organisms; action of physical forces such as heat, light, floating and sinking; change of state, conservation, pressure, magnetism.
Self esteem:	– feeling that one person is a person of worth, valued by others.
Self-help skills:	– working, dressing, eating, toileting, washing, choosing, etc.
Self-image:	– the picture one has of oneself.
Self-reliance:	– the ability to do things for oneself.
Small-scale construction toys:	– could include Lego, small blocks, Constructs straws, Stickle bricks.
Social development:	– how a child learns to live and operate with others.
Spontaneous play activities:	– activities which are not planned but happen as a result of unforeseen circumstances, to which adults and children respond.
Statutory requirements:	– those laid down in law (statute) and/or required under legislation by the registering body or local authority departments.
Stereotype:	– over-simplified generalisation about a particular group, which usually carries derogatory implications, taking a particular assumed characteristic of one person (which may or not be correct) and applying it to all members of that group.
Stimulating environment:	– has pictures/posters, mobiles, toys, mirrors, different textures and colours.
Structured activity:	– a sequenced activity planned to achieve specified developmental outcomes.
Structured programme:	– a series of activities planned in such a way as to achieve developmental outcomes.
Team:	– a group of people working together to common aims and objectives.
Thematic collection:	– collection of articles based on a topic, e.g. a colour, a season, a country, a material, a sense, etc.
Time concepts:	– times of day, morning, afternoon, evening, night, before, after, tomorrow, today, yesterday, next week, next year.
Tokenism:	– people or aspects of their culture are included in the background or in unimportant roles in written and visual materials, through provision of artefacts (presented as unusual or quaint) and opportunities offered to adults and children, but never as main characters or doing worthwhile or important things.
Values:	– the moral principles and beliefs that people think are important and by which they live their lives.

Index